DEC' 2005

Love You Always
Merry Christm

Georgie

STUART McLEAN

Welcome Home

TRAVELS IN SMALLTOWN CANADA

VIKING

VIKING
Published by the Penguin Group
Penguin Books Canada Ltd, 10 Alcorn Avenue, Toronto,
Ontario, Canada M4V 3B2
Penguin Books Ltd, 27 Wrights Lane,
London W8 5TZ, England
Viking Penguin, a division of Penguin Books USA Inc.,
375 Hudson Street, New York, New York 10014, USA
Penguin Books Australia Ltd, Ringwood, Victoria, Australia
Penguin Books (NZ) Ltd, 182–190 Wairau Road,
Auckland 10, New Zealand
Penguin Books Ltd, Registered Offices: Harmondsworth,
Middlesex, England

First published 1992

1 3 5 7 9 10 8 6 4 2

Printed and bound in Canada on acid free paper ∞

Canadian Cataloguing in Publication Data
McLean, Stuart, 1948–
Welcome home: travels in smalltown Canada

Includes bibliographical references.
ISBN 0-670-84069-6
1. Canada – Description and travel – 1981–
I. Title.
FC75.M32 1992   917.104'647   C92-094684-4
F1017.M32 1992

The following were used by permission:

Excerpt from *Keep That Candle Burning Bright and Other Poems*
by Bronwen Wallace, published by Coach House Press, 1991.
Copyright the Estate of Bronwen Wallace.

Excerpt from *The Death of Hockey* by Bruce Kidd and
John Macfarlane, Copyright new press, 1972.

This book
is dedicated to
Tom MacDonnell
1946–1991

ACKNOWLEDGMENTS

This is the last section of this book I am going to write. I just got off the telephone with the production editor at Penguin and she told me if I don't have these final few pages in by noon they are going to start removing limbs.

I have been working on this project for over two years. It will be odd to let it go. A few weeks ago, as I was finishing the last chapter (St-Jean-de-Matha), I began to experience a strange phenomenon when I woke up in the mornings. I wouldn't immediately recognize where I was. It would only take a second or two to orient myself, but it happened enough times that I realized something was changing. I had been away — more than I realized — sunk into this project. I would like to thank the people who came with me and the people who waited while I was gone.

First, and foremost, at Penguin, my editor Meg Masters. The book you are about to read is better and stronger for her help. And Shelly Tanaka, who did the copy-editing and also made it better. Lori Ledingham is the production editor who I imagine is tapping her fingers as I write — patiently, as always. I am also grateful to Martin Gould, the art director at Penguin, for immediately understanding what I wanted this book to look like and finding David Wyman and Wesley Bates to bring my rudimentary ideas to life.

There are a few people connected to each town who deserve special mention. You will meet many of them later on. As well as sharing their lives, however, they also shared their time. In Nakusp, local historian Milt Parent and newspaper editor Denis Stanley. With Maple Creek,

Saskatchewan journalist Brent Lannan and Peter (Quill) Cote of the Federation of Saskatchewan Indian Nations. In Foxwarren, Ron Falloon and Ken Tibbatts. In Dresden, author Don Spearman and newspaper editor Peter Epp. In St-Jean-de-Matha, Pierre-Michel Gadoury and Robert Morin. Newspaper editor Hayden Smith in Sackville. Dorothy and Bernard Agriesti in Ferryland.

I want to thank Professor James W. St.G. Walker of the history department of the University of Waterloo for reviewing my chapter on Dresden. Professor Walker is currently working on a book about the National Unity Association. Donny White, the curator of the Medicine Hat Museum and Art Gallery, did the same for me with Maple Creek. So did Toronto actor Maggie Huculak.

Stephen Beard in London, England and Kate Concannon in San Diego, California both helped research May Bill's story. Thanks also to Peter Gzowski and Farley Mowat for their early support. And my friends Brian Gable and Suanne Kelman who helped as the book evolved.

Peter Boxer who owns Le Marché Vert in St Saveur, Quebec, let me use his flower store as depot for the chapters we were shipping back and forth between Toronto and my family's summer cottage. Debbie McInnis who works there was very thoughtful. Lucie Hall who lives down the lake, let me use her printer every time I had another bit ready to send. In Toronto, Ann Ritchie spent hours on the telephone and in the library helping with research.

I would like to thank my parents, Pat and Andy McLean. Pat is watching the kids swim right now. I am writing this at her dining-room table. This the second summer I've invaded my parents' lives with this book.

My wife Linda Read and my family, Chris, Andy, and Robbie, had to put up with me being away from home a lot. I know that was sometimes difficult. I want to thank them.

I would also like to acknowledge a debt to Mel Hurtig's *The Canadian Encyclopedia*. This wonderful reference was an early companion as I planned my trips. It was a source on everything from silk trains to turtles, from bowling to racism. Everyone in Canada should own a copy.

Finally I would like to acknowledge the generous financial support of the following institutions who helped me with travel expenses:

Air Canada
Budget Rent a Car
The Canada Council
Penguin Books Canada Limited
Via Rail

and
The Ryerson Polytechnical Institute
who gave me the time to get going.

INTRODUCTION

Finally it was Farley and Claire Mowat who convinced me I should write this book. It was Iris Skeoch's idea, and it was a good one. But I didn't see that at first. Iris was my editor at the time and whenever she brought her idea up I would pester her with other projects I thought I should tackle. She didn't let go.

Farley and Claire and I were in Annapolis Royal, Nova Scotia for the weekend when I mentioned Iris's idea. I expected them to take my side. Farley was so enthusiastic (and so dismissive of what I thought I should be up to) that I felt I should reconsider.

Two weeks later a package arrived in the mail from Claire. It was a copy of Berton Roueché's splendid book, *Special Places* — a series of essays he wrote for the *New Yorker* magazine about small towns in America. Before I finished the first chapter I was hooked. I phoned Iris and said OK. OK.

I didn't know how to start.

Matt Cohen was going to France for the year and he gave me his office which happened to be around the corner from my house. I spent the first three months, from September to Christmas, reading. In *The Canadian Encyclopedia* (I read all four volumes) Cole Harris described the inhabited part of Canada as "an island archipelago spread over 4,000 east-west miles."

So that was it.

I was going island hopping.

I started a notebook and began writing things down: themes to cover, places I might visit. Like any journey the hard part was choosing which way to go.

I would not, I decided, visit a town if it had a bank machine.

That was a start.

And if I could find a bowling alley that still used pin boys, I would go to a town like that.

I wanted to find a bus stop somewhere. Maybe in a corner store. Maybe at a gas station. A place where you buy a pop or a coffee with your ticket and sit on the steps outside, your bags beside you. You glance at your watch maybe twenty-five times and before long you're convinced the bus has already passed. Then suddenly the driver is standing there with his paper punch and you have to hurry, leaving whoever it was that brought you standing by the highway, waving, their hand dangling in the air, your face pressed against the window wondering if this was such a good idea after all. Somewhere there was a bus stop with people to talk to.

One afternoon I read that John McIntosh found the apple tree, later to be called the McIntosh Red, and from which all McIntosh apples descended, on a farm near Dundela, Ontario. Then someone told me they thought Olive McIntosh, a direct descendent, and in her eighties, lived alone in a house trailer in Morrisburg and kept a piece of that original tree in a small wooden box. You could write a novel about that tree, I thought — an authentic Canadian relic.

Then I heard there are abandoned outports in Newfoundland where reunions are held. People come to these ghost towns from all over the country and they hold parties that last all weekend. That was something you could write about.

And if I could find a kissing bridge.

And a softball game on a summer evening in sight of the railroad tracks in some town in Saskatchewan.

And a graveyard.

The enchantment, wrote Roueché, of a country graveyard.

One afternoon my wife and I walked up and down rows of tombstones in a graveyard on the Mira River in the Cape Breton village of Marion Bridge. We were looking for her great-grandparent's graves. The land rolled like the ocean. Over here, I said, down on my knees, my fingers tracing the letters on one stone, the inscription slowly giving way to the passage of the wind. As we drove home I told her how moved I was the first time I saw a Canadian military cemetery in France, and she told me again the story of how her mother and father had gone to Holland to find her uncle's grave. Buddy was shot down over the North Sea. The taxi driver who drove Linda's parents into the country, and stayed with them most of the day, wouldn't accept any money.

I wanted to find a graveyard like that. Where the past mattered and people marked the present with what had come before.

I was impressed when I read that Whitecourt, Alberta was named after the postman.

And when I heard that the Lorne Jenkin Highschool in Barrhead, Alberta once offered a course based on the TV show "Reach For the Top." The school, or so I was told, carried Alberta's colours to the national finals six of the last ten years that the program was aired. They won the finals twice. Maybe, I thought, I should go to Barrhead.

R.H. Thomson said I should go to Weyburn, Saskatchewan. He said it was *the most amazing place.*

And a colleague where I teach told me to go to Tillsonburg, Ontario.

"My grandfather was an itinerant preacher," he said. "One day when he was giving a sermon in Tillsonburg he roared the words, 'Seek thee the Lord and Ye shall find Him,' and then he keeled over dead in the pulpit." That's the sort of thing that would make going to church worthwhile. But I didn't make it to Tillsonburg.

Nor to Garson, Manitoba, where they mined the marble they used to build the Centre Block on Parliament Hill.

Or Falher, Alberta, the honey capital of Canada. For a while I subscribed to the Falher paper — a weekly. For a while the town was high on my list.

So was Lindbergh, Alberta (yes, it was named after Charles Lindbergh). There is a salt mine in Lindbergh and enough salt in the mine to last Canada for two hundred years.

There were a lot of places I could have gone.

I wanted to create a tapestry of the country.

I wanted a French town and an English one. A winter town and a summer town. A town where it rained and a town where it never rained. A town in the West and a town in the East. A town in the mountains and a town in the plains. A town that never changed and the most transient of all Canadian communities — a resource town. It has been argued that the prosperity of all the cities in Canada ultimately depends on the staples that resource towns produce.

I wanted to meet the people who lived in these places and talk to them about their lives. Mostly I wanted, like G.D. Hodge and M.A. Qadeer, to write about the importance of being unimportant.

Eventually I chose my seven islands.

Sackville, New Brunswick, rising out of the Tantramar marshes. St-Jean-de-Matha, Quebec, lost in an ocean of snow. Foxwarren, Manitoba, waves of wheat lapping at the end of each dirt street. Maple Creek, Saskatchewan, drifting on the short grass prairie like a raft in the Dead Sea. Nakusp, British Columbia, lost in the roar of the mountains. Dresden, Ontario, floating at the end of the underground railroad. Ferryland, Newfoundland, butting against the chilly winds of the Atlantic Ocean.

I travelled by train and by plane and by boat and by car. I tried to avoid highways whenever I could. I usually took the long way. Over the years I have learned that it usually pays off.

Driving from Sackville to Halifax I detoured through Springhill and Parrsboro. The memorials at the centre of Springhill to the men lost in the coal mines are the most moving monuments in the country. You read the names etched in the stone and you see family after family who lost fathers and uncles and brothers in one morning. I stood there alone on a grey Sunday afternoon, the town empty, as if no one lived there any more, the mines closed, the wind chilly, the parking lot at the Anne Murray Centre empty.

Later that day driving along the Minas Basin between the towns of Lower and Upper Economy I saw two men standing by the side of the road using a pick axe to chop ice from a cliff face.

I pulled over onto the shoulder.

"What are you doing?" I asked.

"Chopping ice," they said.

"Why?"

"We're going to make ice cream."

It was a holiday weekend.

Though I visited bowling alleys wherever I went I never found the pin boy I was looking for. I thought I would. After all, the invention of the string pin setter occurred less than thirty years ago and I was travelling in territory where things didn't necessarily happen quickly. I heard pin boys were still working in an alley about to be closed in Guelph but that wasn't true. They had been replaced a few years ago. Then my friend Big Al (he owns a circus) said there was a shoe store in New Brunswick with two alleys in the back. He guaranteed me there were no automatic pin setters. But by the time I tracked it down the shoe store had been sold and the alleys expanded and modernized. There were four lanes now, the new owner boasted, and no pin boys. Someone told me about a private club in Prince Edward Island that catered to retired nuns. (Why do people ask me if I want to write fiction?) When two different sources, who didn't know each other, told me about the nuns I began to wonder if the club just might exist. I never found it. Someone should.

I stayed in most towns for about two weeks. Sometimes longer. I lived in motels and hotels. I chose places as close to the centre of town as possible. I avoided fancy. Cheap counted.

I filled sixteen notebooks and wrote over three thousand pages of notes. When I finished each visit I would come back home and write for two or three months before going on the road again.

Sometimes it felt like I was travelling through time. I might be standing on a corner, or cutting through a vacant lot, two boys with slingshots in their back pockets would walk by me and I would feel I had left the present and slipped into an era that we who live in large cities have left behind.

An hour later talking to a group of teenagers I would notice their jeans and shirts, the latest colours, the correct brands, and recognize that we are all servants to the television culture, subject to the same pressures and influences no matter where we live.

Once most Canadians lived in small towns. We were a nation of villages. Now nearly all of us (seventy-five percent) live in cities. Between 1900 and 1970 thousands of young people left our small towns and our farms looking for jobs, an education and what they called "a better way of life." These days some people are moving back to small towns looking for the same thing.

"We moved here," says a woman I know, "because the air is clean and we want our kids to grow up in the country where city problems don't exist."

My friend paused. I could almost hear her shaking her head. "We don't want our kids to stay here, of course," she added.

Yet our towns and villages endure.

In their 1983 study of small towns and villages in Canada G.D. Hodge and M.A. Qadeer reported that there were about 9,500 small towns in Canada and that about five million Canadians lived in hamlets, villages and towns. For all the allure of our urban centres, Hodge and Qadeer also reported that between 1961 and 1981 the population of towns and villages actually increased by one million people (an increase of about twenty-five percent).

"If there is one aspect of towns and villages that we find remarkable," they wrote, "it is their persistence, their refusal to die out, their 'staying power.' "

I was welcomed wherever I went. Only once, over two years and among the hundreds of people I approached did I run across someone who didn't want to talk to me.

I could happily live in any of the seven places I visited. Yet more than once in my travels I found myself defending big cities. I'd never want to live in Toronto, people used to say to me. I wouldn't want to live in a place where you don't know your neighbour. But we do know our neighbours, I heard myself saying. Marta who lives next door is from Lithuania. At Christmas she brings things over for my boys. When it snows we try to do her walk before she gets to it. And Sandy on the corner joking with the kids. Bill and Elly phoning to say they have a strawberry pie they want us to have. Ula and Michael across the street. Robert and Laurie. Teresa and Brian. Dr. Fred. Good people I would miss.

Eventually I decided that we all live in small towns. Mine happens to be in the heart of a big city. It is Sam's corner store and Pasquale's bakery, Book City and the library down the street. The teachers who taught my boys this year. The parents who gather at the end of the arena for Saturday morning hockey. My neighbours, my haunts, my family, my home town.

July 22, 1992
Lac Marois
Again

Always, I am amazed at what we tell,
how much faith we put in it.
Never really knowing who is listening,
how they're going to take it, where.

BRONWEN WALLACE

Welcome Home

Maple Creek
SASKATCHEWAN

*It's getting so I don't care for breaking a horse as much as
I used to. I shouldn't say I don't like it, it's just that I'm
getting to the stage where I don't like to be throwed off
so much.*

PANSY WHITE

72 YEARS OLD

RANCHER

I have been driving through the short-grass plains since breakfast. At lunch time it feels as if the white line I am following is running down the centre of an enormous Ping-Pong table. The towns are as infrequent as the cars on the road and look about as lonely. A clump of houses around a grain elevator, a gas station, a general store. Sometimes pick-up trucks appear in the distance, floating at right angles to the highway, held up more, or so it seems, by the surface viscosity of prairie grass than by pavement.

In Wartime, Saskatchewan, I park on the shoulder so I can admire an old eight-sided water tower — a relic from the days of the steam trains. The wooden tower, painted the same brown-red as a railroad station, is made taller by the sprawling horizon.

Wartime was never supposed to be a town. It was just that place on the prairie where they happened to stop building the railroad in 1914. They needed the steel for more urgent affairs. Today there are only three families left here. But farmers come for miles with tanks strapped onto the backs of their trucks so they can fill up from the tower I have stopped to salute.

"Out here you just can't put a value on good water," says Glenn English, kicking the dust beside his 1948 GMC.

"And this is good water," adds Robert Byers. "You can tell the difference between a cup of coffee made with Wartime water and a cup of coffee made in Rosetown."

Sometimes, during spraying season, when farmers need water to dilute the fertilizer they apply to their fields, there will be thirty trucks waiting at the side of the road for their turn at the Wartime tower.

———◄•►———

There are three roads that drop down from Highway 44 towards Maple Creek. Because my map says it skirts the Great Sand Hills, and because it fords the South Saskatchewan

River by ferry rather than by bridge, I choose a dirt road numbered 649.

When I pull up to the crossing, I find the ferry dock is no more than a spit of sand jutting into the river. The ferry is tethered on the far bank. I toot my horn and the boat drifts across to pick me up. The ferryman is Rodney Cocks. He has, he tells me, been driving ferries for twenty-eight years. There is room for maybe six cars on his cable-driven boat. Inside his cabin Cocks has a piece of wood he uses to keep track of his customers. The wood looks like a cribbage board. He moves a nail up the row of holes — one space for every car he carries. Though it is well into the afternoon, I am only the fifth car of the day.

"People aren't travelling the way they used to," says Cocks. "There's just not the money in the country."

I drive south around the western boundary of the Sand Hills and west into a corner of Saskatchewan where trees are so scarce that people refer to them when they are giving directions ("Drive about three miles along Highway 21 and there'll be some trees and then you turn left"). South and west to Maple Creek.

Most towns work up gravitational forces that tug and worry everyone into the centre. Maple Creek spins in a different way. There is something about the gravity here that keeps throwing you out of town. In a country where neighbours sometimes live seventy miles apart, you set off in the morning to walk around main street and in the afternoon find yourself on the back of a horse miles from nowhere. There are supposed to be twenty-five hundred people living in town, but in the phone book it seems that every second resident lists their address as "Ranch" or "Farm."

Maple Creek grew up around the railroad. Jasper Street meets the railway tracks to form the letter T. The rest of the town — homes, stores, fire department, newspaper office, library — is tucked under the arms of the T.

The sign on the door of the town's arena says "No

Sunflower Seeds Allowed Inside." This is a town given to sunflower seeds. When they lean on fences, squinting into the distance and spitting seeds, the men of Maple Creek don't use the first or second person singular. "A fella can get pretty hungry around this time of day" is the correct way to bring up the question of lunch.

It is called dry land farming, and recent years have been drier than usual. In late April, when most Canadian towns are worrying about floods, the notice in the *Maple Creek News* announces the imposition of Watering Restrictions. Odd-numbered houses can water on odd-numbered days. Even-numbered houses on even-numbered days. There hasn't been a good rainfall for six years. The soil is so sandy and poor that it takes about fifty acres of grassland to support one cow. That is why the ranches are so big.

Maple Creek is a cow town. The biggest event every week is the Tuesday cattle auction. You know the cowboys are in town because you can smell the cows. At Hutchings and Sharp on Jasper Street you can buy a leather-grained bull whip for $55. Or a set of spurs ranging from $24.95 to $59.95. You can get metal tips studded with rhinestones to slip on your shirt collars, and belt buckles the size of cantaloupes. People here don't buy these things to dress up. They mean it.

It is a town where the GM dealer tells me that seventy percent of all the vehicles he sells are pick-up trucks. "If they don't buy a half-ton," he says, "they come in here and say 'Show me your big cars.'" It is a town where the local IGA has more bags of seed potatoes for sale (Yukon Gold, Viking, Bintje, Pontiac, Warba) than they have eating potatoes. The cinema (which has been closed for five years) was called the Cowtown. The butcher, the baker and the bar all have false fronts; the old hotel is tin-sided. There are more veterinarians than doctors listed in phone book.

I check into the Commercial Hotel on Pacific Avenue. It faces the railroad yards, the town's two grain elevators and the auction ring. The Commercial is well over one hundred years old and a landmark of local history. The lobby floor is black and white marble tile. The heavy wood and leather chairs have been by the front door since 1883. A buffalo head hangs over the door to the dining-room, a moose head beside the entrance to the bar. Also mounted around the lobby are two antelope, a burrowing owl, a hawk, two mule deer, a lynx, a couple of pheasant, a sage hen and a grouse. A collection of peaked hats adorns a set of antlers behind the front desk. Beside that is a framed copy of the front page of the *Great Falls Tribune* dated October 26, 1926. The headline that day reported the death from "an attack of heart disease" of the great cowboy artist, C.M. Russell. Russell, or so the hotel owner tells me, painted at least three pictures in his room at the Commercial in the early 1900s.

The sign on the stairway (there is no elevator) says "Your shoes must be clean before going upstairs." Over that sign someone has stuck a notice reminding everyone that "Only registered guests are allowed upstairs after 11 P.M." In the 1940s commercial travellers (drummers, they were called) would check in and set up displays in specially reserved showrooms. Maple Creek merchants would shuffle through their stock, and the next evening the itinerant salesmen would drag their six-foot trunks across the road and take the night train to the next town.

Well after ten o'clock on Monday night, truckloads of cattle are still backing up to the east barn of the Maple Creek Auction Ring. The cows and bulls are led off the trucks and into a corral to be inspected. Occasionally a cowboy in the ring daubs a haunch with yellow paint. They'll use the mark to identify the cow at the sale. When I climb over the shoulder-high fence and drop onto the mud, no one challenges my right to be in the pen. Gates are flung open and closed and cows brush against me as they're shunted through a maze of chutes. I feel like I'm a player in a life-sized bovine video game. When a bull starts to snort and paw, I am expected to know enough to make for the fence with everyone else. My safety is my own business.

On auction days, from May through November, Wade Cazes pulls into town and parks his truck in the lot opposite the Commercial. Wade, who operates Cazes' Fruit Stand Ltd from the back of his truck, is from The Hat. That's Medicine Hat, Alberta, an hour west along Highway 1. With a population of over forty thousand, The Hat is where many people from Maple Creek go to shop if they don't drop across the border to Havre, Montana.

Wade spends Monday through Friday on the road. As well as Maple Creek, his circular route takes him through Gull Lake, Cabri and Shaunavon. He is only twenty-five years old, but he is already a master pitchman.

It takes Wade less than half an hour to roll out his awning and spread his fruit and vegetables onto the three folding tables that he carries with him in the back of his truck. Then, with a penknife stuck into a handy cardboard box, he is ready for business.

"Do you like grapes?" he asks the woman walking towards her car.

The woman slows down. Cazes is rolling the grapes in his left hand like dice. When she pauses, he drops the entire handful into the hand she has involuntarily extended.

"They are RED SEEDLESS," he says.

The woman eats the grapes absent-mindedly as she takes in his display.

"How much," she asks, "are the pears?"

Cazes' knife flashes and he holds out a slice of pear at the end of the blade.

"They're ANGELO pears, WINTER pears," he says enthusiastically. "A little bit SWEETER than Bartlett pears. Two dollars for the small basket. Four dollars for the big."

"I'll have a small basket of pears," she says, nodding between bites.

"Which basket would you like?" asks Wade, pointing at the three boxes on his table.

The woman hesitates and chooses the basket that is farthest away. She pops another grape in her mouth.

"What else for you, then?"

She hesitates again.

"How much are the apples?"

"They are RED ROME apples. They are a good FIRM apple. They cost five dollars a bag." Again the knife flashes. Again a piece of fruit is held out.

"But I am *not* selling," says Cazes later, when I tell him he is a great salesman.

"Then what are you doing?" I ask.

"I am standing behind a display of fruit offering people samples and putting anything they want to take home with them into bags."

"Oh," I say. "What about the samples?"

"Sight and taste are your number one senses. If something looks good and tastes good, people will buy it. It's hard not to.

"Do you like grapes?" he asks a woman sailing by. "They are RED SEEDLESS."

"Everything has an adjective," I say.

"People want a reason to buy."

"How much are your potatoes?" another woman asks.

"They are last year's potatoes," he says. "They aren't new crop. But," — there is the slightest pause — "they were grown in SASKATCHEWAN. They're five dollars a bag."

"I'll have a bag of potatoes."

"Which bag would you like?"

On the steeply banked seats around the sawdust auction ring I meet eighty-nine-year-old Royce Smith. Royce was born in Ottawa in 1902. He came west on a settlers' train when he was two years old. The trip took seven days and seven nights, and his parents had to cook their own meals. They sat and slept on seats with wooden slats. His father homesteaded in the spring of 1908 when the range was still unfenced. There were only three other houses along the Big Stick Trail in the twenty or so miles between their farm and town.

"I used to be scared as hell of Indians," says Royce, leaning close so I can hear him over the auctioneer. "I liked to wander off with my dog but my mother was always saying, 'Don't go too far or the Indians will pick you up.' They used to travel through the country in those days by team and wagon and dig up coyote pups. They used to get a bounty for the pelts. They'd also go down to the railroad with buffalo horns. They'd shine them up and sell them to the travellers for hat racks."

Below us an endless parade of cows and calves burst onto the auction floor as if they have been told there is sweet prairie grass on this side of the white gate. When they step on the sawdust they freeze and stare stupidly out at the crowd. Somewhere deep in their cow brains they must sense all is not well. Then they jerk to life and run around and around the ring while the auctioneer ticks off their worth.

———— • ◀————

His name is Jason Wheeler. He is fourteen. He is in grade eight. He is wearing a black western windbreaker with a red horse galloping across the front where a different manufacturer might have curled an alligator. The word "Wrangler" is embroidered over the horse.

I meet Jason at Ranchland Boot and Leather Repair. He is looking for a glove he can use when he goes to the rodeos this season. Jason will travel to rodeos every weekend from May until mid-November. His event is steer-riding. In the winter Jason plays hockey. He won the MVP award this year, but he tells me the rodeos mean a lot more to him than hockey.

"It's more exciting. Way more exciting. The Calgary Stampede is better than the Stanley Cup. When I grow up I want to be a rodeo professional. You see all the real good bull riders on TV and I want to be like them. I want to travel like they do and win money."

Jason lives in town, but he keeps a horse at his Uncle Dan's ranch and goes there at least once a week. His uncle is building him a chute so he can practise this summer. He went to bull-riding school last year. He had to pay his own way. His mother doesn't approve.

"She hates me chewing snuff, too. But everybody does it."

We are walking along the railroad tracks that parallel Pacific Avenue. Jason wants to show me the town's rodeo grounds. He has pried a round disc about the size of a hockey puck from behind his belt.

"I keep it here because my teachers hate it, too." It is Copenhagen Smokeless Tobacco.

"I've never tried it," I say nonchalantly.

Jason brightens.

"Do you want some?"

He offers the tin to me. It looks like it is full of old coffee grounds. I take a small pinch between two fingers.

"Where do I put it?" I ask.

"That's not enough," he says. "You gotta take more."

I pick out more of the moist tobacco than I want.

"That's still not enough. If you're going to do it you gotta get a good wad."

I am not sure if I am supposed to put the tobacco in my mouth or up my nose.

"You put it between your lip," he says, indicating the space between my bottom lip and my teeth.

I drop the tobacco into my mouth. Jason is watching me closely. My mouth feels as if it is on fire.

"It is the strongest stuff there is," he says.

I start to salivate like an old dog.

"It's stronger," says Jason, "if you don't spit."

I thought spitting was the point of it. Baseball players spit. Why shouldn't I? Jason swallows and keeps walking. My mouth is soon so full of juice that my cheeks begin to bulge. What, I wonder, would be worse? To spit in front of the kid, or to swallow the juice and pass out at his feet? I spit. This doesn't seem to offend Jason, so I spit again. I am starting to enjoy this.

We leave the railroad tracks and cross a field of gopher holes, push through a stand of willow that borders a creek bed, climb the fence around the deserted arena and settle, with our backs to the sun, against the cattle chutes. The meadowlarks are singing. The gophers are whistling. A train rumbles through town. I don't know if it is the tobacco, the company or the country, but I feel light-headed, dizzy and fourteen years old.

"I won on a bull out of this chute right here," says Jason, nodding. He has brought his photo album. The pictures are carefully labelled. Jason in his living-room wearing different western outfits. Jason with a vest. Jason with blue jeans and his lucky hat. Jason with his fingers tucked into his belt buckle. Jason in his chaps.

"SH-aps," he says, correcting me. "SH-aps. Not CH-aps."

He has big hands for a boy. Square hands. Cowboy hands.

"The most scared I've ever been was when I got on this one."

He is pointing to a picture of a bull.

"There's a bull we call Paleface, and this one was his older brother. He was really big. It was like climbing onto a barrel, except he was alive. They are all muscle and he was snorting away and when I got on him he got really wild, lunging and trying to get out of the chute."

We talk about the summer. Chasing cows. Snaring gophers. Get some binder twine, he says, and tie a loop like a lariat and put it around their hole and when their head pops up you jerk it. Just before six we walk back across the field and the railroad tracks to the hotel where he has left his bike, unlocked, in the middle of the sidewalk. We have been gone two hours. No one has touched it.

———————— • ————————

There are two barbers in Maple Creek, and their two storefronts face each other across Jasper Street. Joe's Barber Shop is on the east side of Jasper; Darcy's is on the west. Both are one-chair affairs and both barbers are sitting in their chairs reading the newspaper on the afternoon I decide to get my hair cut. I sail doggedly up and down the street looking for a sign that will recommend one establishment over the other. On my third tack I settle on Darcy. It's not often you see a barber with a hacksaw hanging by his chair. There was a time — a time when health care was more direct — when barbers used to bleed people as well as trim their hair. I indulge my curiosity.

"Do you play chess?" asks Darcy Lewis as he wraps a sheet around my neck.

There is a chess board set up on a small table near the wall. A game is in progress.

"I don't play very well," I say.

Darcy looks more like an ex-wrestler than a chess player. His tummy droops over his belt. A toothpick pokes out of his mouth. He slides the toothpick smoothly from side to side as he talks.

"I had a customer who moved into town about fifteen years ago. He couldn't find anyone to play with, so he bought me a book and we started up. He used to come in for a game every morning but he's getting on now and we only play a couple of times a week."

"Too bad," I say.

Darcy, who has been running his electric clippers over my neck, moves to the top of my head. Apparently he doesn't use scissors.

"About a month ago a Czechoslovakian fellow came to town to visit his aunt. She's in the hospital here. He can't speak a word of English, but he came into the store one day and pointed at the board and sat down. I play with him whenever he comes by."

"What's his name?" I ask.

"I don't know," says Darcy. "We can play chess but we can't talk at each other."

Clumps of my hair are drifting down and landing in my lap like tumbleweeds.

"It's not often," Darcy continues, motioning towards the wall with the buzzing clippers, "it's not often you see a barber shop with a hacksaw."

"No," I concede.

"I do woodwork as well as barbering."

"Oh."

"It used to be a lot busier. Once there were six barbers in town and all six of us were busier than the two of us are today. Saturday nights I used to close for supper and then come back. There'd always be a line-up. I'd be here till after ten.

"Some days I come to work and just sit. No one comes in at all. One fellow tells me that folks are getting their hair cut down in the States. You can get it done for five dollars down there and most folks go down once a month anyway. It can get pretty discouraging. So I do woodwork when things get quiet. I work on projects at home, then bring them in here to finish them off."

Darcy holds up a mirror so I can see his handiwork.

"Short enough?" he asks.

"Yes," I say.

He has cut my hair short on both sides but left it long and swirling on top in the style of the early fifties. It makes me smile. The haircut is seven dollars. I give him a three-dollar tip and sit down to see what happens next.

Forty-five minutes pass before the next customer arrives and is sent on his way.

"He didn't pay," I say as the door closes behind him.

"No," says Darcy. "I owed him a haircut. He is a kind of handyman around town and he was over to the house on the weekend to tend to some plumbing. We've been doing this for a couple of years now. I call him whenever I need something done and he comes in here afterwards. It works out good. Otherwise he'd probably never get his hair cut."

"Do you do that with anyone else?"

Darcy motions to the pile of egg cartons stacked in the corner.

"I have a bachelor who brings me eggs. He brings me four or five dozen every couple of weeks and I give him a haircut. I haven't bought eggs for years.

"The day is going fast," he says, looking at his watch. "I've done maybe six haircuts already."

"What do you do when you need a haircut?" I ask. "Where do you go?"

"Across the street at Joe's."

"Where does Joe go?"

"He comes here." We trade. I go there and later in the week he comes here. We never pay." He runs his fingers through his closely cropped black hair. "He really got me the last time. I'm satisfied but sometimes my wife complains. She thinks he cuts it too short."

———— • ————

Elsie Peatch is hemming a festively flowered dress.

"I don't think there is any business where you use your hands like this where you can make money anymore," she says as she knots the end of her thread.

Elsie is the owner and sole employee of The Sewing Room, a storefront operation just down the street from Darcy's Barber Shop. Although she doesn't make dresses anymore ("I don't have the time"), Elsie is the town's tailor.

"The thing about a small town like this is that I can't charge what I could charge in the city. The majority of people who live here couldn't afford it. Like the old guy who brought that jacket in a few minutes ago. If I charged him what I should be charging, the jacket wouldn't be worth fixing. But I never had any idea of being a millionaire, so it doesn't bother me."

Elsie is a war bride. She came to Saskatchewan from Hornchurch, Essex, in 1946. She makes it half-way around the bottom of the dress and pauses.

"The lady who owns this used to make her own dresses. But there's no fabric store in town anymore so she orders her dresses through the catalogue now. When they don't fit she brings them to me.

"I have one old lady who comes down every afternoon. She sits and goes through the rack and if she sees anything that needs to be undone, she does it for me. She'll take out zippers in jackets and open hems and things. She's been doing it for years. It's a big help because these things take time.

"If I offered to pay her she would have a fit. She'd probably stop coming. So I get her something special for Christmas or on her birthday to make up for it. I think she's about seventy-eight years old."

———— •◗ ————

Bill Gilchrist runs the old Whitemud Ranch in the hills south of town. The Sucker Creek runs right past Gilchrist's front door and as it winds by the red and white barns and around a stand of willows, it gives the spread the false feeling of aquatic prosperity. There is no question the ranch is prosperous. Nearly everyone I speak to tells me Gilchrist is someone I should meet, and dropping off Highway 21 into the valley of the Sucker is like driving up to the Ponderosa. If there is a better-kept or wealthier-looking ranch in the surrounding area, I haven't seen it.

Gilchrist, who is sixty-three years old, runs the ranch with the help of his wife, his son, his son's wife and a hired hand they bring on during branding and harvest. Though I ask three times, he won't tell me how big their spread is. A few days later I learn that's a question you aren't supposed to ask a rancher. The economics of the cattle business is so tied to the land that asking a person how big his ranch is, is like asking him his yearly income. The man who sets me straight also tells me Gilchrist works about thirty-seven sections (24,000 acres).

Like many successful men, the morning I come calling, Gilchrist seems to have nothing to do but spend the day with me.

"When visitors come he always goes inside and puts the coffee on," says sometime hired hand Leverne Lund. "He always has time to sit and talk."

Yet Gilchrist's ranch is by far the neatest I visit. The only one painted as nicely. The only one without junk lying around.

"The thing about Bill," says Leverne, "is when he does something he does it properly. He never does things twice. If a machine breaks down he doesn't wire it together so he can keep going. He stops and takes the time to fix it right, even if he's haying."

Gilchrist is sitting comfortably at his kitchen table in front of a picture window that looks over the creek. I know he does things differently from most ranchers in the district, and that's what I want to ask him about.

"We didn't always do it the way we do now. I guess it just takes time for a person to smarten up. But I believe in making mistakes. Anyone who has ever done anything worthwhile always made mistakes, and you might as well admit to them because everyone knows when you've made one. You don't know what's best thinking till you screw up.

"Take the way we hay for example. I have a hay flat down the way. About a thousand acres. For years we tried to work it. We tore it up and seeded all sorts of different grasses.

And none of them ever grew. It took me a long time to work out that nature's got it figured out a lot smarter than we do. You have to learn to live with nature. So we just left the field alone. We just let nature put the grass back on that we had been working so hard to take off. It is very alkali soil down there. Very salty. All it can produce is a low-protein meadow hay. A kind of slough grass. We only get a ton and a half of hay an acre. But it does the job.

"We calve differently than most. Most people like calving in February or March. They keep the calves till the next fall and then sell them. The heavier the calf is, the more you're going to get for it, so you want them born early so there is lots of time for the calf to put on weight. We used to calve in April. After years of dragging dead calves out of snow banks, we started to smarten up. You never see a deer or an antelope calve in April. They calve in the middle of May. Nature has been working at this for years and years and years. So now we calve in May, too. It is so much simpler. The grass is green, the weather is warm. No one is going to freeze to death. I learned that from a neighbour of mine. We had been pretty stupid up till then. I don't want to say what we do is right and what other fellows do is wrong. I'm just saying that what we do works well for us.

"It is a nice way to make a living. Seeing the new calves every year. Bringing down good hay crops. I guess my favourite time is branding. Most people make an affair of it. They bring friends over and get the work done in a day and have a party that night. We kind of stretch it out. We brand maybe five hundred calves over two weeks. We do it in the early morning. I love it. Getting up and hearing the birds singing and the calves jumping around. It's a good physical life. A family life."

"It's four miles to your nearest neighbour," I say. "Do you ever get lonely?"

"Hell, I get lonely in Calgary with people running all over me."

On the drive back to town I start counting the ducks bobbing in the sloughs by the side of the road. Some of them slide through the water like stick puppets. Others bounce on the waves like little ships. I wonder if I can count fifty pairs before I hit town, but I forget where I am when I spot the antelope — three of them standing motionless on the top of a coulee. I have read somewhere that the American pronghorn is the fastest mammal in North America. They can, I read, sustain speeds of up to fifty-five kilometres an hour and reach ninety-five kilometres an hour in short bursts. They communicate imminent danger by raising their tails and the long white hair on their rear ends. The hair flashes in the sunlight and an antelope can allegedly spot the warning from miles away.

Hoping to see them run, I lean on the car horn. Up go the tails and around swing three antelope heads. Spotting my car, they shake their heads and then munch nonchalantly over the top of the coulee and out of sight.

There are three cafes in town. All of them are owned and operated by Chinese Canadians. Each one has its own group of regulars. The Star, on Pacific Street opposite the grain elevator, is where the men and women from the Nikaneet Reserve meet in the morning. The Bel-Air, which caters more to the coffee-break crowd, tends to fill up later in the morning.

Of the three, my favourite is the most idiosyncratic — the B.C. Cafe and Camera Store.

The B.C. is owned by Chuck Wong, an affable fifty-six-year-old restaurateur with a passion for photography. The front half of the B.C. is a camera store. In the frosted glass case by the cash register, where most restaurants offer you a selection of candy bars and chewing gum, Chuck has a spread of cameras and lenses. His open-air office divides the camera store in the front from the cafe in the back. He has a desk right in the centre of the room with an In and Out basket, a selection of rubber stamps, a radio, a box of Kleenex, a pile of papers, a phone and two calendars. Every time I visit the B.C., Chuck is sitting at his desk reading the paper, drinking coffee or trading quips with the regulars in the restaurant. As well as a much-deserved reputation for chicken fried rice, Chuck is known for his honesty. Young men working on the pipeline, who go to work at five-thirty in the morning and don't get back to town until after six, will leave their pay cheques with Chuck to cash or deposit in one of the four local banks. It is the same service his father performed for local ranchers who, in their day, might have had to leave town before they got their cheques from the cattle sales.

Chuck says no one is sure when his grandfather arrived in Canada from Canton. He thinks he might have worked on the railroad in the late 1800s. When he was an old man, Fung King Wong told his grandson that he was teased for wearing his hair in a pigtail when he came to Canada.

The turn of the century was a mean and troubled time for a young man with a pigtail to emigrate to Canada. The country was seized by a spasm of anti-Asian xenophobia in the 1800s when over fifteen thousand Chinese labourers were brought to Canada to work on the Canadian Pacific Railway. These navvies, as they were called, usually received fifty percent less pay than white workers doing the same job, and they were virtually indentured to the Chinese lenders who had paid their fare across the Pacific.

Once the railway was finished, the Chinese were viewed with almost universal suspicion. They were not allowed to vote or practise law, nor could they be elected to public office or serve on juries. Asians didn't get the right to vote in Canada until the late 1940s.

Perhaps it was the Royal Commission on Chinese and Japanese Immigration (1902) that expressed the country's sentiments most clearly. The commission declared that Asians were "unfit for full citizenship . . . obnoxious to a free community and dangerous to the state."

The "entry" tax that was designed to impede Asian immigration was increased from one hundred to five hundred dollars in 1903, and the number of Chinese immigrants dropped from close to five thousand to eight in one year.

If Fung King had stayed in Vancouver he would no doubt have lived in a *fang k'ou*, or bachelor house. The "entry" tax made bringing a wife to Canada prohibitive. It has been estimated that as late as the 1920s there were fewer than fifteen married Chinese women in both Calgary and Edmonton. Fung King's wife would never leave China and never see the restaurant that her husband built and her children and grandchildren went on to develop.

Fung King would have had a difficult time hiring help for his new business. A few years before he arrived in Maple Creek to open the B.C. Cafe, the Saskatchewan government passed legislation prohibiting white women from working in restaurants, laundries and any other businesses owned by Chinese or Japanese.

In 1909 Fung King brought his son George to Canada. Fourteen years later the Chinese Immigration Act was replaced by legislation that to all intents and purposes ended immigration from China for twenty-five years.

Fung's son George went to school in Maple Creek and eventually took over his father's restaurant. As an adult he was sent back to China to meet the woman who would become his wife. They had a son. The boy, Chuck, came in 1951. He landed in Vancouver with his mother on June 7. Three days later they were in Maple Creek. Chuck was sixteen years old.

"When I arrived I couldn't speak any English at all. Not a word. So I went right to work here at the cafe. I never went to school. I learned English by talking to everyone.

"I got married in 1957. I had never met my bride. The marriage was arranged by relatives in Hong Kong. In this country it is different. People wait so long to get married and sometimes it seems to me there is more trouble that way. I've had a good marriage. We've both worked hard. We have a good family."

Chuck has three daughters — Barbara, Joyce and Margaret. Two of the girls have graduated from university and are working in Saskatoon. The third is in her second year at the University of Calgary.

After forty years in the cafe, Chuck has started to relax a little. He is still running the camera business in the front of the restaurant. And the lottery machine. People leave him money with instructions on which numbers he should play when they go on vacation. But he has leased out the kitchen to a Chinese couple from Tompkins, Saskatchewan. The young man who works with them in the kitchen came to Canada from China as a student and was allowed to stay.

"He is pretty lucky, don't you think?" says Chuck, not waiting for an answer as he jumps back and forth from the table where we are sitting to the cash register. "I love this town. I'm never going to leave it. You're lucky to find me here, you know." He is nodding around the cafe. It still has the same tin roof that his grandfather worked under in 1910. "Now that I'm a free man I plan to spend every afternoon on the golf course. I am crazy about golf."

My other favourite spot to eat in town is Currah's Bakery. Carson Currah opened his bakery in 1980, and if you ever find yourself crossing Saskatchewan on the Trans-Canada Highway, you could do worse than drop down Highway 21 into Maple Creek for a coffee and one of Carson's cinnamon buns.

It's an old-fashioned bakery with a screen door and tables and counters piled high with home-baked goods. Carson himself is usually standing by the cash in his white apron, white shirt and white hat.

The range of baked goods would be impressive for any town. For a town the size of Maple Creek, it is staggering. In the bun category alone there are cheese buns, raisin buns, wiener buns, parker house buns, oat bran buns, dinner buns, ham buns, brown ham buns, sub buns, mini buns and, of course, though arguably in a category of their own, cinnamon buns.

You can buy bread sticks and jelly rolls, oatmeal cookies and raisin strudel. For sixty cents you can sit down at one of the five tables and fill your coffee cup as many times as you please.

Harry Braniff is first at the coffee pot every morning. He usually arrives about 5:30 A.M. and settles into the corner chair under the coffee pot. Harry is a retired rancher.

"I come early because I can't sleep. I'm so damn used to getting up early I just can't help it. When I was a kid, Mother would have breakfast ready at five. We'd milk eight cows, feed the horses and be in the fields by seven. Now I get up and read for a while and then come down here. I've got a friend who comes in around six-thirty and we chew the rag. I'm mighty glad we've got this place. Nothing else opens up at that time of the morning."

Leaning on the counter beside the cash register, Carson Currah says there are getting to be fewer and fewer private bakeries across the country.

"It used to be that every small town had a little bakery. But the big companies are pushing them out. What they do is put their bread on special. A guy tried to open a bakery a few years ago over in Leader. Well, Weston came in and dropped their bread prices to fifty cents. The baker lasted two years and then he was finished. Now bread is up to $1.80 in Leader. These companies do this all the time. Even here in Maple Creek the IGA will sometimes put their bread on sale. I don't try to match them, though. You can't sell something at a loss."

Carson nods at a rancher who is backing out the front door with his arms around a bundle of brown paper.

"What I can offer is personal service. I know all my customers. Like Eddie there. Eddie's a bachelor. He lives with his brother. Since his mother died he's been coming in every second Friday. He always takes the same thing.

Twelve loaves of whole wheat bread, one loaf of oat bran bread, four loaves of whole wheat raisin and a dozen crullers. We make up the whole wheat raisin special for him Thursday night. And we make extra crullers on Friday because we know he's coming. You don't get that in a big city. If people come in and ask for something, we'll try to make it. I had a woman the other day asking for oat bran cookies, but she was allergic to flour. Well, that's easy. I can do that. It doesn't seem like much, but that's what makes people come in."

Carson signals for me to follow him behind the counter.

"I want to show you something,"he says.

He takes me to a cluttered desk piled well beyond usefulness with papers and envelopes.

"I want to show you something," he repeats.

He rummages through the precarious piles and smiles as he pulls out a piece of paper.

"I want to tell you about this before I show it to you," he says earnestly, putting the paper face down on the tallest pile.

I nod.

"The store next door," he begins. "The butcher."

"Yes?"

"He has a nephew."

"Yes."

"The boy — his name is Trevor — has cerebral palsy. He can't talk. He has trouble walking. But he used to come and visit his uncle on the weekend. When he was visiting he would come in here and watch me work."

"Yes."

"Come back here with me."

I follow him past the ovens and tables and machines and mixers into the back of the bakery.

"This is the rounding machine. I use this machine to round buns. One morning the boy asked me to let him try it. So I did. He had figured out how to work it by watching me. After that he'd be here every Saturday. He'd come at five in the morning and work with me until nine o'clock. He'd round all the buns, then I'd put them in the oven. He couldn't put the trays into the oven or pull them out. But he could turn the oven on and stop it when they were ready. He'd stand by the oven while the buns were cooking and if anyone came into the store he would snap his fingers or make a noise. He couldn't really call my name, but I would hear him and I would come over and serve them. In the summer when there was no school, he would be here every day of the week, same thing, five in the morning. It was very important to him. He was only twelve years old when he started. He used to bring his mom and dad in to show them what he could do. I never told him anything. He did what he wanted when he was here. Now I want to show you the paper."

We walk back to the desk in the front of the store and Carson hands me the sheet of paper from the top of the pile. It is a poem.

"His teacher gave me this. She wrote it up nice for him."

The poem is called "Happiness."

HAPPINESS
Happiness is the colour
of bread dough,
Happiness sounds like the
mixers turning around,
Happiness tastes like puff pastry
like cream horns,
Happiness smells like cookies straight
from the oven,
Happiness looks like bread loaves
ready for the proofer,
Happiness is being free
in the bakery.

"You know, at the time I never thought anything about having Trevor in the store. But when I read the poem I realized that he is the highlight of all the years

I have been here. He is the most important thing that has ever happened to me.

"A kid like that has a better chance in a small town. If he was walking down the street and needed help he could go to any house in town and they'd help him out."

It is six-thirty now. The bakery should be closed. Carson should have left for home. His family is expecting him for dinner. The screen door is still open. Customers are still drifting in. We are still leaning on the counter by the cash.

"I want," he says, glancing at the clock on the wall, "to tell you one more thing.

"We have a French cop in town. One of the best things that ever happened to this town was the day he came here. He has given this town a whole different outlook about the French. I don't think there is a person in town who doesn't like him.

"Before he came I think all we ever heard was bad things about the French on the radio. Then he arrived and, well, he has changed a lot of attitudes. I remember when he was first here he could hardly speak English. When he was giving someone a ticket he had to ask them for help so he could fill it out properly. Now we have a black cop. He plays hockey with everyone. He's probably changing attitudes, too.

Constable Richard Faucher is pouring cream into his coffee at the small cafe in the Cypress Hills Motor Inn.

"They call me 'Reechar,'" he says, giving his name the French pronunciation. "I think it is a mark of respect. Sometimes kids say 'Hi, Richard,' and I hear their mothers say, 'No, not Richard, Reechar.' It's nice. But I really don't mind what they call me.

"When you graduate from training they always ask you where you want to be posted. I knew you weren't allowed back to your own province so I put down New Brunswick, Nova Scotia or P.E.I. I've always liked the sea. I thought it would be nice to live near water.

"So they sent me to Maple Creek. The summer I arrived — that was 1988 — I think it only rained three times. And each rain lasted about five minutes. I remember thinking, 'What the hell am I doing here?'

"I was scared. I didn't know what to think. All I knew was that I was out west and that they hate the French out here. I was scared that my car would be smashed or maybe my apartment.

"It was like that for people in town, too. A French cop. It was like a prairie fire. Does he hate the English? Will he ticket everyone?

"My English was really poor. It was functional but I couldn't argue or anything. Everyone in town knew I was a recruit. I kept thinking they would try to pull a fast one on me.

"I guess my biggest fear was getting a call on the radio from a colleague who was in trouble. I was afraid he would be talking fast and I would miss something and he'd sign off before I understood. It never happened, but I used to worry about that a lot.

"It took about six months to get the language. People helped me. A lot. They'd laugh at me. And tease me. But they helped me, too.

"It's not only that I have a different language. I also have a different mentality and a different culture from the people who live here. I figured it was up to me to adapt. I am in their home. So I decided to do things their way.

"Once I was investigating a cattle theft — there are lots of cattle thefts around here — and when I went out to see the rancher, he was leading a horse across his fields. He didn't really have time to talk so I got up on the horse with him. I was in uniform and there we were riding across the plains.

"You slowly discover things about the land. Things that are beautiful. Once I saw five antelope as close to me as that Coke machine over there. You don't see things like that back home.

"I have learned lots of things. I've learned that if you arrest a cowboy you don't touch his hat. His hat is just like his horse. They have these expensive hats. So if you are putting them in the jail for the night and you are going to search them, you don't just grab the hat from their head. You tell them what you are going to do and then you take it and put it down on the table carefully. There is a lot to learn.

"My parents came here to visit once. They can't speak a word of English. Not a word. It was beautiful to see the people in town trying to talk to them. Trying to understand. They'd use sign language and simple words. It made me feel good.

"One night we were out for a walk and we went by the Legion and my mother said, 'They are playing *bingo*. Let's go and play *bingo*.'

"I said, 'Mom, I'm a cop. I'd be embarrassed.'

"And she said, 'No, no. Let's go.'

"I said, 'Mom, you don't speak any English.' I was pleading with her but she wouldn't listen.

"She said, 'You can translate.'

"It was a nightmare. People were stopping by our table to meet my parents and I was trying to translate the conversation and the numbers. Because all the time they are calling out numbers. I was a wreck. When we got out I said, 'That's the last time I'm ever going to play *bingo*.' Afterwards people came back to the house for coffee. It was very nice.

"It was my parents' first time out west. They loved it. They loved the town.

"I like the way the people treat me here. It has proved to me that despite language and culture, if you accept people for what they are, they are going to accept you, too."

One afternoon I make the forty-five-minute drive from Maple Creek up a switch-backed mountain road into the Cypress Hills — up over the bench at the top — and down into the accordion folds of the valley where Fort Walsh was built in 1875. The fort was, for a brief period, the headquarters of the North-West Mounted Police.

From a distance the hills rise out of the tawny plains like a mirage. On the road from town the pine trees on the north slopes look like a streak of black between the immense sky and the blond dry carpet of curly native grass called prairie wool. Up close the mirage becomes an island of green — the highest point of land between Labrador and the Rockies. The hills divide the Gulf of Mexico from Hudson Bay. On the far side the water runs south. The Whitemud Creek is called the Frenchman River farther along, and the Frenchman empties into the Milk. The Milk and the Frenchman are the only two rivers in Canada to find, through the Missouri, the Gulf of Mexico.

The hills were one of the last parts of the North American plains that white men would explore. Beaver were not abundant here. And the windblown sea of prairie was too dry to draw anyone with any sense.

Grizzly were here, though, and black bear and elk. In 1871 a Hudson's Bay trader wrote that his post alone traded for 750 grizzly hides and 1,500 elk. Many of the grizzly hides approached the size of a polar bear — one skin measuring thirteen feet from tip to tail.

The hills were one of the last places where large numbers of plains bison roamed freely.

For years the hills were no more than a whisper on the wind, and then they burst like a flare from a sinking ship into history. The flare only shone for a decade — from the spring of 1873 until the autumn of 1882 — but it shone brightly. The town of Fort Walsh was, for a short time, one of the largest settlements between Winnipeg and Vancouver. Sitting Bull, Big Bear, Poundmaker, Wandering Spirit and Piapot came here to seek refuge, set up their lodges and hunt in the coulees and around the sloughs. For a brief moment the hills were centre stage in the tragic drama between white culture and Plains Indians.

I park my car in the deserted Parks Canada parking lot. The fort itself has been rebuilt but hasn't yet opened for the season. There is nothing left of the town site save a few depressions in the ground where foundations used to be. Once there were two hotels, two billiard rooms, a barber, a doctor and a photographer.

I walk along the muddy water of Battle Creek and push through silver wolf willow and red dogwood. The land is the same as it was 125 years ago. I head down the creek, past the fort, to a special spot. To a knoll where the decade was kicked off with a massacre.

It was the spring of 1873. A band of some three hundred Assiniboines was camped on Battle Creek, seeking sanctuary in the timber from the frozen prairie winter. In France, Monet was creating masterpieces in his garden; in England, the British Open golf championship was over ten years old; in America, the New York *Times* was over twenty. There was a suspension bridge over Niagara Falls. They were roller-skating on the east coast, canning salmon on the west, and playing baseball all over. You could buy a carpet sweeper, belong to the Ku Klux Klan or go to see P.T. Barnum's "Greatest Show in Earth" in New York City. But here in the Cypress Hills this starving and desolate band was still sleeping in buffalo-hide tepees.

Across a coulee and beside the creek there were two trading posts and about a dozen American and Canadian wolfers who had ridden up from Fort Benton, Montana. They were looking for forty horses that they had lost to a band of Cree horse thieves. The wolfers, who made their living poisoning buffalo carcasses and then gathering wolf pelts from animals who fed on them, had settled around one of the trading posts for a day of drinking. The Assiniboines were also drinking. They had been given whisky by one of the traders — a reward for returning a different missing horse.

At some point in the day the trader's horse went missing again — stolen, or so the trader assumed, so it could be "returned" again for more whisky. The wolfers, drunk and ready for revenge, joined some of the traders in a visit to and then an assault on the Assiniboine camp. What provoked the gunfire and who shot first has never been clear, though whisky would probably be closest to the truth. When the shooting was over, the wolfers and traders, with their Henry repeating rifles, had killed between fifteen and forty Indians (depending on whose version you accept). One white man was dead. During the next night, Indian women who hadn't fled were captured and raped. Then the traders and the wolfers burned what was left of their posts and fled south into Montana.

The story twisted and grew on its way across the country. In one version two hundred Indians lay dead. The massacre enraged sensitive Ottawa — sensitive mostly to the manifest destiny of the southern union, to Fenian raids and other inclinations of annexation. Ottawa viewed the incursion as an outrageous insult to the newly created international boundary and demanded the extradition of the wolfers. There was a bill before Parliament to establish a force to police the North-West Territories. Its passage was now assured.

The following spring the first three hundred recruits of the North-West Mounted Police set off from Dufferin, Manitoba, on a grueling two-month march. Their orders were to advance to the foothills of the Rocky Mountains, suppress the whisky trade and show the flag. They were to build a network of posts and established a system of horseback patrols throughout the west.

Edward McKay, who had a trading post in the Cypress Hills, wrote a letter to the police, suggesting that a fort be built in the hills:

> ... I think there should be a station there for the protection of all parties, and to stop the traffic of liquor to Both Hf Breeds & Indians. There are two posts engaged in selling liquor in the Cypress Hills, and the

Indians are poor, having sold their all for drink, and many are unable to go to Buffalo — having sold their horses robes & everything for this one article, and are liable to starve & freeze to death. One indian who was drunk going home fell down a bank on to the ice and broke his skull. Killing him instantly. Two American trappers came there, and some Indians being drunk in a [word indistinguishable] they stole their horses & brought them to [Fort] Benton [Montana] & sold them. These Indians are now liable to go to steal some innocent mans horses for revenge. . . .

That summer Inspector James Walsh oversaw the construction of Fort Walsh. The fort was built on the Battle Creek just north of the site of the Cypress Hill massacre. Walsh built his fort next door to Edward McKay's homestead, though if the account of McKay's grandson is to be believed, the exact site had more to do with McKay's five attractive daughters than any tactical considerations. Fort Walsh would serve as the force's headquarters for six years until it was dismantled in 1883.

At noon, as I climb back towards my car, I meet two of the fort's interpretive staff. They are busy preparing the site for the upcoming tourist season. They don't seem upset to see me on the grounds and in fact invite me inside the museum and feed me lunch. After we eat, they graciously leave me to wander through the inside displays.

I am drawn to a photo of James Walsh. He is wearing a fringed buckskin jacket, leather boots that come up to his knees, a hat cocked at a rakish angle, a sword at his waist and a goatee. He has the swashbuckling look of a pirate. He is described as "handsome and flamboyant, quick-tempered and blasphemous, athletic and brave, unconventional and incompliant; a true character, bound to win the idolatry of his men, the respect of Indians like Sitting Bull, and the despair of his superiors."

The forces that brought Sitting Bull and Inspector Walsh face to face in a tepee just east of the Cypress Hills were set in motion by rumours of gold that lingered like smoke over the Black Hills of Montana. The Black Hills had long been a sacred refuge for the Dakota Sioux. During the 1860s, as more and more whites came west, tension between the native and white cultures grew intolerable. The more settlers, miners and homesteaders asked for protection, the more commitments the government broke with the Indians. Embarrassed and then angered by the Sioux refusal to sell or lease the Black Hills, the American government issued an ultimatum. All treaty and non-treaty Indians had to withdraw from the hills. When many didn't comply, the matter was handed over to the War Department.

On May 26, 1876, the assistant commissioner of the NWMP received a memo from the Department of Justice alerting him to the "possibility of the United States' operations against the hostile Indians of Dakota and Montana, on the Yellowstone and Bighorn Rivers, resulting in their being driven for shelter into the Territories, and using Canadian soil as a base for predatory and hostile operations."

Three columns under Generals Alfred Terry, George Crook and John Gibbon converged on the Sioux. They were to meet at the junctions of the Rosebud and Yellowstone rivers.

In the planning, no one had accounted for what would happen at the Little Bighorn. But following the massacre sparked by General George Custer, the Sioux, as expected, fled north into Canada. When they arrived, many of the warriors were wearing odds and ends of U.S. Army uniforms and carrying government-issue guns.

Inspector Walsh set off from the Cypress Hills to meet the war refugees near Wood Mountain. One of his encounters with Sioux chief Sitting Bull was described in a letter from Assistant Commissioner A.G. Irvine to Prime Minister Alexander Mackenzie. . . .

I was particularly struck with Sitting Bull. He is a man of somewhat short stature, but with a pleasant face, a mouth showing great determination, and a fine high forehead. When he smiled, which he often did, his face brightened up wonderfully. I should say he is a man of about forty-five years of age. The warriors who came with him were all men of immense height and very muscular. . . .

. . . Sitting Bull declared he had no wish to fight the Americans, but they had come after him on all sides, taken his horses, land and money, and that he had been obliged to fight. He also says that he will not go back to the other side, as he knows they would take all he had, and destroy all his people. He had come to this country to find peace, and he wished to live in peace; he wanted to trade the buffalo, and that's all he wanted. . . . He believes no one from the other side and he said so. His speech showed him to be a man of wonderful capability. I was much impressed, by the way, when asked by the Priest whether he was going to return or remain; before answering he turned to me and asked "Will the White Mother protect us if we remain here?" On receiving an affirmative reply, he answered "What should I return for? To have my horses and arms taken away? What have the Americans to give me; they have no land? I have come to remain with the White Mother's children."

The ceremony at the opening of the Council was very impressive. After the peace smoke was concluded, the ashes were taken out and solemnly buried, the pipe taken to pieces and buried over the spot. . . .

They all seemed greatly relieved on my assuring them that they would be protected while on this side, and that White men and Indians were punished alike when they did wrong.

I remained in camp all night, and the Indian heart indeed appeared glad. I never saw a happier lot of people. My interpreter said it was the happiest night they had spent for many a weary month.

I might add that I was somewhat surprised at receiving a visit in my tent from Sitting Bull, after eleven at night. He sat on my bed until an early hour in the morning, telling me in a subdued tone his many grievances against the "Long Knives."

I have but little doubt of his future conduct if he remains here, which he assuredly will. . . .

For four years the Americans and the Canadians squabbled over the Sioux. The Americans refused to take the Indians back except as prisoners of war, and the Indians wouldn't leave under those conditions. The Canadians wouldn't force them to leave, nor would they give them the reserve that would allow them to survive.

While the Sioux waited in limbo, Métis hunters continued the wholesale slaughter of the great buffalo herds that the plains culture depended upon. The brutal massacre put the final nail in the coffin of the nomadic tribes. Without buffalo there would be neither food nor shelter.

South of the border the carnage received benign if not official sanction. U.S. Secretary of the Interior C. Delano understood what the death of the bison meant. "I would not," he said in his annual report of 1874, "seriously regret the total disappearance of the buffalo from our western prairies in its effect on the Indians. I would regard it rather as a means of hastening their dependence upon the products of the soil and their own labors."

To their credit, Canadian officials viewed things differently than their American counterparts. In 1877 the lieutenant-governor of the North-West Territories enacted An Ordinance for the Protection of the Buffalo. The legislation called for fines or even imprisonment for anyone killing buffalo for the mere motive of amusement, or wanton destruction, or solely to secure their tongues, choice cuts or pelts. The legislation established a buffalo season, age limitations (no buffalo under two years of age was to be hunted) and outlawed indiscriminate methods of killing. Indians were given more latitude to hunt under the law than whites.

It was, of course, too little too late. By the summer of 1879 the buffalo were gone and the starving tribes around Fort Walsh had been reduced to trading their possessions for food.

At Fort Walsh, Surgeon Augustus Jukes wrote that Indians were

> ... literally in a starving condition and destitute of the commonest necessaries of life. The disappearance of the Buffalo has left them not only without food, but also without Robes, mocassins [sic], and adequate Tents or 'Tepees' to shield them from the inclemency of the impending winter. . . . I saw little children at this inclement season, snow having fallen, who had scarcely rags to cover them.

Starving in Canada and promised fair treatment in the United States, Sioux reluctance began to fade, and one by one the warriors and their families trickled over the border. Sitting Bull was one of the last to go, surrendering at Fort Buford, Montana, on July 19, 1881.

Even the fiercely independent Cree Big Bear would soon capitulate. The confederacy he might have cobbled together with Poundmaker, Riel, Crowfoot and even Sitting Bull was doomed by tribal rivalries, disease and hunger. Weakened and demoralized, he, too, would put his mark on a treaty (December 8, 1882, at Fort Walsh), and he, too, a decade after the Cypress Hills massacre, would leave the hills to history.

By 1883, the "wild and dangerous frontier," as Wallace Stegner wrote in "Wolf Willow," his ode to this corner of the country, "had gone out like a blown match." The match would flare briefly again two years later at Batoche, but soon after, Gabriel Dumont, Riel's canny general, would sign off the rebellion and onto "Buffalo Bill's Wild West Show" as a sharpshooter. It is perhaps altogether appropriate that 1883 would be the first year William F. Cody mounted his western circus. For the free-range prairie was finished. The buffalo culture was dead. Government had come to the west. Sitting Bull joined Gabriel Dumont on Cody's show where, the story goes, he sold his autograph for a dollar and gave the money to children. That same year, a ten-storey skyscraper was built in Chicago. In Montreal the first ice hockey "world championships" were won by McGill University.

It is time for me to leave the park. Before I leave I follow the creek once more down the hill. I look for the last time at the knoll where the Assiniboine were murdered by the wolf traders. I have stayed longer than I meant. Big Bear stood here, I think, maybe Sitting Bull, too, and they looked at the same things I am looking at.

Sometimes you are so close to history you can almost smell it. But every time I think I am close, I reach out and the feeling I am looking for won't come. Something is here, but trying to touch it is like trying to touch fog. Whatever it is I am looking for has eluded me. I drive back to Maple Creek.

———————— •————————

Today there is still a small band of Cree living on the south slope of the Cypress Hills about twenty minutes out of town. About 140 people live here on 3,040 acres. Unlike Sitting Bull, Piapot, Big Bear and all the others who were eventually persuaded to leave the hills, the chief, Kah-Nikaneet (known to the whites as foremost-man) stayed. Authorities kept badgering him to move north where, they said, the land was richer and he could be taught to farm. What they really wanted was to get everyone out of the hills and out of reach of the American whisky traders. But Kah-Nikaneet wouldn't go. He made his living working for local ranchers and kept after the government for a land settlement. In 1913 the tribe got the land settlement he was waiting for. Kah-Nikaneet never saw it. He died in 1911.

Today the chief of the Nikaneet band is Gordon Oakes. He drives the school bus that brings the kids to town from the reserve. Normally the best place to meet him is at the Star Cafe any morning after nine, but Oakes is in California, watching his daughter dance at a powwow in San Francisco. So I arrange to have coffee with his son Larry, instead.

Larry Oakes is thirty-one years old, a band councillor, and thought by many to be the man who will replace his father as chief.

"It was never one of my goals to work in the band office," says Larry, ordering his third cup of coffee in fifteen minutes, "but I guess it's my job to help hold things together until some of the kids who are going to university come home. Then they can take over.

"I always wanted to be a cowboy. I wanted to ride in the rodeo or get into ranching. When you are a kid around here your heroes are always the guys with the big arms who work on the oil rigs. I wanted to quit school in grade nine or ten and go to the rigs. It was my father who persuaded me to finish. Hardly any of my friends did. Most of the Indian kids started to drop out at grade eight or nine. Hardly anyone makes it to eleven. I think my older sister was the first one to graduate. Indian kids don't get the support white kids do. It isn't only the school. The parents don't push, either.

"This is good town to be in as far as being an Indian. Sure, we have our rough spots, but I don't have to hide the fact that I'm an Indian.

"Every year we have the Battle of Little Big Puck at the arena. It's a hockey game between "cowboys and Indians." It started about ten years ago. Tom Reardon, who is a local rancher, and the late Ray Anderson were in the bar talking about who had the better team, so they held a game to find out. It's just kept going. To be on the cowboy team you have to be a rodeo or ranch cowboy. Some of them can't skate at all but some of them are pretty good players. Between the second and third periods everybody gets dressed up. We put on beads and braids and things and they put on chaps and hats. I think the cowboys are up on us in terms of winning, but one year we brought in a bunch of imports and beat them.

"I think some of the imports were surprised to find how well we got along with whites. Last year we one-upped them before the game started. We had a big powwow on the ice and they had to stand around and watch. We fill the arena every year and all the money we raise goes to charity.

"I played senior hockey so I got along with a lot of the older guys fine. They'd joke with me about being Indian. You know. Things like, 'What's the Indian doing here.' Stuff like that. If it's said at the right time it can be funny. But I've noticed if you say the same thing about a white guy, like, 'Hey, honky' or call him 'white boy' or something, he can't take it as good as an Indian does.

"Sometimes I've noticed the white people see us just as Indians. I've heard them say things like, 'That's our Indians,' as if they owned us or something.

"But it's not just the whites. Once I went to a rodeo with a white guy and on the way back we stopped off at a powwow. He was the only white guy there and I'm ashamed to say this, but I was embarrassed to be with him. I was only sixteen or seventeen. But that's no excuse. I guess a white doesn't have a monopoly on those feelings. I never did get a chance to apologize to that guy. I think he knew what was happening.

"There are some things that bother me. Like when a white guy uses a government program to his benefit people call him a smart businessman. Well, when we do it, it's viewed as taking hand-outs.

"But as far as Indians and whites are concerned, we get along here."

Larry's coffee cup was empty again and he twists in his seat looking for his fifth refill.

"Where did you grow up?" I ask as the waitress sails towards us.

"I was born on the reserve. When I was five we moved to town. We were one of the first families to come to town. In those days it was a strange situation to have Indians in town. It was something that people noticed. It was 1964 and we lived in a tent on the edge of town. I think I was the only Indian kid in school. I didn't know how to speak English. I remember there was this one kid who used to pull my ears because I didn't understand him. He thought I was deaf. There was also this little girl who used to come to my place to play. But all she did was give me shit because I didn't understand her. So I used to pretend I was asleep when she came. She didn't like that, either.

"You know we are losing our language. My wife doesn't speak Cree. My kid can't speak Cree, either. We send him to his grandparents to learn and he is learning fast but he isn't fluent. We missed out when he was young.

"It is important to me that he knows the Indian language and Indian practices. We are not a church-going people. And I know some whites think our religious beliefs are just superstitions. Well, I see white men wearing crosses around their necks. Tell me what that is if it isn't superstition."

"What religious ceremonies do you practise with your son?" I ask.

"I don't know if I should even have mentioned these things," he says. He looks up quietly. "But I am proud of them."

"Things like what?" I ask again.

"The Sun Dance, the Give Away Dance, sweats and pow-wows. I want my son to understand these things. I want him to understand the significance behind them. So I make him participate. Lots of kids participate. Do they understand? Probably not. But I didn't understand, either. I did these things because my parents told me to. And then gradually I came to understand the significance of what I was doing."

"What about dreams?" I ask.

"We encourage him to tell us his dreams. Or to tell them to his grandfather. We listen carefully to see if there is any warning in them."

"Why don't you like talking about this?"

"Because I don't want these things to lose their strength. I don't want them to lose their power. I don't know everything there is to know. No one does. You know just what you are meant to know. No more."

———— •·•————

And then it rains. I am woken by thunder one night at four in the morning. I lie in bed for half an hour listening to the sudden downpour settle into a steady hiss. At five I open my window and see that the rain is hard enough to be puddling up the parking lot. It isn't long before a new sound, a more deliberate one, joins the symphony. Water begins to drip through the ceiling in the corner of my room.

There hasn't been a storm like this for over ten years in Maple Creek. Coming as it is in early May, it means that farmers are going to sow their crops into moisture. It means grass will grow where it hasn't grown in years. It means that after ten years of ploughing dry crops under, there will be a harvest. Cattle will be fatter. There will be money again. Cars will sell and people will go to the stores.

It is raining. Phones, I bet, are ringing all over.

It is still raining when I wake up. The wind is blowing hard, sweeping the rain across the streets in angry gusts. On Pacific Avenue I see a cowboy lurch out of a pick-up truck and hunch over to the Star for coffee. He is wearing a bright yellow slicker and a cowboy hat. He has a custom-fitted plastic cover over his hat to keep it dry. It reminds me of a shower cap. He has lace-up rubbers over his cowboy boots.

At Currah's Bakery, Don Dean, who manages a John Deere dealership, has his hands wrapped around a coffee mug and a smile wrapped around his face.

"I got up at six o'clock," he says, "and went out driving. I drove around for about four hours. From about six until ten. I was just driving around to see how widespread the storm was. I drove half-way to Piapot, then west some, and then I drove off the highway and into some fields and sat for a spell. We live according to the weather around here, and this is the best weather we've had in years. This is going to make good grass. And believe me, that's as important to an implement dealer as it is to a farmer."

Everywhere I look people are smiling. They almost look as if they are dreaming. Everyone seems to be saying it might just be rain in town, but back at the farm whole red tomatoes are falling from the sky, and fat heifers, too. Heifers ready for auction are floating out of the clouds and drifting into the fields as if they are wearing parachutes.

———————— • ————————

This afternoon I set off to visit seventy-two-year-old Pansy White. Pansy lives alone on a ranch forty minutes out of town. She runs seventy head of cattle, some sheep, some chickens, two dogs and fourteen horses. Until a few years ago she was breaking the horses herself.

"It's getting," she says, "so I don't care for breaking a horse as much as I used to. I shouldn't say I don't like it, it's just that I'm getting to the stage where I don't like to be throwed off so much."

It's not that she's ready to retire. She still uses a twelve-pound sledgehammer to knock in fence posts. When she hauls manure into Maple Creek, she piles it in her truck with a front-end loader.

"Best be careful on the driveway," she warns over the phone. "It could be pretty slippery from the rain."

I get about five hundred yards down her mile-long dirt lane before my wheels start to spin. Soon I am throwing off clumps of red mud the size of grapefruits. I pull the car onto the grass at the edge of the road, lock it and head off on foot.

At the top of the hill the valley of the Frenchman River is spread out before me like the opening scene of an epic western. Far below I catch a flash of sun off Pansy's tin roof. I can see it will be faster to set off cross-country, so I leave the lane and start overland.

The rain has stopped, but the wind is still blowing. The average annual wind speed in Canada is fourteen kilometres an hour. On the prairies it blows four kilometres an hour faster than the average. Today it is blowing hard enough to knock the hair off a dog. As I struggle over the hills and down the coulees, I have to fight to fill my lungs. I feel as if I am chewing the air rather than breathing it. Half-way to the farm, I discover that by angling my head into the wind and varying how wide I open my mouth I can make sounds, much the way I used to make music by blowing over the top of a pop bottle.

As I pick my way over old wheat stubble that is losing ground to native grass, around the cow pies and over the neat piles of antelope spoor, over rocks worn round by the immense pre-glacial river that once flowed here, over the thick and wiry prairie wool and around a clump of wolf willow near the banks of the creek, I feel it again. The feeling of almost touching something.

Pansy is waiting for me by her door. She is wearing blue jeans and a buoyant blue cowboy shirt. Her auburn hair is barely brushed with grey at the temple. Her forehead is unlined.

"Don't worry about them dogs," she calls in greeting. Her two German shepherds are pounding towards me as if they have been shot out of a cannon.

When the lead dog is about six feet away from me, he leaves the ground. He hits me just above the knees and nearly knocks me over. The second hits a split second later. Their teeth are bared, but their tails are wagging furiously — about the same beat, I figure, as my heart. I smile at Pansy. The German shepherds begin to lick me to death.

We go inside and sit at the kitchen table by the wood stove and Pansy tells me her story. There is a lilt of an accent hidden in her voice that takes me to Atlantic Canada.

Her father, Walter, came from England looking for adventure. He homesteaded on the Whitemud in 1905. The log cabin Pansy grew up in is still standing, more or less, on the creek side of the yard. Pansy remembers Indian families who used to trap muskrat up and down the river, sometimes coming to the house to ask for coffee, sugar or eggs; sometimes setting up their tepees within sight.

"They didn't have no homes. They lived in tents all year round."

The Indians, she remembers, wore ankle-high moccasins with lots of beadwork, and buckskin jackets with fringes.

When she was twelve, Pansy rode five and a half miles across the fields every day to a one-room schoolhouse. It took her half an hour each way. She would go up the coulee, through the bush and out across the prairie. There were lots of deer in those days, antelope and coyote (she pronounces it so it rhymes with "sly boots," rather than the pronunciation I am used to that rhymes with "peyote," the drug).

Like all settlers, Pansy's family lived off the land, picking saskatoons and chokecherries and gooseberries every summer. One winter her father built her and her sister toboggans out of two-by-fours, and they rigged up a pair of harnesses. Her sister had a calf and Pansy had a colt, and they used to drive them all around the yard. In the summer they rode everything they could get their hands on — cows, horses, even the sheep. When they were older they broke horses together. There was always something to do.

"Do you know how to shear sheep?" she asks suddenly.

"No," I say, "I have never done that."

"Oh. I thought you might be looking for a job."

"No," I assure her. "Just stories."

"I have nine great-grandchildren now," she says.

"Do you get lonely, then, out here all by yourself?"

"No. I'm used to living alone now. I've got the dogs and the animals and plenty to do every day. In the winter I may not go into town for two weeks. In the summer I go about once a week. At night I work on my quilts and listen to country music from a station in Grand Falls. I hardly ever watch television. People ask me if I'm afraid to be out here all by myself. Why would I be afraid? This is my home. I think it's whatever you are brought up to. Other people ask me, don't I hate winter? Sure it's cold and lots of times you have to go out in a blizzard. But I can't say that I dislike any of it. It's just part of living."

We walk outside so Pansy can show me the old cabin. There is a dead calf on the roof.

"I flung that up there so the dogs couldn't get at her. I didn't want the dogs developing a taste for sheep."

"What about the work?" I ask. "You can't be as strong as you used to be."

"I can't lift things like I used to. The other night I went out and found a calf that was chilled. I couldn't pick him up and pack him over my shoulders the way I'd like. So I just went and got the truck and put two boards down from the back like a ramp. And I sort of shuffled him up the ramp, leaning on him whenever I needed a rest. He was pretty close to ninety pounds, and they're kind of a dead weight when they're young and cold like that. But I can still handle a bale of hay. Though sometimes I'll use a ramp like I did with the calf."

"Does your family worry? Do they want you to move off the ranch?"

"My family knows better than to talk like that. If something happens . . . well, it happens. I figure somebody will eventually find me. If I get hurt I can just call an ambulance. As long, of course, as I can crawl to the phone."

———— • ————

I meet Jack Moorhead at the auction sale the second Tuesday I am in town. One side of his face is cleanly shaven, while on the other side he has a full beard. One side of him looks like Jimmy Carter; the other like Pete Seeger.

"No reason," he says, smiling, when I introduce myself and ask about the beard. "Just to be silly, I guess. You know how it is. Just to be a little different. I do it every year in the spring and then I grow it back again. I've been doing it for fifteen years now. I think people would be disappointed if I stopped."

Moorhead lives alone on a ranch not far from town.

"I started my baching career thirty-five years ago," he says, by way of apology. "You'll have to excuse the house."

There's a tarpaulin spread over the kitchen floor. The night of the big spring snow Jack had a few calves who were too chilled to stay outside so he threw the tarp down and brought them into the kitchen. He hasn't got around to rolling it up yet.

"I usually give the house a good clean once a year when I go to brand, but last year it just got away on me. You know how it is."

Amid the bags of chocolate cookies there are four jars of peanut butter on the kitchen table. Jack smiles ruefully as he puts a loaf of bread beside the full one and pushes the three empty ones to the side.

"You know how it is," he says.

There is a bucket of eggs on the counter, and on the stove a huge syringe and a bottle of something called Blood Stopper.

"I have quite a habit of going to town to get a square meal two or three times a week."

His apologies are unnecessary. It is, as far as I am

concerned, a perfect lunch. The only lunch that could properly cap the morning we have spent together. Jack allowed me to accompany him by horseback as he wandered through his fields on the daily tour of his ranch. I watched him canter across the prairie — lariat swinging, back-lit by the sky — and single out a calf, rope him and lead him to a weathered corral in the middle of a short-grass field out of sight of everything but the clouds. And even though, when my horse tried to join the chase, I had to get off before I was thrown off, I felt as close to cowboy as I have ever felt in my life.

Now that lunch is over we are in the pick-up and on our way to a pasture where we are going to rope a horse that Jack needs for next week's cattle drive. We have been in the truck about five minutes when Jack stops suddenly in the middle of the dirt road.

"Damn," he says.

We both pop out of the cab and circle round the pick-up to the back of the horse trailer we are pulling. I am not sure what is wrong.

Jack is standing in the middle of the road, hands on hips, staring . . . at a white chicken.

"She must have been roosting in the back of the pick-up," says Jack holding up an egg ruefully. "I usually check before I leave the farm. I guess I forgot."

The chicken rode with us for five minutes before abandoning ship. Jack saw her leave through the rear-view mirror.

And so, I join my first round-up.

"I hope no one sees this," mutters Jack, looking up and down the road nervously.

The two of us, arms outstretched and waving like fools, chase the chicken around the truck like kids chasing a greased pig around a pen. We are so busy yacking and flapping and cutting in the sand that we don't notice the car slide up until the driver has his window half down.

Jack swings around the side of the truck and digs to a stop like he has been shot.

"Oh, hi, Lance," says Jack sheepishly.

"Anything wrong, Jack?" asks Lance, not entirely sure what he has stumbled across.

"No. No," says Jack.

Which is when we round the corner, the chicken and I. At fifty miles an hour.

"Hello," I say smiling.

"Squawwwwwwwwwwwk," says the chicken, ricocheting off Lance's windshield.

"Well, I'll be God-damned," says Lance, smiling condescendingly and heading for town.

"We should have left her for the coyotes," says Jack, watching the car until it sails out of view over the horizon.

Later, with the chicken safe at home, we pull into the field where the horses have been pastured. At first they are five dots on the horizon that I can hardly see. Then as they catch our scent, they are five dots galloping towards us — two pintos, a sorrel, a buckskin and a palomino. Soon they are snorting and stomping and whinnying and muzzling all around us.

There is something about standing in the middle of the prairie and having five free horses gallop up to you that is hard to describe. Whatever the feeling is it's showing on my face.

"You could pretty well move up here, couldn't you?" asks Jack.

I don't need to answer.

Back at the house I ask Jack to tell me about his family.

"My brother Don was killed at Dieppe," he begins. And then he catches himself and begins again.

"My grandfather settled here first. He was an Irishman. He came out in 1874. He was with the North-West Mounted Police."

Maybe my mouth dropped. His grandfather was here before the railroad. He was one of the men who built Fort

Walsh. Who had seen Sitting Bull. Who had been here when Big Bear made his mark on Treaty Number Six in December, 1882.

"Can I show you something?" Jack asks. He gets up and goes into the living-room. He comes back a moment later with five typewritten pages.

"My grandmother wrote this before she died," he says. "She was blind when she wrote it. She taught herself how to type in Braille.

I settle down at the kitchen table to read the pages he has handed me.

> "I was born," it began, "in the year 1876 on the first of April in the little village of Onger, Essex, England ... "

Violet Moorhead came to British North America in September, 1886. She was ten years old. She came with her mother, a widow, who came to marry the man who would be her second husband. Violet was often sea-sick on the ten-day crossing from England.

They took the train from Montreal to Maple Creek, where Walter Peecock was waiting for them. They moved into his ranch four miles from the NWMP barracks.

> It was a great change for her [Violet's mother], as she had never done much housework or cooking and she found it very hard . . . we did not have any modern conveniences at that time, the floors hadn't any floor covering and had to be scrubbed and it was hard work, and we did not have a washing machine but used a wash board . . .

Maple Creek was still a small town. There were only two stores and maybe twenty-five or thirty families.

> . . . the Dixon brothers store was also the Post Office too, and also the Bank as although money was not very plentiful in those days if one had a little spare cash in those days they took it to the Dixon's store where they had a

Vault or place to keep it, and that was all the Bank that we had, in those days we just paid our grocery bill once or twice a year, as that was the only time that we had any money, when we sold some horses, there were not many cattle in those first few years but quite a lot of horses, and the water was delivered by water cart at twenty-five cents a barrel, and not a very large one at that, we had a lot of work in those days, and very few comforts, but everyone was happy.

Out on the ranch it was decided that the girls (Violet had a sister) should help a little, so they milked about twenty cows between them — morning and evening.

Banff was already a summer resort, and for several years their mother supplied the CPR hotel with butter. They shipped between 100 and 150 pounds of butter a week.

It was a lot of work, as we did not have cream separators in those days, and the milk had to be put into cream cans which were very heavy to carry and to keep in a cool place, and they were terrible things to wash and scald, it was a job to churn nearly every day.

In 1894 Violet married Hamilton Moorhead, an officer in the North-West Mounted Police who was with the first regiment of recruits that came to Fort Walsh in the very early days.

. . . it was interesting to hear him talk of those days and about the trouble that they had with the whiskey traders, and while he was in the police a nephew of the poet Charles Dickens was there too . . .

I look up at Jack. He is watching me read.
"She was here right at the beginning," I say.
We sit there in silence for a moment, and then I go back to her story.

I think I should tell you a little about the Sun Dance that we attended on several occasions. We saw a lot of what was called powwows, but a Sun Dance is something that very few old timers have ever seen, and the only reason we saw one was because Father's sister was married to a Mountie and he was sent to a Sun Dance that was taking place at the head of the Piapot Creek in the Cypress Hills, to keep law and order with several other Mounties and he took our family along. It was a wonderful sight to see so many Indian Teepees a thousand or more for they came from all over to attend this dance. In the middle of a circle of small teepees was a very large tent and in the middle of this tent was a large pole from which hung a stout cord. This cord was fastened to the breast of the Indian in this way. A good sized slit was made over each breast in the skin large enough to pass a stout cord through it and was held in place by a thong, and the poor victim had to dance backwards and forwards from side to side of the pole until the skin in the breast broke. Sometimes it took a long time, and it must have been very painful as he had to keep pulling on the cord to break the skin. Around one side of this tent were a number of young squaws with just their faces showing who kept jogging up and down with whistles in their mouths which were made of willow and that they blew all the time. An old Indian sat in the corner of the tent and beat on what was called a Tomtom which made an awful noise and must have added to the poor fellow's misery. At the end of a certain number of days they had a dog feast for they ate dogs in those days, and we were invited to the feast but were quite happy to decline. In those days when the young Indian wanted a girl the Father gave her to the brave who had the most horses or dogs.

The Sun Dance was part of the Indian religion, it was the Making of Braves as they called it. It was a religious ceremony and different from a powwow which was a jolly gathering.

We used to play with the Indian girls, in those days and also used to go in their Teepees and sit down sometimes, they were very nice to us too.

Violet Moorhead died on July 4, 1966. As well as the Sun Dance that she saw on the banks of Piapot Creek, she lived long enough to watch American astronauts rocket into space, to see John Kennedy assassinated. She could have told me about the Sun Dance herself, if I had come sooner.

———————•·—————

I meet Ben Broderick on one of my last days in town. Broderick is an ex-Mountie and now, like many people in many small towns, he has cobbled together a collection of pastimes to help pay the bills.

He is the deputy sheriff for the area out of Swift Current, the coroner, a part-time brand inspector and a sometimes justice of the peace. He ran a honey-bee operation for a while but now works on the pipeline in the autumn and as a security guard in the provincial park in the summer.

When he says, "I'll meet you in my office," he means the front table on the right in the B.C. Cafe. Ben Broderick likes to talk. He is known around town for his stories.

He has a big basset-hound face. He has big ear lobes and a bigger laugh. Mostly he likes to laugh at himself. When he's not working at something, he likes to get out into the prairie with his metal detector. He has an extensive collection of old coins, buttons and rings.

"And I'll be God-damned," he says, "if I can find that God-damn winter camp. I got so God-damned excited about that thing when I first read about it."

Broderick is talking about the camp where CPR rail workers wintered over 1882–83.

"I first read about it in the NWMP report of 1882. The commissionaire wrote to Ottawa that he had sent two men out from Fort Walsh to the camp to maintain law and order due to the influx of prostitutes and gamblers from Montana. Now, the navvies were paid with coin. So I've envisioned this place with lots of drinking and fights and guys stumbling around losing their coin, and I'll be God-damned if I can figure out where the son of a bitch is. Probably in the bottom of Piapot creek coulee, all filled in with mud and flooded. I know the bitch is out there some-where. I also read about it in the memoirs of one of our early pioneers. He says that he travelled from Fort Garry to the end of the steel during the winter of '82–'83 and that he got off the train at the end of the steel and went to Red's Saloon and procured conveyance to Maple Creek with a guy named Quesnelle. The son of a bitch is going to drive me bananas. Shit, I must have spent two hundred hours stomping around that God-damned country, but I'll be God-damned if I know where it is."

Broderick is driving my car for me, waving at and point-ing out landmarks no one else seems to know exist as we roam up and down the country where he came to work and that he can't seem to leave.

"See the gap?" he says, pointing to the valley that runs between the two tabletop hills known as the "west" and "centre" blocks. "That was once one of the largest migra-tion routes of buffalo anywhere. You go up into them hills and you'll see Indian rings and Indian graves all over the God-damn place."

He pulls off the road and we both stare at the rolling valley.

"You can almost see the buffalo, can't you?"

And then we are flying along a dirt side road and then bouncing up a lane that leaves it. Somewhere over the hori-zon someone has uncorked a hole and a dirty black cloud is spilling out of the ground and spreading over the sky. As it rushes towards us and the afternoon gets darker and darker, it feels as if there is going to be a nuclear explosion of rain.

"I want to show you something," says Ben.

Sweet clover growing thick on the edge of the lane brushes the side of the car and then is even closer so that Broderick is almost pushing the car through the bushes. And then the dirt lane isn't dirt anymore. We are driving on grass. To the top of a knoll where we stop and park. We are looking at a field.

"This is Alex Gold's field now. But you know what it was?"

Although he is waiting for my answer, Broderick knows that none is coming.

"This is where A Division came in 1882 when they closed down Fort Walsh. There was once twenty-two buildings in that field."

The wind is up hard now and soon it is raining again. The windshield wipers are slapping out a hypnotic rhythm. As the windows of the car steam up, I feel as if we are suspended on the knoll, alone and out of time.

"In 1919 the Mounties moved out of here and left one caretaker. Then in 1935 they tore down nine buildings but they left all the furniture and all the buggies in storage."

The wind is so strong now it is rocking the car.

"In 1941 the chief historian of the province of Saskatchewan came out here and took pictures of the buildings and he wrote the town and told them that he anticipated that the site would become of major historical importance and wondered if the town would entertain the idea of looking after the grounds until the province was prepared to do so. And the town wrote back that they weren't interested. And you know what happened? Everything was sold off. Every God-damn thing. There was an auction sale. And the buildings were torn down."

Broderick pauses and fixes me with his eyes.

"Now," he says, "let me tell you another story."

He fumbles with the package of cigarettes on the seat beside him, lights one, inhales deeply and leans back.

"In the late fifties they closed down the RCMP detachment at Wood Mountain and moved it down to Mankota. And when they moved it they moved everything, so a lot of the early diaries from Wood Mountain ended up down there.

"Well, it was just a one-man detachment and a friend of mine, Floyd Evans, ended up in charge. I was at Ponteix at the time, which is just down the line, so we used to visit back and forth and one day Floyd told me he wanted to show me something down in the basement. When we go down he pulls out these two great big old lance boxes about twelve feet long and opens one up and out come these God-damn books. Those old bastards used to go out on patrol for weeks. They'd stop in at ranches and sometimes be holed up for days on account of the weather. What they'd do is issue chits to the woman of the house and she would send them in and be reimbursed for the meals she had prepared. Well these were their diaries. God-damn if there weren't books down there written by Walsh himself. We used to sit for hours and read those suckers. Some of them covered the period of the Sitting Bull crisis. So Floyd tells Regina what he has, but no one is interested. They say they got too many books. Even in the fifties the emphasis wasn't on history. We used to talk about taking them. I made him promise me I could have a few, but we never did anything.

"Anyway. Floyd got transferred. And the day he was moved he fully intended to take those boxes with him. But the mover didn't take them. Well, two weeks later Floyd went back to do something or other, but what he really went back for was them books.

"And when he went down to the basement the boxes were gone.

"The new guy said, 'Oh, them lance boxes? I took them to the dump.'

"Floyd went out to the dump. But the boxes were gone. They had been burned.

"We talked it over so many times, you know. I had those books in my hands and why I never took one, I don't know. I guess because you felt guilty because you were in the force and you just never took stuff."

On the way back to the highway we pass the Gold farmhouse.

"See the white stones?" Broderick barks. "The stones in the garden there? See the big white stones in Mrs Gold's garden?"

The windows are too fogged and I can't see the stones, but Broderick isn't waiting for my answer, anyway.

"When they got the land, Mrs Gold wanted to make a garden and she kept finding these stones painted white on one side so she picked them up and used them in her garden. Well, Inspector Antrobus ordered his men to paint rocks white and line the footpaths around the division on both sides. That's where our history is now. In Mrs Gold's garden."

Broderick takes me to his house and sits me down at the dining-room table. He goes to a drawer and comes back with a small brass button. It has turned brown, the colour of rusty soil. There is an eagle embossed on the front. On the back it says "Scovill Mfg Co. Waterbury."

"I found that at the Hudson Bay crossing, right at the edge of the Moorhead Creek [Broderick pronounces it 'crick']. Do you know what it is?"

"Yes. I am holding a button from a U.S. cavalry uniform."

There are many explanations for how the button I am holding might have found its way to the banks of Moorhead Creek. It is unlikely that it fell off the jacket of an American soldier. There were never a lot of U.S. cavalry wandering around what was to become southern Saskatchewan. The most reasonable explanation is that someone else dropped it. In those days Indians liked to tie buttons and other scraps of metal to the fringes on their clothes. They liked the way the buttons jangled as they walked. Broderick believes the button came off an Indian legging — and therefore most likely it was brought to the creek bank by an American Indian — one of the Sioux who came north with Sitting Bull, perhaps. Maybe he dropped it himself, or maybe he traded it to someone else who lost it there.

It is possible — Broderick believes probable — that I am holding something that was cut off a soldier's jacket after the Battle of the Little Bighorn. I turn the button over and over in my hand and bring it to my face.

The next afternoon I come across one of those historical plaques you see beside the highway. I pull onto the shoulder and read the inscription.

> The Fort Qu'appelle – Fort Walsh Cart Trail crossed here, running from north-east to south-west. Used extensively by traders, freighters, mounted police, ranchers and other settlers, it was the main east–west thoroughfare prior to the construction of the Canadian Pacific Railway in 1883.

Across the road from the tablet there is a gate in the fence and two tracks leading up and over a hill. I swing my car off the highway and head up the lane. I get about a quarter of a mile before the mud is too thick to go any farther. Then I bounce another half mile or so on the grass beside the lane. When I can't go farther like that I park and continue on foot.

And that is when I spot it. Heading off to the south-west on about a forty-five degree angle to my lane — two ruts as plain as day stretching over the grassland, dipping over the scrubby hills.

I have read that if you scar the land in the arctic, so

delicate is the ecosystem that the mark will remain there for centuries. And here in this arid and dry corner of south Saskatchewan, where rain seldom falls and grass barely grows, only history lives without effort. And the flutter of cricket wings, the whistle of a gopher as she disappears down a hole with her tail flickering behind her, a meadowlark, the clouds, the sky, the wind. Always the wind.

Dresden

ONTARIO

You can't make a law to make one man love another. I think Premier Frost knew very well the law would not to do that. But it will eliminate the act of discrimination. And of course our personal feelings will come into it later. We'll learn to like each other.

HUGH BURNETT
BLACK CARPENTER
1954

Near the western end of Lake Erie, in a part of Canada that someone is bound to remind you shares the same latitude as northern California, Highway 40 begins its northwesterly run away from the shallowest of the Great Lakes and into the rich agricultural land of Kent County. If you are following the highway north, it is less than an hour and a half over your left shoulder to Windsor and the American city of Detroit, but ahead of you is tomato country. The fields, which crowd up against the dirt concession roads as if they are about to overflow them, are flat and fenceless, and so blessed with water that farmers have to bury pipes under their land to keep it drained.

Some thirty kilometres north of the lake, after you pass through the city of Chatham, Ontario, you'll come on a public golf course on the corner where Concession 9 cuts Highway 40. The sign says "Country View Golf Course," but because the fairways are as flat as Saskatchewan, locals jokingly call their club "Hidden Hills." If you turn here and follow Concession 9 towards the north-east, you eventually meet the banks of the Sydenham River — and there find the town of Dresden, Ontario.

The town fathers long ago recognized that, like me, most visitors would arrive from the south. All that greets anyone coming from the north is a standard highway sign with white letters:

DRESDEN
Population 2,700

At the south end of town, however, where Concession 9 merges with Highway 21 from Thamesville, there is a weathered billboard welcoming you to "HISTORIC DRESDEN CANADA'S LITTLE SARATOGA." Just before the billboard there is another green highway sign:

DRESDEN
Population 2,600

These days it is likely that the figure at the south of town is the more accurate. Dresden isn't growing. In fact, the population hasn't changed considerably since 1882, when it was already 2,080.

To a careful eye the look of the town hasn't altered, either. Though the store-fronts along St George Street have changed hands regularly, the brick façades of the buildings are the same today as they were at the turn of the century. If you stand on the corner of St George and Main and look along the second storey of the town's main street, you can easily imagine it is a Sunday in 1929, when you might have spent the afternoon sitting on the post office steps making bets on what kind of automobile would rattle into view next.

If the billboard (and the racetrack) at the south peg the beginning of town, the end is staked by the river. When you cross the bridge over the Sydenham, all that's left is the high school on your right and the neighbourhood known as North Dresden, and then you are back into the country. Back into the fields that Dresden depends on.

There have been all manner of businesses over the years — four brickyards, an apple-evaporation plant, a sugar-beet factory, a woodworking plant that made wooden hubs and spokes and was once licensed to manufacture the famed Louisville Slugger baseball bat, a failed attempt to build airplanes during the 1920s and, more recently, small manufacturing plants that supply the automotive industry in Detroit. All these enterprises open up like a salesman's smile — sometimes they even prosper for a spell — but they inevitably close. It always comes back to the fields. The town's most enduring and largest employer is the canning plant. Dresden is where Aylmer manufactures all the ketchup they produce in Canada.

There are two schools, two pharmacies, two hardware stores, two video outlets, two pizza parlours, two flower stores, two grocery shops and three lawyers. Two, however, are part time. They come to town a half day a week.

There is a handful of restaurants and one doughnut joint.

"The doughnut shop is where the smokers hang out," says Bea Harris over coffee one morning.

"I wouldn't recommend it," she adds. "Even the doughnuts taste of smoke."

Three new businesses have opened up in the past year — a unisex hairdresser on Main, a clothing store for kids and a second-hand store that sells clothes and furniture. In the same year, the furniture store that sold new items, one of the two grocery stores and a women's clothing store have all closed. So did N.H.S. Die Casting. N.H.S. opened up just after the war and managed to stay in business for forty years, manufacturing things like the inside door handles for Cadillacs. When they closed, 160 people lost their jobs. N.H.S. was the town's second-largest employer.

These have not been easy years. Dresden has become the kind of place you have to leave if you want a night out on the town. There's no movie theatre anymore. The hotel will serve you a drink, but they won't rent you a room. You might take lunch downtown at Marlene's Restaurant or across the street at Dad's Place, but for dinner most people drive to Chatham or Sarnia, or even over the St Clair River into the United States. If they want to buy a new suit or a dress they might go as far as Windsor or London. Even if all you want to do is curl, you still have to drive to the curling club in Wallaceburg.

The houses are more varied than those in most small towns. Some of the largest — three storey brick mansions that sit on generous lots — have been converted into apartments and old people's homes and, in one case, into the town's only funeral parlour. The newer homes are bungalows; the older ones are two-storey and wood frame. Walking along the side streets (which extend seven blocks from St George in one direction and three in the other), I am struck that while many of the houses may be small by city standards, the lots they sit on are larger than I am used to. I am also struck by how quiet a neighbourhood can be. Kids set up their hockey nets in the middle of the street and never seem troubled by the traffic.

It is a well-treed town. It should be. The surrounding countryside was a virgin forest until lumbering began in earnest in 1846. The forest was full of deer, bear, wolves, foxes and wild turkey, and crowded with magnificent trees — the beech with its shimmering bark, the oak with its cathedral branches, the elm, in pioneer days known for its longevity, the walnut, so abundant that it was once used for fence posts, then so scarce that one tree, wrote Donald Peattie in *A Natural History of Trees,* could be worth upwards of twenty thousand dollars wholesale. So desirable that "it is sought by lumbermen in a door to door hunt through the countryside, where owners are sometimes tempted by a small price to sacrifice a magnificent shade tree worth in some cases, if they but knew it, more than their houses."

And, of course, the maple.

Someone tells me that many of the maples around town were planted over one hundred years ago by a Church of England missionary. Thomas Hughes came to British North America from England where he was the headmaster of a school. He was inspired to immigrate by reports he had read about the welfare of fugitive slaves living in Canada West.

Thousands of men, women and children fled slavery in the years before the end of the American Civil War. Most of them settled in the free states of the Union. About 30,000 sought refuge in the Canadas — many helped by the abolitionists whose barns and back bedrooms became known as the Underground Railroad. Most of those who crossed the border settled around Windsor and Chatham. A good number of them made it to Dresden.

Thomas Hughes took a year of theological training in the village of Lambeth before settling in Dresden. He opened a day school and began preaching. He kept a diary.

August 4, 1861: A few strange white people present at the afternoon service. Not more than one or two white people of the village ever come now. Some complain of the room which is certainly most unwholesome this hot weather, but the true reason is a determination not to mix with the colored people.

And yet.

When he gave the Massey Lectures in 1967, Martin Luther King, Jr. spoke of the "historical relationship between American Negroes and Canadians."

Canada is not merely a neighbor to Negroes. Deep in our history of struggle for freedom Canada was the North Star. The Negro slave, denied education, de-humanized, imprisoned on cruel plantations, knew that far to the north a land existed where a fugitive slave if he survived the horrors of the journey could find freedom. The legendary Underground Railroad started in the South and ended in Canada. The freedom road links us together. Our spirituals, now so widely admired around the world, were often codes. We sang of "heaven" that awaited us, and the slave masters listened in innocence, not realizing that we were not speaking of the hereafter. Heaven was the word for Canada, and the Negro sang of the hope that his escape on the Underground Railroad would carry him there. One of our spirituals, "Follow the Drinking Gourd," in its lyrics contained disguised directions for escape. The gourd was the Big Dipper, and the North Star to which its handle pointed gave the celestial map that directed the flight to the Canadian border.

"So standing today in Canada," said King, "I am linked with the history of my people and its unity with your past."

One of the slaves who escaped to Canada was a man called Josiah Henson. He fled north from a plantation in Kentucky. He brought his family with him and they eventually settled in Dresden. Henson was a farmer who described himself as a man of physical strength. He was illiterate, but he was also a preacher of some renown. With help from British Quakers and a group of abolitionists, Henson established a sort of refugee camp and school in Dresden. It was called the British-American Institute. In 1849 he published his autobiography. In 1858 it was reprinted, this time with an introduction by Harriet Beecher Stowe. Henson is believed by many to have been a model for Stowe's influential novel, *Uncle Tom's Cabin.* The only book that sold more copies in its day was the Bible.

Josiah Henson — or Uncle Tom, as some would have it — is buried in Dresden. Just west of town there is a small museum that includes two original buildings from his British-American Institute. Some of his direct descendants still live in town.

It is Henson's story that has drawn me here. I want to believe that Martin Luther King Jr. had it right. That in dark times we shed a little light.

I fear the truth is more complicated.

———— • ————

Today, the tallest building in Dresden, by virtue of the brick tower in its south-west corner, is the Municipal Building at the intersection of St George and Main. The tower is home to Dresden's most striking landmark — the town clock. At night the clock, which is lit from the back, hangs over St George Street like a full moon. After thirty years of silence the clock bell has recently resumed ringing. Patrick Richie — who manages the Dresden liquor store and is also a member of Chapter 92 of the National Association of Watch and Clock Collectors Inc. — spent months working in the tower in his spare time. Richie will tell you that, though there is a bit of play in the hands, the clock keeps pretty good time.

The town council paid Richie for his labour. They continue to pay him in his role of clock-winder and trouble-shooter, but he won't discuss what he makes.

"It's not worth the labour," he says. "You'd have to love it to do it. A watch-maker could make more money putting batteries into wristwatches."

On Wednesday morning outside the liquor store, a stray dog has discovered a game that has Richie baffled.

"Here he comes again," he says, peering thoughtfully over the counter. The mutt is charging the store with the determination of a hound after a rabbit. Just when it seems certain he is going to smash into the glass door, the dog cuts and veers right. He misses by a hair. But he comes close enough to trigger the electronic eye, and the liquor store door swings open. The dog barks and whirls across the street for another pass.

"He started this yesterday," Richie says, shaking his head.

Richie has been working at the liquor store since 1976. He commutes to Dresden from Chatham every morning. It's a twenty-minute drive. He usually brings his lunch and eats at a small table tucked between shelves of Canadian Club and beer at the back of the store. Today he is eating quickly because he has a chore to do. Twice a week, after he has finished his sandwich, Richie walks over to city hall and climbs the flight of stairs and two separate ladders that take him to the top of the clock tower. The two-hundred-pound weights that he is hauling up would keep the clock running for eight days but Richie likes to come more often than that. As he peers over the ledge and onto the town below him he says he is proud of his restoration job.

"There's not that many clock towers left around, and it's sort of nice to hear the bell ringing again. You always know what time it is now because if you can't see the clock you can always hear it. And if the power should go off it'll just keep ticking. It doesn't matter about the hydro to the clock. It brings back the older days."

Old-timers say you used to be able to hear the bell in the old town hall at least five miles into the country. But the town clerk, worried about the condition of the bell tower, had the bell removed and mounted in cement outside his office. He planted flowers in it and, if you looked closely, you could see the crack in the bell casing caused, the story went, by excessive ringing during Dresden's celebrations at the relief of besieged Ladysmith during the Boer War.

The bell at the fire hall used to ring at noon and at nine in the evening to signal curfew for all those under the age of fourteen. The bell at the old McVean factory rang at starting time and quitting time and, like all the other bells in town, at the noon break.

You don't hear town bells the way you used to. It is too bad. A bell lends a certain orderliness to a town — anoints the noon meal with righteousness, resolves the end of the work day with dignity, infuses dusk with a sense of purpose.

Most bells like the one in the Dresden tower are cast in bronze — an alloy of copper and tin. In time of war, like boys taken from their homes and dressed up as soldiers, bells, born as instruments of peace, have been wrestled out of bell towers and returned to the forges to become instruments of conflict.

During World War II, writes the German radio documentary-maker Peter Leonhard Braun, Hermann Göring ordered that only ten bells would be preserved in all of Germany. The rest would be reborn as brass cartridges, copper bearings and tin siding on airplanes. When the churches objected, Göring relented and permitted them to keep five percent of the nation's bells.

So altogether about 47,000 German bells were melted to feed the German military machine.

If you include the bells that were taken from Poland. Czechoslovakia, Holland, Belgium, France, Italy, Austria and Hungary, then 80,000 European bells were silenced by the Nazis.

"In Europe," says Braun, "the guns chime and the bells fire."

After the war, however, the cannons were melted and forged again into bells. And so it is that I look forward to the hourly sounding of the clock bell. It makes me smile. A blessing of bronze. Music from metal. A song of peace.

———————■•■———————

Marlene's is where I have chosen to take most of my meals while in Dresden. The service is friendly, the food home-cooked and fresh. Marlene's is one of the town's social cen-tres. Mornings, before breakfast, a "Reserved" sign is placed in the corner booth, the largest booth in the place. At nine o'clock many of Dresden's businessmen gather here for their morning coffee. This booth, I have been told, is where much of the town's business is decided.

"It is," explains Lillian Steele, who happens to be hav-ing her coffee beside me one morning, "the sanctum sanc-torum." She smiles and nods her head at the corner table. "The morning seminar."

I smile.

"I'm serious," she says. "I'm taking my Master's at the University of Windsor and I have watched professors strug-gle to get seminars going and none of them have come any-where close to those guys. They talk about everything. They talk about world affairs. They talk about local affairs. When the GST was coming in they drew up a petition to get Dresden declared a GST-free zone. Half the town signed it. All sorts of things start over there."

Friday nights at Marlene's, I am told, is like a party.

"You've never seen anything like it," says Lynn Stathis who, with her husband Tony, runs the restaurant. "It fills up pretty full and people move from table to table talking to each other. Everyone knows everyone else. Like I say, it's a party."

When I am not pressed for time I go to the Track Kitchen for breakfast. The Kitchen is a hang-out on the barn side of the racetrack, snuggled up against the backstretch rail-ing. Most of the people who eat here are either trainers or horse owners. There are only ten tables and all but two are beside a window, so you can watch the trotters glide by as you eat. The horses remind me of small planes. Every time I eat at the track I am reminded of country airports with grass runways.

There are about two hundred horses stabled in the low-slung barns at the Dresden Racetrack. Most of the fellows in town who own a horse train it themselves. That means a daily trip to the track, and that means there are plenty of regulars at the Kitchen. More than one of the men thumping around the turf is over sixty. Thirty or forty guys work at the horses full time. For everybody else this is a hobby. The Kitchen is where they come to cry and brag.

There are always rags-to-riches stories at a track, and the track restaurant is always the best place to hear them. You can't hang around the Kitchen for long before someone will tell you that Wilf Duford once paid $500 for a gelding and went on to win over $400,000 with him. Or the time Bill Habkirk paid $175 for a stallion called Camper. For a while Camper held every track record in Ontario.

Stories like that keep people coming to the track. It may just be a hobby, but it is the money that invests the hobby with purpose. When they talk about the show-horse crowd, the guys at the Kitchen just shake their heads.

"Show people think we're crazy," says someone. "Well, we know they're crazy. All they can win is a ribbon."

The talk around the tables is always friendly, usually interesting and mostly unimportant. How come, someone wonders, it's bad luck to knock down cobwebs in a barn?

"Shit," says Jim Eagleson, "I don't know. I was cleaning up in the barn one time and Joe Booth said, 'DON'T DO THAT!' So I've never done it again."

There is racing every Wednesday night and Sunday afternoon June through October. There is a group of regulars — mostly old-timers, most of them with a peripheral association to the track — who gather by the backstretch fence every race day. No one would think to suggest they should pay the two-dollar entrance fee and watch from the grandstand. A few years ago a few guys got together and built a platform back there by the quarter pole for "Tiny" Oliphant. Tiny used to come to the races in a wheelchair and though the platform is barely off the ground it allowed him the advantage he needed to see over the fence. There was usually someone around to run his bets for him.

It's not the best racing in the country but it isn't the worst. If a horse can't make it at Dresden it might be shipped down east for one more try. If it is too lame to run anymore it might be sold to a Mennonite around Elmira. The Mennonites like to have an old trotter pulling their carriages. They like the way the trotters walk. The best-looking ones — the black trotters — often go to the Amish in the States.

"I once got a call from a guy in West Virginia. An Amish guy," says Jim Eagleson with disbelief. "I sold an old horse to a dealer for $300 and it ended up down there. The guy was calling because he wanted to know the horse's story."

Last year there was an average of 1,100 paying customers at the track on race nights. Of course, that doesn't include the boys who watch from Guy Lambkin's backyard. Or, as race secretary Jay Lekavy refers to them, the guys at the Clubhouse.

Whoever owned Guy Lambkin's white clapboard house when they built the Dresden Racetrack refused to sell out. Everything else was bought up and pulled down. But Guy's house is still there — so close to the track you could lean over his backyard fence and touch the horses as they float by. You sometimes hear of apartment buildings around old ballparks that are blessed with a balcony and an obscured view of left field, but few balconies are as blessed as Guy Lambkin's backyard. Every race day about twenty of Guy's friends show up to watch the races with him. The Clubhouse or, as Cal Stephens likes to call it, The Top of the Turn Tavern, is really a garage Guy bought and moved into his backyard for the purpose of watching the races.

"One day he came home," remembers Guy's wife, Margaret, "and he says to me, 'I got a chance to get a nice garage for the car.' And I thought, 'That would be good,' so he bought it, and he had it moved into the backyard, but the first thing I know, I turned around and he had the garage door off and he's putting in a picture window that looks over the track."

"It's like a club we have," says Guy smiling. "Just me and my friends. If the race starts at one-thirty they arrive about twelve-thirty. They park over at the arena. Then we go out back and start comparing notes."

"They go over the program," says Margaret, "and get their notes all ready for the first bet."

"Which is the daily double," says Guy.

They have a runner who takes their bets over to the track before each race. If it is one of the younger guys, he can make it from the garage to the pari-mutuel window in three minutes easy.

"See the gate over there?" Guy is pointing at a large fence that separates his backyard from the grandstand. "The track gave us a key to that gate because we're so good for business."

"They have binoculars," says Margaret.

"And we can hear the track announcer," adds Guy.

"And at the end of the year they have a banquet," says Margaret. "Everybody brings food. And we rent a tent. This has been going on for ten years."

"Last summer we went away for July and August and I left the guys a key to the garage," says Guy.

"It works out well," says Margaret. "They watch over the place for us."

If somebody makes a big hit — say, pockets $300 on the Daily Double — he is expected to buy a beer for everyone in the club. You pay on an honour system — $1.75 into the can by the fridge. The biggest winner ever was Aaron McFadden. He won the Triactor one afternoon and pocketed $1,840 on a $6 ticket. Aaron had brought his thirteen-year-old daughter, Tara, with him that afternoon. She picked the three winning numbers.

The biggest race of the year is on Labour Day. Even the boys at the Clubhouse pay to go to the races on Labour Day. Last year 2,500 paid attendance, which is double the normal rate and pretty near the population of the town. After the Labour Day race everyone heads up to the Legion for the annual chicken barbecue.

———•———

I have checked into a crummy motel about twenty minutes away in Wallaceburg. It is one of these new chains that is notable only for its price. My window overlooks a Pizza Hut parking lot, and several nights I am woken by carloads of kids who come for last call.

Before turning in each night I have been reading Josiah Henson's autobiography. A number of editions of his story were printed, and the ones I have seen vary significantly. The version I am reading, only seventy pages long, is a reproduction of the first edition published in 1849. I read a few pages every night.

Henson was born into slavery on June 15, 1789, on a Maryland farm. His earliest memory was the day his father returned home horribly beaten.

"His right ear had been cut off close to his head," writes Henson, "and he had received a hundred lashes on his back."

The beating had been inflicted because Henson's father had attacked a white man — the overseer on the farm where he worked. The overseer had allegedly assaulted, or maybe raped, Henson's mother.

The family was soon split up. The father was sold to Alabama, says Henson, "and neither my mother nor I ever heard of him again."

Brothers and sisters were sold separately at auction. His mother was bought by a man called Isaac Riley.

My mother, half distracted with the parting forever from all her children, pushed through the crowd, while the bidding for me was going on, to the spot where Riley was standing. She fell at his feet, and clung to his knees, entreating him in tones that a mother only could command, to buy her baby as well as herself, and spare to her one of her little ones at least. Will it, can it be believed that this man, thus appealed to, was capable not merely of turning a deaf ear to her supplication, but of disengaging himself from her with such violent blows and kicks, as to reduce her to the necessity of creeping out of his reach. . . .

Henson was eventually reunited with his mother on Riley's plantation and lived there in appalling conditions during his teenage years. The slaves at Riley's existed on corn meal and salted herring.

"The only dress," says Henson, "was of tow cloth, which for the young, and often even for those who had passed the period of childhood, consisted of a single garment, something like a shirt, but longer, reaching to the ancles [sic]. . . . Our lodging was in log huts, of a single small room, with no other floor than the trodden earth, in which ten or a dozen persons — men, women, and children — might sleep."

Yet he describes himself as a vigorous and healthy boy — "there were few," he says, "who could compete with me in work, or in sport."

He was degraded, starved and abused, but he was also respected. He became superintendent of farm work, and his responsibilities included trips to Washington and Georgetown to sell produce in local markets.

"My master and my fellow slaves used to look upon me, and speak of me, as a wonderfully smart fellow and prophecy the great things I should do when I became a man."

In the winter of 1825, when Henson was thirty-six years old, Isaac Riley, a heavy drinker, suddenly found himself in dire straits as a result of a lawsuit. He entreated Josiah to take all the slaves to his brother Amos in Kentucky and thus prevent them from being seized by the sheriff and sold at auction.

In Kentucky Josiah soon became general manager of Amos Riley's farm. He began to attend church meetings and though he could neither read nor write, he was admitted as a preacher by the Methodist Episcopal Church in 1828.

Encouraged by another Methodist, Henson set about to raise the money he would need to buy his freedom. He received permission to visit his master, Isaac Riley, in Maryland.

> "I . . . travelled leisurely from town to town, preaching as I went, and, wherever circumstances were favorable, soliciting aid in my great object. I succeeded so well, that when I arrived at Montgomery county, I was master of two hundred and seventy-five dollars, besides my horse and my [new] clothes."

Isaac Riley agreed to give Henson his manumission papers for $450 — $350 in cash, which Henson raised by selling his horse and adding the proceeds to what he had earned through preaching, and the remainder due in the form of a note. Henson paid his share of the bargain but the receipt, which was mailed to Amos Riley in Kentucky, set the price of his freedom at $1,000. He still owed a prohibitive $650.

When it became clear that Isaac and Amos Riley were not only going to deny Henson his freedom, but fully intended to sell him in the slave markets of New Orleans, Henson finally determined that he was going to flee with his family to Canada.

> . . . I communicated my intention to my wife, who was too much terrified by the dangers of the attempt to do anything, at first, but endeavor to dissuade me from it, and try to make me contented with my condition as it

was. In vain I explained to her the liability we were in of being separated from our children as well as from each other; and presented every argument which had weighed with my own mind, and had at last decided me. . . . I argued the matter with her, at various times, till I was satisfied that argument alone would not prevail; and then I said to her, very deliberately, that though it was a cruel thing for me to part with her, yet I would do it, and take all the children with me but the youngest, rather than run the risk of forcible separation from them all and of a much worse captivity besides, which we were constantly exposed to here. She wept and entreated, but found I was resolute, and after a whole night spent in talking over the matter, I left her to go to my work for the day. I had not gone far when I heard her voice calling me — I waited till she came up to me, and then, finding me as determined as ever, she said, at last, she would go with me. It was an immense relief to my nerves, and my tears flowed as fast as hers had done before. I rode off with a heart a good deal lighter.

It took Henson and his family about six weeks to reach Canada. They travelled mostly by night through the forest. North of Scioto, they were befriended by Indians and slept in a wigwam. At Sandusky they met a sympathetic Scottish captain who in return for a day's labour took the family to Buffalo on his boat. The next day the captain paid the three-shilling fare for them to cross the river into Canada by ferry and gave Henson a dollar to take with him. It was October 28, 1830.

I threw myself on the ground, rolled in the sand, seized handfuls of it and kissed them, danced round till, in the eyes of several who were present, I passed for a madman. "He's some crazy fellow," said a Colonel Warren, who happened to be there. "O, no, master! Don't you know? I'm free!" He burst into a shout of laughter. "Well, I never knew freedom [could] make a man roll in the sand in such fashion." Still I could not control myself. I hugged and kissed my wife and children, and, until the first exuberant burst of feeling was over, went on as before.

Barbara Carter is the great-great-granddaughter of Josiah Henson. She lives with her husband, Bruce, on their seventy-one-acre farm about ten minutes south of Dresden. Bruce is a Pioneer seed dealer and corn farmer. From May to October Barbara is the site manager for Uncle Tom's Cabin — the small museum on the edge of Dresden that commemorates her ancestor.

We are sitting around the fireplace in the Carters' comfortable living-room. There is a fire burning behind an airtight glass door. Barbara is tired, home late from an auction. She collects American pottery and Victorian furniture, but she didn't see anything worth buying today.

"There's not much I can tell you about Josiah Henson," she says when I ask about the man who has led me here. "Not in the way of family lore, anyway. No one ever talked about him in the family. It's sad to say but it's true. I remember one of my cousins once asked our grandmother for information, but she wouldn't talk. That was back in the days if someone older than you said leave it alone then you left it. My folks never talked about him. They never talked about him at all.

"As far as I understand he went to Massachusetts and Harriet Beecher Stowe got to know of him and what he was saying and that's what inspired her to write the book."

The conversation wanders. We talk about the museum, about Barbara's grandfather, Beecher Henson, named after Harriet Beecher Stowe ("We called him 'Uncle Beech' "). About the weather. And, inevitably, about growing up in Dresden. The Carters are the first black family I have met. In fact, they are the first blacks I have seen since coming to town. But I have been reading another book at night — an unusually candid local history by the ex-editor of the local newspaper.

"No honest attempt to chronicle the lives and times of the people of this community," writes Don Spearman about the blacks in Dresden, "should exclude ... the indignities they suffered and the ignominious conditions under which they were forced to live."

At first I am uncomfortable about bringing the subject up.

"From their first arrival in Canada," Spearman continues, "the blacks were subject to discrimination and derision. There were black-face minstrel shows, and the race in general was the butt of many jokes. They were denied access to places habituated by whites: restaurants, barber shops and pool rooms."

Bruce Carter stands up to get me another beer. We have been talking for an hour now. There has been no mention of colour. They are a comfortable middle-class family. I am worried that if I bring the subject up, I will somehow be drawing attention to something that shouldn't matter to me.

"You're black," I finally say. "It must have been hard growing up here."

"When you are brought up with discrimination," says Barbara, "you know what you can do and what you can't do. So you just abide by the rules and it's not that bad. We knew we couldn't go into the restaurants with our white girl-friends after school, so we just didn't go. I never understood, however, why there were two churches. There were two Baptist churches in town. One for the whites and one for the blacks."

"It was different for me," says Bruce. "I was a very bitter person when I was a teenager. At one time there was not one restaurant in town where I could get a cup of coffee. Toward the end of the war we had German prisoners of war around here. They were working in the sugar-beet fields under guard. The prisoners of war could go into the restaurants, but a negro soldier in a Canadian army uniform couldn't. It was pretty bad. My aunt taught in a segregated school. The last one closed some time in the sixties.''

The Carters' daughter, Gayle, is visiting for the weekend from Detroit. She has been in the kitchen cooking, but she joins us now in the living-room. She is thirty-seven years old and married.

''When I was growing up all my friends were white,'' she says. ''I felt no discrimination at all in school. But I knew outside the school it was different. No one ever said anything but I knew that no one wanted me dating their son.''

''We went down to Disney World a while ago,'' says Bruce. ''We went to the Canadian pavilion. They have a movie about Canada there. It's a tremendous movie — all in the round. But do you know what? There is not one black person in the whole movie. I was watching it and I thought, 'Wait a minute, where am I?' So I sat through it a second time to make sure. It's like we're a non-people. We weren't even in the crowd scenes.''

———— • ————

The juke-box in the bar of the Dresden Hotel favours country artists like Johnny Paycheck and Merle Haggard. Moe Bandy is singing a hurting number called ''Too Old to Die Young'' when I slip in later that night looking for beer and conversation. The basement bar, all that's left of the hotel, is a smoky fellowship of Arborite tables. It is the kind of place where you order two drafts at once. With the kind of pool table where there is bound to be a cigarette balanced on the rim and someone stretching over the felt for a shot they'll probably miss.

There are always plenty of tables to choose from at the hotel. Tonight there are two guys playing pool, three guys from the Kings — the town hockey team (who tied 4 – 4 tonight, thus eliminating themselves from the playoffs) — one old ball player, and maybe ten other customers around the room. The one waitress has plenty of time to chat to the people at the bar as well as serve the tables.

The old ball player is Gerald Cook. He is wearing a red ski jacket, work boots and a peaked hat with a crest that says "WILMOTT FUELS." He is drinking beer with his friend George Segaert.

"There has been a lot of good ball around here," says George, nodding at Gerald, "and this man played most of it."

Gerald Cook is sixty-seven years old. He is also black, although someone had to tell me that. To me he doesn't look any darker than the average Saskatchewan farmer. His face has the same lined roughness. His great-great-grandmother came from Holland.

Gerald played ball in Dresden in the early forties. He was a pitcher. He was scouted by the New York Yankees in the days when blacks were not allowed to play in the bigs. In 1950, when he was playing for St Thomas in the inter-county league, he was given a chance to join a Triple A Yankee farm team in Olean, New York. It was one step away from the majors.

"I had a shot," he says, moving his head back and forth, cradling his beer. "But, ah, shit, that's water under the bridge."

Gerald decided not to go to New York. That was forty years ago, and people in town are still talking about it.

"I was going to go. But I was engaged to be married at the time. I was in love. And I thought, If I go down there I might never come back."

It was 1950. Jackie Robinson had just broken in with the Brooklyn Dodgers.

"Yeah. I watched all them news broadcasts. I saw what happened to him. And I thought to myself, I'm not going to do that. I lived through all that right here in the town of Dresden when I was going to school. I had to get off the sidewalk to let white people go by. I'd get to school OK, but when three-thirty came and school was out, there was lots of times I had to fight my way across the bridge to get home. Those were white guys I was fighting."

Gerald tips his beer back and takes a long slug.

"You've never been discriminated against," he says, looking at me intently. "I know what you're missing and I wouldn't wish it on anyone.

"Imagine how you feel when you're a kid with ten cents in your pocket and you go into a restaurant because you want an ice cream cone and when they give it to you they say, 'Go on. Out on the street now. You aren't allowed to eat that in here.' Imagine living with that. Imagine what it does to you. It's tough. It's really tough."

George Segaert is shaking his head as he listens. George is white.

"Hearing you say that bothers me, Cookie," he says. "I just can't believe that's true. But you're saying it so I know it is."

"It *is* hard to believe," says Cook. "But it happened. Right in Dresden. I lived through it. There were people watched me play in towns around here who used the word nigger. 'Don't you get caught down here after sundown, boy.' People said that to me. That hurt. That's hard to swallow. I used to keep saying to myself, 'This has *gotta* end.'

"Boy it was tough. You see it on TV today. I see it on TV. It still goes on. But not here. I'm glad to live in Dresden today."

"Hearing this makes me upset, Cookie," says George.

"Ah, time is a great healer. You learn to forgive and forget."

Gary McCorkle is fifty-one years old. Gary lives in a bungalow by the racetrack. He, too, is black.

"It was hell growing up," he says to me one morning in the Track Kitchen. "Dad had to take us to Chatham to get our hair cut. The barbers in Dresden wouldn't cut coloured people's hair. There was a restaurant called Kay's. We weren't allowed in there. They wouldn't serve us. I had lots of white buddies at school, but when we came over the bridge and they went into the pool room or them restaurants, I had to go home.

"It was nothing for my mother to wake up on a Saturday morning and there'd be five or six riding horses tied to the clothesline. These would belong to white friends of mine who had slept over. But their parents wouldn't let me stay in their houses.

"I still feel pain for the way I was treated back then. You just don't get over it. I feel hatred for the people who wouldn't let us have ice cream.

"One time five or six of us, we planned this, we got together and went into James Ford's pool room. We walked through the barber shop and turned the lights on in the pool room at the back and he asked us what we were doing. We said, 'We are going to play a game of pool,' and he said, 'You can't shoot any pool here,' so we took the sticks and we broke them over our knees.

"You know what? There was coloured farmers who could have bought those people out — those people who wouldn't serve us. My daddy was one of them.

"People talk about the U.S. and how bad it was. This was as bad as any place in the U.S. The only difference was we didn't have the population. If we had as many people as they did, there would have been riots and killings."

Doug Browning is fifty-four years old. He works in a steel plant in Chatham. He comes back to Dresden every Sunday to attend church with his mother. One Sunday I join him and his mother after church for Sunday brunch at Dad's.

"Jim Ford's Barbershop and Pool Hall? Oh, sure. I remember all that. It was the same with all the barbers in town. If you were black and you wanted your hair cut you had to go to Chatham. Everyone went to Art the barber in Chatham. And Emersons Restaurant. You weren't supposed to go there either. You might go in and sit down but you'd never get waited on. After the law changed and they had to serve coloured people I heard they would salt the food so bad you couldn't eat it.

"They used to say Jim Crow was alive and well and living in Dresden. But that has all changed now."

It has all changed. But the changes didn't come fast and they didn't come easily. And they weren't given. They had to be taken.

Change began when members of the black community in Kent County started to meet at night around kitchen tables to discuss their situation. In 1948, the year the United Nations ratified the Universal Declaration of Human Rights, Dresden's black citizens had to form an organization they called the National Unity Association. In 1949 they sent a deputation to town council.

Their spokesman, William Carter, said they wanted a bylaw "with teeth in it" that would license restaurants and require them to serve people without discriminating. Carter vowed his group would show up at every council meeting until something was done. The meeting was reported in the *Chatham News*. Mayor Walter S. Weese locked horns with Carter in a dramatic debate:

> "Where does council's authority begin and where does it end," the mayor said. "If this was a socialistic state, and the restaurants were owned by the state we would have control, but how can you force any man to serve anyone he does not want to serve. I am against racial discrimination, and I think you know it."
>
> "If you feel that way," Carter replied, "why don't you follow the dictates of your heart?...Otherwise why don't you get off the council?"
>
> "There is no discrimination in my soul," Mayor Weese said.
>
> "Nor is there in your stores," Carter agreed [Mayor Weese owned a self-serve grocery store].
>
> "But, as mayor I am mayor for all the people, and there are intelligent colored people who tell me you are killing their cause."
>
> "I can't think of any intelligent colored person who

would think that," Carter retorted, "but we do have those who lack the guts to stand up and fight."

Mayor Weese inferred that he did not like threats of rowdyism and if it broke out, and Carter agreed, "the police will stop it." Continuing he said, "I have been plagued for weeks by people who say they hear threats of violence. . . ."

Electrifying council . . . Councillor Fry, shoving back his chair, rose to his feet to protest.

"I'm surprised," he said, "at our mayor carrying on a meeting such as this."

Before he could continue, Mayor Weese declared him out of order, and ordered him to sit down.

"I am not out of order," [said] Councillor Fry, "you are the one who is out of order. When you meet a delegation, you hear it, not argue with it. You hear it and refer it to new business for council to discuss. I don't know very much about municipal procedure, but I know that much.

"It seems like I am the only one who has guts enough to get up and tell you so."

Jumping to his feet, Councillor Ernie Willmott, startled council still farther by saying, "Fry, you better take that back and keep your . . . mouth shut, you . . . ."

Coming to council's rescue, Carter quietly observed, "It isn't my place to say what I might think of councillors who call names across the table, but I fail to understand if I am allowed to buy meat in one store, bread and vegetables in another to take home to eat, why I can't enter a restaurant where they are prepared for public use."

Regaining his composure, Mayor Weese said, ". . . This is a big issue. . . . I want it settled. Do you think a bylaw will settle this question once and for all?"

"It will if you enact a bylaw and put teeth in it," Carter replied.

"...We aren't afraid of the restaurant owners. Perhaps we are afraid of enacting a bylaw which is unknown here or in any other part of Canada. We might also fear our ability to enact legislation which we think will not cure the situation. I haven't much faith in legislation to cure moral laws. ..."

"Is it in order for me to speak, Mr. Mayor?" Councillor Fry asked.

"Yes," the mayor replied. ...

" ... If I go back to my store tonight and open up, the police will stop me," he said. "If they can be passed to control me why should they not be passed to control others providing that they benefit our citizens.

"I am in favor of a bylaw to license restaurants, regardless of race, creed or color and let the police commission enforce it. ..."

Speaking for the first time, Councillor George Wellman said, "Councils have side-stepped this issue for a long time. It is too big for a half dozen men. Give it to the people and let them decide by vote."

Council agreed to hold a civic referendum.

Two weeks later the Toronto *Telegram* carried the following story datelined Dresden.

William Carter and Hugh R. Burnett, two Negroes living in Dresden, reported today they had received threatening letters. ...

Hugh R. Burnett said the threat to his life and property had been in a letter postmarked Dresden, sent to William Carter. The letter read:

"Go easy, Mr. Carter. You and Mr. Burnett will be destroyed. Bring on your riots. We are ready for you. We will fix you quick."

The letter was signed with a skull and crossbones.

It was not the first threat Carter and Burnett had received. They had both had anonymous telephone calls

warning them they would be "burned out" if they persist-
ed in their efforts to integrate the restaurants. So had
Councillor Michael Fry.

After delays of almost a year a plebiscite was scheduled
for the following December. By now the situation had
caught the attention of the national press. A month before
the plebiscite, Sidney Katz came to town and wrote a damn-
ing piece for *Maclean's* magazine called "Jim Crow Lives in
Dresden." He found the town's whites "unhappy and stub-
bornly unwilling to discuss the problem."

"You can sense the fear," he wrote, "expressed in the
twin bogies which I heard over and over again. 'Look mis-
ter, would you like a nigger to marry your sister?' and
'Well, *I'm* against discrimination but I got to think of my
business.' "

Katz went to Kay's Grill and met Morley McKay.

He is a burly, black-haired Scot, energetic and nervous,
who fiercely resents interference in his business. "I've
run it for twenty-six years myself," he told me. "Nobody
is going to tell me how to run it now."

Mixing customers, he believes, would drive him into
bankruptcy. He doesn't believe a bylaw, even if passed,
could be enforced. He says that under a democratic form
of government a Negro has every right to buy and operate a restaurant of his own if he feels like it. Negroes who
try to eat at his place "aren't the best type," he says.
"After all, the best type of person doesn't go where he's
not wanted."

McKay used to keep a couple of framed prints of Uncle
Tom over his soda fountain but later took them down.
"I had to," he told me. "The niggers became too cocky.
They used to come in and say 'You show pictures of
Uncle Tom, but you won't serve us.' "

Few Negroes try to get served at the grill now. But
occasionally a carload of colored tourists will wander in
and McKay tells them they aren't wanted.

"It makes me real mad having to go through the whole business," he confessed to me. "Nothing else bothers me as much. It's a feeling I can't quite explain. Do you know that for three days afterward I get raging mad every time I see a Negro. Maybe it's like an animal who's had a smell of blood."

The referendum question was straightforward. "Do you approve of the passing of legislation compelling restaurant owners to serve patrons regardless of race, creed or color?"

The results, in a town where estimates of the black population ranged between 12 and 20 percent, might have been predicted. There were approximately 1,250 eligible voters — 517 voted against the motion; 108 voted in favour.

The National Unity Association led by Carter and Burnett turned to the province. Supported by organized labour and a handful of religious leaders, notably Rabbi Abraham Feinberg, who made speeches in Toronto and in Dresden, Burnett and Carter began to lobby Queen's Park for legislation that would break the colour bar.

After years of dilly-dallying, the Frost government finally gave them the law they wanted. The Fair Accommodation Practices Act was introduced in the spring of 1954. During the bill's second reading familiar bogymen were raised in the legislature. The issue of racial discrimination was "the work of agitators," said C.E. Janes (PC, Lambton East). If it weren't for the work of outsiders from Detroit and people like J.B. Salsberg (L, Toronto, St Andrew) "who went down to Dresden to raise trouble, the two races would be living happily together." Mr Janes painted the spectre of gangs of Detroit thugs crossing the border to sack Dresden businesses. Mr Janes notwithstanding, the bill was passed in April.

Hugh Burnett received more death threats. There were telephone calls and another letter.

"Be careful. No more of this publicity. There is a place in the graveyard for you. We in Dresden don't like it. This is a warning."

Burnett bought a pistol, a .38, to protect himself.

Dresden's blacks might well have thought their battle was over. It wasn't. The law was on the books but no one was prepared to enforce it.

By July, although a number of complaints had been lodged with the minister of labour (who was responsible for administering the law), no legal action had been taken, and two restaurants and all of the town's barber shops were still refusing to serve blacks.

The Toronto Joint Labour Committee for Human Rights sent Sid Blum to Dresden, and he filed a report that detailed the series of snubs his "negro companion" suffered during a tour of the town's four barber shops. The first barber insulted Blum's companion, the second told him he couldn't be served because of public opinion, the third disappeared every time he saw them approaching, and the fourth decided to go to lunch.

The Toronto *Telegram* sent reporter Gordon Donaldson to town in the company of Julian Brooks, 28, and Gladys Grizzle, 20, — two "quiet, well-dressed, well-spoken Negroes."

"I sat in Dresden restaurants," wrote Donaldson, "feeling ashamed and embarrassed as I saw the way they were treated."

At Emersons, the third restaurant, I went in alone and ordered a coffee from Mrs. Annie Emerson. Mr. Brooks and Miss Grizzle entered and sat at the other end of the bar.

Mrs. Emerson saw them and retired to the back kitchen without saying a word.

After a few minutes she came out to sell me a box of matches. She called me over to the cash desk to receive the matches, avoiding the couple. A woman came in and was served with chewing gum.

Mr. Brooks said, "We'd like a coffee and a Coke, please."

No reply. Mrs. Emerson went back to the kitchen.

Mr. Brooks went to the kitchen door and said quietly: "Will you please tell me if we are going to get some service?" No reply. Mrs. Emerson remained sitting in the kitchen.

"All right, if you're not going to serve us will you tell us the reason?" No reply.

Refused for a second time, Julian Brooks and Gladys Grizzle walked out.

By August, eight complaints had been filed with the minister who, the *Telegram* reported, was avoiding prosecutions because he did not want to build up a "martyr" atmosphere. The effective remedy, said the minister, would be a program of education.

The *Globe and Mail,* in a particularly mealy-mouthed editorial, agreed:

> . . . to make people give up discriminatory practices by law is unwise and likely to cause more harm than good. . . . The roots of these practices go far too deep and have been in existence far too long to be eliminated from society overnight by a law, however well meaning.

The *Globe* trotted out all the old weasel words.

> It is regrettable that the Communists have taken a hand in the Dresden matter, as they have frankly revealed in their newspaper. These malicious people are not seeking to extend social harmony, and the anti-discrimination law gives them a powerful springboard of agitation. Those who sincerely wish to improve race relations in this Ontario village should watch carefully that they are not sucked into a propaganda ramp.
> . . . We cannot believe that trouble which has apparently arisen so very recently, after nearly a century of co-existence, represents a social situation as bad as some of the agitators would have the public believe.

... We have every confidence that the good people of Dresden will do their best to find a way out of the situation if left to do so themselves.

The National Film Board came to town and counted nine businesses on main street that were closed to blacks.

In the film *The Dresden Story,* the soft-spoken and articulate Burnett was given the opportunity to confront the rumour-mongers.

ROBERT SCHULTZ (school principal): I think there is a feeling among the people of the town and undoubtedly it is true that Communistic influences seize on opportunities like this and offer their support which is usually accepted by the people involved because they're glad to have any support. But this support is detrimental and I believe that possibly we wouldn't have the trouble involving so many people if it had not been forthcoming.

HOST: Mr Burnett, at the risk of embarrassing you, I'd like to ask you a very direct, blunt question. It's been suggested that you yourself have some Communist affiliation or attachment, and that this accounts for your activity in the association and your interest in this current issue. Would you care to make a statement on this point?

HUGH BURNETT: The question is almost too fantastic to talk about. Of course I am not a member of a Communist Party. I have no affiliation whatever with the Communist Party and I never intend to. It's my job as secretary of National Unity to keep my eyes open for any overtures by the Communist Party or front organizations. . . . We do not intend in any way to be involved with Communists in any way at all. I think it's very silly to even accuse me of being a Communist because I stick up for my rights.

Mrs H.G. French (identified by the National Film Board as prominent in women's affairs) said what was on many people's minds.

MRS FRENCH: The affair of inter-marriage has a lot to do with it.

So did an unidentified man in a pool room:

MAN: We have nothing against the coloured people. They have made a mess in their own nest.

HOST: Do you think they have a lot of support or not?

MAN: They've been backed by the people from outside.

HOST: Who are these people, do you think?

MAN: Well, there are the coloured people from some of the big organizations from the States. There's the Communists looking for trouble all the time. And there is the Jews right behind it.

By January 1955, nothing had changed at Emersons Restaurant or Kay's Grill, although the province, finally acknowledging that the laws of the land were being broken, decided to act. Charges were brought against the owners of the two restaurants. Seven months had passed since the Fair Accommodation Practices Act had become law.

Morley McKay and Anne Emerson were both found guilty and fined fifty dollars each plus costs — the maximum penalty under the law.

Eight months later, however, the convictions were overturned. Chatham County judge Henry Grosch wrote in his judgement that he was not "convinced that the prosecution has satisfied the admitted onus of proving beyond any reasonable doubt that service was denied because of color."

A week later a Toronto labour union disclosed some disturbing things about Judge Grosch's private life. As a private citizen Grosch had attempted, in 1949, to uphold a restrictive racial covenant on some vacation property on Lake Huron known as the Beach O' Pines. The covenant that Judge Grosch had supported said in part that the property "shall never be sold . . . leased . . . or used in any manner by any person of the Jewish, Hebrew, Semite, Negro, or colored race or blood, it being the intention to restrict the ownership . . . to persons of the white or Caucasian races not excluded by this clause."

The minister of labour agreed to bring another case against McKay, who was found guilty and fined $25 and costs of $225.80. This time his appeal was unsuccessful.

Eventually the recalcitrant restaurants either opened their doors or closed down.

The town had always been full of contradictions. There were never any housing restrictions. Black and white lived side by side, said the National Film Board, "as friendly neighbours. No segregation; no coloured district." Children all went to the same school, and among the school children the Film Board found "no sign of any discrimination. They play together, mingle freely. They meet at school and out of school, wear the same sort of clothes, share the same interests." Nor did they find discrimination at the canning plant or the wood-products mill where, they said, "white and coloured work side by side, and very amiably."

Yet when it was all over, Hugh Burnett had to leave town. His carpentry business dried up. Any number of people today, black and white, will tell you that "Hugh got run out of town." He moved to Chatham and later London. He died in 1991.

———— • ————

Caspar Faas came to Dresden in 1952 from Holland. He was a barber — the first in Dresden who would cut a black person's hair. He died when he was fifty-seven years old. Today Caspar's middle son, Joe, is the mayor of Dresden.

Joe Faas is forty-one years old. He is married to Bonnie, who works as a registered nursing assistant at the Park Street Place for Senior Citizens. Bonnie and Joe have two boys — eleven and eight years old. As mayor, Joe collects a

stipend of $3,200 a year. He also works full time at the
Sunoco refinery in Sarnia. Joe works a three-week rotation
at Sunoco, which leaves him time for his job as mayor. He
works three twelve-hour shifts the first two weeks, then four
twelve-hour shifts the third week. He has been on city council since he was twenty-six years old.

"I've kind of worked my way up through the ranks," he
says.

"I treat it like a hobby. You have to like it or you couldn't
do it. Sometimes it's demanding. Sometimes it's enjoyable.
I can't go uptown without someone talking to me. They
want to talk about the sidewalk, or the dogs, or the water
line, or maybe the latest tax increase. Everyone wants to
know why they were hit so hard.

"What about relations between blacks and whites?" I ask.

"As far as I know it's not a problem any more," says Faas.
"If it is, it's not an obvious one. No one has ever said anything to me about it."

One of the town's four policemen is black. So is one of
the six town councillors.

Joe says the hardest thing about being mayor is dealing
with someone who owes taxes.

"I usually go and talk to them myself. I don't have to. We
could just send notices and then, I guess, cut off services.
But when you've lived in town as long as I have you feel you
should go and see people yourself. It's not easy. I tell people that they have to realize it's not my money I'm after. I
tell them that I'm responsible to everyone in town and that
the money they owe, they owe to everyone. I tell them that
it's not fair for them not to pay. I tell them we have to come
up with some compromise. That we're ready to work with
them, and if it's time they need we'll give them time. It has
only happened twice so far, and in both cases we solved
things without going to the extreme.

"I take it all in my stride. I know I have limitations. I can't
change the world. If what I do isn't good enough I'll know
I've done my best. And if my best isn't good enough then

someone else will have to fix the problem. Sometimes you find that people overreact, but if you talk to them, if you explain things, you can usually work things out."

Joe is in the office every day, dealing with the mail, the telephone, signing cheques. There is a meeting of some sort four or five nights a week.

"Sometimes I get home from work and have to rush around and there's no time for supper."

Joe says mostly he enjoys the meetings. He says there is a certain camaraderie that develops among the people working on the town's problems.

"It feels good to help people with their problems. They may seem small to us, but to the person with the problem it's a big deal. It feels good to point them in the right direction — to send them down the right track."

The police force is the largest single item on the city budget ($270,000). After the police comes the fire department ($70,000) and after the fire department, the sidewalks. Nothing, however, has preoccupied Joe Faas more than the question of water quality.

"We've been trying to get fresh water into Dresden for eleven years."

Water from the Sydenham River still meets government standards, but it is getting progressively worse. Only a few years ago every kid in town would eventually muster up the courage to drop into the river from the bridge on St George Street. Some still do. On a hot day you can see kids swing into the river from ropes that are knotted in the trees that line the river banks. But swimming in the river is not a recommended activity in 1992, and most people in town will tell you they aren't crazy about drinking the water, either. They are worried about chemical run-off from the surrounding fields.

"The water may be all right today, but we have to be prepared for the day when it isn't. We want Lake Huron water piped here instead of river water."

Faas looks at his watch and excuses himself. He has

another appointment. Then he has to go to work. We shake hands and he bounds out of the office. The walls of the room where we have been talking are covered with old photos — reeves, wardens and city councils dating back to 1872. I linger in front of the pictures for a while and am once again reminded how important an arena is to all small towns. For there, snuggled among the pictures of the Queen, the framed letter from Pierre Trudeau on the occasion of Dresden's centenary in 1982, down from Diefenbaker's Bill of Rights and Lester Pearson's proclamation concerning Canada's new flag, there on the wall of honour is the photo of Dresden's most recent acquisition — the new Zamboni, the arena's ice-making machine.

———————— ■•━━━━ ————————

Five flights below the bell tower and two flights below the room where Joe Faas and I have been talking, in the basement of the municipal offices, is the headquarters of the four-man Dresden police force. There is one jail cell, one washroom, an office for the chief and a reception area with a counter. On the walls on either side of the door Constable Ken McIntyre has hung two grey sheets, onto which he has glued his police badge collection. "He has other sheets," says Chief Nick Kuipers, "but there is no room for them down here. There are some good ones there. Let me see if I can show you one from a force that doesn't exist anymore."

Also on the wall are three framed illustrations by Norman Rockwell from the cover of *The Saturday Evening Post*. One of them is a picture of a cop sitting at a drugstore counter offering fatherly advice to a young runaway.

Chief Kuipers has chiseled good looks and a deep voice that he projects like a radio news reader.

"Chief here," he says, answering the phone. Or, later, making a call of his own, "It's the chief. Is Paul there?"

Kuipers has been a cop for over twenty years, and he has

worked in bigger cities than Dresden.

"There really isn't that much difference. Not in the crimes. People like to think things are different but sooner or later we get all the things they have in the cities. We get assaults here, and murders, and B and E's. If Toronto gets fifty murders a year, well, the difference is we get one every fifty years. People here are no different to people in Kitchener. Only thing we got going for us is that we are small and there is less of it.

"We have an advantage over city police because we know our people so well. If there is a stranger in town we'll know about it in about five minutes. If we see someone we don't know at night that person will probably get checked.

"You learn the habits of people. Where they go and what they do and who they hang around with. Sometimes my men have solved crimes just because of the way it was done. The other day we solved a break-in because an officer recognized a footprint in the snow. He had taken the trouble to remember someone's footprint. Well, you can't do that in the big city. You don't have the manpower and you don't have the time.

"Our problems are created by less than a quarter percent of the population. I could write down sixty-five names on a piece of paper and eliminate eighty-five percent of our problems. But that quarter percent never goes away. If they move, someone else replaces them."

The telephone rings, and Kuipers scoops it up.

"Chief here."

The town's second-largest employer, N.H.S. Die Casting, is closing its doors. The factory has had a rocky history. Many people in town would argue that it has been mismanaged. This is small comfort for the workers who invested in the company's employee stock purchase plan. They bought stock because they were told it was the only way to keep the company going. Some invested as much as $10,000 and then say they watched helplessly as management redecorated their offices and purchased expensive cars. Tomorrow is the last day on the line, and there is a demonstration planned for 8 A.M. in front of the plant.

The chief is squinting into the phone. "No. I don't expect any trouble and I'm not going to have a car any closer than one thousand yards. If there are problems, that'll be close enough. I don't want to start something by being closer."

Kuipers hangs up and shrugs.

"About a year ago when the recession started to bite, our domestic calls started to go up. When people are out of work there's no money. When there's no money there's more tension.That means there are more arguments and more fights. If times are good and people are working regular we have less problems."

About fifty people show up the next morning at the demonstration. Nearly everyone is carrying a placard. Most of them are also blowing into their mittens and stomping their feet to keep warm. As promised Kuipers has parked the patrol car well up the street from the line of demonstrators. He still catches flak.

"We asked the mayor for help," says someone into a battery powered megaphone, his breath puffing around the speaker like smoke. "What does he do? He sends us the police." The crowd boos. Nearly everyone is wearing a ski jacket and sneakers.

The exception is a tall, elegant, grey-haired man in a brown tweed coat. He is wearing a crisp blue shirt, a tie, gloves that match his coat, brogues and low-cut rubbers. He has a sign resting on his shoulders that says "Keep Jobs in Canada."

He could be a politician out to lend his support. He isn't. He is Alex MacTavish, one of Dresden's two druggists.

"There's a glum feeling over the town today," he is saying to a radio reporter from Chatham. "Every morning you hear of someplace where something is closing down. Well, it's our town this time. It's going to affect everyone. And every part of our community."

Later that night in his family room, Alex MacTavish is pointing out a framed photograph of a Scottish castle. The castle is on a hillside and has been shot from below through a Scottish mist.

"My son gave me that for Christmas," MacTavish explains. "I was in Scotland on a different trip and you know what? I took exactly the same shot. Same castle, same angle, same weather. But my son didn't know it when he took this picture. What do you think of that?"

MacTavish has probably given it some thought himself. He reveals himself to be a careful and thoughtful man. Slumped into the couch, holding his chin in his hand, he repeats each of my questions. Then, running his hand through his hair, he peers at the ceiling and considers his answer.

He came to town in 1961 and bought the pharmacy when the former owner died. Business has prospered. He has thirteen people on the payroll now (there were four when he took over the store), and he has no regrets about leaving the old store in Burlington.

"I went back to see it a few years ago and it was a milk store," he says. "That's probably what would have happened to me. You don't have much of a chance when a superdrugstore moves into a mall next door." He says he has enjoyed the life of the smalltown druggist.

"You get to do things that you couldn't do in the city. The other day a fellow I know got out of the hospital. He had been in for a cancer operation and he came back to town with a prescription. He needed two more days of pills to finish his treatment. But it was a rare drug and there was none in town. And there was none in Wallaceburg or Chatham, either. It was supposed to be my day off anyway so I drove 100 kilometres to London and got the pills and brought them back for him. I left after breakfast and was back by one. If I was managing a store in some shopping mall I wouldn't have done that. But I felt good about doing it. I didn't resent it. For years I have told people if they get a prescription out of town they should bring it back here to be filled. I have encouraged them to come back to town. You see, when people go out of town to see a doctor they have the option of getting their prescriptions filled in the city. I had a reputation to keep. I can't expect them to come back if we don't do our part.

"I know just about all my customers by their first name. You can't trade that off for anything. I go down to the shop every morning, my friends come in, and I get paid for it. Why would I retire?"

There are two pharmacies in town. Both of them have been in business for over 119 years.

———— • ————

It takes only five minutes the next afternoon to walk from the centre of town up St George Street to the concrete bridge and over the river into what is known as North Dresden. It is not an unattractive bridge. However, from the photographs in Don Spearman's book, I prefer the iron one "of the swing type" that it replaced in the 1930s.

The bridge I am walking on in 1991 is the fourth over the river. The first, built of wood in the 1800s, was a toll bridge. In those days the cost of the crossing depended on who you were crossing with. A wagon and two horses cost ten cents; a wagon and one horse, five cents; a horse, mare, ass or mule, three cents; an ox, steer or bull, cow or heifer, two cents; a hog, sheep or other animal, one cent.

The river was once called the Sturgeon and teemed with fine fish. In those days boat-building was an important industry in town and such vessels as *The City of Dresden, The River King, The Hiawatha* and *The Enterprise* chugged up and down the river. River travel was eventually killed by the railway.

Town council paid an $18,000 premium to have the railway pass through town. That got them the rails but only a second-hand engine soon dubbed "John the Baptist" because it had to stop at every station for water.

A five-minute walk from the far side of the bridge, St George is cut by Walnut Street. It is the last street in town. If you live, as Sandy Heatherington does, at 436 Walnut, your backyard butts up against a corn field. In late February, snow is sloped among the ranks of corn stalks like shaving cream on a five-day beard.

Number 436 Walnut is a mobile home. Sandy bought it for $15,000 in 1977. She bought the lot from her sister, had a basement dug and had her second-hand trailer set in place. She has lived here with her husband and two kids ever since. They share their trailer with Bud the budgie, Minuit the "second-hand dog" — a black poodle who sleeps on a blanket under Bud's cage — and Rat, the hamster.

"Kids," says Sandy, "should be raised with animals so they know how to treat them."

Downstairs in the dug basement is a huge rec room — "We have about two hundred people over here every Christmas." On the shelves along one wall, like paintings in an art gallery, is the Heatheringtons' encyclopedia collection. They have the *American Educator, Funk and Wagnall's Encyclopedia, The Student's Encyclopedia, The Family Circle Do It Yourself Encyclopedia, The Young Students Encyclopedia, Funk and Wagnall's Wildlife Encyclopedia, The Illustrated Library of Nature, The Medical Health Encyclopedia*, and what looks like the beginning of a set of something called *Junior Classics*. Obscuring most of the collection from the rest of the room is an oversized television.

On the shelves upstairs are bowling trophies and Sandy's owl collection. And everywhere — on the mantel and covering all the walls — are framed pictures of her kids, Wendy and Joe. I stopped counting at photo number fifty-three.

Sandy is one of the plant workers that Alex MacTavish was demonstrating for. She was the only woman die-caster at N.H.S. Today was her last day of work.

"In 1973 when I was hired they had women's jobs and men's jobs. I didn't want to work with the women on the drill presses and I didn't want to package stuff. I wanted to work the trim press. They said I was too small. I said if I could work on a farm and lift bales of hay then surely to Christ I could lift parts and put them on a press. They said they would try me out and, boy, they gave me a run for my money. In those days there was no weight limit on what you could lift. I could help the men when they needed help but they would never help me. If a tray of pulleys weighed eighty pounds, I had to lift it alone and put it on the skids. They kept saying it was a man's job and I kept saying there are no men's jobs or women's jobs. There are just jobs.

"I worked with a guy called Ron. He was this really shy guy. He didn't talk to me for the first five years. But he watched that I didn't get hurt and I watched that he didn't get hurt. There was no safety equipment back then. We were on incentive. We had to put out two hundred pieces an hour to make $3.31. We'd always try to make four hundred so we could get the full $6.00.

"I saw a young guy lose the tops of four of his fingers, and I saw a ladle of molten metal fall on another guy, and a twenty-four-year-old kid lose his hand at the wrist. You were always getting burned. It comes with the job. Once my hair caught on fire. But I think the men used to get hurt more than the women. They would take more chances. They'd say this'll just take me a second and that's what does it.

"After a while I wanted to be a die-caster. Well, I had the seniority so they had to let me try, but there was this English man there and he thought that a woman belonged at home with the kids. So he got the heaviest dies running, like two-and four-step pulleys, and he gave me a pair of channel locks, which is a fancy name for a pair of pliers, and he told me to 'take them out of there.' So I started to pull the pulleys out and I stayed there doing it for about half an hour. When he came back he checked my work and I hadn't blown anything. There were no holes in anything. So the next day they started me casting.

"All the guys were mean to me. The boss made me clean my machine from top to bottom with a scraper and read all these books. None of the others had to do it. Just me. But I smiled and kept working.

"It wasn't just the boss. My own union brothers picked on me, too. If I went and asked to borrow a tool, they'd throw it at me, like a wrench or something, or they'd stand and curse and swear, not willing to help me in any way. I think they felt I was invading their territory. But the way I figured it, a job was a job."

Sandy was eventually accepted in the plant. By the time it was closed she had been the union steward for eleven years.

She gets up and makes coffee. Her red hair, which tumbles off her head and down onto her shoulders, is tied at the top with four fluorescent shoe-laces. She is wearing jeans and a pair of fluffy slippers.

"You know, they knew they were going to close the plant for months. And they gave us a day's notice. They could have given us more notice. I feel like I have been stripped of eighteen years. I feel like I have wasted eighteen years of my life lining someone else's pocket. I don't regret the people I worked with. They were a great bunch. But the company. I was after the company for years to retrain people. They would never listen.

"And so now what do I do? I think we can make ends meet for the next year. But with my daughter going to university, I don't know. We won't be as bad off as some people who have just bought a house or a car or something. But the company isn't worried about that. We're all just a tax write-off as far as they're concerned. Just numbers. It doesn't seem to worry them that they're killing a town."

It's time for me to leave. We walk to the front door together.

"When I first married my husband," she says, "he didn't know the difference between hay and straw. He didn't have a clue. He had to ask the difference. He's always liked the city. I like the country more."

"Then this is the perfect place for you two," I say, pointing at the neighbours.

"What?"

"This house," I explain. "Your husband can have the front yard. You can have the corn field out back."

Sandy smiles. "Yeah, I guess."

"Good luck," I call from the driveway.

"Luck," she says after me as she shuts the door. "What's that?"

———————— ▪•◄——————

Murray McKim runs what is left of Byron McKim and Son Ltd. Electrical Appliances. Once his grandfather's company was the local distributor for International Harvester farm machinery. It was a million-dollar business. In his father's day, McKim and Son supported a payroll of more than twenty-five. Today all that's left is the remnants of a home appliance store. There are only two employees — Murray, who repairs appliances, and his assistant, a four-day-a-week semi-retired electrician called Igor.

The McKim family sold out of the farm implement business in the sixties. It proved to be a shrewd move. The town's four other implement dealers have all since folded. The last closed its doors in September 1990. Their old showroom and parts department is now a tea room and restaurant called The Lilly Pad.

Murray followed his father into the appliance business and has watched his customers drift away until only he and Igor are left. He has subdivided and rented out the old store-front showroom to a lawyer, an accountant, an insurance company and a real estate firm. He has moved what is left of the family business into a few of the back rooms. If you call he'll give you an address on St George Street, but to find him you have to walk around back. These days you enter McKim and Son off an alley.

Murray's workshop is a testimony to spare time. His latest projects are littered among the out-of-date washing-machine parts — some hunting-knife blades that he has been grinding from scratch and, on the work bench beside a text titled *Carving Bears and Bunnies*, a year's production from his latest hobby — woodcarving. The small pile of half-finished figures includes wooden goats, camels and mules. On another bench is his collection of Coke can art.

In a corner of Igor's workshop, Murray opens a cupboard and rummages around in a collection of old radio tubes.

"We have them all here," he says ruefully. "GE, RCA, Radiothon, Sylvania. They'll never get used now.

"It doesn't pay to repair appliances anymore. It might cost you three hundred dollars to put a new unit in a fridge that is ten or fifteen years old. Well, that's a third of the price of a new one. Used to be we had a full service business here. We sold it and we serviced it. But things change. There are no pure appliance dealers anymore. People shop all over. They go to the Sears catalogue, or Windsor or Detroit, and then they come back and say why can't you do this or that. Sure you can get a better price in the States, but the next time your fridge goes you're going to call up for parts and it's going to be 'Oh, I don't know, we have to order that from Japan.'

"Everything has changed. The manufacturers have changed. They don't make parts anymore. They don't even put numbers on parts. You can't get them, even if you wanted to. My prediction is that before long there won't be any service men left. Service men like me will be antiques. You'll be all on your own. It used to be that service counted. Now all that counts is the price.

———————• •———————

There is no sign of hard times, no doubt about the future, at Dresden's largest employer. The Aylmer canning plant perches on the edge of town like a wealthy uncle. In season, during what is called "Tomato Pack," upwards of 600 men and women will walk, drive, be bused, even flown on chartered jet (Aylmer imports about 150 Jamaicans for six weeks during harvest) to run the loading docks, shuttles, conveyor belts and giant vats that make up the plant.

This is where Aylmer cleans, cooks, processes, bottles and cans every tomato product they sell in Canada. Every bottle of Aylmer ketchup sold from Newfoundland to Vancouver Island comes out the back door of the plant on the edge of Dresden. It's no wonder that people around here talk about tomatoes with the same reverence that Quebeckers reserve for maple syrup.

"You've got to come back in September when the tomatoes are running," says one farmer I meet.

"The town brightens up at harvest time," says Lisa Kerr. "When the Jamaicans come they give a tremendous boost to the economy. The town is busier all over."

Like everyone who comes from the islands to work on the Canadian harvest, the Jamaicans who come to Dresden would rather take their pay cheques home in durable goods than in cash. They buy soap, shampoo, clothing, shoes, tape recorders, radios, even refrigerators, and take it all back to sell, use or give as gifts. They live in bunkhouses on Aylmer's property and arrive complete with four Jamaican chefs and a camp janitor.

Beans and corn may be the backbone of the town's economy, but tomatoes are the preoccupation. Beans and corn are the socks and underwear of agricultural production. A corn field in August is a thing of beauty, but you can see a field of corn anywhere. A field of tomatoes is something to slow down for — a thing to behold. To the south and west of Dresden on the shores of Lake Erie is the town of Leamington, a town that bills itself as the Tomato Capital of Canada. Dresden may not hold the title, but they might be able to mount a fair challenge. And the man to issue the challenge would be Dave Hoyles.

Hoyles worked for seven and a half years with Green Giant all over the United States. He left a fast-track job to upper management because he wanted to bring his family home to Dresden.

"It was a conscious decision to return here. We had been moved something like five times in seven years, and my wife and I started to discuss moving around as much as we were. Neither of us liked the idea of jumping around every two years so I had a show-down with Green Giant and I said, 'Let me settle down or I'll leave.' They said there was still a series of things that they wanted to move me through to round out my experience. So I left.

"I called my father and said, 'Rent us a house,' and he said, 'I guess you're coming home,' and I said, 'I guess we are.' I didn't have a job or anything. I was just coming home.

"I have to admit at first I thought it was the stupidest thing I had done in my life. My wife opened the door on the house that we had rented and burst into tears. It's not a time I relish thinking about. For the first six months I was ready to go back to Green Giant on my hands and knees and beg them to let me start again. I mean, I had moved from a shirt-and-tie job in head office and ended up in a line job here at the plant at thirty percent less pay. It was a completely different ball game.

"But I've always placed a tremendous importance on roots. On the idea of a home town. A base. And I think my kids have that here. There's a sense of belonging. And you get a sense of security from that. We have a close circle of friends and that's important. But we could find that any-where. The whole thing is strengthened here because this is where their grandparents live.

"When they were young my kids spent a lot of time with my father, their grandfather, driving around in his pick-up truck. As they drove around he would tell them things, like This is where I bought a horse, or I got a cow here once. The youngest one was only three years old then and he's always amazing me because today he'll tell me things like 'This is where Grandpa ran over the fox' and he'll know what caused it and how it happened.

"It's not just their lifetime that they're living here. There are lifetimes that were lived before them and they have the ability and the opportunity to know what led up to where they are now. It's the type of thing that you don't get if you're just visiting a place.

"They can take these experiences and go anywhere in the world and have a means of comparison. It may even help them determine what's important to them. We don't drill our kids with what's important. We try to foster an atmosphere where they can figure it out for themselves."

Hoyles is leaning back in a chair at his desk at the plant. He is wearing workboots and a red windbreaker that has "Nabisco Brands" stitched over his heart in white thread. On the other side of the jacket, in a flowing script, is the word "Dave." He is wearing a hard hat, which he takes off from time to time to expose a white hair net. Behind him on a bookshelf he has arranged a sample of all the products that run through his plant. There are cans of spinach, asparagus and beets — whole rosebud beets, sliced beets, diced beets, diced beets in Harvard sauce and shoestring beets. And, of course, tomatoes — tomatoes canned whole, tomatoes with herbs and spices, tomatoes chunky pasta style, tomatoes diced, tomatoes stewed plain, stewed Italian style, stewed Cajun style, stewed Mexican style, bottled and canned as tomato juice, tomato soup, tomato paste and lording over the rest, tomato ketchup.

Although not quite forty, Hoyles is old enough to have attended, from grade one to grade eight, a one-room school house. It was about a mile from the farm where he grew up, and he used to walk or ride his bike to school. His parents ran both dairy and beef cattle, as well as grew crops like wheat, oats, beans and the ubiquitous tomato.

It used to be that vegetables were grown and canned commercially from coast to coast. Each small town in

Canada had its own canner with its own private label. The first stop on the highway towards specialization came when canners in neighbouring towns struck production agreements. The agreements went something like this: "I'll do all the local corn. You can have the peas." Today the industry is so developed that as far as tomatoes are concerned, for Aylmer and sister brand Del Monte, this one plant in Dresden suffices for the whole country. This consolidation gives the canner enormous power — a power they have not been afraid to wield, and a power that has changed forever the character of Canadian farms. In the agricultural world of the nineties, canners dictate everything to their growers who, in the world of agribusiness, are no longer called farmers, but suppliers.

The suppliers (Aylmer needs only forty-four to produce enough tomatoes to satisfy their share of the Canadian market) are only allowed to plant company seedlings. These plants, raised in local greenhouses (as well as being trucked to Canada from Georgia and North Carolina), are the progeny of multi-million-dollar genetic breeding programs. They are production-line plants, bred to produce smaller fruits with tougher skins and more of what is called "solid material." They are oblong rather than round, so they won't roll backwards down the inclined conveyor belts they are meant to climb. Hoyles is particularly proud of his tomatoes' colour. "Our breeding program has enhanced the deepness of the tomato. There is red," he says proudly, "and there is red."

Hoyles also tells his suppliers when to plant, how much to plant, when and how to fertilize, when to harvest, when to ship and how much to ship.

"With what we know about these tomatoes, the predictability of harvest is accurate enough that we can say plant so many today, so many tomorrow, so many next week and you will deliver six loads of tomatoes a day for seven days over a certain week in September."

Hoyles will only buy tomatoes that are mechanically harvested. And with machine harvests you need a field of plants that will ripen at the same time. Gone are the days when hundreds of pickers marched through a field several times during harvest. Today, instead of the discretion of field hands, growers pass over their fields two weeks before harvest and spray the tomatoes with Ethrel — an ethylene dioxide compound. Ethrel is a ripening agent — a gas that induces redness. One pass, *et voilà*, the tomatoes fall into line like military recruits. Then the farmers drive onto the fields with harvesters that, as Mark Kramer describes in his book *Three Farms*, "look like the aftermath of a collision between a grandstand and a streetcar."

In the early eighties Hoyles oversaw a $12 million modernization program that took his plant from a labour-intensive facility to a world-class mechanized tomato production line. Inside, electronic eyes scan each of the millions of fruits that come into the plant and in a fraction of a second elect whether each fruit is red enough to pass muster. Rejected tomatoes are automatically separated from the rest of the harvest. Nowhere in the world is there technology as advanced as this, says Hoyles proudly. "It's seven times more accurate than humans. You don't have to feed it, or fly it up from Jamaica, and it shows up to work every day." When it comes to sorting tomatoes, human error runs at about twenty-eight percent a load. Hoyles's computer is ninety-six percent accurate.

Outside the back doors he shows me a series of pipes and steel tanks that look like they would be happier in an oil refinery than a tomato plant. These are the evaporators that reduce the fresh tomatoes to a condensed paste twice as powerful as the kind you can buy at the grocery store. The paste, a thick gloop with the consistency of liver, is sealed in space-age silver plastic and stored in wooden tubs. Each tub — a square box that comes half-way up my chest — contains what's left of ten tons of tomatoes. Aylmer warehouses the tomatoes as paste until they are ready to manufacture anything from juice to ketchup.

"The paste is sterilized and the bag is sterilized," explains Hoyles. "There is just nothing there that can go wrong. There are no microbes, no enzymes, no bacteria, no oxygen or any other gases that can effect the colour or the taste. It's sitting in a virtually steady state. We had some test batches that we let sit around for three years and when we opened them up we couldn't tell the difference from a batch that was prepared yesterday."

On the way out of the plant we pass a series of rooms piled floor to ceiling with empty tin cans. The cans, which stretch on forever, glimmer in the light. I feel wealthy just looking at them.

"During the tomato pack we'll be going twenty-four hours a day seven days a week, and we'll empty that room of cans three times a day," says Hoyles as we walk past.

"You know," he says as we say goodbye in the parking lot, "there are lots of reasons why tomatoes are better off grown somewhere else. To begin with, look at our climate. We have seven weeks of pack time. California has three months. And we have to start from transplants. Down there they can start with seeds. We think we are doing good if we can pull twenty-five tons an acre. In the U.S. they get thirty-two tons. And they have economies of scale that we can't touch. But we've adapted technology to suit our situation, and this plant moves more whole peeled tomatoes in a day than any of their mega-plants do."

It is lunch. I am hungry and head for Marlene's. I am actually craving ketchup.

Pam, my waitress from the day before, pulls up at my table and with obvious disapproval parrots back my order from yesterday's lunch. One scrambled egg with toast, hold the home fries, did not stand me well in her eyes. Not enough food.

"Are the hamburgers fresh?" I ask. I am still thinking ketchup but I do not like the frozen patties served up at most franchises.

"No," says Pam without batting an eye. "We keep them a week before we serve them."

"I mean," I try to explain, "are they fresh meat or are they those frozen patties you can buy?"

"We get them," Pam says, as if she is talking to someone with a learning problem, "from the packer just over the bridge."

I order the burger. With the home fries.

———————— • ————————

On Friday night there is a teen dance at the community centre. At ten o'clock there are about two hundred kids drifting around the hall. The lights are dim and the music is stunningly loud, but few of the kids are dancing. Most are standing in groups. There is plenty of jittery movement — good-humoured pushing, slapping and shoving in time with conversations that can't possibly be audible over the records — but no dancing.

Well, there is a little dancing. From time to time a person detaches from a group, as if seized by an extra-terrestrial force, and falls into . . . dance. This typically lasts for no more than thirty seconds — sometimes a mere beat or two — and then, as suddenly as they began to dance, they stop.

Sometimes the group takes note of the dancer — the way a group of orangutans might take note of the antics of an irritating adolescent. But more often they overlook the moment the way you might overlook an old man talking to himself on a subway platform.

Only once did I see two people dancing what you might call together. They were both boys. Not touching, mind you, but definitely moving within each other's orbit.

I remember how hard it used to be to ask a girl to dance. Maybe it has gotten harder.

———————— • ————————

The next morning over breakfast at the Track Kitchen, Jay Lekavy launches into a discussion of nicknames.

"I've had about ten over the years," he says. "Dad had the Pontiac dealership in town so there was a time when everyone called me 'Wide Tracker.' I've also been 'O.J.' and 'Blue Jay.' And 'Pot.' That was because my favourite hockey player was Denis Potvin.

"See the guy who just walked in? His dad owns a body shop. They call him 'Fender.'

"A lot of them got their names like that. John Blake's dad worked at National Hardware. One of the things they made out there was called Luster Chrome. So we started calling John 'Luster Chrome.' Everyone in town calls him 'Chrome' today."

I have never been in a town where nicknames figure as prominently as they do in Dresden. In most cases their origins, and often their relevance, seem to have been lost to time. Many of them, one assumes, originated at the arena.

"When I went away to university," says Jay, "I used to talk about the people back home and no one believed me."

Well. Yes.

That's because he could probably talk about most of the men in town without ever using a real name.

There is "Snort" Hooper and his son, "Flip." When Snort opened a shoe store (Snort is an enterprising soul and has, at one time or another owned the shoe store, two different barber shops and various parcels of real estate including the license bureau, a New to You store and a women's clothing store) ... anyway, when Snort opened the shoe store, Peter Epp, editor of the town paper, *The Leader*, thought he should say something about the new store in the paper. Peter's problem was that he only knew Snort as ... Snort. That struck him as indecorous, so being a good reporter he turned to the standard reference, the town phone book. He was, he says, only mildly surprised to find that Snort was (and is still) listed as ... Snort.

There is also "Birdseed" Brewer (his son is called "Tweetie") and "Bus" Pray, "Pickle" Van Daele,

"Gummer" Spearman, "Haircut" Houston and his cousin, "Doc." After toiling for fourteen years in the NHL, Doc (or Ken) Houston is best and, for many, only remembered for the night in 1976 when he punched out Dave "Hammer" Schultz. There's "Skinny" Patterson (who is, of course, fat), "Farmer" McFadden, Tony "The Greek" Stathis, "Buffalo" VanDerMeersch (who is even referred to as "Buffalo" at town council meetings) and "Flower" McKellar. Flower is Paul McKellar who, not surprisingly, runs the flower store on St George Street.

"I couldn't have bought the advertising that nickname gave me," he says ingenuously.

"A year after I got to town, Larry Ennett was clowning around up at the Legion and it just came out of his head. He started to call me Flower and it stuck. That was twenty years ago and now kids my son's age call me Flower up at the arena. When my son was younger they started to call him "Little Flower," and he got into a few fights because of it. He didn't like it. But I never minded. When people think of flowers they think of me."

At McKellar's Flower Store, the afternoon I visit, a delivery man is trying to move more than the five dozen roses that Paul McKellar is willing to buy.

"How about some lilies? I've got a lot of lilies I want to sell."

"Sorry. But I don't have cause to sell a lot of lilies these days."

"They're beautiful Casablancas. This town doesn't buy Casablancas?"

McKellar smiles.

"Not unless you run over someone on the way out of town."

The delivery man shrugs and leaves.

"A Casablanca lily," says McKellar, "is a perfect white lily. One of the few perfect white flowers there are."

I tell Paul that I was surprised to find a flower store on

the main street of Dresden. "I just wasn't expecting a flower store," I say, "and I was astounded when I saw the second one around the corner."

Paul smiles.

"This flower store has been here for a hundred years as near as I can figure." As he talks he paces around a green vase on his work table, arranging flowers for an afternoon delivery.

Every time he pushes a flower into the vase, he screws up his face. Every time he trims a stem, he grimaces. It is as if his mouth is somehow connected to the flowers in his hands.

"It's a rule of thumb that there should be about five thousand people for each flower store in any town. So we are sort of over-represented here, I guess. But my real competition isn't here. It's in Chatham. We don't have a hospital in town. Everyone goes to hospital in Chatham. So I'm in competition with the chain stores in Chatham.

"But it's been OK over the years. I've put two kids through university with this store. You just have to punch and go. It's a seven-day-a-week job. If someone dies and there's a funeral on the weekend, I'll be in here doing the flowers on Sunday."

Paul finishes the vase and holds it up for inspection.

"We're also completely tied to agriculture," he says, grimacing. "If the price of peas and corn goes up, we do well."

Someone comes in the door and he greets them by name. The phone rings and he scribbles an order on a bill with a pen he pulls from the pocket in his green smock.

"This business is more a service business than a product-oriented one. I've almost got to be able to read my customers' minds. A lot of them won't mention money to me. They'll just call and say, 'So-and-so died. Will you please send flowers.' I don't have to ask. I know what they want me to send. It's not a flower business. It's a people business. You can't be successful if you don't like people.

"The trick is in the buying, not the selling. I have eight different suppliers who pass through town and peddle to me. I buy sometimes five days a week. You don't want product going bad on you. These days you get flowers from all over the world. My carnations come from Colombia, the daffs and the iris come from Holland. Used to be that I knew all the growers. Not anymore. There are no carnations grown in Ontario anymore."

Another customer wanders through the front door and there is another huddled conference. Paul smiles and straightens his tie as the customer leaves.

"I always wear a tie to work. It's a clip-on. That way I can take it off if I get cleaning out buckets or start spray-painting flowers. It's just something I've always done."

———■•■———

Up the street it is almost closing time at the hardware store and "Boo" Ellis, eighteen years old, is sprinkling green sweeping compound on the floor by the front counter. He picks up a broom and begins to nudge the compound into neat piles.

Bill Clark is watching Boo's progress from his desk behind the counter. Bill is the fourth generation in the Clark family to operate the business by the bridge. His great-grandfather, William Clark, a stone mason, opened a building-supply business on this very spot near the turn of the century.

"This place has been here so long it's pretty near part of the river," says Clark.

He has records that go back to 1918. Before that it was cash in and cash out.

"According to the books we lost ten cents the first month," says Bill. He pauses and catches my eye before delivering the punch line. "We've been losing money ever since."

Although it is part of the Home Hardware chain, Clark's Hardware has a distinct smalltown feel. You still buy your nails here by the pound. You scoop them out of a wooden bin in the middle of the store, load them into a tin bucket and weigh them on a balance-beam scale. A good percentage of Bill's sales are in bulk — kerosene, plaster, cement, nails. There is a skate sharpener at the back of the store. You bring your empty beer bottles here, too, because the local liquor store isn't set up to handle bottle returns. If you ask, Bill will drop by your house and repair a broken window.

"I'm not crazy to do this. You can't make money doing it. But if there's an older lady or someone who can't get their window out themselves, I'm happy to do it. It's not really a big deal in a town this size. I can do it on my way home for lunch.

"I think service tends to be a little friendlier overall in a small town. You have to rely on your customers day after day. If you aren't treating them right, they're going to go down the street."

In Dresden, down the street would be the Dresden Pro Hardware.

"We sort of share the market between us. He cuts and threads pipe. I don't do that. I sell bicycles. He doesn't sell bikes. He has a larger stock of houseware than I do. I have more sporting goods than him. This isn't something that we have to discuss. We understand that it wouldn't be profitable for either of us if we both went after the same market. We overlap in some things. But that's understandable.

"Business in small towns is dying. It's nothing for people to drive twenty or fifty miles to go shopping these days. So if you're not in the convenience business, you're in trouble. You don't drive fifty miles for a quart of milk. That's why you'll always see a milk store in a small town. Well, it's the same for a kitchen faucet."

Until recently, Clark's used to own and operate the town scale.

"At one time all towns had to have a municipal scale and that was us. We'd weigh anything. Cows, pigs, hay, beans. We even weighed a load of dope for the Mounties. It was one dollar a weigh. Didn't matter what it was. Guys selling scrap would come by and check their load before they went to the scrap yard."

In recent years the scale proved to be more trouble than it was worth.

"You had to shovel it off every day and then cut all around to make sure there was no ice jammed in there. Then you had to pour hot water all around it. I kept a kettle going all day long in case it froze up. When they heard we were going out of it they put in a nice modern scale at McBrayne Feed and Supply. It has heaters underneath."

Boo has finished sweeping and mopping the concrete floor.

"You're going to paint that this summer, Boo," says Clark.

Boo rolls his eyes.

I can tell Bill is anxious to close the store and get going.

"It's been a long week," he says, glancing at his watch.

I gather up my coat and notebook. When I am leaving the store I suddenly think to ask how Boo got his nickname.

"Hey, Boo," Clark calls. "Why they call you that?"

Boo doesn't know.

"His big brother," offers Clark with a shrug, "is called 'Doo.' "

———————— • ————————

Joe Kerr and Bill Glasgow have been lugging cardboard boxes and filing cabinets across Brown Street all afternoon. Joe Kerr is a farmer. He grows corn, beans and wheat on his family's 5,700 acres north of town. It is one of the biggest operations around. Bill is a farmer, too. He grows tomatoes. The two farmers are helping their friend Rob Marchand move into his new office.

Rob is an accountant who is doing more and more work for farmers around Dresden. Farmers who used to take their business to Chatham have started bringing their books to Rob, who comes from a farm family and still farms locally himself. He is typical of young farmers today who must supplement their income with an off-farm pay cheque. Rob is moving into the new office across the street because he needs more space.

At five o'clock the men knock off. They join Joe's wife, Lisa, and Rob's wife, Heidi, among the unpacked cartons and stacks of paper in the new store-front office. Joe and Bill round up some chairs. Rob produces a bottle of rye. The state of the family farm is on everyone's mind.

"You used to see plenty of 200- or 300-acre operations," says Rob. "A guy could have a few pigs, some chickens, maybe some cattle. It was all you needed. Now people have to specialize, because the more specialized you are the more efficient you are. And you have to be efficient today."

"You talk about Old MacDonald down on the farm," says Joe. "The guy with five or six ten-acre fields and some bush. There might be one or two guys like that left. But they're twenty, thirty years out of date. If you find someone like that, take a look at their machinery. They won't have any new machinery. And probably their wife works. She's a nurse or school teacher or something. Otherwise they couldn't afford it. Set-ups like that aren't economic today."

"These days you need about eight hundred acres per family if you want to live the same lifestyle as your buddy who went into a factory right after high school."

"It's because we sell on the world market today."

"United States and Canada have been encouraging farming in the Third World for years. And suddenly we're in a situation of over-production. Yields are up all over. We have all these genetic programs."

"In 1982 a bushel of corn was going for over $4.00. Now it's $2.60."

"And costs have risen three to five percent a year."

"China is a good example. China used to be a net importer of food. Now it's almost an exporter."

"The Europeans are subsidizing their farmers."

"And that's why Dresden is going down the tubes."

"Farming," says Joe Kerr, "went into the recession about six years earlier than the rest of the country. The people who are producing the food are starving."

Ewan Wilson, principal of the Lambton-Kent Composite School, is sitting in his office with his vice-principal, Harold Gillies. Ewan, who is from England, is explaining why he settled in Dresden in 1967.

"It's a great place to raise young people." Ewan has three teenage sons who live with him and his wife on a farm five minutes out of town. "We don't experience the problems that larger cities have. For instance the drop-out rates. They have a thirty percent drop-out rate. We don't have a thirty percent drop-out rate here. And behaviour. I've heard horrendous accounts of behaviour at city schools. We just don't have that here. And vandalism. We don't have vandalism, either. Not like in the city. There's just too much available in big cities."

"Like street corners." Harold Gillies is fidgeting in his seat, his leg bouncing up and down. "We don't have street corners pulling at them."

Wilson nods.

"And franchises. We don't have any franchises in town so there aren't that many part-time jobs."

"Or arcades."

"Or malls."

"Eighty percent of our kids are bused into school. So figure. If they aren't sixteen and they don't have a car, that means they're isolated. They can't just walk to the store. They're less sophisticated and very trusting."

"There's also a certain continuity that you don't get

anywhere else. Everyone in school knows everyone else. Most of the parents come from here. The continuum is passed along."

"Look." Harold leans forward, his foot still bouncing. "In the city you sometimes get two brothers who follow each other through a school. OK. The other day I looked at the school list and I saw there was a Payne boy here. That would be Dr Payne's son. Well, I went to school with Dr Payne. And you know what? When I was a kid, his father, the grandfather, was also one of the town's doctors. So now I am teaching the son of a kid I went to school with and my friend, the kid's father, has taken over *his* father's medical practice. We have all the normal instabilities here. We have plenty of single parents and working parents. But we also have a kind of stability that is probably missing in the cities. You know where people come from. You know their families."

"There just isn't the coming and going you get in the city," says Wilson. "You know your friends are going to be here next year. It's important to the growth and development of a kid to give them that sense of security. That's how fellowship and trust develop."

Harold is nodding.

"I disappointed my parents because I moved to Chatham when I graduated from university. I remember saying that I would never come here to live. I said I was heading for greener pastures. I wanted to go to the big city and do something different. I was away for twelve years. It feels good to be here now. It's nice to be back. Because of the people I know. Because of the roots I have here.

"One day I took my kids on a tour of my places. I took them out to the old sugar-beet factory and out to the railroad tracks where we used to play war and all that stuff. And under the bridge. We used to fish in the crevices down there. I never had enough nerve to dive off the bridge, but kids are still doing that. And then we went back behind the cemetery into what used to be the semi-wilds of Molly's

Creek. We used to go back there and go fishing. We'd take a can of spaghetti and open it up and eat it cold at lunch time. It's odd to think of that. It never occurred to me back then the way spaghetti looks like worms. We'd catch catfish or carp and throw them back. We didn't have movies to go to or anything. It's hard for them to envision that. They keep asking me what we used to do."

Ewan Wilson is nodding. "Today my boys go to the edge of our property down by the river. They go with the dog. They mess around down there. In the winter they skate on it. In the summer they fish. It's a natural part of their day as opposed to a special trip. Sometimes we take the canoe way up the river and float back down.

"You couldn't pay me enough to live in a big city. I might meet six cars on the way to work. My brother-in-law lives in Toronto. That style of life is just not one that I'm fond of."

By five-thirty on Saturday the half-light that comes at the end of a winter day has washed the town in grey. The temperature started to drop when the sun went down and it is getting chilly. Most of the stores on St George Street are closed. The only colour is a smudge of purple on the horizon. The only light from kitchen windows. The only people left outside are children trying to eke the last few minutes out of a dying day.

Over on Hughes Street the five blond Pilon kids — Scott, Lisa, Brent, Kevin and Sarah, aged eight to thirteen — are tobogganing on Cook's Hill. Cook's Hill is no more than a vacant lot between two houses. The ride from the sidewalk on Hughes to the bottom of the hill is only twenty-five gentle yards. But the Pilon kids, who live down the street, come to the hill every day. Between them they have one toboggan, one Krazy Karpet, one turbo tube and two snow boards. They have worn deep ruts down the centre of the hill.

Not far away, in another vacant lot, twelve-year-old Jamie and his nine-year-old brother, Jordan, are playing hockey on the rink their stepfather made. Jamie has stopped the game so he can repair the webbing in one of the goals. He is using a piece of string. The rink is built on a slope and the incline from the goal nearest the sidewalk to the one at the far end is steep enough that the boys could coast from the high goal to the low one. Every few minutes the boys' father peers at them from the kitchen window.

Over on St George Street, at the corner of Trerice, ten-year-old Tammy Hooper is talking with an eight-year-old boy named Gerald. Gerald is on his way to his friend's house. Tammy is out looking for her brothers. Bradley is eleven. Roy is twelve. Their mother wants them home. Tammy will find them in a few minutes riding their bikes over on Davies Street. They don't think they are supposed to be home until the street lights go on. They were going to walk on the river but Roy's ears were too cold.

If Brad and Roy had made it to the river, they would have met John Hawken, Derek Suitor and Jason Timko. They have been playing hockey just down from the bridge since nine o'clock this morning. They used a sheet of plywood to push the snow off their rink. It took them about an hour. The ice is hard and smoother than you'd expect. A few nights ago John's dad chopped a hole in the river and brought a sump pump down and flooded the rink for them. He used a large squeegee to smooth the water off before it froze.

The boys have played all day. They didn't even stop for lunch. Once or twice when they were cold, "mostly on the chin," they went up to John's house and had a drink and warmed up. John lives right on the banks of the river. He has flooded a sort of chute down his front lawn so he can skate onto the river from his porch. Sometimes he climbs up to his house at supper time and eats dinner with his skates on.

The boys are wearing sweat pants and toques. John is

wearing a red Chicago Black Hawks sweater. When they stop skating and stand in a group, leaning on their sticks, they look like veterans from the American Civil War.

They will keep playing until nine or nine-thirty tonight. There is a floodlight on a tree pointing towards the rink. John's dad put it up. But it isn't much help. It is so dark now that only a boy can see the puck.

———— • ————

"Shut the door tight behind you," David Thompson says furtively, peering into the darkness over my shoulder, "or they'll come right in."

Thompson, who is thirty-three, is the newest and youngest of Dresden's four doctors. He came to town in 1984 with his wife, Kim. They came from Hamilton.

"Dr Ruttle, who had the practice before me and lived here in this house, was a twenty-four-hour-a-day man. People have a habit of coming here day and night. He had a back door built into the office so he could sneak out through the garage and go fishing. Do you want to see it?"

David and Kim are proud of their home. They tell me most of their friends in the city are living in apartments. We couldn't afford something like this in the city, they say, as they show off the changes they have made. Megan, who is two, is asleep upstairs. Four-month-old Gillian spends the next hour and a half snuffling in her daddy's arms. "She has a cold," her father the doctor feels compelled to explain. "She doesn't always sound like this."

David and Kim were both raised in small towns. When David went to medical school he applied for an underserviced area scholarship. Accepting it meant, upon graduation, he was obligated to practise in a designated underserviced area — one year for every year of funding.

"We thought very carefully about going to the north," David says. We finally chose a small town. We wanted to live in a place like this because we thought it would be a better place to raise children. A place with fewer bad influences. In Hamilton we lived in an apartment building. There were as many people living in that apartment as live here in town, yet we only knew one other couple. Here everyone knows us and we know everyone else."

"I had a friend down from the city one weekend," says Kim, "and I took her shopping in town. We went to Audrey's Fashions. She only wanted to buy one thing but she couldn't make up her mind between a pair of shorts and a pair of slacks. She wanted her husband to help her choose. Audrey said, 'Take them both.' She didn't mean buy them both. She meant take them both without paying and show them to your husband. And that's what we did. My friend took them both and the arrangement was once she had decided she would mail the ones she didn't want back to me and I would bring them back along with whatever she owed. Nothing was written down. There was no credit card or anything. I'm not sure if they even take credit cards at Audrey's."

"The differences," says David, "are enormous. Just before we moved here I called the post office and told them I wanted to rent a post office box. There is no home delivery here. You have to go to the post office to pick up your mail. I wanted a box instead of General Delivery. Well, they told me there were no boxes available and I said that was too bad because I was the new doctor and I expected to get a lot of mail and they said, 'Oh, you're the new doctor. We've already put a box aside for you.'

"The day we arrived in town one of the councillors — he's the mayor now — showed up at the house with flowers. He invited us to a barbecue that night to meet some people. You wouldn't get that in a large town."

David says practising medicine in a small town is also different from practising in the city.

"First off you get to see people outside of the office. You see how they're getting along. You can see that their osteoarthritis is bothering them when they're limping along the

street. You also get to see them in a family environment. I
can do house calls here. In the city you can't find parking,
or your patients live too far away, or they live in a high-rise
or something. Here if someone is really sick it's not a big
inconvenience for me to jump into the car and scoot over.
I'll do maybe ten house calls a week — for my nursing-
home patients, or for people with limited mobility, or just
for someone who's not well enough to come and see me
themselves. There's no public transport here and no hospital and sometimes it's easier for me to travel than for
them. Besides, it's helpful sometimes to see the patient's
lifestyle. Sometimes that tells you why they're ill and you
can get others involved."

Every night at supper I return to my regular seat at Marlene's. I have taken to sitting at a small table near the back
of the restaurant. My table faces the front door. From here
I can keep my eyes on the comings and goings. One night,
before I have a chance to order, George Higgs comes in.
Higgs is a farmer I met at a Rotary dinner on one of my first
nights in town. He spots me, nods, and to my surprise walks
over and sits down at my table without asking. He almost
apologizes for being late. After we order, Higgs folds his
menu and launches into a lecture about the intrigues and
intricacies of the world sugar market. It is an involved story
that incorporates the Hunt brothers, mysterious Bermuda
head offices, Higgs's role as the last ever president of the
Sugar Beet Growers of Ontario, and the ups and downs of
the last sugar-beet factory in Canada, which he tells me is in
Taber, Alberta. The price of sugar in Pakistan also figures in
his story, which I have difficulty following.

Higgs is a tomato farmer of some success, so when he
pauses for a breath I tell him of my day at the plant. He
smiles and puts his fork down and leans forward. He hasn't
touched his meal.

"I don't know where the free trade is going to take us. But there's no doubt that we're already competing with California and Illinois. When we talk to the canners they're always telling us that we're pricing our tomatoes too high. The threat, of course, is that unless we sell them cheaper, they'll import tomato paste from California. But it's not going to happen, and you know why?"

Higgs leans even closer.

"First trucking. Trucking is getting more and more expensive every day. And second," — he punches the air with his fork — "they have a problem with water down there. You need sixty-six inches of rain a year to grow tomatoes and they're only going to have enough water for twenty-five percent of their crop."

Lynn Stathis comes by our table and tries to induce George to eat something. He looks absentmindedly at his plate and pushes at one of his potatoes half-heartedly. He doesn't bring it to his mouth. "I'm just putting in time," he says quietly after she has gone. Abandoning the potato, Higgs begins to expound on artesian wells in California which, he says, are bound to hit salt water. It is going to be too costly, he notes with satisfaction, to do anything about that.

"We've got the naturals. We've got rainfall, we've got land and we've got the climate." Higgs laughs. He is pleased with himself. "I don't think we have any trouble at all." Then he leans forward again and lowers his voice.

"But the canners won't tell you that."

———————— • ————————

The next morning on an impulse I walk into McFadden's Food Market and wander around the aisles. McFadden's is a country grocery store on the north side of the bridge — the sort of place you'd buy a quart of milk or a box of cereal. My eye is caught by the ketchup display. There are an equal number of Heinz and Aylmer bottles.

"Which one do you sell more of?" I ask. "Heinz or Aylmer?"

The woman who has been watching me more than casually from the back of the store doesn't seem to understand my question.

"Do you sell more of one or the other?" I repeat.

"No," she says finally. "About the same of each, I'd guess."

My tour complete, I walk out of the store and carry on up St George Street. I feel I am being watched. I look over my shoulder and catch the woman peering through the window. She has followed me to the front of her shop and is watching me carefully. I wave. I wonder if she will phone someone and ask about me.

———————————•———————————

Maple Lanes Bowling Alley is the last business at the north end of town. After Maple Lanes come the corn fields. Being the last to arrive on a Wednesday night, I have to park my rented car with its hood hanging over the corner of a frozen field. I wonder vaguely, as I get out of the car, if it is all right to do that.

This is where I have come to spend my last night in Dresden. I am tired. My notes from Maple Lanes, which fill up the last few pages of my notebook, are messier than usual.

Going through the door is like going into a basement rec room circa 1956. I look twice to make sure there aren't pin boys setting up the pins. There is a lunch counter with seven green vinyl stools. Behind the counter, Audrey Weaver is washing coffee mugs. She is working shoulder to shoulder with a Kelvinator that looks old enough to be at home in Murray McKim's workshop. The corners of the fridge are round instead of square, and its white sheen has faded to yellow. There is an Orange Crush clock on the wall.

Tonight is Ladies' Night. The women who aren't bowling or smoking at the counter have settled into a collection of mismatched kitchen chairs around an old kitchen table by the lanes. What is it, I wonder, about bowlers. Why do they smoke so much more than the rest of us?

They are, of course, playing five-pin — one sport Canadians can rightfully claim as their own.

Five-pin bowling was conceived at the turn of the century by a Toronto businessman named Thomas Ryan. Ryan happened to own the first ten-pin bowling alley in the country and was pressed to modify the American game to make it more comfy for some of his upper-class customers. They were having difficulty lifting the regulation bowling ball. During his various experiments to make bowling less (!) strenuous, Ryan had his father shave some standard ten-pins on a lathe. He placed five of these smaller pins on a regulation alley and introduced new rules and a lighter ball. At first the lighter pins flew around the alley with disconcerting and noisy abandon. To deaden the racket, Ryan added a rubber band around the belly of each pin. Today five-pin bowling is said to be the number-one participant sport in Canada. It is also widely played in many of the northern states.

Sitting at the counter at Maple Lanes, it is not long before I fall into conversation with Bonnie Morgan.

"General labour," she says vaguely, when I ask her what she does.

"Oh, yes?" I press. "What sort of work? What sort of work do you do?"

"Oh," says Bonnie, looking away. "Just general labour."

I don't ask again, but I keep looking at her questioningly.

"It's too disgusting to tell. I don't want to make you sick."

"You won't make me sick," I say.

Bonnie looks at me closely.

"I kill chickens," she says. "I've worked at killing chickens for twenty-two years. Eighteen years here in Dresden and then, for the last four years, in Chatham.

"I pull crop. That's the little sack in their throat where the food goes before it goes to their stomach. There's about fifty of us on the line. We do 23,000 chickens a day.

"Some people can't stand it. They can't stand the smell. I guess the smell is disgusting but you get used to it. Other people get motion sickness. I got my daughter a job but she only lasted three weeks. She couldn't take the movement. The chickens are moving one way and the water in the trough below them is going the other way and the motion just gets to some people. It's something like the smell. You have to get used to it.

"You also have to be careful about salmonella poisoning. In the summer it can be really bad. You have to be careful not to put your hands in your mouth. But not only that. Stuff can fly into your mouth and you can get sick enough to end up in hospital. It's easy to get it, but if you're careful you're going to be OK.

"Twenty-two years I have been doing this now. I guess I should have stayed in school. I mean, you're born and raised here and then you get married here. Sometimes I'd just like to go someplace different. When you live in a small town everyone knows your business. Sometimes I'd like to go away and meet new people."

The girl sitting on the stool to my right doesn't look much older than fifteen.

"I'll be seventeen," she says.

Her name is Ida Kay. She isn't bowling. She has come to watch her aunt. Ida's aunt looks more like an older sister. Ida has brought her baby with her. Stephanie is six weeks old.

"Six weeks," I say. "It's a hard time. Are you getting any sleep?"

"It's not hard," says Ida. "I'm living with my parents."

"The father's not with you, then?"

"He's with me. Jeff is nineteen. He works at roofing. We're going to get married in the summer. I'm going to go back to school next year. Grade twelve."

Ida's hair falls down over her shoulders and onto her sweatshirt. Her voice is soft. She seems frightened. Nervous. All the other women here have tight curly hair. Their laughter is loud, almost raucous. Ida seems painfully out of place.

"Don't be nervous," I hear myself saying. "You're doing fine."

"I'm not nervous," she says. "I always fiddle like this. If I'm not playing with my rings I'm fiddling with a cigarette." And then she starts to leave.

"I got to go," she says.

As she slips her daughter into her snowsuit I look up just in time to see Bonnie throw a strike. She punches the air with her fist and then gives a little kick the way golfers do when they sink a long putt. It seems like a good time for me to leave, too.

———————•·————

I return to Dresden over a year later. I go in the late spring when the land is barely brushed with green.

I want to visit Josiah Henson's museum. It was closed for the winter when I was last here. I want to see his grave and go into his house and, if I can, I want to touch things that were once his.

It is a four-hour drive from Toronto to Dresden. I leave home late on a Saturday morning. In Chatham I stop and look up barber shops in the Yellow Pages. I wonder if maybe Art, the Chatham barber that Dresden blacks were forced to visit in the forties and fifties, might still be in town. There are three listings for barbers, but none of them is called Art. I don't expect to find him, so when I look in the White Pages it is almost without paying attention, and I almost miss it. Come on over, says Art.

Number 68 King East is a white clapboard house. There is no sign that says "Barber Shop." I drive by twice thinking I must have made a mistake.

"No. That's Art's," says the old woman I ask on the street. "You gotta go round back."

There is no sign in the back, either. Just a door that leads into a small basement room — a linoleum floor, a space heater, an old tube radio playing the old tunes. Like finding a speakeasy, you have to know it's there.

There is one barber's chair and a choice of five mismatched chairs to wait in. There's a customer in the barber's chair and no one waiting.

"I'm just an old man now," says Art quietly. "These days I just do enough work to keep body and soul together."

Art has been cutting hair in Chatham since 1947.

"I never did put a sign out," he explains. "It's just a neighbourhood place. Everyone knows where it is. The assessor came after I'd been here twenty years and said, 'This is a barber shop.' And I said, 'No it isn't.' And he said, 'If it isn't a barber shop, what are you doing?' And I said, 'I just cut people's hair in my basement.' " He laughs. "I've been paying business taxes ever since."

He gets out a straight razor so he can trim the hair on his customer's neck. He uses a brush and shaving mug to work up the lather he'll need.

"You know what today is?" he says to the man in the chair. "It's the anniversary of D-Day. We shouldn't be here today. We should be having one for old time's sake."

Art and the man in the chair both landed on Juneau Beach. They remember seeing each other.

I have to talk Art into cutting my hair.

"I don't know how to do your hair," he says. He means he does not often cut a white man's hair. It is what white barbers used to say to black men. Art means it kindly. I make a joke about my curls as I climb into his chair, but I can tell he is uneasy.

"I have something you might like to see," he says. He rummages around a cabinet and pulls out a newspaper clipping from a 1958 scandal sheet. He won't talk to me about racism. He says he doesn't know anything, but he knows enough to have kept this two-page feature about Dresden's black community close at hand for thirty-four years. I read the article from begining to end. There is nothing in it I haven't already seen.

My haircut costs $6.50.

It takes half an hour to drive from Art's to Dresden. On the edge of town I park my car and watch three women harvesting a field of asparagus. They are pushing wooden carts down endless rows of plants, bending and cutting each stalk with a small kitchen knife. The woman who can speak English has a thick European accent. We are paid by the hour, she says, not stopping her work. She gives me a handful of asparagus and I eat the stalks raw on the edge of the road.

It takes another minute or two to find the museum on the far side of town. It is a small compound of six weathered buildings in an old apple orchard at the corner of two country roads. One of the old buildings — an unpainted two-storey clapboard house that has been moved (at least) twice over the years — is thought to be the house where Josiah Henson lived at the end of his life. Another, painted red and even smaller, is said to be one of the oldest remaining structures in the area and is believed to be a former refugee slave home.

There are three large tourist buses parked in the orchard when I arrive. The buses left Cleveland, Ohio, this morning at eight-thirty. It took them five and a half hours to get here. They are from the Canaan Missionary Baptist Church.

"We've come for the history," says one man. "So our kids can get an idea of where they came from and what their foreparents did."

"You don't see places like this dedicated to black people in the States," says a woman.

They arrived at about two. They will be gone by five. They will be home at midnight.

The museum takes less than an hour to wander through. By the time I arrive, the families from the Baptist church have seen all they want. Someone is running races for the children in the orchard. I have the displays to myself.

There is a wax figure of a bearded and grey-haired Henson sitting in a parlour chair in the house he is thought to have owned. I squint and look at the figure sideways, trying to make it come alive.

When I come out the buses have gone. There is a small van pulled up at the gate and a family walking through the cemetery where Josiah Henson is buried. It is still used by the Henson family.

The licence plate on the van says Louisiana. The man says his name is Charles Rouillier. He uses the correct French pronunciation. We stand by Henson's grave and talk the way tourists do.

"I live on the Mississippi," he says. "At Paulina. About five years ago, down around Convent and Union, you could still see sheds where they used to keep the slaves. They were nothing but old sheds with galvanized roofs. But there were still shackles in the floor where they used to lock them up. They aren't there anymore. A friend of mine helped tear them down. They were made of cypress. They took them down for the lumber.

"You can still see blacks working in the fields, though. On the sugar cane farms. They live in these little old houses around the barns. They get the houses free but they got to pay for their own utilities. Some of them still don't have electricity."

I can't tell what Charles Rouillier thinks about what he is telling me, and I don't ask. His wife, who has been wandering around with a video camera, calls from the van.

"We have to go," he says.

I drive to town and buy a bottle of Jack Daniels and then go to Marlene's and eat a pizza. When I finish dinner the sun is already begining to set. I drive back to the museum and slip through a split-rail fence and onto the grounds.

Down the road someone is mowing their front lawn with a power mower. I sit at a picnic table under an old cherry tree that must have been here in Henson's time. I open the bourbon, take a drink and wait.

As night closes in, a fox runs through the orchard, her rusty tail streaming behind her like a flag. The Henson family cemetery is just behind me. His house, his bed, his pulpit locked up now.

I take another drink. It is almost midnight. I am not sure what it is I am waiting for.

St-Jean-de-Matha

QUEBEC

Qu'elle est belle la paroisse de St-Jean-de-Matha, avec ses coteaux, ses vallons, ses plaines, ses montagnes, ses forêts, ses rivières et ses lacs.

CURÉ THÉOPHILE-STANISLAS PROVOST
1888

I visit St-Jean-de-Matha in late April, when the rivers are full and running fast and there are still patches of snow in the bush. I come too early for the trees to be in bud, too late to catch the sap running in the maples. All the *cabanes à sucre* are closed, and the few families who actually move into the sugar shacks for the two-week season have gone back home. It is that time of the year when winter lingers in the wind. You can feel it in the morning on the backs of your hands, but you can also sense summer thickening the air somewhere over the mountains — at noon the sun warm on your face for the first time in months.

"Mata" (as the locals call it) is in the foothills of the Laurentian Mountains 100 kilometres north-east of Montreal. The town (population 2,600) is built on a plateau that slopes gently up Rue Principale until it dead ends at Rue Ste-Louise and becomes a hill. Alone at the top of the hill is l'Église de St-Jean-de-Matha — the highest building, built in 1886, on the highest point — so there is nowhere in town you can go and be out of sight of the church. Below the church the houses are huddled together as if in prayer, and along Ste-Louise (the town's oldest street), they are built in the Quebec fashion with their front porches flush to the sidewalk. It is a utilitarian concession — every foot back from the road is another foot of snow to shovel in January.

You can see winter in the architecture wherever you look — the old houses small because they were easier to heat; the brightly painted tin roofs, pitched steeper here than anywhere in the country, because if you let snow accumulate all winter your roof would collapse before spring.

The first houses were built in the 1830s — the first settlers lured into these mountains by the scarcity of farmland in the St Lawrence River Valley. The farmers who tried to scratch their living on the Shield mostly gave up and went into the bush, cutting the trees along the periphery of the vast boreal forest of subarctic Canada. The first sawmill was

built in 1855. There are three in town today. The old farms
are largely gone, but you can still see farmhouses in town
and I count fourteen barns within walking distance of my
hotel (all of them, however, are used as sheds and work-
shops today). There are still some pig farms, more than a
few chicken operations, and even a few dairy herds
around, but no one keeps cattle in town anymore. It wasn't
so long ago, however, that Claire and Adrien Lessard, who
live right on Rue Principale, walked their cows out their
backyard, across Rue Lessard and into the field between
the Caisse Populaire (the town's only bank) and the highway that runs south to St-Félix-de-Valois and north to Ste-
Émélie-de-l'Énergie. Those days may seem long ago, but
the village's last blacksmith, Réal Généreux, closed his
workshop only last year.

These days the main crop in St-Jean-de-Matha is tourists.
Families from Montreal began to build cottages on nearby
Lac Noir in the early twenties. It was the automobile that
opened up the surrounding lakes to the cottagers and
today, in deference to the automobile (and the passing
tourist trade), most of the businesses in town have moved
off Rue Principale and out onto the highway.

Although American snowmobile enthusiasts come here
every winter to tear through the Quebec forests with their
infernal machines, summer is the busy season. Busy
enough that the local supermarket has to increase its sales
staff from twenty-five to over fifty full-time employees for
the summer holidays, and profitable enough that it makes
sense for Isabelle Coutu, who has a fruit store on the highway, to pay $528 a month in rent twelve months a year, for
a business she only opens in the summer.

The week I arrive in town Isabelle is busy readying her
stand — as sure a sign that summer is coming as any other.
At ten in the morning on Rue Principale, old women work
the sidewalks in front of their homes with brooms — sweeping the winter away — while their husbands do things in
their backyards in their checked shirts, suspenders, green

work pants, work boots, their grey hair brushed back, their beards stubbled, their big ears.

It is spring. Everyone is happy just to be outside. The kids riding to school again. I count twenty-six bikes along the school fence. Only two are locked.

I pass over the fancier tourist hotels on the outskirts of town — there are three — and check into the only hotel in the village. Hôtel Mon Repos is more a bar than a guest house. They serve their first beer at eight-thirty in the morning, and there is usually someone in the parking lot waiting for the door to open. The sidewalk in front of the hotel balcony is where the bus stops in town — every morning at eight-thirty on its way south from St-Michel-des-Saints to Montreal. Every night at seven-twenty on its way back.

I am the only guest in the hotel. I share the upstairs bathroom with the owner's teenage son. I have to walk through the bar to get to my room.

There is a barber, a bike store, a video store and the usual collection of convenience stores (*dépanneurs*) where you go for milk, and since this is Quebec, a bottle of wine if you'd like. There is a post office (the only place in town flying a Canadian flag), an elementary school (the *école secondaire* is in St-Félix-de-Valois), one doctor and two funeral parlours. The library, which is in the basement of the municipal building, is open from one-thirty to four o'clock on Wednesday afternoons and from seven to nine on Friday evenings. Nearly every house in town has a television aerial on its roof — sometimes it reminds me of a suburb from the 1950s — yet at night, when I go for walks and look into their front rooms, I am more likely to see families gathered around large tables talking than watching television.

The verb "to chat" or "gossip" in French is *jaser* (pronounced jazz-eh!). *"Que faites-vous?" "Nous jasons!"*

On my first night in town I end up around such a table. Number 186 Ste-Louise is one of the oldest houses in town. It was built in 1840, and the town ambulance driver Pierre-

Michel Gadoury has done such a careful job restoring it that tourists sometimes mistake his home for a museum and knock on the door expecting a tour.

"It's a beautiful house," I say, admiring the pine-planked floor, the antique cabinets, the large wood table, the wood stove in the front room, the plaster walls.

"It sort of chose me," he says, settling down at the table with a mug of strong black coffee. The chairs are wood framed with straight backs, in the style of the Amish. The webbing is wicker.

"I bought it in 1979. I was only twenty-two years old. I was working at my father's garage pumping gas. I had no interest in buying a house. One afternoon I went for a walk on the mountain behind the *église* and when I was walking down the hill I saw the old lady who owned the house working in her garden. It seemed everything else in town was grey except for this house — the house and the garden and the trees around it were shining. I saw it like it was floating out of time — like it was in the old epoch. I stopped and said to the lady, "You have a beautiful house." And she said, "*À toi, je vais la vendre.*" And I said, "*Oui, je veux l'acheter.*" I was thinking about buying a sound system or maybe a car — certainly not a house. But before I knew it I was at the *caisse* asking if they would lend me money. It was all done in a week.

"I think about a week after I moved in a man knocked on the door, and when I answered he looked so surprised.

" 'Is it sold?' he asked.

" '*Oui*'.

" '*Moi*, I want to buy this house.'

" '*Oui,*' I said, '*c'est une belle maison.*'

" 'No, no,' he said. '*Moi*, I want to demolish it and put a new house in its place.' "

Pierre-Michel leans over and smiles. "So, I am happy I bought it. But like I said, it's like the house chose me."

We sit at the table in his front room for hours listening to the music of Gilles Vigneault. People come and go and I am introduced but I forget their names. One of them is

Jean-Pierre Gravel, who lives here with Pierre-Michel. When he introduces himself and asks about my book, I launch into a lengthy description of my travels across the country — about the things I have seen and the things I plan to write about. He nods reassuringly as I go on, encouraging me to continue, and I am thinking that maybe I shouldn't have worried so about my French. I'm doing just fine. This is . . . easy. When I can think of nothing more to say I pause and smile. Pierre-Michel smiles back. There is a silence which lasts a beat too long. We stare at each other awkwardly. My heart sinks as I realize he hasn't understood a word I've said.

"And what is your book about?" he asks politely.

The afternoon slides into evening, the evening dips into night. We drink wine. We eat. We talk. On the wall there is a picture of the dreamy Émile Nelligan, the legendary Quebecker known for his sad and nostalgic poems. There is a fire in the wood stove. There is only one light on, hanging low over the table as if this was a pool room. Smoke from the stove mingles with smoke from strong French cigarettes and twists in the dim light. Someone lights a candle. Someone changes the music.

Georges Brassens is singing "Les copains d'abord."

"I like this song," I say.

"C'est la chanson de la maison," says Jean-Pierre Gravel expansively. He is sitting at the far end of the table. He jumps up and leaps onto the hot stove and dances on it in his sock feet. Suddenly everyone is singing so loud that you can't hear Brassens anymore.

There is more wine and more cigarettes and more talk — coming so fast now that I can only follow snatches of the conversation. And here is Vigneault again and Jean-Pierre standing close beside me unbuttoning his shirt.

He wants to show me something on his chest.

A tattoo.

A *fleur-de-lis.*

It is over his heart.

"C'est la musique vraiment nationaliste," he says. He is talking about Vigneault.

He shakes my hand solemnly.

"That's Louise," Jean-Pierre says later, pointing at a woman with red hair at the far end of the table. "She used to be *ma blonde* but she doesn't have a boyfriend now. She would be perfect for you."

What is he saying?

"C'est l'amour. C'est l'amour that makes these little towns go round."

I have drunk too much. Fragments of conversation flick by like skiers passing me on a hill.

Duplessis.

"He's still here in our hearts. We don't necessarily like him but he's still here. We refer to him often. It was an epoch — good or bad — that's not important. What's important is that he's still here."

Quebec City.

"You must go. You must go. Go in the summer. Go between July 15 and August 15. It's magic. There are musicians and jugglers everywhere."

The volunteer fire department.

"We are volunteers but we get paid. Twenty-five dollars for the first hour. Twelve dollars for every hour after that. Twenty dollars for a practice."

Tibi.

"Ah, Tibi. You could meet him in one of the hotels. He must be . . . How old is Tibi? Maybe he's seventy. If the church steeple needed painting he would paint it. If someone drowns they call Tibi and he looks at the river and he says, 'They're there.' "

The poster on the wall by the kitchen says: *"Un référendum sur la souveraineté et rien d'autre."*

"Que penses-tu de la souveraineté?" someone asks.

I don't know what to say. There is a pride here I admire. As much as nationalism repels me, so too am I drawn to the sense of community it fosters, the feeling of common cause. I feel more comfortable around this table — the smell of the wood smoke travelling along the black stove-pipe before it slips through the wall, the rough plank floor, each board more than a foot wide, the jackets hanging on the pegs by the door, the old casement windows, the antique armoire — this smoke, this wine, these people making me more comfortable than I often feel in my home town, and in many ways fighting a familiar battle: defending a community of values, a language, a culture and its beliefs before the maw of continentalism.

What do I think of *souveraineté?*

If only they would take us with them.

The next morning I wake up to the sound of geese flying north. I shower and go to the little cafe on Rue Principale for breakfast.

"Do you have any *céréale?*" I ask.

"*Quoi?*"

I am sitting at the counter. The young woman who has come to take my order doesn't understand my French.

"*Céréale.*" I repeat. "*Avez-vous la céréale?*"

"*Ah. Oui.*"

"*Quelles sortes avez-vous?*"

"Frosted Flakes."

"*C'est tout?*"

"Frosted Flakes *et gruau.*"

"*Quoi?*"

She goes away and comes back with a box of Quaker Oats.

"*Je vais prendre le gruau.*"

"*Tu veux ton gruau froid ou chaud?*"

"*Chaud,*" I say. "I'll have it hot."

After breakfast I go back to Pierre-Michel's. Jean-Pierre Gravel wants to take me for a drive. Jean-Pierre is twenty-

six years old. He works at a Canada Packers chicken farm
in St-Félix-de-Valois. He has been taking correspondence
courses for the past two years to complete his *école secondaire*. Next year he hopes to go to college and take
agronomie. He wants to work with flowers.

Jean-Pierre takes me first to the Chutes Monte-à-Peine
— a waterfall on the Rivière l'Assomption on the edge
of town.

"It used to be nudist here," he says as we scramble
through the birch and pine forest on our way to the cool
air at the bottom of the falls. "When I was a boy I would
come here with binoculars."

We squat on a large rock — spray off the water driven
into our faces by the wind — our world reduced to the
roar of the falls, the white of the birch, the green of the
pine, the perfect blue sky, the rock black, wet, slippery, the
water boiling.

"I was in France last year," says Jean-Pierre, lighting a
cigarette. He is wearing jeans, black boots, a green checked
shirt and a sweater. "People used to think I was from *Bel-
gique ou la Suisse*. When I said I wasn't from Europe they'd
say, *'Vous êtes Canadien?'* and I'd tell them, *'Non, Québécois.'*
They used to say, *'Pouf. C'est la même chose.'* "

Our next stop is the graveyard. It is on the side of a steep
hill. It is the best view of town you can find — the only place
that looks down on the church.

"Oui," Jean-Pierre says as we walk through the tombstones, "I am a nationalist, but not an extremist. I am not
a racist.

"I would like to see western Canada one day. But I have
to learn how to speak English first. I am afraid if I went
before I would have problems. I'm afraid of being
snubbed. I know there are people who hate Quebec. There
are extremists everywhere. I hope to learn English at
college."

Half-way up the hill we stop in front of a tombstone.

"This is my brother's grave," he says. "He was killed in

a car crash. Before his accident he went all the way to Vancouver. He liked it. He said it was nice."

Below us a motorcycle is twisting along the road from town. It makes me think of Steve McQueen in the movie *The Great Escape.*

We drive north along the country roads, along the Rivière Noire and the Rivière Blanche.

"My grandfather used to live there," says Jean-Pierre, pointing at a house in the trees. "He used to make alcohol in the bush."

Somewhere on every *rang* we pass a *croix de chemin.* Here in Matha it is the Knights of Columbus who erect these roadside crosses. May is *le mois de Marie,* and every Wednesday night in May, seventy-five to one hundred faithful gather at the *église* at seven-thirty and travel by bus to one of these crosses and say the *chapelet.* They gather at the cross, sing, pray, and then return by bus to the *église* for mass at eight o'clock.

We drive up to Ste-Émélie and down to the edge of Lac Noir where Jean-Pierre parks by a trail at the edge of the road.

"This is the Pain de sucre," he says, pointing at a squat mountain. "We are going to climb it."

We follow a mud road that soon narrows to a trail. The trail switches back and winds over a rock fall. There is a life-sized religious statue waiting for us at the top of the mountain, her arms open in greeting, her head knocked askew.

"Vandals," says Jean-Pierre.

On the peak behind the statue there is a large cross that lights up at night like the cross on the top of Mount Royal in Montreal. It is windy on the summit. We sit on a large flat rock, the world stretched out before us.

"I like high places," says Jean-Pierre. "There is an impression of magic in places that are high. It is like an energy that comes out of the earth. You fall into a sense of well-being. Of relaxation. It's like making love to a woman.

C'est vraiment une jouissance."

Sometimes he would use words that I do not understand. *Jouissance.* I carry a dictionary with me and whenever I am stumped I ask him to stop while I look the word up. If I can't find it I give him the dictionary and tell him to find it for me.

"Oh," I say, my finger tracing the word on the page. "*Jouissance* — pleasure, enjoyment, delight, sensual pleasure, climax."

He smiles and keeps going.

"I think the mountains change the character of people. It's hard to explain, but it's special. You can sense the magic. It comes out of the ground. It comes up out of the rocks."

All around us the grey Laurentian Mountains roll — south towards the St Lawrence River, north towards the arctic.

Below us is Lac Noir, mottled silver and white like the side of a fish, like a mackerel sky. The ice pulling back from the shore. The water, where it has already overflowed the ice in places, dark and cold. Soon the ice will rot and sink. Soon the cottagers with their power boats and electric mowers will be here to worry the quiet. Today there is just the wind.

"I want to know more about nationalism," I say.

Jean-Pierre sits up.

"The separatists want to shut the door between Canada and Quebec. I think that's too extreme. I am a nationalist. We have our own language and our own culture here. I am in favour of a form of separation, but I want to leave the door open between Canada and Quebec. I want autonomy *pour nous autres* but I want to leave the door open for cultural and economic exchanges."

"What about the United States?" I ask.

"They are cowboys. They invade us with their ideas and culture and politics and television and cinema. I think of them as Rambo — big arms, little heads."

"Canada and Quebec are like cousins. We come from the same family. The U.S.A is like a neighbour. A big machine that wants to run over everyone. They are very different from us."

"Us," I say. "Who is 'Us'? Is it Quebec. Or is it Canada?"

"Both of us. Canada is more of a gentleman. Canada has more class. Canada is more calm, more quiet, more humble. And more intelligent. Less exhibitionist. It's easier for Quebec to have relations with Canada than with the Americans. With Canada we can sit at the same table and talk things over. You can't talk things over with the Americans. With the Americans it's only business that matters. It's a culture of Big Macs and TV. It's not a culture that interests me.

"I want Quebec to become a country but I want also to remain a partner with Canada."

I try to explain that many English Canadians also fear American culture.

"We worry about Rambo, too."

I tell him my two sons and all their friends in Toronto go to school in French. Not just French class, I say, but all day long. Jean-Pierre is surprised to hear this. At first he doesn't believe what I'm telling him.

"Why?" he asks.

"I don't know," I say.

"It is funny to hear this," he says. "It changes some of my ideas."

"Me, too," I say. "Me, too."

———————— ● ————————

That afternoon Pierre-Michel Gadoury takes me to meet his grandfather. Donat Gadoury is eighty-four years old. He is in the *Guinness Book of Records* — the strongest man of his age in the world. He once knocked out a cow with a single punch, and he can, allegedly, lift over four hundred pounds with one finger. Donat and his second wife Germaine live in an old farmhouse on Rue Laurent. Germaine is eighty-six. When we arrive Donat is out in the garage — working.

"He works all the time," says Pierre-Michel as we cross the yard.

Donat's son, Réjean Gadoury, believes his father developed his strength after he sold the family farm. He bought a truck and made a business buying and selling lumber. But he would transport anything, and it so happened that when he got his truck the village began replacing the wooden sidewalks with cement. There were no loaders in those days, so whenever Donat carried gravel or sand he had to load and unload it by hand. He had seven sons, and after school they would help their father. They used to have competitions — the boys on one side of the truck and their father on the other. Donat always won.

"Sometimes," remembers Réjean, "my father used to lift up the front of the truck — just for fun."

When they talk about strength in Matha, they talk about *la force*. Donat says *la force* is hereditary. Michel Gadoury (Donat's father) believed *la force de la famille* came from Donat's grandmother. The story was that Délima Lafrenière used to stand in the parlour and throw sacks of grain up to her husband, Léandre, who would drag them across the loft and return for another.

Pierre-Michel opens the garage door and we slip into the cool shed. Donat is fiddling at his work bench. He does not seem surprised that we are here. Lots of people have heard about his feats of strength. One day three vans with twenty-five Americans stopped in town and asked where he lived. He welcomed them all into his house.

Standing by the bench in the dim light Donat Gadoury doesn't look big enough to be a strongman. And he doesn't look old enough to be eighty-four. He has the lean look of a farmer you might meet at the gas pump at some out of the way Saskatchewan garage. He has a certain dignity. He looks like he knows why he is here.

There are two huge spoked iron wheels mounted like

dumbells on an iron bar in the middle of the garage. Each wheel is about three feet across and weighs three hundred pounds. They are from an old stationary engine. Donat shakes my hand and without a word walks over to the home-made weight. He grasps the bar as if to lift the six hundred pounds, then smiles, steps back, and motions me to try first.

I might as well try to fly to the moon. I can't make the bar shift along the floor, let alone lift it in the air.

Donat rubs some rosin on his hands and lifts the bar three inches off the ground. He holds it there for about ten seconds before setting it down gently. He is five feet seven inches tall. He weighs one hundred and sixty pounds. He is eighty-four years old. And he is smiling.

When television talk show host Michel Louvain asked him if he lifted weights to stay in shape, Donat said, No, he split wood. He splits four or five cords a day. Before he splits the wood he cuts down the trees himself. He takes his son's truck and goes into the bush alone. Last year he cut about three hundred cords of firewood.

The greatest day of Donat's life was October 1, 1988. It was the day the judges from the *Guinness Book of Records* came to St-Jean-de-Matha to see if he was as strong as people claimed. The town made a big affair of it. There was a dinner at the Centre Culturel. Tickets cost fifty dollars each, and all five hundred were sold. Even the member of parliament, Robert de Cotret, was there. Profits from the dinner were used to erect a bronze bust in Donat Gadoury Park.

Donat wore his blue dress suit that night. He sat on stage and ate with the dignitaries. There were many *hommages* — speeches and telegrams from around the world. When the time came for him to lift, he took off his jacket and went onto the stage in his white shirt, tie and dress pants. The record he had to beat was 800 pounds. He started at 500 and moved up to 600. Then 700 and 800. Everyone was afraid for him. After all, *monsieur,* he was an old man.

Donat cleared 841½ pounds without breaking a sweat.

The hall erupted. A man pressed up against him with tears streaming down his face. There were men and women crying all over the hall. They were crying for joy.

Donat was upset. He could have kept going but in the confusion it was impossible. A week later on television he lifted 1,000 pounds.

We follow Donat back inside his house and sit in the front room. He walks over to his bedroom door, reaches up and grabs the door frame with his fingertips. While we watch, he does a chin-up on the door frame. He lets himself down slowly. It is an impressive feat. There is no more than an inch of wood to grip with his fingers. The door itself is decorated from top to bottom with a hand-painted mural — a wilderness scene that includes a lake, some mountains, five trees and seven birds.

"André Roger did that," says Donat.

Roger, it turns out, is also in the *Guinness Book of Records*. He is the world's fastest artist. He apparently turned up in Matha one day wanting to do something for Donat.

"You should have seen how fast he painted that," says Donat, shaking his head as he settles into his chair.

"You are not," I say to Donat quietly when we are all sitting, "the first strongman to live in St-Jean."

He smiles.

"No," he says. "I'm not."

Louis Cyr was the strongest man who ever lived, or so they say. In 1895 in Boston, Cyr lifted a platform with his back. Eighteen fat men were standing on the platform. Their combined weight was 4,337 pounds. It is said to be the most weight ever lifted by one man.

Cyr was born in St-Cyprien-de-Napierville, Quebec. He lived at the turn of the century — before professional sport, Hollywood, television and all the other organized distractions — in an era when the public imagination could be seized by something as pure as a feat of strength.

Sometimes as many as ten thousand people paid to watch his demonstrations.

For a spell he owned a circus and travelled through Quebec with a caravan of horse-drawn wagons — his father travelling a few days in front of the show as bill-poster and publicist. When Cyr joined the Barnum circus, he was one of the few employees who were invited to eat at the owner's table. He performed in Paris and London. There is a photo of him in England (where he spent two years) between two dapple-grey horses that belonged to the Marquis of Queensberry. The horses are facing in opposite directions and Cyr, wearing a low-cut singlet, tight leotards and high laced boots, is holding a harness above the crook of each elbow. He won one of the horses from the marquis by restraining the team as they were driven in opposite directions.

There is a life-sized statue erected to Cyr's memory where Rue St-Antoine runs into St-Jacques in St Henri, Montreal. Hardly anyone goes to see it. The statue is in a working class neighbourhood. I found it one day by accident. It is, I think, my favourite monument in the country.

I once climbed up on the concrete platform and stood beside the statue and tried to imagine what it would have been like to stand beside Cyr. He weighed over three hundred pounds. His thighs (thirty-six inches) were as thick as my waist. His chest (sixty inches) was almost as round as he was tall (five feet ten inches).

Cyr married a girl from Matha and came here to live when he retired. He is buried in the graveyard at the edge of town.

And Donat Gadoury remembers him.

"He used to come to our house in a *calèche*. My father would play the harmonica and Cyr would dance. He ate too much. My mother used to say, 'When Louis Cyr comes I have to put on extra food.' He used to eat enough food for three men. Sometimes after church he would go to the black-smith and people would gather and he would lift the anvil."

We talk about Matha and early days in the village. "I started to work in the bush when I was fourteen," says Donat. "When I was seventeen my appendix burst. I was in the hospital in Montreal for sixty-four days. My father used to come every week on the train to visit me. When they said I was going to die he took me home. That was in August. When I didn't die they said I would never have my health." He looks at me carefully to see if I am following his story. Then he smiles broadly.

"When we came home in August we said *une neuvaine*— that's nine days of prayer to St Joseph. The first time I went out of the house was for midnight mass at Christmas. After that my father gave me little jobs to help him in the bush. I used to drive the wagon. I got better."

As we get up to leave Donat pulls out a newspaper story written by a Montreal reporter.

"If you write that I knocked out a cow don't write that I punched it in the head," he says, pointing to the article. "I didn't punch it in the head. I punched it in the side. I knocked the wind out of it.

"The cow was *méchante*. We were trying to control her. I didn't hurt her. After a few moments she opened her eyes, took a deep breath, and got up. But she was shaking all over."

We leave Donat's and walk back to Pierre-Michel's house. "I have some things in my basement that you should see," he says. We climb down the worn stairs and wind our way to the front of the house. There is a large wooden chest against the stone wall.

"This used to be Cyr's," he says. "He used it for costumes on his *cirque*."

The chest is enormous — taller than a table. I try to imagine men lifting it when it was full. I try to imagine Cyr's horse-drawn caravan creaking from village to village, the chest on the back of one wagon, Cyr leading the parade — his long flowing hair, his goatee, his tall silk hat. Once in Boston he lifted a horse, a big Percheron imported from

France. He owned a restaurant in Montreal and each night when the room was fullest, his wife would call for help from behind the bar. He would reach over and she would sit on his extended hand and he would lift her over the tables as if she were a bird.

Pierre-Michel and I swing the lid of the chest open and peer inside. The chest is musty and dank and empty of everything but memories.

"How did you get it?" I ask.

"Someone called me a few years ago. They had seen a notice in the newspaper. There was going to be an auction in Montreal. They were going to sell a collection of Louis Cyr's possessions. The collection belonged to his grandson who was very sick. I had two days to find some money so we could bring these things back to Matha. There was a town council meeting that night. I went and asked for money to buy as much as possible. They refused. They said it was not part of the budget. The next morning I phoned Béton Louis Cyr (a cement firm on the edge of town, one of the town's largest businesses). They said it didn't interest them to buy things that belonged to Louis Cyr. I asked them just to lend me the money and they told me they couldn't make a decision that fast. The important thing was just to buy the stuff. We could worry about who was going to pay for it later. But no one wanted to help. Finally Diane Trudeau and I each made a loan to the *Société d'histoire de St-Jean-de-Matha*. We each gave $250 and Robert Morin took it to the sale and bought four objects. He got that little statue over there, Cyr's *porte-manteau* and two framed pictures.

"Later we got his bed, that rocking chair by the window, a charcoal drawing of his wife and this chest. We could have bought the entire collection for eight thousand dollars."

Over and over it is the same thing. History slipping between the fingers of the people who care. Relics and icons turning to dust in some dump. Stories rotting and thrown away like bad meat.

Pierre-Michel is shutting the chest.

"There was an enormous rocking chair," he says. "An admirer had made it for him. It was huge. They say he used to sit in it when he lived here. I would have loved to have got that."

The next afternoon I return to the graveyard on the edge of the village. I want to visit Cyr's tomb. I start at the top of the cemetery and walk back and forth along the rows of stones, working my way down the hill.

It doesn't take me long to find Cyr's marker. It is a three-tiered concrete base with a cross on top. It is not the largest stone in the graveyard.

> Ici repose
> Louis Cyr
> Champion
> des hommes forts
> époux de
> Émélina Comtois
> déc le 10 nov 1912
> âgé de 49 ans et 1 mois
> son épouse
> Melina Comtois
> déc le 28 oct 1917
> âgée de 54 ans

There is a rumour in town that Cyr is not buried in this grave. He died in Montreal and they say no one in Matha saw the corpse. Some people believe his body went to the medical school at the Université de Montréal. There was a woman, Marie-Louise Archambault, who died last year. She used to live opposite the cemetery and said she could remember the burial. She said the casket had big locks all around it.

I reach out and touch the stone. I have thought about this man for so many years that it feels odd to find such a modest memorial in such a simple place.

I stand quietly for a few minutes and then turn to go. But instead of leaving the graveyard I feel an urge to continue my walk by the rows of stones. When I get to the middle of the cemetery I see that I am not alone.

There is an old man walking up the hill. At first I wonder if he is a caretaker who has come to check on me. Then I see that, like me, he is walking back and forth across the hill — working his way up as I work my way down. He is talking quietly to himself as he walks by the graves. Praying, I think. In a few minutes we will pass.

"Bonjour," I say.

"Bonjour."

"Il fait beau aujourd'hui."

"Oui, monsieur. Il fait beau."

He stops and takes off his hat and runs his hand through his hair.

His name is Clément Ayotte. He is sixty-five years old. He was a dairy farmer until he sold his farm two years ago. You can see my land from here, he says, pointing across the valley.

"Do you come here often?" I ask.

"Not too often," he says. Then he shakes his head. "Last night I went for a walk with my neighbour, Paul Archambault, and he started to talk about Léopold Marcil. He said he knew Léopold Marcil well and I said I remembered him, too. Then he said I was too young to remember Léopold Marcil. But I do remember him. So I want to find his grave and see what year he died.

"Bonne chance," I say.

"Oui, monsieur."

We shake hands and he walks off whispering to himself — not praying, but reading the names on the stones under his breath. Gravel, Gadoury, Rondeau, Généreux, Geoffroy, Ducharme, Desrosiers . . .

As I work my way farther down the hill, I count nine wooden crosses among the granite and concrete tombstones. Some of them are obviously home-made, the rough carved messages blessed with the love of a child's letter. I am almost back at my car when Clément Ayotte's voice rings through the cemetery.

"JE L'AI TROUVÉ!"

And again.

"JE L'AI TROUVÉ!"

We meet in the middle of the hill.

"I found it," he says. "I was nineteen years old when Léopold Marcil died. At nineteen you can remember things."

He is pleased with himself. I hold out my hand. We shake.

"Félicitations."

"Oui, monsieur."

———————— • ————————

I settle on Le Cuistot on Rue Principale as the place to eat. There is a larger and more extensive restaurant on the highway, and I could walk there in five minutes, but I like the idea of eating in the village. There are ten tables and a counter at Le Cuistot. Usually I sit at the counter and flip through the *Journal de Montréal,* a Quebec tabloid that becomes my source of news during my stay.

Today at lunch, while Normand fixes my sandwich, I consider the ways I could order french fried potatoes.

Frites, frites avec sauce (petite et grosse), and what must be one of the sillier foods invented in the last decade: *poutine (mini, petite et grosse). Poutine,* in case you have missed it, is french fries mixed with cheese curds and then covered with gravy.

It is an invention that contravenes a rule I have always followed as far as food is concerned: Don't eat anything that squeaks. It's a handy rule which covers both cheese curds and mice.

Le Cuistot offers a variation on *poutine* I have not seen before — *Poutine Italienne (mini $3.55, petite $4.10,* and *grosse $4.65).* I don't ask.

For a few days now I have been wondering about the transport trucks — huge grey three- and four-axle semi-trailers turning off Highway 131 and shoving their way through the middle of town. Sometimes one goes by every five minutes. Even when it is quiet, an hour never passes without a truck growling along Rue Ste-Louise.

"It's garbage. For the dump," says Jean-Pierre Gravel. "We are a nice little village but we are also a dumping ground. They bring garbage here from Montreal and Ottawa. It's a big, big controversy."

The dump, Centre de valorisation et d'élimination des déchets de Lanaudière, is on an abandoned farm about three kilometres from the centre of town.

When it opened in the 1960s, the dump was designed to serve Matha and some of the neighbouring villages. For years no one paid it much attention. That all changed in the autumn of 1988.

"Suddenly the dump was open twenty-four hours a day," says Robert Morin, who is the secretary for Action Écologie, the local environmental group. "It began to smell and people began to wonder what was going on. We made an official complaint to city hall. They told us there was nothing to worry about. They said the dump was a model site. They said the garbage was buried every day. We didn't believe them. The next day we rented an airplane and flew over the site and took pictures. It was the first time we saw the sludge. There were six pools of black sludge the size of six hockey rinks. It was raw sewage. All of it was uncovered. They were bringing it in so fast they couldn't keep up with it.

"The first thing we thought was that we'd turn to the ministry of the environment. We thought they'd help us. And maybe the hardest thing about all of this — we have been fighting this site for three years now — the hardest thing has been realizing we have to fight the minister as well as everyone else. We've had to use the Freedom of Information Act three times to get information from the minister.

"We started to check everything really closely. We checked plans and permits. Everything. We soon discovered that the owner was burying garbage on a part of the land which he had no right to use. It was a lot that was designed to act as a filter for leakage that came from the rest of the site. They were doing this right under the nose of the minister's inspectors, and they were doing it for six months before we discovered and reported it.

"They admitted there was a problem and it was around then that the local owner decided he had had enough. In 1989 he sold the dump to a firm in Boucherville — Services Sanitaires Transvick."

At the time of the sale, according to the Montreal *Gazette* (July 20, 1991), the dump was "a disaster: illegally overfilled in some areas, poorly maintained, classed by the Quebec Environment Department one of the three hundred most dangerous sites in the province."

Most of the garbage was still coming from the region, but the new owners began to haul more and more from the outside. Trucks began to appear from as far away as the Ottawa Valley, Hull and a number of municipalities around the island of Montreal.

A reporter from Radio-Canada, Christine St-Pierre, caused a stir when she followed a number of Transvick trucks from the community of Brossard. She discovered that Transvick was collecting recyclable material from Blue Bags and then hauling it to the Matha dump. St-Pierre calculated Brossard was paying Transvick $110 a ton to "recycle" the loads they were throwing in the dump. The fee for picking up garbage at that time was in the neighbourhood of $30 a ton.

At first many people in Matha were suspicious of Action Écologie. They were perceived by many as trouble-makers. When they went to council meetings the mayor would try to deflect the group, claiming that questions concerning the dump were not the city's concern. The dump, said the mayor, came under the jurisdiction of the minister of the environment. Action Écologie questioned the mayor's perspective. They said he was protecting the company and a sweetheart deal the village had struck with the dump's new owners. In return for favourable zoning, Matha was allowed to dump municipal waste for free.

Today the green and white Action Écologie sign is nailed onto porches all over town. When Transvick announced it wanted to expand the dump, 2,400 people signed a petition against the proposal. These days, like birders who can casually spot the difference between a Canada and a Kirtland's warbler, there are plenty of people in Matha who can glance at a semi and tell you where it has come from and what it is carrying. One of those people is Michel Archambault.

Michel Archambault owns a garage opposite the graveyard. It is a country garage — the last business on the road between the village and the dump. It is as clean and roomy as any garage I have ever been in. Fan belts and other spare parts hang neatly, according to size, along the wall. There is a rocking chair and two straight-back chairs in one corner. People often come to sit and talk while Michel works. Garage Michel Archambault has become a sort of centre for those who oppose the dump.

You can't buy gas from Michel, but you can bring your car here to be repaired or have the oil changed. On the day I visit he is working alone — about to install a new engine in a 1984 Nissan Micra.

"The guy who owns this car brought it in last December," says Michel. "He told me not to start working until he had enough money to pay me. That was — what? — almost six months ago. I got the call last week to go ahead."

I settle into one of the chairs as he rubs his hands with an old rag.

"My father was a farmer. So was my grandfather," he says when I ask him where his environmentalism came from. "This is their land. The house where I live has always been in the Archambault family. I like the earth. But I didn't want to work on it." He looks around the garage. "I like this.

"I'm very careful here. When I built the garage [in 1974] I built special oil traps into all the drains. See this?" He is down on his knees pulling the cover off a drain in the floor. He dips his hand into the oily water. "See? I built it so the oil couldn't escape. No matter what I spill it stays here and I can get at it. When I change people's oil I collect it in those drums over there. I give the old oil to the sawmill and they re-use it as a lubricant."

He opens a cupboard under a work bench and pulls out a large bottle of detergent.

"This is biodegradable," he says. "I use it when I wash the floor. I get it specially from the Ford Motor Company. If you are a mechanic you should pay attention to these things. I don't think all garages are like this, but they could be."

Michel keeps a pair of binoculars on his bench. He also has a 35-mm camera that is loaded and ready to use, a small Panasonic tape recorder he can clip onto his telephone, a CB radio and a notebook.

"I call it my agenda for the environment," he says.

He is not the only person in town who keeps a camera handy. It is there in case there is an *événement* he wants to document. Someone has already snapped photos of a truck driving through town with garbage spilling out the back. Sometimes Michel climbs the hill behind the grave-yard and takes photos of the dump. There is an old water cistern back there, and a rotting ladder you can use to climb to the top if you are careful. They call it their obser-vation post and sit there for hours watching the dump.

Michel has figured out how to use his binoculars as a tele-
photo lens, and he has taken some good shots from the top
of the cistern. He hasn't worked out the frequency the
transport trucks use on the radio yet, but he keeps notes
of likely positions and thinks he might figure it out one day.

"It's not important, that part. It's like a hobby. It's
just fun."

He says he knows the dump is not as bad as it used to be.
He says he knows they are no longer dumping in the controversial filter lot, the *zone tampon,* but, he says, they
haven't cleaned it out, either.

"I compare it to an old car. If I want to sell you an old
car, I'll show you the top all waxed up, but I might not tell
you the frame is cracked and rusted.

"It's the same at the dump. They've cleaned up the surface, but not underneath. They don't tell us what's underneath. And it's what's underneath that counts. If the frame
is rusted, the car is finished.

"We've had tests done. We know there's a problem.
There are spots where it's leaking phenol above the ministry guidelines. We've found one spot where the levels are
sixteen times the ministry's norm."

As I say goodbye and prepare to leave, I receive an unexpected lesson in the politics of language.

Michel is reaching for a repair manual. He wants to
check something on the car he is about to disassemble. I
watch as he flips open the heavy hardcover book and runs
his oil-stained finger down the index.

"Wait," I say as he starts to return the book to the shelf.
"Isn't that all in English?"

He closes the book and shows me the cover.

Chilton Automotive Service Manual, 1984.
Chilton Book Company
Chilton Way
Radnor, PA.

"They only come in English," he says matter-of-factly.

"But you can't speak English," I say.

"No, but I can read it. I have to. All the manuals are in English. I work with these books every day.

"I can't speak to you in English," he says. "I wish I could. If I try, the words don't come. But I can read these books. I guess I'm used to them. It's hard sometimes when there are new words. Like fuel injector. I learned that first in French. Then I'd see it in the book and I didn't know what it was."

There is a computer at the far end of the garage. Michel has to use it when he is working on new cars which, these days, seem to have more computer chips in them than anything else. He likes his computer. He says it is a helpful tool. He is happy to show it to me.

He flips a button on the side and familiar green letters glow on the black screen.

"Diagnostic Function Menu," they read. "Press desired function: 1. Data Stream, 2. Code Description, 3. Prom. ID."

Michel presses a number and the letters dissolve. A moment later they reappear: "No data at ALCA connector. Press Mode EXIT."

The program, probably written in the United States, is, of course, only available in English.

I once knew a man in the insurance business. He operated a brokerage house in Montreal. Many of his clients were French-speaking. Yet most of the policies he issued were in English. I used to wonder what it would be like if you lived in a place like, well, a place like St-Jean-de-Matha and your insurance policy arrived in the mail and it was written in a language that you did not understand and could not read.

"They would be very expensive to translate," my friend told me when I asked.

Maybe. But they are in French now.

Wouldn't you vote for the party that insisted that your insurance company send you a policy in a language you could read? In a referendum on the future of Quebec, which way do you think Michel Archambault would vote?

———————— • ————————

Donat Gadoury is on the telephone.

"Let's shoot some pool," he says.

I do not play pool often, and when I do, I am not very good. But I have always enjoyed the game. I like the symmetry of the table, the colours of the balls against the green felt, the click of them striking one against the other. I like the controlled violence of a hard shot snapping into a side pocket, the elegance of a kissed ball lingering towards a corner. I like the balance of the cue and the harmony of light and smoke and sound that hovers over a pool hall. Most of all, I think, I like what the game does to men. It makes them move more carefully. Sometimes, absorbed and unselfconscious, even clumsy men can become balletic when they play, sinking slowly, elegantly over the table. Quietly, quietly, the cue centres, eyes drifting along the wood, flicking across the table like a snake about to strike, the cue pulling back, steadied by the thumb, motionless. . . . Then! The white ball jumping forward like a grenade.

There is a table in the front room of the bar in my hotel. Twenty-five cents a game. You push your quarter into the slot on the side and the balls fall into a receptacle at the end of the table.

Donat Gadoury is eighty-four years old. How good could he be?

"Can I get you a drink?" I ask.

"Oui, merci," he says, shrugging.

I order a beer for myself. The bartender seems to know what Donat wants. He asked me for white wine but I think the bartender pours him a Dubonnet.

Donat has to explain the rules to me. I break. Then he begins to call his shots without seeming to refer to the numbers painted on the balls.

"Quatre par le sept," he says, lining up his shot.

"Tiens-là!" he says, as the ball disappears.

He tells me that he plays in the pool tournament every year. He won three of the last four years.

Donat moves around the table like he is stalking a rabbit. As he prepares each shot, I can see he is lining up the next one in his mind — planning where the cue ball should come to rest. When I prepare to shoot I am only wondering about the probability of sinking something. Anything.

He wins the first five games.

In the sixth I inexplicably sink five balls in a row. I have never had a run like it in my life. I never will again.

"Good," he says as the fifth ball drops.

It is the first and only word of English I ever hear him say.

I actually win the sixth game. When it is over I reach out to take his cue. He thinks I want to shake hands and there is an awkward moment as we both adjust to each other's expectations. I put my cue down and as I extend my hand again I remember how hard his grip was the first time we met.

I take his hand and squeeze it with all my might. It is meant to be a joke. I am trying to say I can be a strong guy, too. I have never squeezed anyone's hand as hard as I am squeezing Donat Gadoury's.

He doesn't appear to notice. This is crazy, I think. I get up on my toes and lean even closer, putting my entire body into my handshake. Donat senses me shifting positions and looks directly into my eyes. He looks up just as I am leaning closer. He thinks I want to kiss him. He leans forward and kisses me. He still hasn't noticed my grip.

"Would you like to come to supper?" he asks.

Germaine has a piece of steak on a plate that she is going to fry for her husband.

"There's not very much," she says.

"It's OK," I say, still thinking about my handshake. "I'm not very hungry."

There are home-made pickles on the table, salad, bread and butter.

The television is on in the other room. Jeopardy. In French.

"It's a good show," says Donat.

I can't believe it. I am talking to him about Jeopardy. It's just like visiting my parents.

———— • ————

One day after lunch I end up in front of the book racks in the Pharmacie Jérome Landry. There are two racks of paperback books among the skin moisturizers and sunglasses in the main street drugstore. One rack is completely given over to a collection of over-sized Danielle Steel paperbacks. There are fourteen different titles in the edition — all translated into French. They cost $16.95 each. The other rack offers, also in French translation, books by Barbara Taylor Bradford, Robert Ludlum, Agatha Christie, P.D. James and Judith Krantz. I spot only one Canadian author that I recognize. Lucy Maud Montgomery. There are three Montgomery titles — all in French and all with the familiar television characters on the cover.

———— • ————

Another afternoon when I have nothing to do I decide to go for a walk around town. When I turn the corner from Rue Édouard onto Dumais, I almost walk into a sawmill. There are thousands of logs still covered with bark stacked right up against the street. I wonder how I could have missed them until now. The mill is closed today, but I can hear a chainsaw around the next corner.

In a vacant lot in front of their house, André Roy, fifty years old, and his father, Germain, seventy-seven, are cutting firewood for next winter. It is a job they have done together for the past thirty years.

"I put in a new wood furnace this spring," says André. "For the last thirty years I've used a five-gallon oil drum. But I couldn't get insurance anymore so I had to get rid of it."

Germain picks up an axe and stands one of the pieces of birch on end. It is thirteen inches long.

André smiles at his father.

"He likes this," he says.

The old man lifts the axe behind his head and pulls it down with a grunt onto the upended log. It sinks into the wood. He has to wiggle the axe handle back and forth to free it. The second blow lands at precisely the same spot and the wood flies apart. He puts the axe down and carries the two pieces to the wood pile. He reaches for the chainsaw and moves towards the next log.

André picks up a piece of one-by-two that they use as a measure. It is thirteen inches long and painted red so it won't get lost on the ground. He takes the axe and moves along the log cutting a notch every thirteen inches. Germain pulls the cord on the chainsaw and begins at the first notch.

A cord of wood stands four feet high, eight feet long and thirteen inches deep. In Montreal a cord of wood costs seventy dollars, delivered. In Matha a cord delivered to your house is forty dollars. André figures he pays twenty dollars a cord for these unsplit logs.

Last winter he burned fifteen cords to heat his house. The salesman who sold him the new high-efficiency wood furnace told him he won't have to burn that much this year. André is not so sure. He is putting away fifteen cords to be safe.

———— ◗•◖ ————

It is Saturday. I have a problem. I don't know what to do tonight. I have been thinking about this all week. I have three choices.

There is a show at the Auberge Mirador, a club on the highway just north of town — "C'est la faute à Elvis." *"La revue,* "says the poster, *"la plus populaire au Québec,* "already seen by 275,000 Quebeckers and featuring some of the "best young Québécois singers."

I know Quebec has a feel for Elvis Presley that is unrivalled in the country. This would, I think, be an opportunity to explore the lure American culture exerts even here in Quebec. And Elvis, hovering over the whole affair like . . . like what? A cherub? A drug-crazed demon? Uncle Sam himself? All of the above?

There is also the Festival du Bûcheron at the Centre Culturel. *Un soirée du "bon vieux temps."* Bûcheron means woodcutter. This is a night of tradition — old men in *ceinture fléchée* step-dancing to the fiddle. Beer, baked beans, the spoons. *Une vrai nuit Québécoise,* if you want to see something *"authentique,"* says Pierre-Michel.

And in St-Félix-de-Valois? At the salle des Chevaliers de Colomb (the Knights of Columbus hall) — *Super Gala de Lutte.* Wrestling. The Insane Warrior (Sex Symbol '92) vs Monsieur Rock 'N' Roll. Jeff "The Smart Boy" from (gasp!) Toronto vs Serge "Power Machine" Jodoin, de St-Damas. In a hall that can't seat more than two or three hundred people.

See?

In the end Elvis is cancelled. I go to the wrestling.

The salle des Chevaliers de Colomb turns out to be like any other church hall between Montreal and Trois-Rivières. Just large enough for the smart (rented) red, green and yellow wrestling ring in the centre of the room, with enough space left over for four rows of wooden folding chairs around the walls. At eight o'clock, the announced starting time, I count about 150 people in the audience. The room looks full.

We have been watching the wrestlers arrive, alone and in pairs — all sporting the same haircut (short on top, long at the neck), all carrying gym bags. They walk through the hall and, as the promoter directs them, through one of two doors at the far end of the hall. Later in the evening I learn that both doors lead to the same cramped dressing room behind the stage, which all fourteen combatants share.

Kathy, who is eighteen, arrives with her boyfriend, Michel Lamothe, who, the poster says, will soon be fighting Stéphane "Pretty Boy" Veillette.

When she sits in a chair near me I introduce myself. To my surprise, she speaks perfect English. She comes from North Bay.

"I came down here last summer to meet my father — who I didn't know. He left home when I was very young. While I was here I met Michel and I decided to come back and be with him. I wanted to get away from my problems at home."

"Your problems?"

"My mother remarried when I was two," she says. "She died when I was eight and left me with my stepfather.

"After she died it was hell. My stepfather started drinking. He would slap me and grab me and throw me around. I used to have bruises and stuff. I was eight years old. My brother and I were kind of left alone. I was older than he was and I had to take care of him.

"When I was sixteen I moved out and lived with my boyfriend's parents. Then I lived in a foster home for a month. That was when my real father started writing letters. He lives around here. I came to see him last July. I spent about a week. It was kind of . . . It wasn't what I expected."

"Tell me what happened?" I asked.

"Well, you kind of expect to have a dad who is rich. When I got here it turned out that he was on welfare. I only stayed a week. I was upset. I went back to North Bay. Things weren't so good there, either. I was engaged to be married. I'd been going with a guy for two and a half years but I didn't like him anymore. He was really sweet to me. He gave me everything. He even bought me a sports car. But it had kind of faded away. I didn't want to marry him. I said I'd met somebody. I said I was moving. I wanted a new start.

"While I was here visiting my father I met Michel and he had written and asked me to come back. So I did. I rented an apartment by myself. Social Services helped me. Now Michel and I are going to move in together. I've been with him for nine months. Things couldn't be better.

"I think I'll stay here in Quebec. I like it here. Michel and I talk about getting married in two years. It's better than what I had in North Bay. My stepfather didn't want me. It felt like nobody wanted me. I didn't have anything to lose when I came. It couldn't have been any worse.

"I do miss speaking English, though. When I came here my French wasn't great. I couldn't tell a story or anything like that. Michel doesn't speak English. But it's not all that different here. Except for the language. They think the same and eat the same and do the same things. It's just the words that are different."

"I gotta go now," she says. "Michel is on soon."

"A lot has happened," I say.

"I've learned a lot. I've learned you should never give up. There's always someone out there who's going to love you. If you keep looking there's always someone who's going to take you in."

I stay for the fights but I don't really watch them. I only write one thing in my notebook. The New Beastie Boys (a tag team duo from "New York City"), I scribble, both speak French. Their manager, "Miss Trouble," strides around the hall during their fight blowing a shrill whistle and yelling "Shut up" at the crowd.

I get up to leave before the final event is over. On my way to the front door I see Kathy sitting alone in the corner. I go over to say goodbye.

"I don't have anything else to say," she says. "I don't want to talk anymore." She is looking around the room anxiously.

"What's the matter?"

"I'm already in trouble for talking to you," she says. "Michel is mad at me."

I start to ask why and then think better of it. The best thing I can do is go away.

"Good luck," I say. I try to give her a reassuring smile. She's not looking at me.

It is eleven-thirty when I pull into town. I drive over to the Centre Culturel to see what is happening at the Festival du Bûcheron. I am surprised to find the hall still packed. The man at the door tells me they sold over five hundred tickets. There was an NHL playoff game tonight.

Most of the people here are over fifty, most of them in plaid shirts, most of them drinking beer and many of them dancing. Joseph Beaudry, sixty-seven, is alone at the microphone. He is singing what are known as *chansons à répondre*. The back-up band, all wearing cowboy hats — drums, two guitars, a fiddle and accordion — look like they've been lobotomized. When Joseph sits down they begin *les sets carrés*. Nobody needs a caller to tell them what to do. They all know the steps.

Donat Gadoury is here gliding from table to table like a senator. A deep blue cardigan with the insignia of the Montreal Canadiens over his heart, a plaid shirt, an almost regal presence. But I don't feel like staying here, either.

There is a band playing back at the hotel. I get into bed but the music is right under me. I'm not going to sleep until they stop playing. I am too tired to read, too discouraged to go downstairs for a drink. The last time I look at my watch it is quarter of three.

———————————◆•◆———————————

There are no policemen in St-Jean-de-Matha. But there is one police badge. It is silver and professional-looking and is heavier than you'd expect. Yves Charron carries it in a

leather flip wallet just like the cops do on television. Mostly
he keeps it in his briefcase on the front seat of his maroon
Ford Tempo. Yves is an *officier responsable du règlement de sta-
tionnement.* He is, in fact, the *officier responsable* — Matha's
one and only traffic cop.

It is not a full-time position. Yves works full time at a
youth detention centre in Joliette. He says writing traffic
tickets is more a calling than a job.

"I don't do it in the sense of making money," he says, sitting at the table in the front room of his house. "I do it to
contribute to the municipality. As a service."

It hasn't made him the most popular guy in town.

"People want to kill me when I give them a ticket. The
first time I gave a ticket last year the guy got in his car and
drove it right up against me and started to push on me with
the bumper. They're just not used to it. They think they're
in the country. They think they can park anywhere.

"When I give a ticket in the summer, when the tourists
are here, it isn't rare to have twelve or fourteen people
gather around me and, yes, I check my back. They don't
like it at all. They don't like the rules and they don't like
me. People say things like they're going to kill me. I
don't believe they're really going to kill me. They just say
that. But you don't know. So I'm always checking. I had a
woman once who was parked across the front of a driveway. When she came out and saw me writing a ticket she
said, 'What are you doing that for? This is my uncle's
drive.' She was really angry. She stuck her nails right
into me."

Yves doesn't have a uniform or a squad car. All he has
are his badge and a book of tickets (every infraction comes
with an automatic ten-dollar fine).

"When I started the municipality didn't know what to
pay me. So they began paying me by the ticket. I got five
dollars for every ten-dollar ticket I issued. After a while I
realized I wasn't covering my expenses. So I started going
really hard. If I saw a car parked incorrectly I didn't give it

a chance. Out came the book. After about a year the mayor said, 'OK, OK. You have to slow down.' That's when they put me on a salary. I get one hundred dollars a week. I have to provide my car and pay for the gas.

"The good thing is that I know nearly no one. I've lived here for twelve years but I don't mix much. I could give a ticket to the mayor, or the doctor, or one of the councillors, and I wouldn't know."

———— • ————

One night Jean-Pierre Gravel takes me for a walk into the hills behind the church.

"This is where I grew up," he says. "I know these paths like the back of my hand."

When we come out of the woods he wants to show me the inside of the church. In a hall behind the altar twenty children are pressed around three large tables, studying for their confirmation. Another group of twenty come on Sunday after mass.

"Let's go see Louise," says Jean-Pierre.

Louise Geoffroy lives with her mother on Rue Durand. By the time we arrive at the Geoffroys' side door, her mother is in bed. Louise is sitting at the kitchen table with her cousin and her cousin's wife, talking.

When Jean-Pierre tells them we have come from the church it is not long before the conversation wends its way to Curé Bernèche.

"I was born at home," says Louise, "in 1956. I only weighed four pounds. They put me in the wood stove to keep me warm. They say I cried without stopping. They called for Dr Lessard and he came and he said there was nothing to do. He said I was going to die. So my father phoned Curé Bernèche. He came here to the house and looked at me and said, 'Give the baby castor oil.' I was fine from that moment on."

Everyone at the table nods.

"He could do miracles."

"*Vraiment.*"

"*Certain.*"

"There was a fire in a swamp. In the roots. It was moving towards Matha. There was lots of smoke. They called Curé Bernèche. He walked through the forest in a line between the fire and town. Wherever he walked, the fire stopped."

"The house. The house."

"There was a house on fire. Whose house was that? Mme Savignac? Her house was burning and there was another building beside it. Was it another house or a garage? It's not important. There were two buildings side by side, very close — maybe three or four feet apart — and one was on fire. They called for Curé Bernèche and he came and he walked between the two and the fire went down just like that. After, they called the fire department, and they came and put it out. But it didn't spread. That's the point."

Louise stands up and leaves the room without a word. When she comes back to the table she is carrying a small red suitcase — something a vaudeville magician might have had on a stand beside him. She opens the lid.

"There is a picture here somewhere," she says. The suitcase is full of snapshots. She is looking for a picture of Curé Bernèche.

"Here's one of my father," she says.

It is 1957. Her father the taxi driver is standing by an early Bombardier Ski-Doo. It looks like a Volkswagen on skis. Dr Lessard is standing beside him.

More Ski-Doos. A big one rolling across a field of snow. It looks like a loaf of bread, it looks like a tank, it has little portholes running down the side. Yet another, small and square. And a rectangular one with sculpted edges. But no picture of Curé Bernèche.

"Wait a minute," says Louise, getting up again. "I know."

She comes back a moment later and hands me a small

framed picture of the priest. He has a brushcut and is wearing glasses. He is frowning.

"It was by my mother's bed," she says.

M. l'abbé Albert Bernèche was born in St-Barthélemi in October 1887. He came to Matha in September 1942. He was the *curé* for twenty-five years. He died in 1967.

Twenty-five years have passed since he said a mass, heard a confession. Yet all the while I was in town he kept popping up, unbidden, in conversation.

"The legend was that he knew everything," says Réjean Gadoury one morning. We are sharing an elegant breakfast at La Montagne Coupée, the new *auberge* Réjean built. The inn is perched on top of a dramatic cliff on the south of town.

"I remember when I was fifteen or sixteen I went to a dance in Joliette. It was in a club. You weren't supposed to be there unless you were over eighteen. The next morning during mass I remember Curé Bernèche saying, 'It is not correct for little Gadoury to go dancing on Saturday night. The parents of this child should take better care him.' I wanted to slide under the pew. My father turned crimson. How did he know I went dancing? Everybody believed he could perform miracles. He could turn the wind. He could heal people."

"Do you really believe that?" I ask. "Could he really perform miracles?"

Réjean Gadoury throws his hands up in the air.

"What do I know what I believe?"

"You know what you think."

"Now? Today?"

"Yes."

"No. I don't believe that anymore. But then! He was like a father to the whole parish. He knew all his little children and if you did something wrong it could be very dangerous. He had the reputation of a saint. We all believed he could make miracles."

I go to visit the present *curé*. There is a small handwritten sign on the door of the presbytery. "We are Christian Catholics," it reads. "Respect our faith."

"What does that mean? What is that for?" I ask the woman who answers the door.

"It is for the Jehovah's Witnesses," she says.

There is a desk and three chairs in the foyer. It makes me think of a waiting room in a doctor's office. There is a picture of Pope Jean-Paul II on the wall. Nothing else. The woman motions to one of the chairs. I sit down. She goes to get the *curé*.

On Sunday I go to the late mass. I sit alone near the front. There are four antique hooks screwed along the back of the pew in front of me. I wonder what they are for. When I notice there are similar hooks along the backs of all the pews, I realize they are there for our hats.

The vaulted ceiling is painted blue and white and pale green. The stations of the cross adorn the walls along both sides of the church. Above the priest and looking down on the congregation, a life-sized plaster Christ hangs from a cross — blood on his hands, thighs, feet and heart, blood trickling over his chest.

The effect is profound and guilt-inducing. He died. He suffered. And I drank beer and watched hockey in the Bar Général last night. In the very front row there is a young boy, maybe ten, sitting alone. He is watching the candles on the table in front of him. They are in glass jars — yellow, red, green, deep blue, flames flickering. The light shimmering, glowing. Something to watch. The boy leans over and fiddles with one of the jars.

Curé Roger Latendresse is wearing a white robe with red trim. The altar boy serving him is actually a young girl with braids, hot pink socks, red shoes, black leggings and a pink jumper. The *curé* is wiping his silver goblet carefully and folding a linen napkin over the top of it as if he were about to make it disappear.

"Religion," says Curé Latendresse, settling behind the desk in the presbytery waiting room, "is Love.

"That's all. Love. It is about the Love we have for God. It is about the Love God has for us. And it is about the Love that is among us. That's the foundation. All the rest is just accessory. It is only there to show Love."

The *curé* takes the *pain consacré* from the *tabernacle*. He holds the plate to the sky. The congregation comes forward for communion. They are each given a piece of the host. Only the *curé* drinks wine.

"It is all right to do it just with the bread like that," he explains later. "They aren't missing anything. Christ is present in both. It's not like there is half of Him in the bread and half of Him in the wine. For special ceremonies we use both the bread and the wine. But on a normal Sunday we just use the bread. Why? There are lots of people here and people are in a hurry these days. They worry about health, too. Not everyone wants to drink out of the same glass anymore."

After the mass is over I go to the candles. It costs twenty-five cents to light one. I put $1.50 into the box. I try to light a different colour for each quarter.

———————————————

Claude Bégin, who is the owner and manager of the Supermarché Provigo — the largest grocery store in town — does not like the idea of opening on Sundays.

"I have no choice," he says. "I have to open. The store in St-Félix is open on Sundays now."

Bégin bought the Provigo a little over a year ago. Like most of the businesses in Matha, the Provigo is on the highway (briefly renamed Chemin Louis Cyr as it sweeps by the village).

Before coming to Matha, Claude Bégin spent sixteen years in Montreal with the Steinberg chain.

"It was a big change moving to a small town," he says. "In Montreal nobody knew me. I used to work in a jacket and tie and spend all my time in my office. I was an administrator. Here I spend a day a week in the meat department and a day a week in fruits and vegetables. I spend twenty hours a week on the cash wrapping vegetables and carrying people's orders to their cars. If I'm not on the floor people say to me, 'You weren't here yesterday. Where were you?' Some people shop here five or six days a week. They want to talk to me. I talk about the weather maybe fifty times a day. But I like it.

"It's so different here. More than one customer has come to me and said, 'I saw your house the other day. Nice house.' If I'd told my customers in the city where I lived they would have looked at me and said, 'So what?'

"But it was hard when I first came. The old owner had a certain way of doing things. He had built this place and run it for twenty years. And here I was, a city boy taking over. It was a big event around here. People don't like change. They hate change. And I had to change some things. We have an in-store bakery and the old owner used to make his own sugar pies. Well, he could afford to run the bakery three hundred hours a week and still make a profit. I can't afford that. I had to cut back. I'm getting my sugar pies from Ontario. Some people don't like that. People talk.

"Some of the old customers used to come to me and say, 'Things aren't the way they used to be.' That was tough on my morale. I'd smile and listen. But it was hard.

"It was difficult working with the staff, too. There is no union here. That's rare in the grocery business. A few weeks before I arrived, the union came to town and went door to door. They told people they knew me from Montreal. They said I was a tough guy. The employees said they would give me a chance.

"Well, it was hard at first. I wasn't used to coping with

things when there was no grievance sheet. It's more like a family here. If there's a problem you have to talk about it. I had to change the way I worked and I wasn't good at it at first.

"I was always comparing things to the city. I used to say things like, 'In Montreal we'd...' Finally my staff said, 'Well, you're not in Montreal anymore.'

"There is a different attitude to work here. For instance, no one takes coffee breaks. They'd riot in the city without a coffee break. On the other hand they don't rush around here like they do in Montreal. If business slows down here then everyone slows down.

"I like it better now. I'd have to say that this is the best staff I've ever had. My life has changed for the best. It's true that I worry more than I used to. I own the store now. But the stress has been reduced by about eighty percent."

Claude glances at his watch and fidgets in his chair.

"Do you have to do something?" I ask.

"It's time for me to go and bag orders."

"Twenty hours a week," I say. "Why do you do that?"

"I like it," he says. "This is where I have the closest contact with my customers. I see what they're buying. I carry their food to the car and open the trunk and see the competition. I see bags from other places. Even here in a small town people shop around. They go to Joliette, or St-Félix or St-Gabriel-de-Brandon. When they leave I give them a smile. It is the last thing they see. It's important for our reputation."

As Claude heads for the front of the store, he picks up a green apple from a fruit bin and invites me to do the same. On my way out, apple in hand, I stop in front of the wine display — bottles of Beaujolais and Burgundy imported from France in tankers, bottled by the Quebec Liquor Board, and sold in grocery stores both large and small across the province. At the front counter I ask a young woman about the tobacco leaves I saw advertised on my way in. She reaches below her cash and pulls out a package that looks like a stick of French bread. The raw leaves are honey coloured and wrapped in cellophane.

"You can make a carton of cigarettes with that," she says. "People chop them in their blender. You just have to add a bit of water. Then you can roll your own."

"How much?" I asked.

"For a carton or a package of leaves?

"Both."

"For a carton it's $40; $4.99 for the leaves."

Before I leave I write down the name of the local farmer who supplies Claude Bégin with his maple products — maple syrup, maple sugar, maple jelly, maple butter, something called *tire*, which is like a bucket of maple taffy, and *pain de sucre* — a hard lump of maple candy.

———— • ————

Jean-Marie Latraverse is seventy-three years old. He lives alone on his farm not far from town. Sitting in his rocking chair, his boots drying in front of the wood stove, his blue sailor hat pushed back on his head, he looks as if he might have spent much of life in a cafe in Marseilles. In fact he spent it as an architect working in Montreal. He bought his farm in 1963.

"The land was waiting for me," he says, his strong voice sailing across the room. "I like nature. I like women, too. But nature is more steady than a woman. Nature will always be there. A woman can leave you all alone. You're never alone when you're with nature."

Jean-Marie's wife died in 1970.

"Two weeks after she died her best friend came over to see me. 'You must be lonely,' she said. An hour after that we were in bed making love. It keeps you young, making love. I try to make love once a week.

"Shall we go and see the sugar bush?" It is more a statement that a question. He is already half-way across the room.

"My life is simple now," he says as we climb into my car. "We use plastic hose. We have five thousand spigots. We used to do it the old way. I used to have buckets and two horses. I stopped using the horses seven years ago. It's too bad. That was the real McCoy. And the quality was better. Turn right here.

"With a bucket, if the water isn't clear you can throw it out. With the hose, cloudy sap gets mixed up with all the rest of it. But it's so much easier with the hose. At the next corner you have to turn right. That's it.

"I still have forty-seven years to go, you know. I had a bad accident a few years ago. You're going to turn up ahead again. To the right. I was nearly killed. For six days it was sort of life and death. See that house over there? The man that lives there makes violins. He makes six at a time. Anyway, I had a meeting with The Boss up there." He gestures towards the roof of the car with his thumb. "St Peter and I had a chat. He said, 'I am not ready for you, Jean-Marie.' He said, 'I'll see you in fifty-four years.' Add it up. That was six years ago. I have some time left. I am going to live to be 120. That's why I'm not too worried. OK. Here we are."

The *cabane à sucre* has been closed for almost two weeks. Jean-Marie's partner, a young farmer who is earning his share in the business with his labour, has been here all day cleaning the tubing. During the run the man brought his wife and children here and they slept on mattresses in the cabin.

"The spirit of Henry Ford has invaded the bush," bemoaned Thomas Ripley in his book *A Vermont Boyhood*. And yet even here, with plastic tubing snaking through the sugar bush, much still remains.

Every farmer still has his own *cabane à sucre*. And the maple moon (as the Ojibwa called it) still coincides with the first whisper of spring. The cry of a crow cuts through the pale sun and a farmer finds himself standing in the middle of his hillside sugar bush. He can see clear across the valley — the trees as straight and bare as barnwood, the rolling hills mottled like the side of a cow. He sees a white ocean of granular snow and, where the snow has melted, spongy brown islands of last year's leaves — pools of decay compressing under his boots, the wonderful smell of the earth.

A maple bush during the spring run is a happy place to be. A place of wet wool and aching muscles. Men and women stumbling around in the snow, pants and gloves wet, hands and feet cold. After you've stayed up a few nights tending the evaporator you can almost imagine the trees breathing — in and out, in and out — the sugar water running up and down under the bark.

Maple syrup is only made in North America. Seventy-five percent of it comes from Canada. Ninety percent of that from here in Quebec. The nutrient-rich sap (the final syrup contains potassium, magnesium, phosphorus, manganese, iron, zinc, copper, tin and calcium) is anywhere from two to five percent sugar. It is stored over the winter in the root system of the tree and starts to flow towards the stems and branches when the days are warm and the nights still cold. The sap moves up and down the tree with the temperature. As soon as the buds burst, the liquid turns cloudy and the sugar content nosedives. A tapped tree (it should be at least fifty years old) will give up about seven percent of its total sap, apparently without any harm. There is another run of sap in the fall and some people have tried to tap their trees twice a year. But the weather is not as favourable in the autumn and autumn syrup has a bitter edge.

"It's the difference," says Bertrand Champagne, who for thirty years was the local buyer for an American wholesaler, "between eating *un chip ordinaire* and *un chip barbecue.*"

The alchemy happens in the sugar shack. In a few short hours the cold clear sap is mysteriously transformed into golden syrup. The tang of wood smoke from the fire-box mixes with the sweet-smelling steam that billows out of the evaporator. The happy aroma gets into everything. A sugar shack, writes R.D. Lawrence in his book about maple syrup, is like "a steam bath built inside the heart of a volcano."

Standing in the bright April sun it is easy to imagine the sugar bush in operation, easy to regret not being here.

"We have some of the best trees in Quebec," says Jean-Marie proudly. "And if we have the best in Quebec it means we have some of the best in the world. They're all sugar maples. The water is different." He catches himself and laughs out loud. "Listen to me. It's a pleasure to talk like this, but I sound just like an American."

Not many producers fared as well as Jean-Marie Latraverse this spring. There is a glut of maple syrup in Quebec. The government agency that buys syrup from the producers has not yet sold the last two years' production. It is being stored in barrels. The surplus is in the neighbourhood of twenty-eight million pounds of syrup. The price is way down. In the mid-eighties you could get forty-five dollars a gallon. This spring you might have to take twenty-five.

The problems began when the American Food and Drug Administration changed the regulations governing what could be labelled maple syrup or maple sugar. Products once had to contain fifteen percent maple syrup by volume to use the maple name. As of 1976 anything containing just two percent could qualify.

At the same time the bottom fell out of the American market, the Quebec government was subsidizing farmers to expand production. The production increased by over twenty-five percent.

So this spring many farmers like Laurent Rondeau, who has a sugar bush and a small dairy farm on the other side of the highway, stopped producing syrup before the run ended.

"I stopped after six days. It wasn't selling. *Ouf,* I could have sold it. But for a ridiculous price. So I stopped. Lots of guys stopped production early. In the past the American companies bought our syrup. But not anymore. I stopped early last year, too."

Laurent is the fifth generation in his family to work the 140 acres he owns on the Rang St-Guillaume. He took over from his father, Viateur, who took over from his father, Napoléon, who took over from his father, Emanuel, who took over from his father, whose name Laurent can't remember. Today Laurent needs an off-farm job to survive. Like so many other farmers in Canada, he drives a school bus during the week. And like so many other farm children, his sons and daughter have left the land. His oldest son is an electrician in Montreal. His daughter is in Trois Rivières studying to be a teacher. His two other boys are also away at school.

Just fifteen years ago Laurent used horses to collect sap in the spring. He had three. He still cuts fifteen cords of wood every autumn for the fire-box.

It is just after supper when I stop at his farm. A sign nailed to a tree, *"Sirop d'érable à vendre,"* catches my eye and I pull into the drive. Laurent seems happy to leave his sister to finish the evening milking. We walk through the twilight across the muddy barnyard and into his *cabane à sucre,* only a stone's throw from his house. Behind the *cabane* a hill of grey maples rolls into the sky. Laurent is wearing old work clothes, tall rubber boots, a hat and glasses. There is a pair of snowshoes hanging on one wall. The old red work sleds are piled on top of each other in the middle of the room. He pulls out two chairs, lights a cigarette and we sit in the gloomy shack for an hour talking.

"When I work on the farm I work for myself," he says. "I don't have a boss. I like the fresh air. I don't like town."

I ask him about politics.

"That is something very difficult to deal with," he says. "Should Quebec separate from Canada? There are those that say it would be good and those that say it wouldn't. It's very complicated. It's hard to know if it's good or bad. It's right to have French as the number one language. But it's not correct for them to pass a law that says there can be no English on a sign. I think we can live together."

"Are you Canadien or Québécois?" I ask.

"Québécois," he says without hesitation. But then he adds, "I am Canadien also. We haven't separated, not yet. I am still Canadien."

Back in my bed I can't stop thinking of maple syrup. What a telling state of affairs. Our national tree — the symbol on our flag, for heaven's sake — bled for years so we could sell the bulk of whatever we produced to Americans for cash. Now they have re-defined it for us — cheapened it — and left us with what? Ottawa has decreed that the Canadian army will purchase Quebec maple syrup and serve it in army cafeterias from coast to coast in an effort to consume the surplus. The image of jugs of maple syrup sloshing up and down mess hall tables — "Not again?" — is anything but reassuring. Now I read that Nova Scotia has complained. What about *our* surplus, they're asking.

———————— • ————————

Donat Gadoury keeps coming up in conversations. Jean-Marie Latraverse mentions that he sometimes hires Donat to work in his sugar bush, cutting trees.

"I asked him when he was going to retire," says Jean-Marie. "He told me he'll stop working when he gets old."

A few days later I visit the Centre au coeur des femmes, a women's drop-in centre in a basement apartment on Rue Ste-Louise. Louise Bélanger works at the centre.

"At the begining the men in town were afraid of this place. We are a little bit feminist and I guess a lot of men over forty are afraid of women who decide to say, 'I'm good for work outside the home.'

"But Donat is for the centre. He has been an example for the younger men in town. For me, too. He is a simple man, but he's also a wise one. When you talk to him — I don't know, it's hard to explain — he's like a father. He has something great yet he remains so simple. We like him."

Louise introduces me to Gail Jurewicz, a thirty-eight-year-old mother who comes to the centre regularly. Gail has recently moved into the area from Montreal where she was raised in English. Now she and her children are living in a French milieu.

"I didn't want to bring my kids up in the city. I wanted them to have fresh air and space around them and peace.

"When I first saw this place I thought, 'A women's centre? In St-Jean-de-Matha? What kind of people are going to be there?' But it's a wonderful place. There is a word in French — *accueillant* — I don't know if you have a word like that in English. It translates as 'welcome' but it's not the same. It's a *warm* welcome.

"It's not always easy to integrate here. At first they think you're a weekender. The area is so full of chalets. It takes a while to put down roots and to get people to trust you. The centre is the first place where I felt I belonged. The first two years, I was at home with the kids. When I finally had some free time I didn't know what to do. So I came here. Every Tuesday afternoon there's an open meeting. Sometimes they rent videos and we have a discussion afterwards. Sometimes there's a guest speaker. We've talked about old age and poverty. We've talked about menopause. We've talked about non-traditional jobs. And grieving. And the feminine condition. Like I said, I stay at home with my children. And that gets validation here. They say it's OK to stay at home with your kids. They make me feel good."

Louise Bélanger has been listening to us.

"When I moved here it was easy for me because of my children," she says. "I think it is more difficult for a man. My husband is a welder. It took him four years to find work. Most of the little companies around here are family-run businesses. So when you're looking for a job it can be hard. You have to compete against family. When my husband finally found work it was in St-Michel-des-Saints, about a hundred kilometres north of here. It took him seven years to find a job in Matha.

"I think it's different for a woman. The women of Matha are more receptive to things from the outside — both ideas and people. I think men have trouble because this is just a little village and there are only so many jobs. I think maybe the men are afraid this new guy is going to take their job away from them. I think they also feel protective. They want to protect their village and protect their traditions and protect their identity. It's like 'This is my corner. This is my place.'

"All the same, we've found helpfulness and humanity here that we never found in Montreal. It's a real community. People think of each other. They want to know what each other is doing. They take the time to find out what each other feels. They take the time to live. That's very important to me. The way they live here is the way I like to live, too. When I lived in Montreal I often felt alone. I'm never alone here. In Montreal I was always running. People here aren't always running after something."

———————— • ————————

Albert Chartier has been drawing the cartoon *Onésime* for forty-nine years. He is considered by some to be the father of Quebec cartoonists. There are two awards handed out to comic book artists every year in his name. One is called the Albert Chartier Award; the other is called the Onésime. His full-page strip appears once a month in the *Bulletin des Agriculteurs,* a monthly farm magazine with a paid circulation of about forty thousand. Year after year when the magazine does its readership survey, readers report that the long-suffering Onésime, who reminds me of Dagwood Bumstead, is their favourite feature.

Chartier lives with his wife on the top of a mountain that overlooks Lac Noir. He is eighty years old.

"How time flies," he says laughing. "How did it happen? I don't know. I only feel twenty.

"The other day I was joking with the waitress in the restaurant where I go every morning. She said, 'I'd love to have you for my —' I thought she was going to say, my chum, or maybe, my father, but she said, 'I'd love to have you for my Grandfather.' I guess I *am* getting old."

It takes Chartier half an hour every morning to walk down the hill to the restaurant on the highway ("I do it for the exercise"). He leaves at eleven. He drinks two coffees and reads *La Presse* ("I love that paper. It has good journalism. Good editorials"). He arrives home in time for lunch two or three hours later. He exercises every morning for half an hour before his walk. He also smokes and drinks beer.

When he was young Chartier spent two years in New York drawing panel gags for Big Top Comics.

"I was going to go to Tahiti on a freighter but the war put an end to that. So I went to New York instead.

"I'm a pacifist. I'm not a killer. I didn't want to go overseas. I passed my physical and my dossier went to the *fusiliers Mont-Royal.* I had a friend there and somehow my dossier got lost on his desk. They never bothered me again. If it had been a question of defending our country, that would have been different."

Chartier came back to Canada in 1942 and drew cartoons for *Maple Leaf Magazine.*

"That was my war effort. Drawing gags for the troops."

After the war Chartier did cover illustrations for weekly magazines in the Norman Rockwell style that was popular at the time.

"People thought I was pretty good. I was no better than anyone else. It was just because I'd been to New York. It's like we say in French, 'You have to go somewhere else to be recognized at home.' "

"We say that too."

"You do?" He looks surprised.

Albert did covers for *Le Samedi* ("Le magazine national des Canadiens"). His cartoons appeared in *Weekend* — the

English magazine that came with the Saturday paper. When his work appeared in English he signed it "Al" Chartier.

In the 1960s he drew a bilingual comic strip about the history of New France that was syndicated across Canada by the Telegram News Service.

"You had to turn it upside down to read the English. It was suppose to promote bilingualism."

"I am a federalist," he says when I ask. "I think we should get to know each other a little more. We're just like strangers in this country. When Quebeckers go on vacation we stay in Quebec or we go to Florida. And when we go to Florida we hang out together. There are French papers and French radio down there.

"Recently a group of Quebeckers went to the Calgary Stampede. They were welcomed. They had a good time. I saw it on TV. We should do more of that. What do you think? Do you agree?"

He is standing now, waving his hands in the air. He is a short man, balding. He has a white beard. He looks like an elf.

"For heavens sake, it could be so simple."

"Do you talk like this in your cartoons?" I ask. "What does Onésime say about politics."

"Oh. Onésime doesn't say things like this," he says. "I have to be careful not to offend anyone. If Onésime said things like that he would offend half our readers."

Our conversation drifts to other things. I ask about Curé Bernèche. Could he do miracles?

"I remember a man once who was planting trees on a Sunday," he says. "You weren't supposed to work like that on a Sunday. Curé Bernèche saw him and shook his head and said, 'Those won't grow my boy.' And it was true. Whatever he said, was a fact. Oh, there are lots of stories. It's funny, most of them concern fire."

"Did you learn your English in New York?" I ask.

"No," he says. "I went to the High School of Montreal for grade ten. I was the only French kid there. It was my idea. I thought it would help me in my career if I could speak English."

"Was it hard?" I ask. "You must have had some tough times."

"No, no. I made friends fast. I helped everyone with their French homework. I helped them with their art."

He tells me he didn't find it hard to fit into Matha either. He used to work local people's names into his comic strip. When it was maple syrup time Onésime would visit a local *érablière.*

When it is time for me to leave we say goodbye at the door, and I walk, alone, along the path to my car. As I am pulling out of the driveway Albert Chartier appears out of the trees. He leans down to the window.

"Send me a picture of your children," he says. "I would like to see them. No. Send me a picture of your whole family. All of you. Together."

I find it a strangely touching request.

"Why?" I ask.

"I don't know," he says. "You either like someone or you don't. I like you. I would like to see your family."

———— • ————

I pay another call on Curé Latendresse. I have been reading William Humber's *Cheering for the Home Team: The Story of Baseball in Canada.* In the appendix — a list of the 143 Canadians who had (as of 1983) played in "the Big Time" — I find the name Augustin J. Dugas, outfielder, born 1907, St-Jean-de-Matha, Quebec.

No one in town seems to have heard of Gus Dugas. He is not buried in the graveyard, but I wonder if the *curé* might have a record of his birth.

"Oh, yes," he says. "I heard of that before. An American came here once asking for information. He was travelling all over Quebec to wherever ball players had come from. I couldn't tell him anything. I think the Dugas left early on to the United States."

The great migration of French-Canadians into the mill towns of the Northeastern United States began after the Civil War and continued in waves until the depression of 1929. During *la grande hémorragie,* more than 900,000 men and women left rural Quebec in search of work in the textile mills and shoe factories in the New England states.

Many of the grey stone mills are still standing today, some of them still working, and wherever you see them — in towns like Lawrence, and New Bedford, Massachusetts; Manchester and Nashua, New Hampshire; Biddeford and Lewiston, Maine — you can flip through the phone books and see the footprints the Quebeckers have left. Though many families have anglicized their names (Blanche becomes White, Boisvert becomes Greenwood) and just as many others have forgotten how to pronounce theirs, there are still those who honour their roots.

In June 1992, the *Globe and Mail* reported that four hundred people gathered in a Manchester parish hall to celebrate St Jean Baptiste day with *tourtière, fèves au lard* and *soupe aux pois.* The *Globe* speculated that fully a third of those living in New Hampshire today have French blood running in their veins.

It was once possible to live totally in French in pockets of New England. There were bilingual parochial schools staffed by nuns that were still open in the 1960s. Today, though there are still churches where you can hear a mass in French, and Manchester has a French bookstore (La Librairie Populaire), living in French is no longer possible. Television inoculated the homes with English and today in many Franco-American families only the grandparents can speak French.

Louis Cyr himself went with his family to Lowell, Massachusetts, and worked in the mills. Like others, the Cyrs scraped together every last cent they owned for the train trip — a journey they believed would bring them prosperity and a better life. When Cyr retired in Matha he built himself a large house on Ste-Louise in the New England style, complete with gables and turrets and a widow's walk.

Though still standing today, his house has been covered with aluminum siding and converted into apartments.

It seems everyone in Matha has a relative of some sort living in Lowell today. Donat Gadoury's daughter emigrated in 1957. Cécile Tellier (pronounced Tell-yer in Lowell) worked in a "stitching place" for thirty-three years. She sewed aprons and dusters and cheap cotton dresses.

After thirty-four years she says she still speaks French better than English — "My tongue is all mixed up" — but she does fine in her new language.

Cécile returns to Matha every year for Donat's New Year's dinner. Since her husband died she is thinking of moving back home, but her two daughters are settled in the States and it would be hard to leave them.

She tries to talk to her grandchildren in French. The ten-year-old will repeat what she says, but the seven-year-old thinks she sounds funny when she speaks and her third grandchild ignores her. She has taught her two littlest ones a French song.

The young ones enjoy their annual trip to Matha (Cécile calls it "St Gene" when she is talking with her sons-in-law) and when they play with their Quebec cousins they seem to get along.

"I'm not sure how they communicate," says Cécile, "but they understand each other. One bunch speaks English and one speaks French, but they play cards and other games together."

Gus Dugas (the ball player) probably moved to Lowell when he was young — perhaps worked a spell in the mills himself. According to Humber, Dugas played 125 games in the Big Leagues. He had 3 home runs, 45 hits and a batting average of .206.

———————————— • ————————————

One evening I go for a walk and end up on Rue Amélie. It is a dead-end street on the edge of town and appears to be where the rich people live. The architecture of the sixteen homes I count has nothing to do with the clapboard walls and steep tin roofs that characterize the rest of town. The houses here are large and modern and could have been plucked out of any suburban development and set down on these spacious lots. The garages alone are larger than many of the homes that crowd the Rue Ste-Louise. I find it almost vulgar, and wonder why anyone would choose to live here. The only thing these people seem to have in common with the rest of the village is the woodpiles in their backyards.

Though it is an easy walk from my hotel, Rue Amélie is considered far enough away from the centre of things to warrant rural mail delivery. There is a mailbox at the end of every paved driveway. Everyone else in town has to pick up their mail.

The next time I see Louise Bélanger I remark that if the names painted on the mailboxes of Rue Amélie are any measure, a surprising number of married women in Matha have retained their maiden names.

"That changed about fifteen years ago," says Louise. "When I had my third child [he is twelve now] we had the choice of giving him the name of the father, or the mother, or both. At work I use my maiden name."

———————— • ————————

Poultry is a big business in the Matha area. Inevitably I end up on a turkey farm. It is just down the road from Jean-Marie Latraverse's house.

"Too bad you couldn't come back in a few weeks," says Bruce Scott, the farm manager who is showing me around. "We'll be breeding the hens." It takes me a few moments to grasp that he means *artificial* breeding. Remember, we are talking turkeys.

He takes me to a separate barn where they keep the toms — sixty-five-pound turkeys larger than an eight-year-old boy.

Someone is, apparently, actually paid to masturbate these genetic monsters, collect the semen and drive it down the road to the hen-house.

Scott shows me the breeding manual from Hybrid Turkeys Limited. "Steps to follow in milking a tom ... page D-4." I wouldn't make this up.

———— • ————

When I arrive at Marc Pelletier's house he tells me the turtles have been mating for over three hours.

Sometimes you get stuck in a theme. Animal sex is not something I am actively searching out, but when I keep running into it like this I decide I might as well go with the flow.

"Once the male penetrates the female," says Pelletier shaking his head, "his penis enlarges and he can't take it out. He's trapped. He'll have to wait a few more hours before he can withdraw."

Pelletier is kneeling down in front of his living-room aquarium. He is a school principal in nearby St-Charles-de-Mandeville. Turtles are his hobby.

"The penis is actually in his tail. It's a funny-looking little thing. It's the same colour as beef liver."

I met Pelletier at the community centre one night. He was helping at a bingo — a fund-raiser for École Bernèche.

"You should come over to the house," he said. "But not tomorrow night. Tomorrow we're having a spaghetti dinner at my school. It's another fund-raiser."

"That," says Pelletier, moving to the next aquarium, "is a wood turtle." He is pointing at a turtle with a gnarled shell.

"It's supposed to be the most intelligent turtle in the world. They say a wood turtle can find its way through a maze. When they mate, the male tries to bite the female's head. It makes it easier for him to enter her."

I didn't ask.

"The problem is they only mate in the water. And a mating can last as long as twenty-four hours. The male gets over the female and keeps her under him. If the water's too deep, she won't be able to breathe, and if she's not strong enough to drag him to shallow water she can drown."

Pelletier has thirty-five different turtles in various tanks around his house. Most of them are in the basement. Some of them hibernating in a fridge.

"That's a diamond-back egg." He is pointing to a small egg lying in a plastic yoghurt tub. "It was a good egg, but I don't think it's going to hatch. It's been there a few months now."

In the wild, turtle eggs can take two to three months to hatch. Sometimes painted turtles will lay eggs in the summer that will not hatch until the following spring.

Although they have existed largely unchanged for at least 150 million years, there were no turtles (or any reptiles, for that matter) left in Canada during the last ice age. Biologists speculate that most turtles spent the ice age in the south-east corner of the continent and have since migrated into Canada along the Mississippi and Ohio rivers. Today there are turtles in every province except Newfoundland and Prince Edward Island. The notion of such a methodical and thorough migration is sobering.

"Can I see the ones in the fridge?" I ask.

We go downstairs. Marc opens the fridge door and pulls out a comatose wood turtle. She is lying in a plastic tub.

"I've had her in there since November 10th," he says. "It's the safest way for them to hibernate in captivity. If I left them in the yard there would be a fifty percent chance they wouldn't make it through the winter. In a natural state they would bury themselves in clay or mud."

I ask him about the turtles you buy in pet stores. They are usually red-eared sliders, he tells me — a common turtle of the southern Mississippi River system. They live long lives and can grow to be about a foot in length. It is not, however, a turtle native to Canada, and you aren't allowed to import turtles anymore.

"What dealers do is import turtle eggs," Marc says. "That's not covered by the law. I think they bring in about 200,000 eggs a year. These days if you buy a turtle at a pet store it's probably going to be a female. The temperature an egg incubates at can determine a turtle's sex. In captivity breeders just want eggs to hatch as quickly as possible so they keep them as warm as they can.

"I am going to an international symposium of turtles of the world in New York in August."

Pelletier and I go back upstairs. We settle on his couch and talk about history and politics and beaches we both like to go to in Maine. We get out his atlas and I mark my favourite spots on it. Inevitably the talk drifts round to language and the future of his province.

"I don't believe our language is in danger. I don't believe that our language will die if we are prepared to work for it. It won't be the fault of the English if we lose our French. It's our language. It's our responsibility. We have to take care of it. Yes, students have problems writing these days. But that isn't a political problem. It's a sociological one. But how would I vote if I had to choose the future of Quebec? I think I would vote for sovereignty. But I'd hesitate before I cast my ballot. And I'd hesitate for a lot of reasons. I'd wonder if it would really change anything. I think it would be very hard at first. If everyone understands that and agrees to it, well, OK. Then we can do it. But people today are ready to go on strike over the difference between one and three percent. What's going to happen if we separate and the government says, 'We're building a new country here and we can't give you this and that?' These are the questions I'd ask myself if I was going to vote about the future of Quebec.

"The arguments," he continues, "are good on both sides of the fence. There are good reasons to say yes and good reasons to say no. Quite honestly I think most of us will be mixed up.

"Fundamentally I guess I believe in an independent Quebec — but with less passion than I did in 1976. Probably because I'm older.

"Here in Matha it is much less passionate than in Montreal. In Montreal there is more confrontation between the two languages. If you go downtown you might have to ask for something in English. Here you aren't confronted by that reality."

———————— • ————————

It is 8 A.M. Yannick Roy, twelve years old, grade seven, is going to be early for school. He was up earlier than usual this morning. His little brother was crying.

Yannick is wearing blue pants, a blue jean jacket and a red corduroy 49er's hat. When he gets to school he will meet Jean-Philippe Lepage who is wearing a black T-shirt that says "The Simpsons" across the front. He'll also meet Maxime Soulière and Jeanvier Beaudoin. Jeanvier bought two fresh packs of hockey cards this morning, one at the *dépanneur* and one at Vidéo Matha. He will open the cards in the school yard and the boys will compare their collections and talk about trades.

At 8:15 the bus that brings the kids who are in wheelchairs pulls right into the school yard and up to the side door.

The driver lifts Stéphane out of the bus and passes him to Laurent Smith. Laurent helps with the special children at École Bernèche. Stéphane is five years old. He cannot walk unaided. Laurent puts him down, takes his hands and begins to walk backwards into the school — a kind of human walker. Stéphane seems to be falling asleep.

"Away. Let's go. You can do it, Stéphane." Laurent Smith keeps a constant quiet chatter going while the two of them stumble along the corridor.

Stéphane is in the classroom now. He is sitting on the floor with his back propped up against a wall. Eleven-year-old Danny, grade five, is sitting cross-legged in front of him. Danny is a volunteer from the regular stream. Like the other student volunteers, he will stay here until the first bell rings. He is trying to put Stéphane's leg into a plastic brace. His mouth is pursed. He is concentrating with all his might. Stéphane still seems to be only half awake. Like Laurent Smith, Danny never stops talking to Stéphane.

"Hey, Stéphane, wake up. *Lève-toi.* Ah, good. *Bien.* Hey! Don't do that, Stéphane."

Stéphane has just reached down and undone a strap.

Danny has started to talk to himself now. It isn't easy to get Stéphane's sneaker on over the brace.

There are four special children in this class. Sophie (who is seven years old), Caroline (who has a wonderful smile and is nine), Steve (who is thirteen) and Stéphane (who is five). Three of them have cerebral palsy, the fourth has a degenerative neurological condition known as Allen Vorden Spatz Syndrome. Each child has a student volunteer hovering over them as they enter the class. Helping. Holding. Hugging. The volunteers are all tender and careful. I find the moment profoundly moving.

"Do you like to do this?" I ask Danny.

A smile lights up his face as he nods. "I like to play with him," he says, referring to Stéphane. "It makes me happy to help."

As well as coming in the morning, Danny also helps on Thursday afternoons during class time.

The kids are sitting in a circle now. All of them are in wheelchairs. Steve is struggling to tell us about his weekend. There is a Ninja Turtle backpack hooked onto the back of his chair.

I slip out of the room and look for Laurent Smith. I find him in the cafeteria handing out milk cartons to monitors dispatched from each class. When he has finished, he takes me to a small office and we sit down. He is going to tell me about his life.

"My great-grandfather only spoke English," he begins. "He came from England and lived in the Eastern Townships. His name was Ernest Smith. He married a French woman and started to speak French. He had four children. My grandfather, Victor, was one of them. Victor learned English from his father but he spoke French, too, of course. His son, my father, was Gerard. He was the one that came to Matha. He was a watchmaker. He used to travel all over, living in hotels, repairing clocks and watches. He could speak both languages but he did not transmit English to his children. We only spoke French at home. All I can speak is French.

"I have two brothers, Marcel and René. René is in the Canadian Armed Forces. He is stationed in Israel. He married a woman from New Brunswick. The last time he came back to Matha was for the funeral of our father, Gerard. He stayed at our house. When he comes here it's like meeting a stranger. He tries to speak French but he has lots of problems. He is in the process of losing it. At his home they only speak English. He looks for words.

"His wife has made a big effort to learn French. She used to come to Matha to visit my mother, and she thought that it was right to speak to her in French, so in the army she made an effort to find French friends and speak to them in French.

"It was important to René that his kids speak French. And they can speak it, but they live in English, and when they come here they are too shy to speak too much.

"My brother is himself English now. He has forgotten his roots. Or maybe not. Maybe he has found his real roots — the English inside him from his great-grandfather. I never thought about that before. It's funny how the wheel turns and turns. Do you want a coffee?"

Laurent gets up and goes to the staff cafeteria and fixes himself a coffee. He comes back, settles down and continues his story.

"I worked in Ontario for five summers. I used to go for three months every year and pick tobacco near Tillsonburg. After the tobacco harvest was over we used to go to Florida and pick oranges. When I was working in Ontario I had a rage against the English. I hated them. When I came back to Quebec I realized that it wasn't the English that I hated. It was my ancestors. I didn't like having English ancestors. For a long time I never talked about this. I was ashamed of it. I wanted to be a real Québécois."

For fifteen years Laurent Smith travelled with a motorcycle gang.

"J'étais un motard," he says.

If he needed money he sold drugs or stole. He spent a month in a Mexican jail. The jail was like a huge hole in the ground. The guards stayed around the rim. The prisoners milled freely below. There were no doors on their cells. It was the law of the jungle. The rule of strength. Laurent was sexually assaulted. He only got out because his friends showed up with five hundred dollars and bought his freedom.

"It wasn't easy," is about all he'll say.

Back in Quebec he was consuming two twenty-six-ounce bottles of tequilla a day, plus a hit of heroin. After he tried to kill himself three times, a friend took him to an Alcoholics Anonymous meeting in St-Félix. It was February 2, 1978.

"I remember," he says. "After the meeting we went back to my friend's house and he said, If you want to get clean you have to be tied up. I agreed. They tied me to a bed with leather belts. They attached both legs and both arms. It was one of the worst times of my life. After three days I begged them to let me up. I screamed, I cried, I . . . I was so angry. I was crazy. They wouldn't untie me. And I couldn't get free. Oh, I tried. A doctor came every second day to check on me. At the beginning of the fourth week I began to understand that maybe this was good for me. They set me free after a month.

"A month after they let me go I started to work a little at my friend's restaurant. It was very difficult. I was very tired. I didn't have any strength. I didn't have any resistance. If I worked for an hour I had to sleep for three. I would go for an hour or an hour and a half at lunch. Then I would go home and sleep. Then I'd return for maybe an hour at dinner. I was always tired. I wasn't drinking or taking drugs or anything, but I was still feeling depressive and crazy. My friend said I should get help. I went to the hospital for alcoholics and took a twenty-eight-day cure. After that I was ready. I started working with alcoholics."

A teacher pokes her head in the door and says something to Laurent.

"Just a minute," he says to me as he stands up.

He leaves me alone in the office and comes back a moment later carrying Stéphane. He sets him down on a changing table and begins to unbutton the boy's pants. Stéphane has soiled himself. Laurent is going to change his diaper. He slides the boy's pants deftly down to his knees. He has done this a thousand times before. While he cleans the boy he continues to talk.

"One day I saw an ad in the paper. The school board needed a monitor on the bus to help with handicapped kids. It was only four hours a week but I applied. When I went to the interview I warned the woman that she might have problems. I told her people would want to know why she had hired a drug addict. She said she was ready to take the chance."

He has finished cleaning Stéphane. He bends down and whispers something in the boy's ear. He blows on his face. He pats him on the bum.

"Hey, Stéphane," he says. "You're ready to go back?"

He picks the boy up carefully in his arms. He has been working for the school for thirteen years now. He is full time — here in the building thirty-five hours a week. Changing diapers. Helping in the washroom. Opening doors. Loading and unloading the bus. Helping teachers

in the classroom. He has a bushy red beard. He is wearing
bright turquoise running shoes, rainbow coloured sweat
pants and a pink, blue and purple Ocean Pacific T-shirt.
He looks like he is on the way to the beach. As he carries
Stéphane out the door, I can feel tears in my eyes.

———— • ————

It is always hard to leave. When it is time to go I always
feel as if there is someone I should visit, someone I
should say goodbye to. I have eaten breakfast and lunch
nearly every day at Le Cuistot, the little cafe on Rue Principale. After I settle accounts at the hotel (seventy-five
dollars a week), I drop in for one more bowl of soup.
The same young woman has served me nearly every day,
yet we have barely spoken during my entire visit. Her
name is Marie-Hélène Préville. She is nineteen years old.
Her father, Normand, who is forty-one, owns the restaurant. Strangely, today, she lingers by my table and chats.
Does she sense I am leaving?

She tells me she isn't going to school anymore. She says
working in the restaurant is her full-time job. She has a
boyfriend. His name is Mario. He owns a trucking company. He is teaching her how to drive a semi-trailer. She
wants to drive a school bus one day.

She takes my order and disappears into the kitchen.

She brings me my soup without a word.

I keep thinking of Laurent Smith. Of Donat Gadoury. Of
Jean-Marie Latraverse's maple bush. Is there any symbol
more enduringly Québécois than a grey maple bush
against a grey sky. Pancakes and fiddle music. Woodsmoke
and wet wool.

When they want to highlight the difference between
Quebec and Canada, graphic artists have appropriated the
maple leaf and assigned it to the Canadian camp. They use
the *fleur-de-lis* for Quebec. One night, sitting at the bar in
my hotel, I idly try to sketch a *fleur-de-lis* on a napkin. It
comes out looking like a maple leaf. Like Laurent Smith,

and his brother René, my drawing drifts beyond my control from one culture to the other.

On the way out of town I drive by the church, then down the hill, down Rue Principale, past the *croix de chemin* where Rue Principale meets Chemin Louis Cyr, then onto the highway and out of town. Out of the mountains and onto the plains of the St Lawrence River. Soon to Montreal and then by train to Toronto.

Oh, Quebec.

Three times larger than France

Seven times larger than Great Britain.

Child of the maybe ten thousand men and women who came here from France before 1760.

"My Canada," reads the bumper sticker popular in the rest of the country, "includes Quebec."

Sackville

NEW BRUNSWICK

I've scraped quite a few cats off the road over the years. It's not part of my job. But I do it anyway. The first time they asked me I should have said no. But I didn't. And once you've done it once it's hard to stop. Oh, well. It's not that big a job to pick a dead cat up.

ROBERT STEPHENS
DOG CATCHER

At the geographic centre of Sackville, New Brunswick — which itself likes to lay claim to lying at the geographic centre of Canada's Maritime provinces — is the intersection of Bridge and Main streets, and Sackville's only traffic signal. It is one of those traffic signals that, once in every sequence, shows red in all four directions. Every time that happens, all the cars have to stop, and while they wait, pedestrians cross the street on the diagonal as well as corner to corner. For a moment it looks like a game of Parcheesi come to life. It is a pleasing ritual to watch — made more pleasing when you consider that here at the centre of things, once every 40 seconds, things almost stop.

Time, in fact, has stopped here at Bridge and Main — for the time being, anyway. The town clock, erected by the Lions Club in 1967 on the occasion of Canada's one hundredth birthday, was recently taken down.

"It didn't rotate and was showing two different times on each side," says Sackville Redevelopment Inc. co-ordinator Sheila Cole in *The Sackville Tribune-Post*. "It was an embarrassment to have it there so it was taken down."

A new 14-foot, four-sided, $20,000 tower clock will be going up in a few months. The tower, says the paper, will contain "Sackville's familiar duck motif, as well as a directory panel where special events and public service announcements can be advertised." The paper also says the driving factor behind the new tower is the public's displeasure with not having a clock in the downtown core.

Sackville (population 5,470) may be big enough to have a downtown core, but it's still small enough that if you are five dollars short at the cash register at Johnstone's Save-Easy, they'd rather give you credit than reshelve your groceries, though they are likely to record your name and debt. There are three schools in town: one elementary, one middle and one high school. There is a movie theatre with one screen that features two different films each night. The drugstore is on the corner by the traffic lights and is actually called the Corner Drug Store. There is a bookstore and four taxi cabs. The taxi cabs are all station wagons, the better to shuttle students from Mount Allison University up on the hill to Steve's Tavern down by the train station. The cabs don't have meters. The fare usually has more to do with the number of passengers than the number of kilometres covered. A typical three-minute trip from the university to Steve's might run to thirteen dollars — a dollar for each undergraduate stuffed into the back.

This is a town that understands tradition. There was a time when the political party you supported determined where you were buried. There are still two funeral directors on Bridge Street and still those who would tell you that Conservatives go to Campbell's and Liberals go to David Jones. A town where Mrs Helen C. Beale wouldn't think of going downtown to mail a letter without putting on a dress, white gloves and a hat.

"Oh, yes," says Fran Smith, offering me a plate of Rice Krispie squares. "You'll feel you've died and gone to heaven when you meet Helen Beale. She is one of the finest teachers anyone ever had. She taught me, and I'm seventy-eight."

Even downtown, Sackville is a town of large lots and kitchen gardens. A community where all the homes seem to be white clapboard and all the businesses red brick. Along Bridge Street many of the buildings, houses and businesses feature late-Victorian architectural flourishes. It is a style that gives the street a regal feel and the town a veneer of wealth and affluence more typical of New England than Maritime Canada. On Sunday at eleven you can hear church bells ringing all over. Drive off the main street and down any number of side roads, however, and some of the trailers that are strung together make you wonder whether downtown isn't a false-fronted movie set, an artfully preserved illusion created for, or perhaps by, moneyed parents and the affluent alumni of Atlantic Canada's wealthiest university. The university has brought outside elements that most small towns have to do without, but beyond the genteel and treed main street, Sackville is really a blue-collar town. A town built by foundry men and farmers, shiftworkers and shipbuilders — most of whom are out of work today.

Sackville was once the centre of one of the most successful farming districts in Atlantic Canada. Perhaps nowhere in the country does farm land have a more uniquely Canadian pedigree. The first settlers were French Acadians who came to what they called "Près des Bourques" in the late 1600s. The early French dyked thousands of acres of marshland, reclaiming bogs of "floating moss, swamps, lakes and oozing streams." In 1754 the settlement had a population of eighty-nine Acadians. In November, 1775, however, the community was razed by a British force during the shameful expulsion of the Acadians from eastern Canada. It was the next wave of settlement — the British who came in the 1760s and '70s — who began to clear the inland forests in earnest. Why the two groups couldn't get along doing that is hard to fathom.

Marsh hay once made Sackville rich. Sweet hay from the marshes was swept up by marsh carts with strangely offset wheels and then shipped as far away as Newfoundland and even Great Britain — to feed pit ponies and high-stepping fillies — for those were the days when horsepower meant what it said. As everywhere in the country, the farm economy around Sackville has not fared well in the twentieth century. The internal combustion engine dropped the coup de grâce on the business of exporting hay, and today the squat marsh hay barns dot the lowlands around town like pieces from a forgotten Monopoly game.

The two foundries forged wood, gas, oil and electric stoves as well as furnaces and heaters. The Fawcett stove which was still being manufactured in 1990 pre-dated Confederation by fifteen years. But both foundries are closed today. One has been torn down. All that's left of the other is a compound of imposing brick buildings and two shippers who, for over a year, have been packing up inventory and selling it across the country furnace by furnace. When the Enterprise Fawcett foundry closed in 1990, some men who were able to find work went from $1,000 to $250 a week overnight. There are always rumours that a new owner is thinking of reopening the plant — no one knows when, but it might be soon. Soon, for those to whom it matters the most, could mean anything from next week to next century. Most important, however, soon means maybe, and maybe means maybe it isn't over. When the foundries closed, the town lost more than seven hundred jobs. It lost a lifestyle as well.

Like the sons of coal miners, Sackville boys would report for duty at their fathers' foundry the day they were old enough to work. It was more than a first job. It meant joining a community. Going to the Christmas party with everyone. Staying after hours to enamel a set of trays to take home. The molders union established in Sackville on March 1, 1889 was one of the first unions in Canada. Yet after ten, twenty, sometimes even thirty and forty years of service, no one from either foundry has a pension worth speaking of. Most have none at all.

People miss the foundries terribly. Not the work. Well, yes. The work. But mostly that sense of belonging. And there sits Mount Allison on the hill, getting fatter and fatter. When the foundries closed, the university solidified its dominion over the town. Kids from all over snapping up the best places to live, wearing their baggy Levis and the big leather belts they have made at the Harness Shop. The boys favour penny loafers or cowboy boots and Ralph Lauren shirts — it seems every second boy owns the pale blue and white striped button-down. The girls all have big gold hoop earrings and oversized cable-knit sweaters that they get from Eddie Bauer or L.L. Bean. There used to be fights between townies and gowns. But, like the foundries, the fighting is over for now.

Some people in town grew up with the idea that the university wasn't a place for them to be. And they have never been there. Never. Other people thought differently. "Our kids aren't going to work in no foundry. They're going up on the hill." Four years at university is as good as a one-way ticket west. Like all small towns, Sackville's greatest export is her people.

If everyone remembers the foundries — and everyone does — hardly anyone can recall the shipbuilding days. Crossing the silted-up Tantramar River on the edge of town, it is incredible even to think of Sackville as a place where ships were built.

The river, as Charles Moffat explained in a 1946 book about the town ("the official book on the most central town in the Maritime Provinces"), "pursued a circular course and formed a loop around a section of marshland now known as the Ram Pasture. The Ram Pasture neck wore away by erosion and an island was formed thus creating a direct course for the tides from Cumberland Basin to pass up the river. The shipping facilities were located in the portion of the river thus cut off and soon were marooned by the deposits from tidal waters."

So Sackville, sitting on the narrow arm that joins Nova Scotia to New Brunswick, was left high and dry. The last sailing vessels came up the river in 1922. There is a street called Landing, but it doesn't reach the water anymore. The wharves, like the water, have disappeared, though traces of the docks linger opposite the CNR station like old men lingering around a seedy bar.

What hasn't disappeared from Sackville is the small-town ideal of local businesses that serve a local community. Sackville somehow missed the "malling" of North America. The town sailed through the sixties and seventies with its downtown neighbourhood intact. Sackville is a place where people stop at the post office for their mail, and on street corners for their conversation. The bowling alley is just down from the bank. There are no muffler shops, no fast-food franchises, and not a lot of neon. There is no mall on the edge of town.

Real estate developers have a nose for places like Sackville, so, in spring, 1990, when an out-of-town consortium petitioned town council to change the zoning of a parcel of property on the edge of town, the reactions were predictable. The developers wanted to build. They weren't quite clear at first *what* they wanted to build, but the zoning changes they requested would have let them build just about anything. At first they said they were only planning a hotel, but when pressed admitted they were thinking of a "destination" hotel. In the development game that is code for a hotel with stores or, more likely, a mall with a few rooms for rent. The mayor and many others in town were mesmerized by the three million dollars the developers were promising to spend. More than a few were excited by visions of a shopping complex as big as you might find in Moncton. Some people weren't quite so sure.

The issue split town council down the middle and culminated in what is now referred to as the "long meeting" in October, 1990. Council, which was not accustomed to such attention, had to convene at the Legion. The room was packed by 7:30 P.M. From the opening gavel the mayor, who led the pro-development side, was challenged by the deputy mayor, who led the opposition. The meeting swung back and forth all evening. The mayor was forced to read into the record all the letters he had received opposing the project. After each letter citizens stood up and voiced their opinions. Those who were there say the mayor, who is also the owner of Campbell's Funeral Home and normally a sanguine man, had to struggle to maintain his composure. When the final vote came, it was well after midnight. Council had tied. Four votes for development, four votes against. Mayor Campbell had to cast the final ballot and predictably came down on the side of the mall. Everyone filed out quietly.

The development issue unleashed unfamiliar passions onto the front page of *The Sackville Tribune-Post,* a paper used to gentler concerns like these:

From the "Town Notices" of February 13:

* It has come to our attention that Michelle Kilfoil from Institute for Map Publishing has recently been approaching business owners concerning advertising for a new Town of Sackville map.

We would like to inform the business owners that this map has not been accepted as the official Town map for Sackville and that any work on the production of this map has been done solely by Institute for Map Publishing.

From the paper of March 27:

* *Was Not the Human 'Jake'*
Maurice (Jake) Fisher is not the "Jake" referred to in a letter to the editor in last week's *Tribune-Post.*

The "Jake" to which the letter was dedicated was the family pet dog found shot dead.

From the back page of the same edition:

* *Hiccup Help*
Say your standard remedies for hiccups don't seem to be having an effect? Stand in front of a mirror and while taking short shallow breaths, slip a cool spoon handle into your mouth and touch the uvula (that small lobe hanging at the back of your throat) until the hiccups stop.

Finally, this notice from February 13:

* The Bank of Nova Scotia, Sackville wishes to advise the public that Mildred Wry will be retiring after 41 years of service with the bank on February 14.

The branch will be holding an appreciation day for Mildred on February 14th.

Coffee and donuts will be served.

By the time I arrive in town, plans for the mall have been laid to rest. The developers may have won their battle at council, but their plans have sunk into the morass of the 1990s recession. Things in town have more or less returned to normal. Even Mildred is back at the bank. Her retirement lasted barely two weeks before she was called in to help out for a spell.

We meet at a lunch counter across from the bank one noon hour. She is wearing slacks, and her hair is permed in tight brown curls. She tells me about the going-away celebration I missed.

"It was like a big birthday party. They had balloons around my desk and a sign up on the wall. Except I didn't even see it until the day was half over. I wore a new blue two-piece dress. It was the first time I wore it. When I came to work one of the girls, one of the loan officers, had brought in her own curling iron, and she took me downstairs to the ladies' room and did my hair before we opened. All day long people would come in to make a deposit and come over and wish me the best. They brought me presents, too. I got flowers, two potted plants, some cards, two boxes of chocolates, a pair of earrings, some little paper notes, a nice — it could be a candy dish, it's on a pedestal — maybe it's a cake dish, for squares and things. One customer gave me fifty dollars in an envelope. And there was this little coloured vase. I'm not sure what to use it for. It's made of pink glass and it's in the shape of a goose. I don't think you could use it as a cream pitcher, but it is something to that effect."

Mildred is nervous talking to me. She is not sure she should be in a book.

"You're not going to use my name, are you?" she asks.

She won't order a coffee or a tea. She keeps looking at her watch. But we both know she is not due back at the bank for another forty-five minutes.

She is only back at work temporarily — filling in because the bank is short-staffed. She says she misses her job. Even at home she hasn't left work completely.

"Customers still call me at home. Older people, mostly, who don't remember things as well as they used to. They call and say, 'I wouldn't say this to any of the others but I am worried about my savings certificate. I can't remember when it's due.' One phoned me at home last night. She was confused about something someone had told her. I pacified her and told her not to worry. I told her the bank would phone and clear things up. I've had a number of calls like that.

"Your customers get to be like your family, and it's your job to look after them. For me being at work is just like being at home. People may come and go, but you remember them — although I remember people's account numbers better than their names. I might forget their name but I would never forget their number."

———————— •·•———————

I am not in Sackville long before I learn that life in town swings around the post office. Everyone goes for mail once a day. Most days are planned around these visits, which are as much about conversation as they are about correspondence. In Sackville you do things either before or after Post Office. Some go two or three times a day, just in case.

I can't go for mail, but I do evolve my own routine. I eat breakfast in the Marshlands Inn where I am staying. I have a room on the top floor. ("It used to be the turnip room," I am later told. "That's where we used to store the turnips.") It is a charming room under the eaves, and though it has neither bath nor television, it does have a toilet sequestered behind a linen curtain that hangs on an elegant silver rod. Most important, it is only nine stairs up from Room Thirty-five. That is where Her Majesty Queen

Elizabeth rested during her visit to Sackville in 1984. Downstairs in the lounge, where a pot of hot chocolate is waiting for me every night by the fireplace, I can look at the guest book, kept carefully in a glass case, which Elizabeth herself signed. She wrote simply, "Elizabeth, September 26, 1984," and when someone corrected her, she changed the six to a seven. It is an awkward and messy correction and when I first saw it I wondered why she didn't tear out the page and start over. After a while I come to like it. It is the only mistake I have ever seen the Queen make.

I eat lunch every day at Mel's Tea Room on Bridge Street. Most days I order the chicken sandwich. The chicken is actually carved from a real bird. The white sliced bread is always fresh.

Mel's is the kind of place where James Dean would feel at home. Or where Frankie and Annette would share a float. There is a marble soda fountain with extra-high stools that look like golf tees, sixteen straight-backed booths to stretch out in, and a room in the back with a few benches and a pay phone that has, for fifty years, served as the town's bus station. Up front there are racks of magazines, books, cigarettes and assorted groceries.

The cover of the menu reads, "Mel's Soda Fountain and Sandwich Bar." Inside the menu at the bottom of the page there is a warning: "Broken or missing dishes will be charged to the customer."

In case that isn't clear, the warning is repeated: "Customers will be held responsible for any damage to furnishings, broken or missing dishes, etc."

Such is life when you do business in a university town.

"My mom came to Mount Allison," a girl tells me one day. The girl is herself a student. She is sitting in one of the booths, smoking and sipping a milkshake. "My mom used to come here and get malteds."

For some unfathomable reason, everything at Mel's seems
to come in threes. There are three coffee pots behind the
soda fountain (each with a Styrofoam cup stuck in the top
to keep the coffee hot), three milkshake machines ($1.35
a shake and yes, you get the extra that comes in the silver
canister). Every day Minerva, the wife of the owner, bakes
three pies and slips them, one on top of the other, into the
vertical pie rack on the counter. Today, in the grocery section, there are three jars of peanut butter, three contain-
ers of Cheez Whiz, three loaves of bread. On the counter
by the the cash register there are three blocks of fresh
maple cream wrapped in waxed paper that isn't stuck or
sealed in cellophane but is simply folded closed. Beside
them is an old-fashioned scale used for weighing the
chocolates that come from the Ganong factory in St
Stephen. The unpackaged chocolates are displayed on
trays behind the counter. A quarter pound costs $1.35,
and you can choose Peppermint Patties, Bridge Mixture,
Willow Crisp, Maple Buds, Turtles, Chunks or Macaroons.
In a glass display case under the counter there are three
lonely boxes of chocolates on a shelf that could hold many
more.

Everything about Mel's could hold more. Especially the
booths. There is always plenty of space here. Yet even
though it opens at seven in the morning and doesn't close
until midnight, and even though I come in often and at
many different times of the day and night, I never walk into
Mel's and find myself alone. It may never be crowded, but
it is never empty. There is always enough space, even at
noon, for someone to spread their books around a booth
and fiddle with an essay and a cup of tea. They could sit
there all day long and no one would bother them.

That's what Sally Scott is doing the day I meet her. Like
many of the regulars at Mel's, Sally is a student at Mount
Allison. She has short blonde hair and is wearing a pink
cotton kangaroo pullover. She is poring over the catalogue
from Joyce Wieland's retrospective at the Art Gallery of

Ontario. She is working on an essay. Wieland, she says, is "an incredible artist."

She seems happy for the interruption when I ask if I can sit down for a moment. She pushes the book away and lights a cigarette.

"I come from a small town. This place," she says, nodding around the cafe, "feels like home. It's comfy. I always sit in the same place and they always bring me an ashtray. I like it best in the morning when only half the lights are on. I can stay here for a long time and they don't mind. I can concentrate here. I've been coming here so long that I know what's going to happen so nothing distracts me. I always see someone I know. One of my roommates just had a cup of tea with me. It's a classic place. It's friendly. Has anyone told you about the butter trick?"

"No," I say.

"Is it your birthday?"

"No."

"Well, when it's your birthday you'll be sitting here and the waitress will walk by and put a pat of butter on your nose. She does it to everybody. Did you see the gum under the tables?"

I peer at the underside of our table. It could be a Joyce Wieland canvas.

"That's fifty years of gum," says Sally enthusiastically. "Every table is like that."

———— • ————

There is no gum under the tables at the Vienna Restaurant. Though only a step down the street from Mel's, and also a place where you can drop in for coffee, the Vienna aspires to greater things. The twelve tables are draped with white tablecloths and then covered with glass. Paintings and prints by local artists, with price tags, hang on the walls.

If Mel's is where students collect, the Vienna is where Mount Allison faculty come for coffee and lunch. On a

Tuesday afternoon, writer Ann Copeland and I sit at the window table in the Vienna and watch the snow melting on the sidewalk.

Ann Copeland was once a nun — a sister in the Ursuline order. Born and raised in the United States, she taught English and music at a series of Catholic schools until she returned to school — to Cornell — to study for her PhD in English.

Now married, Copeland moved to Sackville in 1971 when her husband was hired to teach English at Mount Allison. She came dragging recommendations that she turn her PhD thesis, on U.S. poet Wallace Stevens, into a book. Instead of writing the book, she worried about it. Then she decided what she really wanted to write was fiction. With a three-year-old at home she had no place to work, so when the chaplain from Mount Allison offered her a storage closet in the basement as an office, she moved a card table, a chair and a lamp into the room, hired a babysitter and went there two mornings a week from nine until noon.

She gave herself five years.

She was writing stories about nuns. Above her, in the vestry, someone practised the organ. Her first collection of short stories, *At Peace,* was published in 1978.

I ask her if Sackville is a good place to live and be a writer.

"Oh, yes. It is a good place to live. No one locks their doors here. It's a good place to raise kids." She pauses. "The other side is that it is seductively comfortable. And that is dangerous because you can shrink your sense of possibility."

"Why," I ask, "don't you write under your real name?"

Copeland pauses.

"So I can have a space where I am not a mommy, or a daughter, or a wife, or whatever. It is my way of pushing my borders out. It is important to know one's vulnerabilities. I know that otherwise I would be unable to consider some things that I should consider when I am writing fiction.

This is my way to clear a little space. You never get rid of your mother looking over your shoulder. This is my way of getting rid of my mother, of clearing up an inner space."

The next morning when I come downstairs for breakfast at the Marshlands Inn, there is a coat waiting for me.

"Ann Copeland brought it," the man behind the desk tells me. (Except he uses her real name.) "She was worried that your jacket wasn't warm enough. She said to use it while you're in town and just leave it here and she'll come and get it when you leave."

———————• •———————

On another morning at the Vienna, I meet George Stanley. Stanley is one of the six current members of a Sackville institution known as the Owls (to some as Bill's Tea Club). The Owls is an ever-changing confederacy of retired men who have at times numbered as many as fifteen. They muster at the Vienna every morning at eleven for coffee and conversation and have been doing so for over twenty years. There have been occasions, when a regular was sick, when the Owls have convened at a home or around a hospital bed.

But after twenty years the Vienna is as good, or better, than most homes. No one has to order. The waitresses know who drinks tea and who drinks coffee.

As each man drops into his place each morning, the first thing he does is dig out a handful of change and pass it over to Max Walker.

"This is Max," says someone by way of introduction. "He doesn't say much."

Everyone else more than makes up for Max's reserve. Max keeps busy sorting the mound of coins into piles. Max used to be an accountant. He'll pay the bill, but he won't leave a tip. Twice a year, at Christmas and Easter, the Owls leave a special envelope for their waitresses.

"If you write about us," warns Dan Shrieves, the ex-chief of police, "whatever you do, don't call us codgers. Someone once called us codgers."

"What is a codger, anyway?" wonders David MacAulay.

"I don't know," says Bill Sawdon, retired owner of *The Sackville Tribune-Post.*

"I asked Don once," mutters someone else menacingly. "He said he didn't know. But he didn't like it, either."

"Someone should look it up."

"I want to talk to you about two things," I say the next afternoon as I settle onto the couch in George Stanley's study. "Louis Riel and the Canadian flag."

"Ah," he says. "We have had a longstanding relationship, Riel and I."

"Then let's start with Riel," I say.

Stanley is wearing a white shirt, a bright red tie, a brown sports jacket and green corduroys. The sports jacket has leather patches on the elbows that need re-stitching. Sitting in his extensive library among autographed photos of the royal family, Stanley looks very much like an ex-governor general. He is, in fact, the ex-lieutenant governor of New Brunswick, an ex-professor, military historian and biographer of Riel.

Stanley grew up in Manitoba listening to stories about the North-West Rebellion. As a boy he met men who had fought at Batoche. At first he is reluctant to talk about Riel. That was all a long time ago, he says. But he smiles when I voice the question that has nagged me for years.

"Why is it," I want to know, "that in every second museum I visit in this country, there is a foot-long section of rope and a sign claiming it was cut from the noose used to hang Riel?"

"I wondered about that, too," says Stanley, running his hand through his unruly white hair. "And I have an explanation.

"My explanation is this. During the years that they were

agitating to hang Riel, the Orange Order dispatched their members to political meetings with bits of rope. There is enough supporting evidence to corroborate this — that they were waving these pieces of rope at meetings to wake up the public to the idea of a hanging. Well, afterwards there were all these bits of rope — every Orangeman had one — and some of them were handed down. Children were told that this was a bit of rope that helped to hang Riel. I have seen enough rope in these little museums to fashion a pretty long cord if they were all spliced together. You understand that there will be people out there who will swear their grandfather was at the hanging and he got the rope and gave it to their father, and so on. Well, it's just not so. It was not a part of the tradition — it never was — to cut up pieces of rope at a hanging and distribute it to the curious."

"What about the Canadian flag?" I ask.

"What about it?"

"You designed it, didn't you?"

"Yes. It was my idea."

"Tell me about that."

"It started with a request from a friend of mine. He happened to be a member of parliament and was on the flag committee. He knew my interests in history and heraldry and he asked if I would write a memo for the committee on historical flags in Canada. He suggested if I had any ideas of my own to include them in my memo. So I drew up some pictures and included them."

"Where did the design come from?"

"One of the images I have carried with me all my life is a photograph I saw when I was a boy. It was a picture from the 1928 Olympics in Amsterdam of Percy Williams breasting the tape and winning a gold medal for Canada. He was wearing a white jersey with a red maple leaf on his chest. It's an image that has always stuck with me.

"I was dean of arts at Royal Military College at the time I wrote the memo and I must admit that I modelled my flag on the RMC one. RMC has a mailed fist in the middle instead of a maple leaf. Did you know that the first symbol of the St Jean de Baptiste society was a red maple leaf? Not many people do. So it works, you see.

"Anyway. When I was a boy I remember spending countless hours drawing flags, and I was determined that this one would be easy to draw. The solution was to stylize the leaf. My friend called me near the end and said there was a problem. He told me there were thirteen points on my maple leaf and we couldn't have a flag with thirteen points. I said that was easy. Just take off two at the bottom — one off each side. That's why the leaf is flat at the bottom."

"There was a blue one," I say. "The one where the red leaf was between two blue borders. The borders were supposed to represent the sea. Was that yours, too?"

"No. No. No. We had to fight that one. I didn't want red, white and blue. It is almost the American national anthem."

George Stanley throws his head back and starts to sing.

"Three cheers for the red, white and blue."

He stops and fixes me with his eyes.

"We had to get rid of the red, white and blue."

———————— • ————————

Perhaps no one in Sackville has embraced George Stanley's flag with more grit than Bob Edgett.

Edgett is a large man with big hands. His face has a gentleness that reminds me of Gordie Howe. He has the same soft toughness, the same clarity of vision. Gordie Howe just wanted to play hockey. Bob Edgett just wants to be a boxer.

Edgett's is the classic boxing story. He was the kid who used to cry when he was picked on. The kid who was afraid to fight. The kid who went to the gym to build himself up and then went on to win four Maritime championships, a Golden Glove championship and finally a Central Ontario championship, by scoring two knock-outs in two consecu-

tive nights at Massey Hall in Toronto. He fought Yvon
Durelle twice and trained with him before all his big fights.
Then he lost a kidney, had to step out of the ring and vowed
he'd help anyone who wanted to step into one. He opened
the Bob Edgett Boys Club in 1953. He has been running it
ever since. Three nights a week he pulls up to the club with
a vanload of boys and runs them through a two-and-a-half-
hour workout. Then he drives them home. He has been
running his club single-handedly for thirty-eight years. On
weekends he takes his boys on trips. They have fought in the
Yukon, Australia, Toronto and many of the north-eastern
states. They travel in Bob's van. He bought the current one
three years ago. It has already gone through three motors.

The clubhouse is a white wooden building with red trim
that sits on a hill on the edge of Sackville.

"It used to be the entrance to the Mount Allison gym,"
says Edgett. "They were going to tear it down, so they sold
it to me for $100. I moved it out here for $140. The city
gave me the land free as long as I run the club. They gave
me a 99-year lease."

The clubhouse has the feel of a locker room and the
decor of a construction site. Like all boxing clubs, the walls
are papered with old posters, schedules, newspaper articles
and photos of boxing stars from other eras. Six bare light-
bulbs hang from the ceiling along with three punching
bags, two speed bags and a duffle bag stuffed with old
clothes and mattress filling. ("That's an upper-cut bag,"
says Edgett. "I made it myself.") It is impossible to walk
more than two steps in any direction without bumping into
something. At the far end of the room there is a sign hanging over the boxing ring — "Be a Good Sport." Edgett
points to the sign more than once that night.

"That's the main thing," he says. "That's what it is all
about."

Edgett is standing beside the ring with his arms crossed
thickly over his chest. He is wearing a beige prison-guard

shirt. (He has just retired after thirty-three years as a guard at Dorchester Penitentiary. He goes back at least once a week to visit prisoners and colleagues.) Tonight he looks more like a marine drill sergeant than a prison guard. He is watching his boys. There are fifteen here tonight. The youngest is six. The oldest, whose arms are as round as the little one's waist, is over thirty. He is wearing sweat pants, a singlet and a crossed-out tattoo on his right shoulder. The boys are all stuffed into the ring and shuffling around and around together. They are shadow boxing. Each time a boy throws an imaginary punch, a hiss of air seeps out of his mouth. It sounds like a boxing ring full of steam pipes.

"You ever boxed before?" a young lad asks me.

"No. Not really."

"It's pretty good. It makes your nose bigger, anyway."

The rhythmic thumping of the speed bag.

Explosions and grunts from the heavy bag.

"That guy served time at Dorchester." Edgett is pointing to the thirty-year-old with the obscured tattoo.

"What did your tattoo used to say?" I ask.

"I'd rather not say," he replies politely. "It was a mistake putting it there. That's why I blacked it out."

"But what did it say?"

"I'd rather not say."

Now two boys are sparring in the ring. The rest of the kids are working out on various equipment — the heavy bags, the upper-cut bags, the double-end bag. One small boy is standing on a wooden block so he can reach the bobbing speed bag. The two youngest kids are using the sit-up board as a slide. One of the boys in the ring has a nosebleed.

"Time," says Edgett. Everyone moves to a different station.

The noise of the bags is hypnotic. The slapping rhythm of the speed bag launches the room somewhere out of time.

"I'm pleased all to pieces," says Edgett. "Some of these

kids, I taught their fathers. Now they bring their kids here. Sometimes I see the fathers' moves in the kids. The kids sometimes do things that their dad used to do. Sometimes you had someone and his nose used to bleed easily. Then his kid'll come and his nose will bleed, too."

Like many veterans, Edgett carries a portfolio of his past campaigns in his wallet. He hands me an envelope of snapshots that have been thumbed through thousands of times. Pictures of Bob and Yvon Durelle.

"A great friend of mine," says Bob. "He has no hair in this one. It all fell out when he was booked for murder."

"Did it grow back?"

"Oh, yeah."

And Bob with Joe Walcott, Archie Moore, George Foreman, Floyd Patterson, Joe Fraser, Ernie Shavers, Angelo Dundee. Pictures of Bob with his boys. In the club, by the van, on the road.

"This is New York City. We've been to New York seven times. We've won 61 out of 103 fights in New York City."

Pictures from prisons where Bob's kids have put on demonstrations. I recognize the rug that lines the clubhouse ring.

"We take it with us to demonstrations where there is no ring," says Edgett. "We roll it up and put it in the back of the van. I got it from a carpet factory in town. It was remnants. We put it together with duct tape."

Edgett pulls one photo out of the pile and hands it to me.

"That's Barry Wood."

He is holding a picture of a young man with a sweet smile who looks about fifteen years old.

"He was the best kid I ever had. He was killed in a car accident about a year ago. I still can't believe it. I still think I am going to see him. He was eighteen years old. Nicest kid you could ever have met. I never heard him swear, ever. He was on his way to the Commonwealth Games and he got killed. The games weren't anything more than a step towards the Olympics. He would have gone to the Olympics."

Edgett nods in the direction of a man who has stood quietly by the wall all night. He has the shy reserve of a farmer.

"That's Barry's father. He lives about sixty miles from here. He comes down three nights a week. He brings his grandson now." Edgett nods towards Patrick, the six-year-old. He is wearing a Teenage Mutant Ninja Turtle T-shirt.

Wade Tower, who is eighteen years old, is working on the speed bag.

"I've learned a lot from Bob. He has taught me if I want something the only way I'll get it is to work hard. I wanted to go to the Nationals and I got there. I went running every night. I won a silver medal in 1988. I have learned how to be independent. I have a job. I cook at the university on weekends. I get up at five in the morning and work until three. It's not easy. I have the job because I want to save money so I can go to university myself. If it wasn't for Bob I wouldn't have the job and I wouldn't be going to college.

"The club gave me something to do on Friday nights instead of going out with friends. I look at some of my friends and see what they do on their weekends and I realize how much better off I am. Some of them have dropped out of school. Some of them are into drugs pretty heavily. Others are drinking. A lot of them have bad relationships with their parents. This place taught me how to respect people.

"You look at this place — it may not be much — but what we lack in money we have in spirit. It's like a big family. That might sound corny, but it's true. You'd have to be with us on the road to see the heart we have. We go to New York City and all we have are sneakers, tank tops and ripped jeans. The kids there will have fancy boxing boots and shorts and robes and all that. But all that stuff does is make them *look* good.

"Bob is like a father to me. He's like a father to every boy who comes in here. If the world was full of people like Bob

Edgett the world would be all right. He teaches you how to treat other people. I love that. I love showing the little kids stuff. I'm probably going to be a teacher."

For years Bob Edgett has paid for everything himself. He mooches around town raising money any way he can. You can't get a red windbreaker at Frenchies in Amherst, Nova Scotia, or the Salvation Army in Sackville because whenever one comes in they put it aside for Bob. He picks up the jackets every month or so and takes them to his friend Darren who stencils "Bob Edgett's Boxing Club" on them. That way the kids have something to wear on road trips.

"It's easier," says Edgett, "to keep track of a van full of kids if they are all dressed in red."

A few years ago someone left Edgett $50,000.

"It was like manna from heaven. I use it to fix the club. Buy equipment. Stuff like that."

As we prepare to leave I introduce myself to Barry Wood's father. He takes me on a tour of the clubhouse, pointing out newspaper clippings about his son that are taped around the room. Then he pauses in front of an empty wall.

"That was Barry when he was twelve," he says.

I am not sure what he is talking about. The wall looks blank to me.

"This is a year later," he says, running his finger over the empty boards.

A wave of anxiety floods over me. Then I see what he is talking about. There is a faint ladder of pencil marks climbing the wall. There is a scribbled date beside each one. His fingers linger on the lines. I think of the wall at home where I have marked my own children's growth. I think of a woman I know who lost her husband. "I have become obsessed with details," she says. "I go over the smallest thing again and again in my mind."

There is something special about Bob Edgett, and people

who sense that want to be in his orbit. He's a saint, says Fran Smith. We are sipping tea from bone china in her living-room. I can't imagine her even *thinking* of going to a box-ing match. He's a master, she goes on, at taking three weeks to plan something spontaneous.

"If one of his boys needs glasses and the family can't afford them, he'll speak to someone who'll speak to some-one else and then the glasses will mysteriously appear and Bob will look surprised and say, 'Oh, that's great.' He's a strategist. He would have made a marvellous general."

Edgett has an advantage over most people. He knows what he wants and he's not shy to say what he needs. That, more than anything, makes people want to help him.

The old milk truck sways onto the parking lot by the university at the same time every night. Bill Maxwell, who is at the wheel, bought the truck second-hand for three hundred dollars about a year ago. As the truck shudders to a halt in the middle of the empty lot, two young men step out of the darkness. Another night at Mr Chips is about to begin.

Bill and his wife, Linda, will stay in the parking lot until midnight. For the next four hours they will sling home-made hamburgers, hot dogs and French fries out a window Bill cut in the side of their truck.

When Maxwell lost his job after thirteen years at the Enterprise Foundry, his dream was to open a garage.

"I lost my shirt with the garage," he says without any remorse, "so I thought I'd try this out. It's an old-fashioned operation, but it's a living."

According to the menu painted on the side of the truck, Bill and Linda make their living with four items. Ham-burgers and onion rings cost $1.50 each. Hot dogs or French fries are $1.00. The "home-made fries," says the sign, are "peeled and chipped daily."

Inside the van, Bill and Linda rub elbows as they cook. Bill works the grill. Linda does the fries and onion rings and leans out the window to take orders.

"I'd hate to do the burgers," she says. "I'd be afraid I was going to screw them up."

"It depends what you are used to," says Bill, sprinkling steak spice over the grill like snow. "If she had started on the burgers she'd be fine."

Linda has a greeting for every customer. She seems to know all of them by name.

"What'll it be tonight, Terry?"

"You're looking a little sleepy today, George."

"That's all, Beth?"

"After four years you get to know the students," says Bill. "You get to know them and you get personal with them."

"On cold nights," says Linda, "we invite the kids in. You wouldn't think they would come to us when it was below zero. Well, we've had five or six in here at once."

"It can get so crowded I can hardly cook," says Bill. "But you wouldn't want to see them outside when it was real cold."

"The mayor comes in most nights," says Linda.

"He usually sits on the picnic cooler by the door," says Bill.

Bill and Linda keep canned pop in the picnic cooler.

At ten o'clock the temperature in the back of the van must be 150 degrees.

"You might find an onion ring or two in there," says Linda as she hands an order of chips out the window.

"Do you want bacon in your burger, Pete?"

"Bacon?" I ask.

"I started doing bacon last summer," says Bill. "I don't advertise it because it's hard to do when it gets real busy. It gets too greasy and can get into the buns."

"How much is the bacon?" I ask.

"Officially?"

"Yeah."

"Officially it's twenty-five cents. But mostly I don't charge. It depends on what kind of a mood I'm in."

A boy who has come with a list peers into the window.

"Two burgers with cheese, two all dressed with bacon, three hot dogs, two fries and two orders of clams."

"Clams?" I ask.

"I don't advertise the clams," says Bill.

"We use them as something to fall back on," says Linda. "Like if we run out of something."

"How much are the clams?" I ask.

"Here, or in town?"

"Here."

"They're $2.75 here; $5.50 in town."

"Same clams?"

"Same clams," says Bill.

"Same clams," says Linda.

Around midnight two girls arrive at the window. The snow still has a long way to go before it is completely melted, yet one girl is wearing shorts. Her friend orders fries and a burger. The girl wearing the short pants hangs back. "Do you want anything?" asks Linda.

"I don't have any money," says the girl in the shorts.

"Well, do you want anything?" she asks again. "You can pay next time."

The girl orders fries.

As Bill hands her the grease-spotted bag, he turns to me.

"She'll be back tomorrow night with the money. And she'll buy something else."

Then he smiles.

"Try that at the Marshlands Inn."

———— • ————

Before she died, John Wightman's mother lived in the Drew Nursing Home. John, a bachelor, was devoted to his mother, so when he retired from the military fifteen years ago, he took a room in Sackville. He visited his mother every day. He kept her room spotless. He washed the walls more than some people thought necessary. He liked to take walks. He started to drop by the railroad station. Neil Horsman was the ticket agent back then.

"He would come by around ten. Then I would see him again after lunch."

John had time on his hands. His visits became more frequent.

"It was a place for him to hang out. He would come and chin-wag and watch the people coming and going. One day I was busy doing tickets and the train came in and John said, 'Look, you're busy, I'll take the freight off for you.' And I guess that was the start of it. He sort of took the freight over as his job."

There have been a good number of ticket agents since Neil left the station, and with each one John's tenure has solidified. He shows up at the station for every train now. He is a fixture — almost an employee.

Roger Bourque is the current agent.

"At first I didn't like the idea. I had nothing in common with him and I didn't need the help. He'd come in the morning and make toast in the little kitchen. I think one of the other agents had made a deal with him. He would let him use the fridge and stove in return for doing the luggage. His mother was ill at the time and then she passed away and I thought he wouldn't come back, but he's still here. He comes every morning and makes me toast and smokes his pipe and reads the paper and then when the train comes in he wheels the luggage out. He still walks a lot. He swims, too."

John has brought a radio to the station. He listens to the noon news every day. Sometimes he washes his clothes in the sink by hand. He wears khaki wool sweaters with patches that he was issued in the army. His hair is cut short in the military style. With his pipe in his mouth he looks like a British captain in charge of a small country airfield.

He is shy. The station is his home now. His place.

———— • ————

I go for a haircut at Eddie's Barber Shop on Thursday morning.

"You Eddie?" I ask hopefully, swinging into the chair by the window.

"Nope. I'm Butch."

"Is that Eddie?" I nod at the other barber.

"Nope. That's Bobby. Eddie was my father-in-law."

"Oh. You worked here all your life, then?"

"Nope. I worked sixteen years as a spot welder at the foundry."

Like most barber shops, there are more barber chairs at Eddie's than there are barbers. In Eddie's case there are three chairs and two barbers. The middle chair — the old-fashioned one with the porcelain bottom and the porcelain arms and the two leather strops — used to belong to Eddie. Butch and Bobby have left it the way it was, in the middle of the room. They use the chairs on either side. They have, however, put away the brass spittoon.

"We left it out for a while, but we kind of got upset at people spitting at it and missing," says Butch.

On the walls over their chairs are two stuffed rabbit heads mounted on wooden plaques. Each rabbit has a set of horns.

"How do you like our jack-a-lopes?" asks Bobby.

Beside one of the jack-a-lopes is a framed picture.

"That's Eddie there," says Bobby. "The people he is with (there are three men and one young boy in the photo), that's four generations of the same family. Eddie cut all their hair."

Stuck into the mirrors at various angles are postcards, each one addressed to: "Bobby and Butch, The Barbers, Sackville, New Brunswick." On each card there is a single handwritten question. The first one I pick up reads:

Hello Guys. Have you ever wondered if feather pillows
are getting more comfy would it
be because down is up?

The next one says:

Hello Guys. Have you ever wondered if firemen have
bigger balls than policemen, would it be because
they sell more tickets?

Both cards are signed "Willi Ponder."

"He won't admit to it, but we get one of those every time
Bob Edgett goes out of town," says Bobby.

Bobby is cutting a little boy's hair. The boy's mother is
slumped into one of the seats along the far wall. The boy
is getting a rat tail, and he won't stop talking. "I am going
to be the third kid in my class with a rat tail," he says. He
has said it five times.

"I went to barber and hairstyling school for a year," says
Butch, sensing, perhaps, my anxiety.

"Oh," I say.

"It's too bad you couldn't have met Eddie."

"Did he have regular customers?" I ask.

"Dr Barnhill used to come in for a shave every day. You
would have liked the doctor. You could set your clock by
him. He'd come in between 9:45 and 10:15. He did that
every day from 1956 until he died in — when was that,
Bobby, 1985? He even came in on Sundays. Eddie would
come down to scrub the floor in the morning and the doctor would come in at eleven when everyone was at church.
That way no one knew they were here. Every second Sunday Eddie would give him a brushcut.

"What hours do *you* keep?" I ask.

"Officially we open at eight o'clock, but I try to get here
at 7:40 because there is always someone waiting to get a
haircut before work. On Monday somebody always comes
in early to fill us in on what happened on the weekend.
Who got caught drinking or who was in a fight. You get the

news here before it's in the paper."

A haircut at Eddie's costs six dollars. A shampoo is three dollars. Butch didn't charge me the extra two dollars for the head rub with the quinine lotion.

"We just started using the cash register a year ago," he says, making my change. "We used to put our money in a drawer. Each barber had his own drawer."

———— • ————

The Vogue Cinema was built in 1946. Little has been done to it since. The theatre holds 350 people. There are sixteen rows in front and seven in the balcony at the back. Each night as they wait for the first show, the audience is washed by pale blue lights that glow behind the art deco moulding. There are two shows a night.

The Vogue is owned and operated by Sheila Cole. Sheila is twenty-eight years old. She bought the theatre after graduating from the University of New Brunswick with an MBA. Seven nights a week she sells tickets from the ticket booth in the small lobby. When everyone is in the theatre, she helps at the candy counter.

Sheila is one of the fifty-three independent theatre owners in Atlantic Canada. She is also the only woman in New Brunswick who holds a projectionist's licence. To get her licence, Sheila had to apprentice for three hundred hours and then pass a written exam.

Running a theatre in a small town is not without problems. Sheila may be the only game in town, but that doesn't mean she doesn't have competition. There are nine theatres in Moncton, only forty-five kilometres away, and two more fifteen kilometres away in Amherst, Nova Scotia.

"What I try to do," says Cole, sitting in her office during the first feature, "is keep my prices down. I keep them about $1.50 under Moncton and 50 cents under Amherst."

Sheila has to rent the films she shows from distributors. The rental fee is not a fixed fee but rather a percentage of her box office. For first-run movies the percentage can be as much as sixty to seventy percent of the gate. If she waits until movies have been out for three to six weeks, the cut drops to the forty percent range. At $6 ($5 if you are under sixteen) a ticket Cole cannot afford to bring in movies during the first few weeks of their run.

"I also have to pay for my posters. They cost $8 each. If I send them back I get a $2 credit. But I keep them and sell them to the students. The previews cost money, too. It costs $6 to rent them for the first week and $3 for the second. It all adds up. The chains can make some of it up at the canteen. The chains have a return per patron of about $3. Mine is $1.75. I only charge $1 for pop and popcorn. I wouldn't want to think of going higher. There are a lot of kids around here who might get $5 or $6 a week allowance. I wouldn't feel good putting my popcorn prices higher."

"What about videos?" I ask. "Have videos hurt your business?"

"No," she says, "they've helped. They hurt at first but in the long run what they've done is make people want to see movies again."

Upstairs, Sheila's sister, Lisa, is waiting in the projection booth for word that she can begin tonight's film.

The typical movie arrives at the theatre on five or six separate reels. Each reel runs twenty-odd minutes. Modern multi-screen theatres have up-to-date equipment that allows projectionists to splice those reels together so an entire film can run on one spool. This means one projectionist can run as many as five movies simultaneously.

The Vogue doesn't have that kind of equipment. The Vogue has two Strong Super 175 projectors. Each one is about the size of a furnace.

Lisa is sitting on a chair in the corner of the crowded projection room behind the balcony. She is wearing sweat pants, leather desert boots and an olive green sweater that is too big for her. Her long hair is piled up on top of her head. She smiles when I climb into her room. I like her right away. I think she is pretty. She puts her book down. She is reading *Hamlet*.

Lisa shows me a hole in the projection booth wall through which I can peer down on everyone in the theatre below me. It is at moments like these that I love my work. I like being behind the scenes.

The first reel begins to clunk around the projector. Lisa smiles.

"Between each reel you can watch the movie, read or write."

For a while we watch the movie together through the small hole.

"You write?" I ask.

"Yes," she says.

"Is that what you write in?" I point to a book on a table.

"Yes."

"Poems?"

"Yes."

"Can I read one?"

"Yes." She nods after every answer, as if she is monitoring her end of our conversation and is pleased that she is getting it right.

"Choose one for me," I say.

Lisa screws up her face and flips through her book. She doesn't look up for a few minutes.

"I can't do it," she says. "You choose one. The ones signed Jane are the ones I wrote."

"But your name is Lisa."

"Yeah."

A bell on one of the projectors starts to ring. It sounds like someone's roast is ready to come out of the oven.

"That's the signal that the reel is going to end," she says.

I follow Lisa around the first projector and over to the second.

"The cue is going to show up in about thirty seconds."

"What is the cue?"

"It is a dot in the upper righthand corner of the screen. It will flash for about a second, and when it does I have twelve seconds before the switch."

I am watching the screen carefully. I am afraid I am going to blink and miss the dot.

"Me, too," says Lisa.

When it comes, Lisa starts counting out loud. She has her left hand on the projector, her foot on a pedal on the floor and her right hand on the sound button on the wall.

"When I get to ten I start the projector. Two seconds later there will be another cue on the screen. When I see it I push the sound button and the foot pedal at the same time.

"The good thing about this job," she says, smiling, as the projectors switch flawlessly, "is that you only have to work every twenty minutes."

Lisa says that it is hard to find a day job in Sackville. She says she wants to go out west and earn enough money so that she can go to England.

"What about school?" I ask.

"I was at U.P.E.I. last year. I didn't do so well."

"You didn't have a good time?"

"No. That was the problem. I had too good a time."

On West Main Street, hovering on the edge of the business district, I stumble onto the Sackville Harness Shop. It is the last business in North America still making long-straw handmade horse collars. Appropriately, the collars are being stuffed and stitched in what might be the oldest building in town. The front of the store has been traced back to 1845.

Inside, the air is heavy with the smell of leather. The wooden floor, first running this way, then running that way, and then this way again, is worn and tired from seventy years of trade.

What little machinery there is in the store is black, belted and oily. Each piece looks like an ancient sewing machine. Several are powered only by crank or foot pedal. "The British United Shoe Machinery Co., Leicester England" reads the flowery gold-leaf script on one. Most of the work here is done by hand.

There are three men working in the shop today. That's down from the peak of nine who were employed after World War II when the shop had to scramble to catch up on back orders.

As well as the horse collars (ten dollars an inch, the average collar being twenty-five inches), you can also buy harnesses of all sorts, halters, reins, sleigh bells and men's leather "purses" (wallets with a cowboy motif). There are two saddles in the store, one hanging from a beam, the other on the front counter. Both in for repair.

The radio in the shop is tuned to FM 104 — "Back to back country favourites."

> You got to dance with who brung you
> Swung with who swung you
> Life ain't no forty yard dash

Cowboys. When I was five I owned a black cowboy hat with a string that tucked up under my chin. I had a black shirt, black pants with fringes, a bandanna, gloves (also with fringes), spurs and a set of leather holsters. I wore my six-shooters — heavy silver cap guns with pearl white handles — backwards in my leather holsters like Hopalong Cassidy, pistol grips pointing frontwards so I could cross draw. Left hand over the body to the right gun. Right hand, likewise, to the left side.

Though I tried, probably for hours, I never mastered with acceptable grace the art of twirling my six-guns around my fingers the way my heroes could. Hoppy could spin his guns by the trigger guard like a pinwheel and then make them magically disappear into his holster or, if need be, slap them into the palm of his hand ready for action. All my cowboy heroes could get their guns swinging with the careless abandon of a Yo-Yo. My friends and I stuck to pulling them from our sides and arguing over who was dead and who was just winged. I got you. No, you didn't, you missed.

The low point of my career as a cowboy happened one Saturday morning before breakfast. It is a moment I shared with my father — a moment we have never spoken of. Yet it stands out in my mind as clearly as if it happened yesterday.

I had, as was my custom on Friday night, worn my black shirt and pants — the ones with the fringes — to bed. I wore them under my pyjamas. My guns and hat were slung over the bedpost. I wanted to be ready for action at first light. I had something I wanted to try. Something I had seen on television.

My mother was already downstairs when I got to my parents' bedroom. My father was still asleep, and that's how I should have left him. I should have asked for my mother's help. But this seemed to be a thing men should share. He had, after all, been in the war. I took one of my guns from my holster and approached the bed.

"Dad," I said, holding out the pearl handle of my six-shooter. "Take this and tell me to put up my hands."

My father stirred restlessly.

"Just hold it," I said, forcing the gun into his hand. "Point it at me and tell me to put up my hands."

"Hands up," said my father, one eye peering through God-knows-what fog.

I stood beside the bed in my black cowboy shirt and pants with my hands triumphantly in the air — just the way Hoppy held his hands on TV when the bank robbers surprised him in the cabin. And then, smiling just like Hoppy, I drew my foot back and, with the astonishing strength of a five-year-old cowboy, I kicked the gun my father was pointing at me. To my amazement, and my father's great surprise, my foot landed on the fleshy spot where his hand joined his arm and, just like on television, the gun flew out of his hand. Unlike the bad guy on TV, my father sat up quickly, as if he had been shot. Holding his wrist and peering at me with a stupid expression, he made a queer choking sound that made me think of a stuck pig.

The world seemed to freeze there for a moment, between my father and me — him sitting in bed holding his wrist and staring at me stupidly, and me, just as stupidly, standing by the bedside staring back.

It had never occurred to me that I would hurt him. I was trying to kick the gun, not him. I couldn't believe that he was angry at me. Especially not after the feat I had just performed. Then, as we stared at each other in stop time, I noticed the gun, which had left my father's hand and had described a graceful arc towards the bedroom ceiling and was now heading down again. End over end it tumbled in slow motion on its trajectory from the ceiling towards my father's head.

It landed on his forehead with a dull thud followed immediately by an explosion. The impact set a cap off. In his dazed state, my father may have actually believed he had been shot. Maybe the whole incident collided with some hideous dream from the war. I have never asked. I remember him reaching out with his hand to grab me, but being both awake and alert, I managed to get out of the way. He lurched towards the bathroom, blood streaming from his forehead. I ran to my mother.

"Dad's bleeding like a stuck pig," I sobbed. God knows what she thought she'd find as she bounded up the stairs. I waited sobbing in the kitchen. Ten minutes later my mother came down.

"Dad's gone back to bed," she said. "It's OK. He's just a little tired." She gathered me in her arms and pulled me close.

"It's OK," she said. "Come on. Cowboys don't cry."

———————— • ————————

I realize I have been at the Harness Shop for well over two hours now. In that time Gordie Atkinson has fixed a lead line, made a belt and done some leather stitching. He has also taken an order for a dozen calf halters. For the last half hour he has been leaning against the front counter talking to a middle-aged man who looks like a farmer. After a half hour of pleasant chat, he asks the question most shop owners open with.

"Is there anything I can do for you, Ross?"

"Oh, no," says the farmer. "I'm just putting in time."

Gordie returns to his workbench and for ten minutes the farmer pokes around the front of the store by himself. He is almost out the door when he turns.

"I might like to put up a sign that says 'Horse for Sale.' Would that be OK?"

It is almost an afterthought. But it isn't. There was something on his mind after all.

———————— • ————————

I visit the farmer the next afternoon. His name is Ross Cole. He is forty-one years old. Like most people who farm today, Ross has an "off farm" job. He drives a school bus. I want to meet him because Ross still works with horses.

When I arrive he takes me out to the barn and shows me his rigging. He has three horse collars. They were all made at the Harness Shop.

"It's plain and simple," he says. "I like horses. That's why I use them. I like the smell of them. And they're good to work with. Horses don't tramp the ground like a tractor. After you work your ground with a tractor, it can get as hard as cement. A horse leaves it nice and broken up."

Sometimes people stop their cars on the side of the road

to watch Ross working his fields. Sometimes they ask if they can take his picture.

"People like it. Everyone is used to machines."

Ross also works a wood lot behind his family's farm, and he still uses a horse when he works in the bush.

"I like the horses because they are quiet. I like it in the bush when it is quiet. I throw a blanket over the horse and give her a feed bag and then it's just me and the horse and the quiet.

"Everyone thinks I'm crazy. They think a horse is too slow. That I can't cut as much wood as they can because I can't haul as much out of the bush with a horse as they can with a tractor. What they forget is that you have to buy a tractor and pay for the fuel and the parts. A horse is a lot cheaper than a tractor. And a horse will always start no matter how cold it is. Another thing is that horses don't get stuck."

Ross Cole is not the only person around logging with horses. I hear about a big outfit on the other side of Fredericton that has ten or twelve horses in the bush. They say the horses don't trample the small growth, so the loggers can be more selective about what they cut. And during those winters when it snows before freeze-up and a tractor can't make a good road — well, boy, that doesn't bother a horse. Not at all.

Ross cuts pulp wood for the paper mills, logs for lumber and a bit of firewood. He heats his house with wood (fifteen cords a year), and his wife Valerie does all her baking and cooking on a wood stove. When we get back to the house, Valerie is in the kitchen making tuna sandwiches.

"We have brown bread or home-made white," she says.

"Home-made white," I say. "You cook it in the wood stove?"

"Yes."

"Is it hard? I mean, getting the temperature right?"

"You get used to it."

"Your wife makes bread, does she?" assumes Ross.

"Oh, yes," I say too quickly. I don't know why I lie. I don't, I think, want them to think less of us.

———————•———————

That night I decide to eat dinner at the Marshlands Inn for the first time. It has seemed too formal to me up to now. I have been more comfortable with the casualness of Mel's. The cosiness of the Vienna. But tonight I am tired and feel like a change.

In the parking lot I pull alongside a blue Chevrolet. The back seat is piled to the window with bags and boxes. The two women standing beside the driver's door are deep in discussion.

"Moving?" I ask.

"Sort of," one replies.

"Are you checking in?"

"We are trying to decide if we are going to go in and eat."

"It's very nice. Would you like to join me?"

Their names are Margaret and Judy. Margaret is fifty-five. Judy is forty-eight. They have driven from Amherst, Nova Scotia, where they have just finished packing their mother's life into cardboard boxes. Their mother is living in a "home." They are on their way to Saint John.

"At first I thought it was going to be terrible," says Judy. "Being there without her. But it wasn't. It was a relief. It took ten nights. After all the furniture was out we bought two foam mattresses and slept on the floor. We sorted through everything. Then we called the Salvation Army, had work done around the house and finally rented it for the next year."

"I got irritable this morning," says Margaret. "I guess it just builds up inside you. Every once in a while I'd say, 'Are we doing the right thing? What if she wants to come back?' "

"Then I'd say she's not coming back," says Judy.

Margaret lives in Montreal. Judy lives in Saint John.

"She wanted to be independent," says Margaret. "She wanted to keep living alone. She wanted to stay in her house and look after her cat. And we all wanted that, too. We didn't talk about her failing memory. In fact, at first we pretended it wasn't happening. Then we started to cover for her."

"She got an abscessed tooth, so I came to stay with her for two weeks." says Judy. "I had to. We had to make sure that she would remember to take her medication. When I arrived, she was limping, but she couldn't remember how she had hurt herself.

"Later I found a note. It said, 'I, Flora, if I don't remember tomorrow, I fell and hurt my ankle.'

"When I talk to her now she says, 'I'm fine. But I find myself living in such a peculiar place. You'll have to come and see it.'

"Once she asked me what she had done to get there. 'What did I do,' she said. 'Whatever it was I won't do it again.' "

"It is a big dilemma," says Margaret. "She was surviving. She was healthy enough. Maybe she should be alone."

The meal is over. We are drinking coffee.

"You never used the word Alzheimer," I say.

"No," says Margaret.

"We never used the word," says Judy.

"We always say memory loss," says Margaret.

"We haven't told anyone, I don't know why."

"I think we feel like we are betraying her."

"Mostly I just want reassurance," says Judy. "I want somebody to tell me we did the right thing."

Judy pauses and picks at her plate. There is a silence that is longer than it should be. Then she looks at me.

"The thing is, of course, I'm still not sure."

———— • ————

The big news in the next day's paper is that the bus will no longer be stopping at Mel's.

"50-YEAR TRADITION BROKEN . . ." reads the headline in the *Tribune-Post*.

Anyone in town considering travel on SMT bus lines should go to Wiley's Quik Mart on East Main Street because that's where the service is now located.

The decision by SMT to move to a new location breaks a 50-year tradition of having the service at Mel's Tea Room on Bridge Street. . . .

Gary Wiley, proprietor of Wiley's Quik Mart, said he was approached by SMT to consider running the bus service out of his East Main Street location. Wiley said SMT was going to move the service whether or not he agreed to take it on.

"If it wasn't me it was going to be somebody else," he said.

According to Wiley, SMT cited safety as the main reason for removing the service from Mel's. He said with reduced train service SMT has been using larger buses and needs more room to park and turn around.

Wiley expects the change to his business to be a positive one, yet feels badly for the loss to Mel's Tea Room owner Bernard Goodwin.

"I feel badly about Bernard losing the service. It's been there all my life. I grew up in Bernard's back yard, I played with his boys, I hung out at his business," he said.

I decide it is time to talk to Mel. Or rather Mel's son, Bernard. Bernard began working at his dad's restaurant after the war. He took it over when Mel died. That was in 1953.

We have been nodding at each other all week, Bernard and I, but we haven't spoken more than pleasantries.

Bernard chooses one of the front booths, so he can keep his eye on the cash.

"I may have to get up," he says. He is wearing grey pants

and a soft plaid shirt. Apart from Bob Edgett, Bernard is the gentlest-looking man in town.

"I didn't start out in the store," he says quietly. "I spent five years in the RCMP. I was in the Musical Ride for a while."

If I have learned anything in journalism, it is that everyone has a story. You hear the damndest things in the most unexpected places. I am talking to a seventy-six-year-old man who has run a cafe in Sackville, New Brunswick, for the past fifty years.

"The Musical Ride?" I say.

"That's all we eastern fellas were good for. The western fellas were all brought up on horses. But the instructors never liked their riding style. They could teach us anything they wanted. So it was always easterners who ended up in the Musical Ride."

"Did you tour?" I ask.

"All over. Down to San Francisco and pretty much all over Canada. When the war broke out we were at the Exhibition in Toronto. They came and woke us up that night and we went out with the Toronto police. There were about thirty-five of us. We went all over the city arresting German people and Italian people. We got quite a few. There were a lot of us out that night."

Mel served overseas during the war. He was stationed in Cambridge and flew bombing missions over the Ruhr Valley. He was sent to Moncton in 1945 and came home on weekends to help his father.

"Dad needed help. That's why I came. When I was a kid I used to make the fire for Dad every morning. I did that for a couple of years, I guess. I would sweep the floor. That's how I made my spending money. I delivered parcels for him, too. So I guess I have worked here all my life. Except for nine years."

Bernard married in England and he and his wife had four children. His wife died, and when he married again he married Minerva who has worked at Mel's all her life.

"I guess Minerva has worked here as long as I have," he says. "She does most of the baking. She does pies every day. And roasts all the chickens. We raise all our own chickens at home. I've got about 150 hens today. I sell eight to ten dozen eggs every day. They are $1.60 a dozen. Nice brown eggs. I grow the chickens to maturity and then kill them off. Most of those chicken places kill them at four or five pounds and sell them as quarters. We let them grow to ten pounds before we use them here.

"We also grow all our own vegetables. All the potatoes, carrots, turnips, peas, beans, cauliflower, tomatoes, squash and pumpkin comes from the garden. I've always liked to work the garden. That's what I do when I'm not here. It all helps out, I guess.

"It's a quiet life here. But we don't mind it. It's slower. But I never liked the big cities. I always found them kind of lonely places. Here you know half the people in town."

At the back of the restaurant, beside the empty and dark "Bus Waiting Room," is an office that can't have changed much since 1918 when Mel first opened the restaurant. Inside there is a wooden desk, a filing cabinet and a big black safe. The wooden chair that matches the desk looks as if it is going to fall apart the next time someone sits in it.

"Roger has been talking about getting a new one," says Bernard.

Roger is Bernard's son. Roger, already middle-aged, shares the business with his father. One day he will take over.

"I told him to go ahead and buy a new chair over a year ago. I don't care, myself. I never have time to sit down."

"Will he do all right?" I ask. "Is Roger going to get rich?"

"He won't make a fortune," Bernard says, smiling. "But he'll make a living."

Not bad, I think. Not bad in a town the shipbuilders left a long time ago. Where the foundries have all closed and the hay fields no longer bring wealth. Not bad to start a little business and pass it on to your son. Not bad after seventy-three years to pass it on again.

Foxwarren

MANITOBA

*Hockey is the Canadian metaphor,
the rink a symbol of this country's vast stretches of water and
wilderness, its extremes of climate, the player a symbol of
our struggle to civilize such a land. . . . Unsure as we are
about who we are, we know at least this about ourselves:
we are hockey players, and we are hockey fans,
and once we could say we were the best.*

BRUCE KIDD
JOHN MACFARLANE
THE DEATH OF HOCKEY

I wanted to visit a town where hockey still mattered. I called Ken Dryden. Ken told me to call Bob Strumm.

"He is an assistant coach for the Detroit Red Wings," said Dryden. "He used to scout in Saskatchewan. He knows every little arena there is."

"I want to go somewhere in Saskatchewan," I said to Strumm when he returned my call. "A place with an arena and a home team, a cafeteria, a gas station and not much else."

"Foxwarren, Manitoba," he said without a pause.

"Saskatchewan," I said. "Somewhere in Saskatchewan. I want to watch a town team, in a town where hockey still counts."

"You want to go to Foxwarren," he said.

———————— •• ————————

"You want to stay here for two *weeks?*" The woman on the telephone had a soft Ukrainian accent.

"Yes," I said. "Two weeks."

Pause.

"*Where* are you calling from?"

"I told you already. Toronto."

Pause.

"*Toronto.*"

"Yes."

Pause.

"But how are you going to get *here?*" She sounded incredulous.

"By plane to Winnipeg. Then by car."

Pause.

"You want to stay here over a Saturday night?"

"Is that a problem?"

"No. No. That's no problem."

"How much, then? If I stay two weeks can you give me a special rate?"

Pause.

"You sure you want to stay here two *weeks?*"
"Yes. Maybe more."
Longer pause.
"How does twenty dollars a night sound."
"Twenty dollars would be fine."
The Kent was the only hotel in town.

———— • ————

There are parts of the prairie where you are never out of sight of a grain elevator. You can glance at your rear-view mirror, and just as one elevator vanishes out the back, the top of another will poke over the horizon in front of you like a telephone pole. In western Canada, prosperity is calculated in units of verticality. Oil rigs, grain elevators and silos measure the land.

Thirty kilometres east of the Saskatchewan border, Foxwarren, Manitoba, offers little vertical warning. It comes on you suddenly, for it is a town with no surroundings save for fields of grain. It is as if the town was dropped down a long time ago in the middle of someone's acreage.

You have passed by places like Foxwarren hundreds of times. They are the towns just off the highway. You might have stopped at the gas station. You might have seen the sign pointing towards town and wondered who could possibly live there, and what they could possibly do.

Most of Foxwarren is sandwiched between the Yellowhead Highway on the north and the railway tracks on the south. You can walk from one side of town to the other in less than ten minutes. Most of the streets are still dirt, and if they don't end at the highway or the railway tracks, they end in someone's grain field. It is the kind of town where you can hear every dog bark and — if you've lived here long enough — know whose dog is barking. If you are in the washroom in the hotel bar, about the farthest place you can get from the train tracks without leaving town — you'll still hear each train rumble by.

On any given Sunday there are fewer than twenty people at either church service, though if someone dies, they
invariably have to put up loudspeakers in the church basement and, if the funeral is large, erect another set on the
lawn. Foxwarren is the kind of town you come home to
when you die. You may live in Winnipeg for thirty-five
years, but if you were born here you'll probably want to be
buried here, too. The local funeral parlour has a twenty-
four-hour toll-free line. It is, however, in Russell, two towns
to the north.

The telephone listings in Foxwarren take two and a half
pages in the regional phone book. There are numbers for
141 households. If you ask around, most people will tell
you that about 150 people live in town. If you look up the
police, you will see that, like the funeral parlour, they have
a Russell number. The ambulance comes from Birtle, the
town to the south.

People who live here know the different steps to dances
like the Heel and Toe Polka, the Cross Country Waltz, the
Ranger Waltz, the Boston Two Step. They know the difference between the Buffalo Glide as danced in Manitoba and
as danced in Saskatchewan. They live close enough to the
boundary to dance both.

"We can dance for three hours," says Helen Burdett,
"and never do the same dance twice."

When there is a dance at the Leisure Centre and they
break for refreshments around ten at night, it is called
lunch. You eat your big meal at noon and it is called dinner. You have supper in the evening. Lunch is something
you get at weddings, dances or funerals.

It is the kind of town where you get married young, in
the kind of country where summer mornings are blessed
with that special kind of peace that comes when you know
everybody for miles around.

The Kent Hotel turns out to be a box of a building. There
is a bar downstairs — the only one for miles — and nine

rooms over it. The favourite drink in the bar is rye and Coke. Elsie, the owner, and the woman I spoke to on the phone, has two bottles of rye side by side in the liquor dispenser so she can pour two shots at once. As I sign the register (Stuart McLean, Toronto, March 12, 1991) I notice that the last guest checked out over two weeks ago.

Aside from the hotel there is one general store, a cafe, a post office, a gas station, a credit union, two churches and two grain elevators, but there's not much else.

The elevators lord over the town like fortresses left behind by some occupying army. The architecture of these giant rectangular bins has barely changed since the first one was built in Gretna, Manitoba, in 1881. At their peak in the 1930s, there were not even six thousand grain elevators in the whole of Canada. The number seems impossibly small. There were seven once in Foxwarren. The two that remain are, of course, both beside the train tracks. The elevators are the only cause that trains have for stopping here anymore.

Both elevators are covered with aluminium siding, and they flash unequivocally in the noon sun. Sometimes at the end of the day, when the light hits them right, they appear to melt into the land. Walking along the tracks my first morning in town, I am surprised to see a door in one of the elevators marked "Office." It has never occurred to me that someone might work in one. I thought the elevators, like giant silos, were just places where you left your crops.

I open the door, climb the stairs and step into Lou Deeley's office. Deeley is the local agent for Manitoba Pool Elevator. He works in a sizeable room with the kind of large rectangular windows you see in a radio studio. The window looks out at the weigh scale and the chutes where the farmers dump their loads of grain.

Deeley's office reminds me of a ticket office in a railroad station. There is a computer by the window that looks out of place. It is the only thing in the room made of plastic. The floor is yellow linoleum; the trim, the counter and the table are all wood. There are little brass weights for the hand scale Lou uses to grade the grain.

Deeley has worked in elevators for forty years, and the doctors have told him he should have quit long ago.

"It's the dust," he says. "They tell me I shouldn't work in the dust, but what can you do. You have to make a living. Some people get farmer's lung or emphysema. I've had to take pills for five or six years now to help me breathe. Some guys wear a mask, but I don't like that because my glasses fog up."

The elevators aren't as bad as they used to be, but there is still plenty of dust. Even here in the office you can see it drifting in the morning sun.

Deeley wipes his finger across the window-sill and holds it up.

"See? I wiped that off two days ago, and it's dusty again."

A three-ton dump truck rumbles up the platform outside. Garth Jacobs slouches into the office. A moment later he's back outside pulling a handle, and the dumpster on the back of his truck starts to rise. Golden pellets pour out the back and disappear into the elevator like a load of sand. It takes less than two minutes to empty the truck.

"That's wheat," says Deeley's assistant, Ken Ewbank. "That's the bread and butter of the prairie."

"Quite a few loaves of bread going down that hole," says Garth. "Though when you sell it like this you can't buy yourself that much bread back."

Ewbank scoops a few handfuls of the grain as it pours out of the truck. Back in the office he spreads it on the counter so he can grade it. He assesses each truckload for fungus, moisture level, colour and percentage of foreign material. There are eighty-five different categories into which he can classify the load. It may be Spring Wheat (the best wheat grown in Canada), Canadian Prairie Spring Wheat, Winter Wheat or Utility Wheat. It may be Number One Red, Number Two or Number Three. If the crop was frozen, immature or mildewed, he will classify it as Canada Feed.

Ewbank is counting individual kernels now with a pair of tweezers. It will take him five minutes to finish. What he finally settles on will determine how much Garth gets paid for the 457 bushels he has just delivered. Ken jots down some figures then punches the results into the computer. A printer clicks into action and spits out a cheque for $1,371. The same load would have brought $1,850 in 1985. That's a drop of twenty-six percent.

"Another day, another dollar lost," someone mutters as Garth heads out the door. No one laughs.

Lou Deeley is fiddling with a calculator on the cluttered desk in his inner office. Grain isn't supposed to be measured in bushels anymore, but none of the farmers who live around here like to work in tonnes. So while the paperwork might be metric, the conversation isn't.

"We put through over a million bushels last year," says Deeley. "That used to be a big deal for one elevator. But they are taking so many rail lines out that the elevators are consolidated now. You have to do two million bushels to amount to anything today.

"Everything used to go by train. Lumber, coal, people, the mail. Now it all goes by truck. You just don't see the trains anymore."

Outside, Stan Souch is holding a familiar seminar.

"There is nobody left in the country."

Souch, who still farms a half section (320 acres), rocks back and forth and jingles the change in his pocket as he talks.

"You feel kind of bad about it. You hate to see your home town go. But there is nothing you can do to stop it going. You can't survive on a small farm anymore. Not with the price of grain where it is. It's ridiculous. So you have to fold up or you have to get bigger. Look at Ray Gadd. He took over the McCaig quarter, and he farms Tom Vaughan's quarter, and Reg Gadd's land, and the Williams place — there is a half a section there — and the Mispelons' place, and he bought the Alex Hay half, and he bought Lloyd Parton's half, and Jack Mitchell's place, and the Little half and the half that belonged to the Hamiltons. All these people were four-horse farmers. They all had a few cattle and a few chickens. There were families that lived in all those places. Families that shopped in town. And they're all gone now."

The economics of farming has changed dramatically over the past fifty years on the Canadian prairies, and the changes on the farms have had a profound impact on Canada's small towns. You have to be big to survive in the modern world. The era of the family farm with six cows, four horses and the quarter section of prairie (160 acres) that was deeded to homesteaders under the Dominion Land Policy is over.

The change began slowly. It started after the war. At first everyone wanted to get rid of their cows. Milk cows tied you down. It was hard to go to the curling bonspiels if you had six cows in your barn.

It used to be that every second town had a creamery. Everyone with cows (and pretty near everyone had cows) kept their milk and sold their cream. The creameries would come two times a week — right out to the farm — and pick it up. Then they'd put it on the train. Hell, you could make a living on a *quarter* section.

Things speeded up when they started paving the roads. Better roads meant farmers could go shopping in town, and that meant they didn't have to produce everything themselves.

"There used to be seven elevators right here in Foxwarren. Now there are two," says Stan Souch. "There used to be sixteen buses at school. Now there are three, and they have to go further and further to fill them up. There used to be three garages and three or four machine shops. There were a couple of restaurants and a doctor, and a barber, and a pool room, and a bank. There is nothing like that anymore. They took the station away twenty years ago. They built the schools in the bigger towns. And the buses came and took the kids away. There used to be sixteen people on the phone line between Andy Low's house and town. There are two now."

Everyone in the elevator office has stopped what they are doing. They are leaning against the counters in their stained jeans and jackets, arms folded over their chests, heads nodding in agreement as Souch goes on.

"The town of Foxwarren will be gone soon. Look at the list of sales in the country every year. Every sale is another vacant farm. Every vacant farm is one less family to support this town. There'll be nothing left here. It's like the butcher store. It sat there for a while and then it goes back to the municipality for taxes and then they just take it down with a back hoe and cart it out to the dump. If they don't do that the skunks will take over. They didn't even bother to take the freezer out before they knocked it over — or the fridge or even the cupboards."

There is a senior citizen living in every second house in town, and every time a senior dies their house dies with them — sitting vacant at first, then, like the butcher store, bulldozed to keep the skunks away. There used to be three kids coming out of each of these one-bedroom homes. Not anymore.

Foxwarren is not even an official town now. It's run by the municipality of Birtle.

Souch is looking only at me — still fiddling with the money in his pocket — as if he is embarrassed to look at his friends.

"I don't have to worry. I'll be gone before it's over. That might sound funny to you. But it's true. You get to my age, you go away for two weeks and another fellow you used to know is gone. And the way the trend is today — they're talking about putting elevators so many miles apart — well, these elevators will be gone, too. They've closed up the curling rink. They have to scrape all around the country to get enough guys to make a hockey team. The writing is on the wall."

I follow Ken Ewbank outside to the chute and watch another truckload of grain spill into the elevator.

"Funny," I say absent-mindedly, letting the funnel of wheat run over my hand like water. "All this grain and they don't have cereal at the cafe. I had to eat eggs this morning at breakfast."

———— • ————

All my mornings in Foxwarren begin at the cafe.

The morning after I mention to Ewbank that I favour cereal, Patricia Graham greets me at the counter with a bowl and a box of corn flakes.

"I brought you some cereal in from home," she says matter-of-factly.

She doesn't mention why she might have done this, and I don't ask. It is my first experience with small town communication, and a lesson I file away. Whatever you say gets back to the person you said it about.

The cafe is tucked around the side of the gas station. I usually walk across the parking lot at about 8:30 A.M., and things are usually humming. The day officially begins at 7:30 in the morning when Pat Graham puts on the first pot of coffee. She starts every day by shaking a jar of vinegar over the coffee pot.

"If I don't do that," she says, "there'll be an awful-looking scum on top of it."

After the coffee is going, Pat starts her soup. She makes a new pot every day. The favourites in town are her beef barley and beet borscht. She also makes her own pies — $1.30 for the apple or raisin; ten cents extra for the pumpkin, rhubarb, coconut, banana or lemon.

She opens for business at eight o'clock. Seven days a week. She closes only three days a year — Christmas, Boxing Day and New Year's.

By 8:15 the place starts to fill up. There are five tables against the walls and six stools at the counter — room for twenty-one paying customers. Twenty-two if Pat gives up the stool at the far end of the counter where she often has a coffee going. A full house in the morning is about fourteen people. Usually the same fourteen.

In the mornings, Pat is the only woman in the joint. Her tight brown curls the only hair on display, her pointed frames the only glasses worn with an eye to fashion. All the men — sitting at the tables, almost creating a fog now with their steaming coffee and cigarettes — are wearing windbreakers and peaked caps.

The talk this morning begins, as it does every morning, with hockey. Theoren Fleury, a boy from the town down the road and playing for the Calgary Flames in the NHL, has scored forty-six goals this season. There are still nine games left to play and still some people on coffee row who believe Theoren might score fifty. Last night at the arena, Fleury's father, a grain farmer who has never declared more than $15,000 on his income tax form, shook his head and smiled when asked about his son's $1.2 million contract. "We don't," he said, "talk about money. Never."

This is grain country — a place where harvest time is the only time you make money. The rest of the year you spend it.

The Spokane Chiefs played last night in the Western Hockey League, so they are next on the agenda. The WHL (Junior A hockey) is one step away from the big leagues, and Foxwarren native Pat Falloon plays for the Chiefs.

One of the regulars on coffee row is Pat Falloon's father, Ron. Last night Ron and his wife, Diane, drove their 1986 Buick down a rutted lane to a small hill in the middle of a field not far from their farmhouse.

"If I angle the car right," says Ron, "I can pull in the Spokane station that carries the game."

Ron and Diane took a bag of popcorn with them and sat in the car until the game ended. Whenever they were chilly, Ron turned the engine over and ran the heater.

"I tried just about everything before I found that spot," says Ron. "One night I went driving to all the high places within twenty miles. I'd get the game, but it would fade in and out. Another time I ran a wire from the car to an old windmill and tried to use it as an antenna. But it didn't bring the voice in any better. It just made the static louder.

"I have talked to other parents about this. Ray Whitney's father, who lives in Fort Saskatchewan, sometimes goes up on the roof with his radio to pull in Spokane games. Chris Rowland's dad drives down to a lake where he lives. Someone told him he'd get reflections off the water, and that would improve the reception.

"To be honest, I never really expected to get the station at all. But some nights it comes in real clear out there."

Ken Tibbatts is in the cafe this morning with his grey checked pork-pie hat pushed back on his head. The crest on his jacket says "Foxwarren Falcons, 1984 N.C.H.L. Champs." The bar on his arm reads "Coach." Tibbatts, more than anyone else here, embodies Foxwarren's dedication to hockey. Every fall after his crops are in, he spends hours on the concrete floor of the town's arena putting in the ice. Every season he quietly digs into his own pocket to pay travel money to some of the out-of-town players he recruits for the town team, the Falcons. All season long Tibbatts lumbers around under the stands, sharpening skates and taping sticks. Many say he is the reason the arena is still going.

Tibbatts and Falloon and the other men who are either leaning away from or hunching over their second and third cups of coffee are, every one of them, grain farmers. They have, however, another calling — a higher vocation. For above and beyond anything else, they understand, feel and follow hockey in a way that few Canadians can anymore. They are not, largely, interested in the NHL. Theirs is the world of town hockey.

The Falcons are an "intermediate" team. They play in the North Central Hockey League against neighbouring towns such as Russell, Shoal Lake and Roblin. This is the community-based hockey that Bruce Kidd and John Macfarlane elegized in their lament on hockey (*The Death of Hockey*) — town games scrubbed out by town teams before three and four hundred fans in tin-roofed arenas on Friday nights.

Hockey is more a faith than a sport in Foxwarren; the men around these tables are no more faithful than most in town. It is nothing for anyone here to drive 120 kilometres any night to watch the Falcons play in Birtle or Binscarth or any of the other towns on the local circuit. There is probably not a rink in western Canada where they wouldn't find someone they knew. They've eaten more onion-soaked hamburgers than anyone should during a life and watched too many games in arenas with holes big enough that you could throw a cat outside without aiming. And late at night they have followed snowploughs home along drifted-in highways, hunched over the steering wheel and peering into the blackness. That's what winter is about. You wait for the snow to melt so you can plant your crop. And while you wait, there is hockey. And while you wait for the next game, there is always time for another coffee.

"I don't," says Patricia, "serve the coffee. And I don't keep tabs. Everyone pours their own. If they want a refill they get it themselves. It's fifty cents a cup and twenty-five cents for every refill. They tell me how much they owe when they leave."

Some mornings coffee is free.

"Like when someone has a sixty-fifth birthday, they'll put a sign up front that says 'coffee today is on . . .' Well, whoever is having the birthday puts their name down, and then if you take a coffee you sign your name and I add it up at dinner. Or when someone wins money at bingo or something. There was free coffee for ten days when Ken Tibbatts and his pals won the lottery. I think they won $23,000 each."

There is always something to talk about and sometimes something to do. The first order of business after coffee every day is the mail.

———————— • ————————

The Foxwarren post office is not much bigger than a double garage. It looks as if Canada Post might have bought the prefab structure from the same people who supply Canadian Tire with their tool sheds. It is not the prettiest building in town but, like the cafe, it has much to recommend it. It is on the corner of two dirt streets whose names I never did discover, in what is more or less the centre of town. Donna Hodgson is the postmistress, and she is the sixth person (three men, three women) to hold the job since the post office opened on August 1, 1889.

Albert Laycock, the first postmaster in Foxwarren, held the job for thirty years. William MacGranachan, who followed Laycock in 1919, holds the record for longevity, finally stepping aside for his son, Ronald William Mac-Granachan, in 1956.

"I'll probably be the last postmistress in town," says Donna matter-of-factly. "These days when a postmaster resigns they usually close post offices like these and replace them with Superboxes. I guess that could put pressure on me if I ever won the lottery. I'd have to think twice about what I was doing to the town if I quit. You'd just hate to see it happen. They're always taking things away from small towns. The last thing we lost was the high school. Thank goodness we still have the rink. It's about all we do have."

A brown pick-up truck pulls up to the post office. Donna excuses herself and pulls a handful of mail from one of the 161 rented letter boxes.

"People are supposed to use their keys and get their own mail from the other side of the wall," she says, "but hardly anyone uses their key. They come right into the office and I know why they're here, so I get the mail out and hand it to them. I do everything. I'll make out money orders and even lick the stamps. In a small town you have time to do that sort of thing."

While she is chatting with the woman from the pick-up truck, I wander over to the picture of Queen Elizabeth that is hanging over the post-office boxes. The picture is so large I can see her fingernails. It is the first time I have ever noticed them. The Queen, I write in my notebook, seems to have nice nails.

Donna brings a letter back to an old wooden desk in the corner of the office. She picks up a date stamp that looks like a hammer. The worn wooden handle has been repaired with tape. It looks as if it could be the same one Albert Laycock used in 1889. Every morning Donna has to use a pair of tweezers and a crochet hook to change the date. She hits the letter two times.

"You want to do it twice so you cancel the stamp with the first one and give them a clear reading on the envelope with the second. That way they can see when the letter was mailed. Not everybody does that. But they should."

After everyone has picked up their mail, the parade from the cafe continues across the railway tracks and over to the Leisure Centre. The Leisure Centre, which occupies the old Legion, was putatively built for the town's senior citizens. And at least ten seniors show up every day for dinner. At $2.75 it is a bargain. Though you have to be over sixty-five to enjoy the noon meal, that doesn't stop everyone else in town from dropping by every morning for a game of pool or another cup of coffee. The Leisure Centre acts as a clearing house for the town. If you are driving to Birtle to do some shopping, as likely as not you will drop by the Leisure Centre and let someone know where you are going. It reminds me of a teen club I used to hang around in the summers long ago, except none of the regulars here are teenagers.

The guys from coffee row usually pull into the Leisure

Centre around nine-thirty every morning. When they arrive they go downstairs to the pool table to play a cut-throat variation of snooker called golf. The pockets are numbered, and each player around the table plays a pocket in sequence (this is one round). A missed pocket (or a miscue) counts as a point against the player. The player with the most points at the end of the game has to pay a penny a point to the centre. The only time I see most of these men without their windbreakers or peaked hats on is during the morning golf game.

Those who don't play golf gather around the lunch tables upstairs for more coffee and conversation. A loonie (dropped, on the honour system, into one of the loon piggy banks) buys you three or four coffees and a muffin if you want one.

Talk around the table has the frankness you'd expect in a town where many of the streets are still dirt. On the morning I visit, one young woman is trying to decide whether she should go, this evening, to Birtle for the male stripper or to Russell for the bingo.

"I vote for the male stripper," I say hopefully, wondering if I might be invited along.

"Yeah," she replies wistfully, "but it's big money at Russell. Two thousand dollars for fifty-eight numbers."

Jean Falloon, who is wearing a sweatshirt with "Lottery 6/49" printed across the front, seems to be giving the evening's options careful thought.

"Do you know," she says unexpectedly, "that I was fifty years old before I saw a calf born? Dean would never let me in the barn when a cow was calving. I think he was embarrassed. I helped with other things, but I didn't go out there when there was a calving. I knew he didn't want me there so I didn't go. Can you imagine? I was twenty when we got married. That means I was on that farm for thirty years before it happened."

"What happened?" someone asks.

"Before I saw a calf being born."

"What happened?" they repeat.

"Finally one night one just came. We were out in the barn together and a calf just came and that was that. My first after all those years."

"I was raised on a farm," says Diane, who is also sitting at the table, "and I never saw a cow born, either."

"When I was pregnant," says Jean, "I was always shy. I was always self-conscious about going out. Now, my God, they have those sweatshirts with the big arrows pointing at the baby. Things sure have changed. I think it's a good change. I like this."

———— • ————

The only store in Foxwarren used to be called Hector's Shopping Centre, but when Reg Gadd took it over in 1972, he changed the name. Now it's called Reg's Shopping Centre.

Reg used to farm, but he always had a yen to be in the store business so when the opportunity came up to buy Hector's, he jumped. Reg still owns a half section a little over a mile out of town. His nephew farms it now.

Reg's has the cosy feel you expect of a good country store. There is a reading lamp beside the cash register, a ceiling fan above it, and a spool of string dangling from the ceiling that Reg and his wife, Catherine, use to tie up the flaps on cardboard boxes so they'll hold more. There is a little grey file box full of index cards where charges are recorded. Individual items are noted in blue ink. Totals are added in red.

There is a set of mounted antlers on the wall behind the meat counter.

"The dog dragged them home and I had them fixed up," Reg says. "Someone once said I should get a hunting licence or I might get in trouble."

A handwritten sign near the front door says, "Donations will be accepted here for the Chris Rice Fire Fund." Rice is a farmer from Binscarth who had a fire in his trailer and lost all his possessions. Reg says the donations are coming in "fine."

The store is wide and spacious. The floor is wood and almost a hundred years old.

"It came out of an Indian residential school that was built in 1894," says Reg. "It was moved here from Birtle when the school was torn down in 1936."

The groceries at Reg's are lined up on the left side of the store; the dry goods on the right. Among the rubber boots, work gloves, mitts, toques and towels there is a selection of broadcloth and quilt batting.

"A lot of the women in town like to quilt," says Reg.

Two days a week Reg arrives at his store at 5:45 A.M. to help unload produce that arrives on semi-trailers from Winnipeg. After the delivery he goes home for breakfast and a shave.

"We open at 9:00 A.M. except during seeding time. We open at 8:00 A.M. then. It's not official. It may be 8:30. People know that as long as the car is parked out in front, then we're open. We're here until 6:00 or 6:30 every night. It can be hard," he says, "but I don't strain myself. I do a lot of talking during the day."

Reg will be seventy this year. Both he and Catherine are old enough to qualify for the senior's dinner at the Leisure Centre, and that is where they eat. But neither of them has any intention of retiring. Like Donna at the post office, they worry about what would happen if they quit working.

"I don't like to think about it," says Reg. "I hope someone would take over. A community needs a store, but I just don't know what's going to happen. I do know that as long as we have our health, we'll stay here. I don't have a crystal ball, but I hate to think of the place closing down. Maybe a younger person could take it. They could work longer hours and pay less wages. Business isn't bad. I mean, it's what you'd expect considering the population is getting smaller and the times are hard."

No one in Foxwarren would want to see the store close. But if it did, if it came to that, most people figure they could muddle through. They could shop in Birtle or Binscarth.

What they really worry about is the arena.

———— • ————

The Foxwarren arena illuminates Foxwarren the way the Roman Catholic Church used to illuminate Quebec. Hockey in Foxwarren is a faith, a theology and a creed. In Foxwarren you don't go to a game as much as you give yourself to The Game. You don't *enjoy* hockey. You believe in it. Even the unfaithful find themselves caught up in the arena. They attend games the way many people attend church. They go to the hockey equivalents of the high holidays — playoff games and the weekend tournaments. No matter how you fight it, if you live in Foxwarren you can't escape the arena's gravity.

Slipping through the flapping wooden door into the arena is always surprising because somehow it seems larger in there than the town itself. As if the men who built it, and it was built with volunteer labour — managed to bring more of the prairie into the building than there is outside. On the ice, under the arched wooden roof, they have captured the essence of western Canada. The flatness of the land. The vastness of the sky.

It is fitting that the first time I visit, Tom Scantlebury should be pulling the ice machine around the rink with an old red tractor. Appropriate that here in the middle of the prairie they'd work their ice as well their fields with a tractor. It is a Massey-Ferguson 175, and the two front tires lean in on a wonky angle as if they are about to collapse.

They can't afford a Zamboni here — an "ice pony," as one young boy I know used to call them — but the tractor has the same mesmerizing effect on the ice. Round and round it goes, making the world new again.

Scantlebury is the arena caretaker this year. He moved his family to Foxwarren from Birtle, where he lived all his life. They moved because Tom thinks his eleven-year-old son, Thomas, will find the Foxwarren hockey program more challenging. Birtle, he says, is leaning towards recreational hockey. Last year when he coached in Birtle, Tom took a team to the provincial championships, and they didn't even ask him back.

"They thought I was too competitive," he says with disgust. The ice is finished. It looks like a freshly painted floor. Like a harrowed field waiting for weather.

"They thought I was horsewhipping my kids to do what I wanted. They didn't like me.

"When my boy started playing hockey, I gave the game up. I figured I had my turn, now it's his. In Birtle they're more interested in playing old-timers than letting their kids play. I look at hockey as an attitude-builder. If you want to keep your kids out of hot water, keep them on ice.

"That's why we came here. They get all the ice time they want here. If no one is using the rink, the kids can have it. Lots of people have keys. Or they can come over to my house and ask for a key and throw on a row of lights and play. There was a bunch of them in here last night shooting the puck around till nine-thirty.

"I had a crack at Junior. I don't know if I didn't have the desire or what. Maybe I didn't have the coaching. I wanted to make sure my kid has the right coaching. There are people in this town that know hockey. When I used to play hockey I was known as a bit of a ruffian. Maybe if I had someone who had grabbed me by the scruff of the neck back then I wouldn't have been like that."

Scantlebury tells me he is thinking of buying a house and staying in Foxwarren. He is renting the house he is living in this year. His rent runs him three hundred dollars a month. He has his eye on an empty house two blocks from the rink that he thinks he can buy for two thousand dollars. It needs a coat of paint, he says, but it is beautiful inside. It has all the original wood.

A man pokes his head around the door and shyly asks Tom if he has any broken sticks. Tom tells him that there's a stack in the furnace room but that he should just take the fibreglass ones.

"He uses them for chasing cows," Tom explains. "I got another guy who likes the wood ones. He makes bowls out of them."

―――――•―――――

That night a winter fog settles on the fields around town. It gathers so thick in spots that truck drivers rumbling down the Yellowhead Highway towards Winnipeg have to pull off the road and wait it out. One of them actually checks into the Kent — the only other guest during my entire stay. He has a beer, a pickled egg and two pickled sausages for supper. Then he wanders upstairs to bed.

By morning he has gone, but not the fog. Outside there are only shades of grey. The world looks like a black-and-white photograph. It is hard to tell where the snow in the fields turns to fog and where the fog merges with the clouds. Some time before dawn the vapour in the air begins to crystallize on the trees and telephone lines and fence posts. The combination of the fog and the hoar-frost makes the world old, long-haired and venerable.

―――――•―――――

There is a big game in Foxwarren tonight. It is supper time, and Tom still isn't ready. He has to mop out the dressing-rooms, wash the plexiglass that surrounds the rink and edge the ice. As always on game nights, Tom is not alone in the rink. Ken Tibbatts is in a tiny room downstairs — the "snake pit," they call it — sharpening skates.

"I used to make ice with a little wee bob-sleigh with steel runners and a barrel," he says. "I've put in the ice for years and years. We have some of the best ice around."

Tibbatts is warming up to what is clearly a favourite subject.

"We have excellent ice now. In March you couldn't find better ice anywhere. But in the dead of winter it's not as good. It gets too cold in the arena. Even with the refrigeration plant off it's too cold. The ice gets too hard and it starts to chip.

"You want soft water for great ice. Our problem is that our water is too hard. If we had Binscarth water we would have better ice. We have too much iron and calcium and magnesium for good ice. We built a huge cistern to catch rain water for the curling rink, but it didn't work so good. It leaked into the water table. So we bought a 2,000-gallon tank and used it to haul water for our curling ice. We got it from Merv Gadd's well over in the Snake Creek Valley."

Hockey has been Ken Tibbatts' life. The winter he turned seventeen, he and another boy moved off their farms and "bached" together in town so they'd be closer to the rink. It was the winter of '41–'42, and Foxwarren won the Northwestern Collegiate Hockey Shield. It's still hanging in the front hall of the school. Ken and Murray used to go to the rink every night and stay until it closed. Then they'd go back to their room and do homework. At twelve-thirty, when the "Flyer" came through town on its way from Winnipeg to Edmonton, they would turn in for the night. They cooked on a hot plate and ate a lot of venison — they called it "jumper meat." When they ran out of venison, they made stews and soups out of potatoes. There was only one bed for the two of them. They had to go home to the farm if they wanted a bath.

"I often think about that winter," says Tibbatts. "We weren't the best hockey players in the world, but we were in shape. We hardly had enough players to make a team. Me and Alan Kristinson used to play defence sixty minutes straight. We never left the ice."

Not so long ago Tibbatts had a dream of assembling a

team in Foxwarren that would challenge for the Allan Cup
— the trophy awarded to the best senior amateur team in
Canada. The dream almost materialized. The idea was that
Foxwarren local and NHL pro Ron Low and his friend
Butch Goring would both take a year off from their pro-
fessional hockey careers to play hockey for fun and free.

"We could have done it," says Ken. "It could have come
together." A little groundwork was done, a little bit of
money was collected.

"It's not going to happen now. Ron and Butch are too
old."

Now Ken has other matters to occupy his mind.

"I worry that the rink is going to close. It's getting to be
too much for a town our size to keep up. And it's getting
harder every year. We have hardly no revenue coming in.
And it costs an awful lot to keep going. I made a promise
to myself that I'd keep it open until my grandsons had their
shot. Hockey is important to me. I love the game. Hell, I
don't know how to put this. It's important to the town, too.
If we didn't have the rink I don't think there'd be a town
left. There's hardly anything left, anyway. It used to be a
thriving place, you know. There was a car dealership and a
couple more grocers and two implement dealers. None of
them are left. If the rink closed up that would be it. It's the
heart of the town. If it closed, people would go elsewhere
to play hockey. And if they aren't coming to town to skate,
they aren't going to come to shop, and before long the
town will just blow away."

The rink has already begun to shut down. They used to
keep the ice in until school was out. They'd cover it with
sawdust at the end of the hockey season and then plough
the sawdust off for the summer hockey camp Ron Lowe
and Butch Goring ran. But they can't afford to do that
anymore. In 1990 they stopped putting ice in for curling.
It was getting too expensive. Now the curling rink is dark
and hard to see through the great length of glass on your
left as you come into the arena.

Ken Tibbatts isn't the only person who is worried about the arena. The whole town is worried.

Garth Graham is a dairy farmer.

"Our fathers and grandfathers built it with their bare hands, and I'm so darned proud of it. But I'm scared, too. We might not be able to keep it going. It's getting so expensive. Hydro is a son of a bitch. It's closed, it would be terrible. It might be the straw that broke the town's back. I don't know what we'd do. We all grew up here and had such a great time here. It would be horrible to walk away. You see your kids on the ice and you think of yourself when you were young.

"It's not like we let it go. We put the artificial ice in and the new roof up. All of that was paid for by donations and volunteer labour. The only reason we can keep it going at all is because everyone chips in."

The arched wooden roof is tied together by a thousand cross-hatched wooden beams. It makes the arena look more like a barn built with a wooden Meccano set than anything else. At the far end there is a metal extension added twenty years ago to lengthen the ice surface by twenty feet. It also serves as a stark reminder of what a thing of beauty wood is. There are five rows of rough wooden benches on either side of the ice. The benches go up to where the roof starts to curve. The bottom two rows are painted red, the top three blue. Many people, however, choose to watch games from the stacking chairs by the kitchen. The view through the rink-wide glass window behind the Visitors net may not be as good, but it's a lot warmer in the "waiting room" than in the rink. In January and February it is so cold inside the arena that they leave the plant off.

It costs four dollars to go to a Falcons game. On a good night maybe three or four hundred fans show up — about double the number of people who live in town. Over the winter the responsibility for running the kitchen is shared — a week at a time — among families from town. You can get a coffee or a hamburger at all the games and most of the practices.

There is always some scheme under way to keep the rink solvent. There is a big smorg (smorgasbord) in the fall which draws over four hundred people, an annual car rally, a social, a stock show and a barbecue in the summer. And bingo. Someone is always selling tickets for something. But it is still close to the bone.

Tibbatts gets up and stretches.

"I should take you out to meet Andy Low," he says. "He's the best coach the town has ever had."

———— • ————

In a town where hockey is holy, eighty-year-old Andy Low is a full-fledged archangel, though, like all deities, he is better viewed from a distance, better seen through the gauze of sanctity. The day we come for lunch it takes him five minutes to shuffle his walker out to the kitchen from his main-floor bedroom. He sinks thankfully into the nearest chair, his tongue darting in and out of his mouth like a lizard's.

Like Foxwarren itself, Andy's future is uncertain. He is worn out, but he is still alive — as he says, "running the clock out." Like many old men, Andy has become the embodiment of a better era — living proof that the stories everyone has heard actually happened. With his old age he blesses everyone else with youth.

He doesn't go out anymore, and not many people come to the farm where he lives with his brother. Miracles, though, are still ascribed to him.

The night in 1948 when he chartered a train and sold tickets and the entire town went to Neepawa for the championship game. They dubbed it the Whisky Special. It started at the end of the line in Inglis, and people who had never been in a hockey rink in their lives swung aboard at level crossings and even in the middle of the prairie, stomping and shivering in the darkness as they waited in their fields to be picked up. Low wouldn't let his players on the train. He wanted them sober at game time, so they had to go by car. When the train pulled into Neepawa, you never saw a rink fill up so fast in your life. Old Pratt the lawyer spent the whole night trying to keep people out of jail.

The night Flynn got in the fight. They were rolling around on the ice and after a while Flynn got the guy's finger in his mouth and was biting down hard — Jesus, you could hear the guy screaming all over the rink. Flynn was scared to let go. He thought the guy would kill him.

The time Andy and Ken drove right across Manitoba to Kenora, Ontario — over five hours one way — to pick up the hockey player who had moved east to work at the pulp mill. They went to get him so he could play in a weekend game and had him back in time for work on Monday morning, and that's a long drive, boy, especially in the middle of a snow storm.

And the night they followed the snowplough into Swan River, and they didn't get there until 11:30 at night. There was no changing room in the arena, so they strung up a curtain and the guys changed behind the curtain. They had the whole team crammed into one car that night. Nine guys plus their equipment in a 1935 Chevy. God knows.

But the age of miracles has passed. The years since Andy Low and his boys helled around have melted away. The town is dying and everyone knows it. One day the houses will be gone and the wind will blow over the grass and when the trains blow their whistles at the crossing there won't be anyone left to hear it.

———— • ————

My stay at the Kent Hotel soon settles into a comfortable rhythm. Though there are nine rooms upstairs around the wide L-shaped hall, I am the only guest. There isn't room for many more. Elsie, the owner, occupies five of the nine rooms. Room One is where she keeps her linen and towels. Room Two is her closet where she dresses and applies her makeup every morning. Room Three serves as her attic. She stores her Christmas decorations there. She has an ironing board set up in Room Four. And keeps a jigsaw puzzle on the bed.

"I got it for Christmas a year ago," she says. "It is a picture of a lake. Once in a while I kneel down by the bed and work on it."

Elsie sleeps in Room Nine.

She has put me in Number Six — farthest from the stairs — at the end of the hall. At night, to turn off the hall light, I tug the string that hangs from the ceiling half-way along from the bathroom. I get so I can do it without slowing as I swing down the hall.

Elsie has accepted my arrival as she might accept the visit of some distant relative. I come and go as I please — not quite part of the family, but not entirely a stranger, either.

I make my own bed. I leave my door ajar at night. When I go out in the morning I don't lock the door behind me. I have no choice. Elsie hasn't given me a key.

"I opened it yesterday," she said, the day I arrived.

Apparently, at the Kent, it is the vacant rooms that are locked. The occupied ones — or mine, at least — stay open.

I wake before Elsie every morning and slip down the stairs and across the parking lot to the cafe for breakfast. I learn how to let myself out the front door without jarring the bell that she has hanging there, as if she was running a country hardware rather than a hotel. Elsie, having stayed up to close the bar, sleeps until past nine.

While I don't exactly have the run of the place, before long Elsie is granting me special privileges.

One afternoon, stopping in at the bar, I ask for a glass of tomato juice.

"It's expensive like that," says Elsie. "By the glass."

She opens a new bottle and pours me a glass of juice. She replaces the bottle in the corner of the cooler.

"That's your bottle," she says.

From then on, whenever I am thirsty, I walk behind the bar, open the cooler and fill a glass from my bottle. When I check out Elsie charges me $1.65 for the juice.

"You only used the one bottle," she says.

Elsie spends most of her days in the bar — chatting, serving drinks and smoking. She sits at a corner table that gives her a view of both the television and the front door. Her seat is padded with a square of carpet remnant.

She and her husband bought the Kent in 1964. It was never a wild success, but then, it was never meant to be. It fed them, they paid off the mortgage and managed to send their six children to college or university. Elsie used to cook dinners and still will if anyone asks — it is part of her licensing requirements — but no one asks. When her husband died in 1975 she carried on alone — running what has essentially become a bar.

Since Elsie added the pool table, there is room for thirty-one chairs in the Fox's Den. As well as drinks, she sells chips, pickled sausages, pickled eggs, beef jerky, and Hot Rods. She keeps pizzas and a submarine sandwich called a Chuckwagon in a freezer in the back and warms them up in a microwave. Twice I watch her cut off customers — her neighbours — and once call a local farmer to accounts when he gets rowdy. I also watch him apologize the next day. It doesn't surprise me when she tells me she has never let a drunk take a pack of cigarettes upstairs to bed. I can imagine both the confrontation and the outcome.

Elsie takes a lit match and singes the ends of her filter tips before she puts each cigarette in her mouth.

"A bus driver taught me that. I do it so I don't inhale fibres from the filter. It makes sense to me. It makes better sense that I quit. I dragged out some cassette tapes the other day and I am going to give it a God-damned good shot. I quit once for four months and I thought I had it made. But you're in the bar all the time. One day I took a puff. I thought I could take just one puff. But you can't."

———— • ————

Everyone at the cafe is talking about Ben Low's oil change this morning. Ben took his truck in to the Esso yesterday and Bill Crawford drained the oil, replaced the filter and then sent Ben off without adding new oil. Ben only got about a mile down the road before his oil light came on. Bill took the tow truck out and added the oil on the side of the road. It looks like Ben didn't burn out the motor. This morning, sipping coffee and twisting in their seats so they can peer at the gas pumps, everyone has an opinion about what Bill should do to make up for his mistake. Bill's problem is that he isn't a local boy and he has only been running the station since the fall, and everyone has been watching to see what kind of job he'll do. Most say he isn't as careful as Donny Hudson used to be, and this morning there are some who believe he'll never make it.

"Are you going to take *your* car there?"

By lunch the joke is if you do take your car to Crawford's for an oil change, what you do when he is finished is back out of the bay, roll your car to the pump and ask him to fill your tank and check the oil.

———————•—————————

The Foxwarren School is an impressive two storeys of brick and mortar just up the street from the arena. There are sixty-one children enrolled there. It is small enough that the phone numbers of each student, plus the teachers, support staff and the odd emergency number have been typed onto a single sheet of paper and posted by the school's only telephone. School begins in kindergarten and continues through grade eight. After grade eight, students are bused to Birtle. There are, on staff, two full-time teachers, two half-time teachers and one teacher who has a seventy-percent load. Students are summoned to class by a wood-handled bell that is kept on a shelf by the front door. There is a hand-written schedule pinned to the wall beside it.

Phil DeCorby teaches in all the grades between three and eight. He is also the principal and one of the two full-time teachers.

"We used to have a bell on top of the school that you pulled with a long rope," says DeCorby. "It must have weighed a half a ton. It was probably up there ever since the school was built. That was 1917. The bell tower rotted out and last summer we thought it best to bring it down. I have been here twenty-two years and I hated to see it go. It felt like we were tearing the school down the day we took it off.

"They wanted to put in a buzzer but we fought that. So now we use the hand bell. It has its advantages. You can look at the clock and if your lesson's not over you can finish off before you go into the corridor to ring it."

DeCorby and I are talking in the staff lunchroom.

"I am never in my office," he says. "We just use it to store records."

Most of the grades are doubled up. Some of them are tripled.

"That's not easy at first," says DeCorby. "You have to learn how to keep one group busy while you're teaching the others. You have to hand out worksheets to one group and then shift to another group and teach them a lesson. It's kind of like being one of those plate spinners they used to have on Ed Sullivan. But I've always felt it doesn't hurt a kid to hear a lesson a second time. Maybe we're not covering some of the details as well as we could, but I have always believed we're turning out independent learners."

Outside, a train whistle splits the winter afternoon. We both look up as a freight bisects the tall school window. The sky is winter blue. The snow is white. Wheat rolling east. New cars rattling west. The story of Canada in the window every day.

The clatter of the train would be hard to talk over, so we watch it pass without speaking. How wonderful, I think. A prairie school where there must be silence every time a train goes by.

At the turn of the century and for thirty years after that, the tracks on these prairies were haunted by the most romantic train in Canadian history — the silk train. Silk that arrived in Vancouver by boat had to be shipped to the Lakehead. Because the cargo was so valuable, and because it deteriorated almost as erratically as the silk market fluctuated, matters of both speed and safety tormented the men who ran these trains. To prevent moisture damage, the silk was wrapped in special paper before it was sealed into box cars. The box cars were made airtight with carefully varnished wood panelling. The trains, sometimes as long as fifteen cars, were dispatched from Vancouver with armed guards and no other passengers. They rocked across the country to Fort William, fifteen hours faster than any other run. They were given priority over all other trains on the tracks. Once a train carrying Prince Albert (later George VI) was shunted onto a siding to wait while a silk train burned past.

The freight that is passing the school is gone, the clatter fading under the high sky. I wonder what it must have been like when the trains were steam. Standing on the prairie, could you see them before you heard them? And after they passed, how long would they linger in the sky?

The school is silent. I can hear a music class practising for the Marquette Fine Arts Festival. They are singing "Land of the Silver Birch."

Judie Bewer teaches language, art, health, French, and family life.

"When I came here I couldn't believe they kept a school open for seventy or eighty kids. I used to teach in a school that had one hundred children in kindergarten. Here I have six.

"I love the small school concept. I've done a lot of thinking and reading about it. I think this is the best way to get a fully rounded education — to be a kid in a small school. I believe in all the techniques we use here: peer coaching, cross grades, individualized programs, close contact between the students and the teachers. The kids become more independent learners.

"I *like* what my students do. I *love* the fact that my students go to another school and go right to the top of the class. If you only have six kids in a class, you can do a lot of things. You can make a difference. You can connect with your students. You can move the bright ones faster than they'd normally go.

"The thing about a school this size is that everyone is important. Kids don't slip through the cracks. There is no one on the bench during a volleyball game. We have a Christmas pageant and everyone sings, acts, dances and speaks on stage. If a kid isn't here, the kid is missed. You don't get that in a big school."

Marlene Low teaches half-time. When she graduated from university in 1970 she wanted to live in a large city. But she married Jack in 1974 and moved to Foxwarren, instead. Like Judie Bewer, Marlene is committed to the small rural school.

"Everyone has to participate to get something going here. Kids don't get lost in the crowd. They get lots of individual attention and they get a good education. Peer pressure is not as great as it is in the cities. For better or for worse, the kids are protected here. One thing city kids have over us is that they're a lot more street-wise. I know some kids here just can't cope in the big cities. They have been so protected, all they can do is stay on the farm."

As we walk by the dark wood trim that lines the high-ceilinged halls, principal Phil DeCorby says that, like every farmer and business person in town, he is concerned about the future of his enterprise.

"When I came in the fall of 1968, there were 135 kids here. Now there are 61. A lot of the farms have consolidated and a lot of families have left the area. So far the trend in the province is to keep the small schools going. But if the division office changes, it could be the end of the rope. If they wanted to close us down there's lots of room for these kids in the school at Birtle."

As we pass the locked front door, he says he is more concerned about the building itself than any shift in government policy.

"The mortar is letting go and the outer layer of bricks is leaning out. The structure is sound. There are actually three layers of bricks, but it's a major repair job. It might cost $140,000. And they might not want to do that."

So far DeCorby has dealt with the loose bricks by erecting a fence around his school. The fence prevents anyone from getting close to the outside walls. The only way into the school is through a temporary wooden tunnel that leads to the side door.

"Mr DeCorby?" Two grade-seven girls pop out of a classroom. "We are doing the experiment and we can't figure out how to do the lightbulb thing."

DeCorby excuses himself.

"We eat lunch at noon every day," he says to me as he turns to go. "We have a microwave and a fridge. You're welcome to join us any time you'd like. Just drop by."

It takes less than three minutes to walk through the parking lot and across the field, from the side door of the school to the side door of the arena. And so, one lunch time, I find Kris Finch — thirteen years old, grade seven — alone on the ice. Stick, puck, gloves and skates, twisting, digging, twirling, alone in his imagination like a figure skater. He has only turned one bank of lights on — electricity is expensive — so the arena is even darker, older, colder, more mysterious than usual. I slip into the stands and watch unseen. He is rushing the net now, flicking the puck high, puffing the webbing like smoke. There should, I think, be smoke on the ice. The smoke should come up to his knees.

Amber Beasley is twelve years old and freckled. On the
edge of becoming a young woman, but still with a few summers of girlhood left. She is wearing a pink sweater, black
cords and black ankle boots. Her smile is mischievous and
full of life.

"We live right on the edge of the valley. So on a hot day
I can follow the cow path down to the river. My favourite
spot is where the cows water. There are lots of gopher holes
there. And lots of rocks on one side. I take my bathing suit
with me and change down by the water. There is no one
there but the cows. There is a fence across the water where
the river is deep and I can swim under it. It is deeper under
there because there's a beaver dam. Once or twice I've
gone skinny-dipping. Sometimes I see a beaver or a
muskrat. But no one else.

"On one side there are willows. Sometimes I catch frogs.
You have to be like a cat. You have to jump first. If I get one
I bang its head against a rock and dissect it and use its legs
for fish bait. You get jackfish, mostly. I bring them home.
Other times I go with my parents and we take a frypan and
cook them by the stream. Sometimes my sister and I take
our raft down there. I guess it is my favourite spot."

Colin Stanchuk is thirteen. A serious boy.

"I live on the crest of the valley near a gravel pit. We fool
around down there on our bikes. We build jumps and try
to make it to the top and stuff. Sometimes we go down by
the river, to the pasture where the cows are. Or we have
races on the dirt roads along the valley. I can go just about
anywhere I want on my bike, though I do have limits. I am
not allowed on the highway. Or past the Angusville Road
or the Copping's Road or the Davidson's place.

"There are only about five of us in each grade at school.
The kids in my class are like my brothers and sisters. But I
know everybody, even the kids in kindergarten. Some of
the kids in kindergarten are my friends.

"In the fall I help my dad with the haying. Last year I

drove the tractor. I've been driving the tractor since I was nine. It feels good to drive it during harvest. It feels like you're free. There is no one around. You're not cooped up. Just the fresh air. I guess I feel important when I can help like that. More grown up.

"One day, when I was ten, we were down the road at my uncle's farm, which is about a mile from our place, and I told my dad I wanted to go home. Usually he drives me himself but this time he said, 'Get in the truck.' Then he said I could drive myself home. At first I thought he was joking, but he threw me into the cab and started to show me the gears and the clutch. He said, 'Don't go too fast,' and 'If you meet a car go to the side of the road.' He said if I got brave I could put it in second gear. I didn't want to meet anyone because I didn't know what they would think. I was afraid I wouldn't be able to pull over far enough so they could get by.

"When I got home my mom heard the truck and thought my dad was home. Then she looked out the window and, boy, was she surprised.

"It was sort of scary the first time but now I can ask and he'll let me have the truck most any time. He trusts me. He knows I won't go out to the highway. Sometimes I drive the truck down the valley and shoot birds. Magpies and crows."

Lunch is over.

Kris Finch is in the dressing-room below the stands wiping his skates.

"Yes," he says earnestly, "I'd like to be a hockey player when I grow up. That's my dream. I sort of want to grow up to be another Pat Falloon. He's a good guy. Just such a . . . I don't know how to say it. He's put Foxwarren on the map. He has got our name on TV. Heck. It makes us all proud to see a guy make it bar none. I'd like to give as much to the community as he did. I don't know whether I have the ability. Some do, some don't.

"For now I just want to put as much into my team as I can. I want to be a leader.

"In the fall I came and watched Ken put in the ice. Then I helped lay the lines and circles down.

"This is a good town to grow up in. In the summer we go bike riding. There are all these little nooks and spots that are nice to visit. Sometimes we go up into the hills and watch the deer jumping. Me and Chris Low were biking down in the Snake Creek Valley one day. We made a sort of bridge over the creek with a piece of wood and then we went up the hill. It was sunny and hot and Chris said it would be neat if a buck jumped out and just as he said it a deer jumped out of the bush about fifty yards away — close enough to see it in detail. We kind of stood there in awe with grins on our faces.

"There is another valley we go to. It's so green down there and you see rabbits all the time with little ones and birds. There's birds all over."

Back at school Judie Bewer is getting ready for her afternoon class. She watches Kris walking back across the fields from the rink.

"Hockey colours everything that happens in this town. It is the major contributor to a kid's self-esteem, and to the family's esteem.

"I had a girl in one of my classes. She came from a family of three girls. Her dream in life was to have a brother so she could have a hockey party. If there's a tournament, then the whole family goes out of town to the tournament.

"There's an old proverb. Do you know it? It is almost if you play hockey well then you are good-looking and can sing well, too. And that's scary for kids who don't quite measure up. It worries me. I see it in the classroom. After a tournament, if they play well they work better. If they don't get to play, or they don't play well, their self-esteem is rock-bottom.

"I have seen men do cruel things to kids because they

have to choose between winning or playing all their kids. Kids in this town start getting benched at seven."

Judie has four boys, and she and her husband pulled them out of the local hockey program ten years ago.

"It took us about a half of one winter to make the decision. One weekend my husband sat in the Russell arena for ten hours. It was a wonderful winter day and on the way home one of the boys cried for two or three hours because his team didn't win the tournament. And my husband came home and said, 'This is not fun. We are not going to do this anymore.' We told the kids if they quit we would take them skiing to Lake Louise. I think one of the kids is still bitter about that."

———————•·•———————

One afternoon, walking west of town, I am attracted by a stand of trees. As I get closer I notice the fence by the road. The wrought-iron on the gate reads

Foxwarren Cemetery
1870–1970
These gates erected in honour of our pioneers

I climb over the fence and walk between the stones, reading the inscriptions. There have been no visitors since the last snowfall. I go back twice to the Ryan family plot — four graves surrounded by four tall pines in the centre of the cemetery. There is no snow under the trees — the pine needles on the ground remind me of campsites on the Canadian shield — but something about the stones keeps drawing me back. I crouch down and run my hand against the oldest one.

Frank C. Ryan, Grandfather 1875–1939
Ellen Ryan, Grandmother 1876–1972
Laurence R. Ryan, Father 1899–1978
Dina J. Ryan, Mother 1898–1975

Suddenly it is as clear as day. If I had come just twenty years earlier, I could have talked to people like these. Even fifteen years ago history was still alive. Even ten years ago I could have met men and women who saw the Plains buffalo, who might have heard of Riel from their parents, who might have seen him when they were children. But I am too late. What was I so busy doing?

Months later, at my desk in Toronto, I will run across Frank C. Ryan again in the Foxwarren history book. I will learn that he worked for the Pinkertons police force at the turn of the century. He worked undercover for the forerunner of the FBI in the great gangster city of Chicago, posing as a mail clerk. When his cover was blown, he fled to Manitoba with his family on the CNR "Turkey Trail" and took his wife by buggy over five miles of rough prairie — a ride she never forgot — to the ranch they would settle. In 1918 and 1919 he grew more registered wheat and oats than any other farmer in the province. He died, in seeding time, of a blood clot — a complication of a broken leg.

Friday night. Seven o'clock. The bar at the Kent Hotel. Ron Falloon is here, and a few others. Maybe twelve people in all. The television is on.

The telephone rings. Elsie picks it up and peers out the window into the dwindling light.

"What's happening, Elsie?"

"The cops," she announces to everyone. "The bastards are parked at the back door."

Like passengers on a cruise ship who have been told there are dolphins on the starboard side, everyone in the bar heads for a window.

Ron Falloon sighs and orders another rye and Coke. He can't leave now. No one can. No one is going to walk out of the bar and climb into his car in front of the cops. Everyone settles down to wait them out.

"There is more wisdom in the bottom half of a bottle of whisky than the top, anyway," says Ron.

Half an hour later the cops pull out of the parking lot. Everyone watches carefully as the red tail-lights crest the hill and turn the corner towards Birtle. But no one leaves.

"They were moving too slow," says someone, returning to his seat sceptically.

———— • ————

Dinner at Isabel and Bill Johnston's. I met them in the bar at the hotel one night. They phoned a few days later and invited me for a meal.

After we finish eating, Lou Deeley from the grain elevator arrives. He has a Foxwarren bumper sticker and a grain elevator hat he wants to give me. Ron Falloon, who has also been at dinner, is concerned that I roll the peak of my new hat before I put it on.

"We wouldn't want you to be a flat peak, Stu."

I look around the room and, sure enough, the peak of each man's cap has a pleasing roll so it is higher in the centre than on the two ends.

"Does that serve a purpose? Or does it just look better?" I ask.

"We think it does," says Ron.

Later, in the hotel bar, I notice Ron quietly pick my hat off the table and work the peak for a few minutes. Apparently I haven't achieved a satisfactory roll yet. When he sees me watching him, he grins, but he doesn't stop working.

———— • ————

The Falcons are playing at home tonight against Roblin. It is the third game in a best-of-five semi-final series leading towards the league championship.

Sometimes hockey can be like poetry. When the passes click one, two, three, and a winger bursts from the side of the rink with nothing between him and the goal, the game is stripped to its essence — a man who wants to put the puck in the net and a man who wants to stop him. You wonder how a game that moves so fast can suddenly freeze like that — the winger and the goalie moving together across the front of the net as if they are dancing a ballet. Sometimes it *is* a ballet.

Somewhere over the years I have lost touch with the dance. I don't even know how many teams there are in the National Hockey League anymore. This is why I have come to Foxwarren. I want to find hockey again.

But what am I looking for? Do I simply want to travel through time — to my childhood, perhaps? Do I want to share with my children the sense of simplicity I felt when the world spun on Saturday nights, when the Montreal Canadiens took the ice and that soft maritime chant filled our den — "Good evening, ladies and gentlemen and hockey fans from coast to coast. This is Danny Gallivan at the Forum in Montreal . . ."

Hockey used to matter to me. In my memory the morning paper was more important then — more compelling when hockey news was all the news I wanted.

In those days we marked our lives with winter. Learning first to stumble around the rink on cumbersome double-bladed devices called cheesecutters or bob-skates. Little children with our arms stretched wide. The letter T come to life. ("You're a tree. Walk like a tree.") Rinks of fallen kids flipping on the ice in their dark snowsuits like baby seals. Graduating to our first grown-up skates when we reached kindergarten.

We played hockey before we could tie our own skates. When I was nine my mother fastened my skates at home, and I walked six blocks along the sanded sidewalks to the local rink.

Once we learned how to move on the ice, we had to

confront the mystery of stopping. To skate full speed towards the gate and then to . . . stop. To thrust your hips sideways so your skates bit and the ice shaved up around your feet in a shower of snow.

The first time you lifted the puck off the ice was a holy moment. The black disc tumbling in the air. A slap-shot soaring above the ice. The sound of the puck on the boards. The convergence of stick and puck — of wood and rubber.

But my search goes beyond memory, to a feeling that if I can understand hockey again, I can maybe understand my country. For surely hockey is a key to this land — the perfect Canadian game played on the perfect Canadian medium in the perfect Canadian season.

It *was* more than a game. It was a national preoccupation. The dramatic tension that was set ticking every time the anglo Leafs from Toronto faced off against Les Canadiens from Montreal was once a psychodrama that allowed us all to act out our deepest feelings about our nation.

The Rocket Richard riots outside the Montreal Forum in the spring of 1955 were the most significant sports riots in our history. Many would say they had as much to do with politics as they did with sport.

When Howie Morenz died in a Montreal hospital in 1937, he lay in state at centre ice in the Montreal Forum. This veneration, followed by his funeral, also held in the Forum and attended by over ten thousand fans, confirmed what we knew all along. It may have been our history, but it was our religion, too.

It is how we learned about each other. How else would a farmer in Foxwarren have known how to say, "Maurice" or "Richard" with such unselfconscious *élan?* It never occurred to anyone that they were speaking another language. They weren't speaking French. They were speaking hockey.

When Princess Elizabeth came to Canada in October, 1951, she was taken to Maple Leaf Gardens to see a game.

It was the first game of the season, and before it began, the future queen walked out to centre ice to drop a ceremonial puck. Toronto was playing Chicago. Chicago won 3-1.

It never occurred to anyone that Elizabeth might have preferred to do something else that night. We watched her as carefully as we watched the game. It was as if we were introducing our best girl to our mother.

Maybe after everything, we loved hockey because we were good at it. We were the best in the world. Beyond the faith, the myths, the legends, beyond the thrills, the smells, the lights, the heroes, it was simply something we did well.

And now Toronto only plays Montreal three times during the regular season. Our game is full of American teams and European players. We have hired mercenaries and proxies to fight our battles.

Why did we let go?

Does the answer have to do with a study by a Dallas pollster which ranked NHL hockey fortieth in terms of overall popularity in the United States — behind tractor pulls, body building, billiards and high school football, and just ahead of snowmobile racing. When the pollsters asked Americans to identify the sport they most hated or disliked, thirty percent of those polled identified hockey.

Have we given up on the game because we no longer see it through our own eyes? Is everything we feel filtered and mirrored by American television? Could it be as simple and insidious as that?

I have come to Foxwarren not expecting to answer my questions, but maybe hoping to find the game again. Thinking that if I can't find it under this wooden roof, under these home-made beams, among these farmers who care for it still, where will I find it?

The light is bad, the dressing-rooms are crowded and dirty, the arena has holes in it and the crowd is chilly, but the ice is hard and cold and, above all, cared for.

This is hockey pure and simple. No hype, no hoop-la.

Three or four hundred fans have, like me, paid four dollars to watch tonight's game.

I wanted passion. So here it is.

I buy a hamburger at the canteen. It comes wrapped in silver paper and is burned almost to a crisp. I have to throw most of it out.

When the teams take the ice I have my second disappointment. The players from Roblin are wearing the green, gold and white of the Minnesota North Stars of the National Hockey League. They even call themselves the North Stars — the Roblin North Stars.

Bev Wotton is here, though her son Scott lives in Dauphin, almost two hundred kilometres away, where he plays hockey for the Dauphin Kings (Tier Two Junior A). Her other boy, Mark, lives five hours away in Saskatoon ("Closer than most"), where he plays for the Saskatoon Blades (WHL).

Scott and Mark are both teenagers. And, like other young men from town, they have forsaken town hockey to enter the seminary of the junior leagues. They live in buses and board with strangers and play in places like Brandon, Swift Current, Moose Jaw, Medicine Hat, Neepawa and Winkler. Once young men had to go to war to have their names inked onto the town's Honour Roll. Today this honour is bestowed by professional hockey — the NHL — which, for one of the Wotton boys at least, is only a step away.

"I cried when they left," says Bev. "It was really an empty feeling. I knew they were going away to lead their lives, but at the same time I knew that our years as a family were over. You worry. You worry if you taught them enough while they were at home. And whether they can look after themselves if they get into a scrape.

"At first when they left I used to fill the pot with potatoes and there was no one there to eat them. We had to eat warmed-up potatoes every second night. Then when they'd come to visit I was used to cooking a small amount and there wouldn't be enough to go around.

"It was strange. In the mornings I didn't have to get up an hour ahead of time because there was only the two girls left. And all of a sudden two nights a week we could sit and do nothing. At first we couldn't fill the time. We couldn't seem to settle down.

"For the first month or so my husband didn't let anything show. But I know he missed having the boys around to talk hockey or farming. He took to going out to the shed. He made picture frames and things. He framed all their mementoes. The pucks they scored their first goal with. Their team pictures. Things like that.

"One boy might make it. There are agents interested already. But he can't be drafted until next year. He's still too young."

And now the game is under way. My notes begin with a careful cataloguing of the Foxwarren team:

Blair Lee farms with his dad. He used to play Junior with the Brandon Wheat Kings.

Allan Tremblay is a Mountie in Rossburn. Sometimes, when he pulls swing shifts, he can't make the games.

Danny Tremblay also misses games sometimes. Danny works in a Saskatchewan potash mine.

Robbie Ewbank has three kids and works at the department of highways. Once he played with the Melville Millionaires.

But my notes, which begin in such detail, trail off soon after the action begins. I don't even remember who wins.

There is a high stick. And then another. High elbows in the corner. And a fight. And then another. I am close enough to the ice to see it too clearly. This is not why I have come.

I find myself thinking about Andy Low. Is this the way it always was? Somehow the game seemed purer when I was young. In my memory even the fights were . . . Were what?

Honourable? Just? Dignified? Who has changed? Me, or the game? I can't ask Andy Low. He isn't here tonight. Even though several people offered to bring him, he won't come to games anymore.

The next night I drive to Russell to watch the thirteen-year-olds play. This is more like it, I think, as I watch the player and the puck both heading towards the goal, the puck and the crowd rising as one, the puck rising towards the net, cheers rising towards the ceiling.

And then, just as I begin to enjoy myself, Kris Finch — the good-looking boy who wants to be Wayne Gretzky, the boy I wanted to be — circles at centre ice, head up as the play drifts in the opposite direction, and catches the opposition centre looking down, dropping him cold with a high elbow. They have to use smelling salts before they can help him to the bench.

I came looking for the heart of Canada. Is this what we have become? Chippy? Aggressive? Even when we play? Dressing up like Americans. Naming ourselves after American professional teams.

There is no disillusionment more complete than the disillusion that comes with lost love. Once I was enchanted by hockey. Maybe you don't see things clearly when you are under a spell.

On Sunday evening I am invited to Ron Falloon's house to watch his son Pat on TV. The Spokane game is being carried on the Sports Network — one of the few games of the season. About twenty people are sprinkled around the living-room — sipping beer, following Pat's every move and making bets on whether he'll be interviewed in between periods. At the end of the second period the phone rings. It's for me. It's Elsie from the hotel. She is phoning to tell me she is going out and wants to know what time she should be back to let me in. Several hours later I suddenly realize I didn't tell Elsie (or anyone else) where I was going to be.

———— • ————

On Sunday night, as usual, there is a smorg at Pat's Cafe:

Breaded pork chops
Sweet and sour chicken wings
Baked potatoes
Casserole
Vegetables
Sliced tomatoes
Jellied salads
Tossed salad
Raw vegetables
Buns and butter
Tea or coffee
Dessert
Adults: $5.95
Children under ten: $3.00
Pre-schoolers: free

Instead of going to the smorg I get in my car and drive thirty minutes to Russell. The sign on the local motel says POOL/SAUNA. I continue into town and buy a polyester bathing suit at the local clothing store. When I return to the motel I walk past the front desk as if I were a registered guest.

I find the pool without too much difficulty and lift a motel towel from a pile that belongs to a family playing in the water. I change into my new bathing suit in the men's washroom and collapse in the sauna.

Two hours later I order a steak in the motel dining-room and drink a half bottle of wine. After dinner I go to the Russell movie theatre, not even looking to see what is playing when I buy my ticket. It turns out to be an Arnold

Schwarzenegger movie — *Kindergarten Cop* — and, all things considered, a pleasant surprise.

On the way home I pick up a Wisconsin radio station on the car radio. It is a phone-in show. A state politician, Representative Roberts, is touting a bill before the local assembly. He wants to make it mandatory to refer to bowling "alleys" as bowling "centres."

———————— • ————————

Cindy and Neil Falloon attracted a lot of attention in Foxwarren when they began to remodel their house.

"It was," says Cindy, "a big deal. People would drive by during the day to see what was happening. Sometimes they would park their cars and come in and have a look."

Cindy and Neil decided they were going to live in Foxwarren when they got married. Cindy had already tried Winnipeg and she had only lasted three months.

"I was working as a secretary. I rode the bus with the same people every morning. One morning I turned to the lady I rode with every day and said, 'Hi. How are you?' and she looked at me like I had propositioned her."

Cindy was brought up in Binscarth and had always thought Foxwarren kids were decent.

"They seemed to turn out nice."

Cindy wanted her kids to turn out nice, too. So she and Neil bought their house in the centre of town.

"It was 1984 and I think it cost us $6,500. It's just a three-bedroom bungalow, but it's on three lots, and not too long after, we bought a fourth lot and put a pool in. I think it cost us $200 for the extra lot.

"Neil works as a mechanic in Russell and I work at the GM dealership in Birtle so between us we do all right. When we bought the house we were making maybe $45,000 a year. We could do anything we wanted with that kind of money. We went to Hawaii for our honeymoon. We went to Jamaica for a holiday. We have two new vehicles.

And we paid cash for everything. Our friends who live in the city spend their whole lives paying off their houses. We will be debt-free by the time we're thirty."

Cindy and Neil gutted the bungalow and put in new windows ("they cost half the renovation"), a hardwood floor, new kitchen cabinets, new Gyproc walls, a hot tub in the living-room, a new TV, a new stereo, plants and pictures of the family on the walls. It is the sort of renovation you see a lot in larger cities, but not the sort of thing people are used to seeing in Foxwarren.

We are sitting in the kitchen, Cindy and I. She is fixing a pot of coffee. In the bedroom around the corner Neil is trying to coax his two-year-old son to sleep.

"He's not usually like this," says Cindy. Kevin is throwing a temper tantrum.

"When Kevin was born we got a swing set and a sandbox and put up a fence around the backyard. We figured we needed the fence because we shouldn't let him run out on the street. We've never closed him in there yet. You just don't have to. It's not as if there's any traffic. It's sort of silly, really. We looked everywhere for that fence. We wanted a certain kind of fence. We painted it brown so it would match the trim of the house.

"We know that if we ever had to sell the house, we'd never get our money back. But we have no intention of moving. We like it here. Oh, sometimes I go through phases of wanting to leave. My best friend moved to Edmonton. And she told me all the things they were doing there. And here I am in Foxwarren and the highlight of my life is watching my husband play hockey. I mean, if Neil didn't play hockey there'd be nothing to do. We go to all the games. And, of course, you have to join every committee in town because if you didn't join, there'd be no committee."

Neil emerges from the bedroom shaking his head. He opens a beer and joins us at the kitchen table. I recognize him from the Falcons game. He wore number 15. He had an "A" on his jersey. The Falcons don't have a captain, but they do have three assistant captains.

"It's a good town to bring up kids," he says. "We've had kids visit from the city and they're just so different from the kids around here.

"We had a group billeted with us for a hockey camp one spring. We told them to lay their equipment out on the lawn to dry. Well, they thought they shouldn't because someone would steal it. I said, 'Who's going to steal it? The sixty-year-old man who lives on that side of us, or the ten-year girl who lives over there?'

"They thought we were pheasants. That's what they said, 'pheasants.' We had a brand-new car, but they thought we had to be poor because we lived in the country.

"They didn't know anything. They didn't know how to shell a pea. We took them out to a dairy farm where we get our milk.

" 'This is where we get milk,' we said. And then I asked them where they got their milk. 'From a store,' they said. 'Well, where do you think the store gets it?' I asked. 'They make it.' That's what they said. 'They make it.'

"Some of the cows had ribbons in their stalls from the fair. They thought they were race cows."

On my way back to the hotel I take an inventory of the Falloons' backyard. Besides the pool, the sandbox and the swing set, there are three plum trees, three apple trees, two cherry trees, a raspberry patch, a clump of black currant bushes and a corner of gooseberries.

———————◼•◼———————

The next morning is my last day in town. As I pay for breakfast, Pat points at the soup pot.

"It's my beet borscht," she says. "You'll be here for lunch, right?"

She is fixing the soup specially for me. It is her most popular, and she wants me to try some before I leave.

"I'll be here," I say.

After breakfast I go back to the hotel to settle with Elsie.

The bill is already written up, but it doesn't look like enough to me. She has charged me less than eight dollars a night. When I try to give her more, she refuses.

"I hardly rent out a room these days. I have hunters that come in the fall, but that's about it. Years ago I got a lot of truckers. I used to rent maybe three or four rooms a night. But over the last fifteen years all the truckers got sleepers on their cabs. And in the summer people just pass through now. Poor people keep driving. People with money want to stay in motels."

"At least keep the change," I say. She does. But she insists on giving me a hat in return.

"HAVE A KOOL ONE AT THE KENT" read the white letters across the blue background.

We go outside and I take her picture standing by the front door. In the picture she is wearing a grey sweater, blue slacks and sneakers. She is smiling. The sign on the door behind her says "COME IN — WE'RE OPEN."

I drop by the arena for a last look. There are seven kids on the ice fooling around. Three boys and two girls are playing hockey at one end. Two girls are practising figure-skating routines at centre ice. It's March. The season is almost over. Soon the ice will be gone.

Four women are sitting, feet up, sipping coffee in the waiting room.

"What are we going to do this weekend?" I hear one of them ask as I leave. "We haven't got a hockey game to go to."

Over in the school a group of moms, dads and kids are gathered around the piano practising for the music festival. They are going to sing tomorrow in Binscarth. They are singing "Blue Moon." I can hear them from the arena parking lot.

I should go and see them. Say goodbye. Wish them luck. But it is getting late.

I have to go to Pat's and have my soup. I have to leave.

Nakusp
BRITISH COLUMBIA

If I was to tell you the truth, I would tell you that when we moved here I felt like I had come home.

EDITH IZAIROVICH
THE VILLAGE BREAD AND BAKERY SHOP

It was the magistrate's wife, Mrs Mamchur, who slammed the door of the Broadway Cafe in Weldon Taddy's face. This was twenty-six-years ago, mind you, but Taddy still remembers the moment fondly.

"It was our first morning in town. We were in the process of moving up from Edson, Alberta. It was the moment when I knew we were doing the right thing."

Mrs Mamchur, of course, had the right to shut the door on whomever she pleased. It was, after all, her cafe. But it wasn't the slamming door that reassured Weldon. It was the sign that Mrs Mamchur slid into her restaurant window as she pulled down the blind.

It was noon. The sign read: "CLOSED FOR LUNCH."

"I guess I figured that this was the sort of town I wanted to live in. Kind of laid back and relaxed.

"Later I learned that it was a regular procedure. Mrs Mamchur had twelve or fifteen customers who came for lunch every day, and she used to close down for an hour while they ate."

Nakusp seems to engender such epiphanies in people who pass through town. Take Bob Nowak, for instance. In September, 1971, Bob and his wife, Judy, stopped in Nakusp on their way to Calgary. This wasn't a holiday. They were moving to Calgary. Bob had a new job waiting there.

"We stayed in Nakusp for four days," remembers Bob, "and on the fourth morning we looked at each other and said, 'This is really nice. We should stay here.'"

So Bob phoned his employers and said there had been a change in plans. He said he was sorry but he wouldn't be coming to work.

"I could see my future laid out in front of me. If I had gone I would be living in a subdivision and driving a station wagon. I didn't want that."

Bob never left Nakusp. He owns the town's delicatessen today. He lives in a dome. With Judy.

———————— • ————————

Founded only at the turn of the century, Nakusp (pop. 1,374) is still young enough that almost everybody remembers where they came from. Those who were born here stay on, even though finding a job these days takes as much imagination as diligence. Those who arrive stay for precisely that reason. They've come to get away from it all.

The town is ringed by mountains; the mountains, as likely as not, ringed by clouds. At the foot of the mountains, and therefore at the edge of town, lies Upper Arrow Lake.

The lake at Nakusp's back door, which defines the town as much as the mountains, is really a widening in the powerful Columbia River. A widening that grew wider still and actually swallowed part of Nakusp in 1968. That was after Canadian politicians inked the controversial Columbia River Treaty with the United States. For a cash payment, British Columbia agreed to build three dams on the Columbia, in effect turning it into a huge reservoir. The water level is regulated to provide America with flood control and hydro-electric power. That the dams were at the same time flooding out Canadian towns didn't prevent the project from going ahead. At high water, which was when I visited Nakusp, the lake lapped pleasingly around the edge of town. But from high water to low there is a seventy-foot drop in the level of the lake. It's not so pretty at low water, they tell me. Come back when there is five hundred yards of mud and sand between the shore and the lake and see what you think. Sometimes in the summer when the water is low, the wind blows across the exposed sand, and there are sand storms in town.

So Bay Street is under water, and Broadway — the only street left in town with a name — is now the main street in Nakusp. The avenues — First through Eighth — run north–south away from the lake. The streets — Broadway, then First, Second, Third and Fourth — run east–west, parallel to the shore.

The streets and avenues are paved, but the laneways that wander between them are still dirt. I walk on the lanes whenever I can, and by the end of my stay have looked into most of the backyards in town. I learn that nearly every house has a woodpile and garden, and nearly every garden a stand of sweet corn.

This is a town that can still afford vacant lots. A place where every vacant lot has a diagonal path bisecting the tall grass. A community where packs of seven-year-olds can safely wheel around downtown on their bicycles like a flock of crows.

The high school is opposite the bakery. The bakery is beside the pool hall. What else could a mountain-ringed teenager need besides a puff pastry and a vast plain of green felt?

Fifty-three-year-old Bill Robison teaches grade seven beside the classroom where he himself was a grade seven student.

"They advise you not to teach in your home town," he says one afternoon, leaning on the white steel railing that stretches along the new lakeshore promenade. "But I've never regretted it. When they offered me the job I didn't even hesitate. I teach local history. And when you love a town so much you're just a better teacher."

The town paper, *The Arrow Lake News*, comes out on Wednesday. Each week its Letters to the Editor column spills off its designated page to season the rest of the paper. Lately the town has been treated to a spirited argument over flatulence penned by two letter-writers who have been signing themselves Cornelius Burke, Major (ret) and Dr. P.B. Pedageese, B.S.

In May, on another matter, publisher and editor Denis Stanley, who bought the paper from his father (who had himself taken *his* father out), felt it necessary to print the following reminder:

LETTER POLICY
This week the *News* had a letter to the editor from Josef Knittelbour of Ravenhaven, B.C.

It is the opinion of the editor that this is not a real person in a real town but rather a nom de plume. The letter was mailed from Fauquier.

It is the policy of this newspaper to print letters using a nom de plume but the letter must be signed with the right name and address of the letter writer which will be held from publication if requested.

However, the editor must have the correct signature for legal purposes.

It is just the right paper for this out-of-the-way town whose sense of news is kindly out of step with the big city dailies. It may not be noteworthy when someone from Nakusp leaves town to go to university, but it is news the spring they graduate — and newsworthy enough for a photo of the graduate somewhere in the paper.

"Hell," says Glen Olson, who runs the marina in the south-east corner of town, "Denis'll put your picture in the paper if you catch a trout over twenty pounds. And we'll put your name on that trophy over there."

Glen is pointing to a trophy that is balanced on a shelf by the wood stove. He has engraved four names on it since he introduced it five years ago.

"Hell," says Glen's father-in-law from his seat beside the coffee pot in the middle of the bait store, "Denis'll run your picture if you land a fifteen- or sixteen-pounder."

"But you won't get your name on the trophy," adds Glen.

The town is as still and quiet as the lake at dawn.

A circuit judge visits once every few weeks.

The automobile licence bureau in Nelson sends a driving examiner up once a month. He has seven appointments during the month I live at the Selkirk Inn.

There is a dentist in town, but most people still make the hour-plus drive to Nelson or Vernon to have their teeth looked after.

There is a hospital, but they don't do operations.

There were more new houses built in the past year (twenty) than in the last ten years combined. Not exactly a boom, but something.

Half of the new homes were built by locals. The rest by Albertans who plan to use them in the summer or Europeans (mostly German) who say the mountains remind them of home.

As for local business, the sports store is closing, but someone has plans for a bookstore and someone else is going to try their hand at antiques.

There is no mall. Just a main street with a lot of false-fronted buildings in the old western style. There is a movie theatre, a large and well-stocked supermarket, two schools, two bakeries, three gas stations, a shoe store, five restaurants (six if you count The Hut Drive Inn at the end of Broadway) and a private bus that makes a run to Nelson a few times a week.

In the evening the streets are empty. So empty that at the close of one day, while walking down Broadway, I could imagine I was walking in the sweet quiet of dawn rather than the dusky moments before dark. The only sound was a helicopter thudding a fire crew back from a day's work in the bush.

When night finally settles on Nakusp, the town's teenagers take over, wheeling up and down Broadway like bats. A pick-up truck stops beside a parked car, a head pops out the window and there is a hurried conversation before the pick-up speeds off. Some nights they go to a place known as the Car Wash — a small beach along the road to Revelstoke, where a drain pipe conveniently spills water on the sand below. Other nights to the gravel pit. If someone's parents are out, it's a house in town. If you are a teenager in Nakusp, you might find the town boring and claustrophobic but there's always a party somewhere.

Every working day at noon a steam whistle punctuates the town's resolve. The whistle was saved from the SS *Minto,* an old stern paddle-wheeler that called Nakusp her home port. The *Minto* was retired and then, sadly, burned in the middle of the lake on August 1, 1968. It was teacher Bill Robison's birthday.

"There is a picture of her burning. I have never been able to hang it in my class up to now. It upsets me too much to think that we didn't save her. I am going to see if I can put it up this year. I want to remind my kids that we didn't do our job."

The *Minto* was originally built to go to the Klondike. But when the Klondike went bust, they shipped her to Revelstoke in a thousand pieces and then by barge to Nakusp. That was in 1898. The ways where she was built are still visible at low water in front of the hotel.

As recently as 1959 there was no road running north out of Nakusp. Until she stopped running in 1953, most people who wanted to go to Vancouver rode the *Minto* up the Columbia the same way Mark Twain rode the sternwheelers up the Mississippi. The boat used to back out of Nakusp after breakfast and edge into Arrowhead around noon. At Arrowhead you caught the local train to Revelstoke. The local shunted back and forth along the track, stopping every five minutes to drop milk cans at every farm in the valley. It took two and a half hours to cover the thirty miles. At Revelstoke you swung aboard the Transcontinental just in time for dinner and the overnight ride — in a berth if you were lucky — to Vancouver. The sight of the Transcontinental hissing into Revelstoke with its snazzy white-trimmed wheels and its white-gloved porters was no small beer to someone living in Nakusp.

These days you can drive to Vancouver from Nakusp in under eight hours. Time saved, maybe, but something lost.

Those who rode the *Minto* — and there are lots of people in town who remember her well — will tell you that it is cheering to hear her whistle again. They will also tell you the whistle doesn't sound the same as it used to.

"It sounds different because they're blowing air through it instead of steam," says Bill Atherton. Atherton is sitting on a bench in the Caribou Cobbler shoe store. He has dropped in for a chat. Atherton worked on the *Minto* as a deck hand for a brief period and rode as a passenger on the boat's last trip. "I had a thing about that boat," he says.

"I rode the *Minto* when I was young," says local historian Milt Parent. "I used to love to watch the fireman coal it up and stoke the fire. I used to love the smell of the steam and the oil. The smokestack sounded like a giant breathing. They didn't cover the wheel at the back because of the ice in the winter. They didn't want the ice getting jammed up in there. So you could stand at the back of the boat and watch the wheel going around. Each time a paddle hit the water there was a slapping sound and then the water would froth as the paddle stirred up the lake and that would give you a rainbow in the mist that comes off the surface. Standing by the wheel was like watching fence posts go by on the highway. And all that frothy water. The grease dripping off the wheel looked like honey to me. It looked like something you could eat."

"The *Minto* was a real workhorse," says Pete Coates, who worked on her in the forties. "She'd ferry men and horses and supplies back and forth to the logging camps all along the river. We hauled a lot of hay. We'd dump hay on pretty well every trip. The men would spend three or four months in the bush, then they'd come to town and check into the hotel until they were broke. The hotel used to have a smell all its own. Anyway, if they wanted her to stop they used to build a fire on the shore, or maybe fly a flag. We'd run her right up onto the beach and then back her off. She only drew about three and a half feet of water at the stern, empty or full. Maybe she'd go six inches lower with a real heavy load.

"There were a couple of staterooms, and sometimes people would come aboard and live on her for as long as a week. They'd do two round trips. After a few days they'd be just like one of the crew. I think we had about twenty-four people working on her. That includes the mail clerk, the purser and two cooks.

"The lake was beautiful. Every trip you'd see something you hadn't seen before. Coming up on a moonlit night with all her lights on, she was just like a little city moving along the water.

"Watching her when she came into town was as good as going to the show. Everyone would stop farming and come and have a look. Oh, they'd have some cream to deliver or a load of vegetables, but what they really wanted was to see the boat."

"The whistle has more of a honk now," says Bill Atherton. "A kind of hooting honk. It used to be more melodious. It had a haunting quality that just isn't there anymore. I guess they can't install a steam generator on main street just for the whistle, but I claim they could get the same sound if they injected some water into the air stream."

Bill Atherton isn't the only person I'll meet who'll voice that theory. The tenor of the *Minto's* whistle is important in Nakusp. An echo, maybe, not only of the boat, but of the communities and farms she once served that, like Bay Street, lie at the bottom of the 130-mile reservoir that sloshed up their valley.

The picture of the *Minto* burning that Robison wants to hang in his class hangs over the fireplace in Murphy's Landing — the bar at the Kuskanax Lodge.

"They gave her a Viking funeral," someone is bound to say if they see you looking at the picture.

As if the words somehow added dignity to the affair.

Maybe.

But there is no disguising what people really feel.

They shouldn't have burned her and they are ashamed they let it happen.

Nakusp was settled during the Slocan Valley mining boom
in the late 1890s. The Nakusp–Slocan Railway was completed in 1893, but the dream of building a smelter in town
faded when Trail, to the south, completed theirs first. Ore
would never do more than pass through town. It came
from the mineheads in the mountains by rail and was
loaded onto the steamers that slipped down the river to
Trail.

Though the town may have lost the smelter, they did
have their railroad, and one thing you could say about a
railroad in the late 1800s was that it had a tremendous
appetite for timber. The logs were burned for fuel, the timber went for ties, cribbing, trestles and stations. Thus
began the logging industry that the town has risen and
fallen with ever since.

Nakusp is essentially a one-company town. Like all
resource-based communities it has ridden the booms and
endured the busts. Today the only show in town is a logging company that is broke. The bush is shut down. Not a
logger is working. The mayor has struck an action committee. People are scared the town will go under.

For years British Columbia governments have allowed
the logging industry to rape the interior of the province in
order to pay for the prosperity of Vancouver. Industry has
been clear-cutting the forests faster than it can regenerate
them. Cutting down trees is a twilight occupation. Logs are
becoming less accessible and more costly to get to. Now the
government wants to establish the tourism industry. But
you only make minimum wage working in a motel, and you
can't expect a logger to jump at the opportunity to change
beds for a living. Out in the bush you can make $250 in
a day.

Not so long ago one of the biggest log drives in western
Canada tumbled down the Columbia River at Nakusp's
front door. Today a single tug hauls the logs down the lake
in huge mile-long booms. It travels about three miles an
hour and makes the trip about once a month.

In the days of the river drives you'd go to the Leland Hotel if you wanted to meet a logger. The bar in the hotel was so thick with men who worked in the woods that on a winter evening it smelled more of spruce and wet wool than it did of beer. There was a blackboard on the wall where anybody who needed a man would write the particulars of the job. Sometimes you couldn't sit down and order a beer without someone offering you work. And they didn't want you tomorrow, boy. They wanted you to start now.

Today if you are running a logging show and you're looking for somebody to work in the bush, likely as not you'll go looking at Shaw's.

Shaw's is, ostensibly, a chainsaw store — a place a faller can buy a new saw or take his old one to be fixed. But it's also part hiring hall and part coffee shop. It's patronized by as many retired loggers as men who still work in the bush. They begin arriving at about nine most mornings, drop some change into the can by the coffee pot and sit by the front window swinging their legs and swapping stories.

"They do more logging in here than they do in the bush," says owner George Scott, himself an ex-logger.

"And the trees are bigger in here," adds a voice that floats up to the front counter from somewhere near the back.

A new chainsaw costs one thousand dollars. A faller working full time in the woods will have to stop and sharpen his blade once a day. He will replace the blade every three weeks and buy a new saw every year.

In Nakusp the model of preference is made in Sweden and is called a Husqvarna. The most popular model weighs sixteen pounds and has a saw blade about twenty-six inches long.

The key to any logging show is the man who brings down the trees. And the key to falling trees properly is understanding what is going to happen when they hit the ground. Not only does a faller have to lay down each tree so it doesn't hit a stump and break apart; he also has to make sure it's easy to pull out of the woods. If he doesn't lay the top of the tree right on the skid trail, then the skidder man is going to rip it apart when he drags it away to the stage.

"That's George Walker," says Bill Atherton, nodding out the window of the shoe store. "He used to be one of the best fallers around." The man he is speaking of is pushing a shopping basket of groceries along Broadway.

Walker is half Indian. His mother was native; his father was Irish. He is moving his shopping cart full of groceries along the street with a tentativeness that makes me think of old man wheeling an IV along a hospital corridor.

Walker lives with his son Tim in a worn-out house behind the Imperial garage. He is fifty-three years old.

"I was a logger most of my life," he says, sitting at his kitchen table. "I started as a choker man but I liked being faller best of all. You had no one telling you what to do. There was just you and the trees. And it's the highest-paying job there is in the bush. I was getting $22.60 an hour and I was working ten-hour days."

George hasn't worked much in the bush since his leg was crushed in a "Cat" accident over ten years ago. The throttle of the Caterpillar vehicle he was driving stuck, and while he was trying to fix it he was thrown off, and his leg was run over by the tread.

"It wasn't easy work. You had to pack in your power saw, two gallons of fuel, a quart of oil, your tools, an axe, your lunch and a wedge belt. That's a lot of weight. In my days the saw alone weighed forty-five pounds. If it was winter you had your rain gear and your snowshoes, too.

"When there's snow you really shouldn't be working more than six hours. After six hours you're going to be tired. That's when you start making mistakes."

There are many ways of falling a tree, and loggers sit in bars and spin away hours arguing about what someone might or might not have done with a chainsaw.

George looks at the table top carefully.

"Every tree is different," he says, not looking up. "Some trees, when you approach them you're scared. Even up close you can't figure out which way they're leaning. And there's all sorts of other stuff to think about. Like the weight of the limbs. You got to take into account which side of the tree is heavier. In winter you have the ice factor, too. Ice can pull a tree around. And if there's rot in the trunk, that can effect the way it falls. And you got the wind factor, too.

"Sometimes it's leaning the opposite way you want to take it out. You can have everything against you and you can still make it fall where you want. You do your under-cut, your side cut and your back cut, but you leave just enough of the meat in to hold it up. Then you bang in some wedges to lift it some, and then you hit it with another tree. You drop another tree on it to push it over the way you want. But you got to be careful. You have to make sure you knock it over and not just knock it loose. Otherwise it can come back on you. You have to know what you're doing in there."

Like all craftsmen, the men who work in the bush have evolved their own vocabulary to describe the things they do and see.

Contractors, or "gypos," who are mostly freelance oper-ators, contract to log a block of land. They sign an agree-ment with a logging company to take so many loads of logs a day off the block at a certain price. Once they have a con-tract, they have what's known as a "show," as in, "Bill Miller has a full phase show up on the Falls Creek Road." A "full phase show" means that Bill has to fall the trees, "skid" (drag) them out of the bush, load them onto trucks and take them to the "dump," which around Nakusp more than likely means putting them in the lake.

A full crew on a full phase logging show could be as many as seven men.

The faller drops the trees with a chainsaw.

The chokerman sizes up the trees where they fall and bundles them into "turns" (drags). He fastens the drags together with steel cables known as chokers.

The Cat driver hauls the drags up to the landing, or "stage." He uses a Caterpillar-driven vehicle (sometimes a surplus army tank) with a blade on front for cutting a road and a winch in the back for hauling the turn.

A skidder operator does the same thing as a Cat driver, using a vehicle more like a big farm tractor than a tank.

At the landing the buckerman measures the butt log (the first and biggest log cut off the tree) to company specs and trims the trees.

The loaderman sorts and "decks" (piles) the logs using a vehicle that is essentially a front-end loader.

The truck driver hauls the loads to the dump.

When they talk about bringing down trees, loggers, like farmers and firefighters and others who work hard with their bodies, will tell you that it's something that gets into your blood. Some of them say it's the thrill, others the danger, others the joy of a perfect morning.

"I remember one autumn day," says George Walker, running his hand through his hair. "To me the autumn is the best time to be in the bush. There are no flies and no bugs. Anyway, I remember this autumn morning. It was nice and cool and the sun was slanting through this stand of hemlock and fir where I was working. There was thick moss all around and the trees were a perfect size. About 150 feet high and $3\frac{1}{2}$ feet round at the stump. Well, I moved from tree to tree putting undercuts in while the Cat was pulling the logs out. Then when he was gone all I had to do was go back and tip them over one after one. At one point I was going so smooth I'd have one starting to fall before the one before it hit the ground. That was a nice day. I remember that."

"We used to put an axe handle in the ground," says logger Mac Falkiner over supper at the Lord Minto, the town's classiest restaurant. "We'd try to drop the tree right on the axe handle. It was like a target. You'd try and drive the handle into the ground. But those were in the days when we did selective logging. We used to call it high grading. You only took out the trees you needed. And if you didn't fall them right, then you couldn't get them out of the bush."

A "widowmaker" is a tree that has a loose limb wedged somewhere amongst its branches. Maybe a bough from a neighbouring tree has broken off in a storm and snagged in a crutch on its way to the ground. If he can't see it, a faller has no way of knowing the limb is there until he jars it loose and it crashes down on top of him.

A "schoolmarm" is a heavy branch that grows straight out from the trunk and then makes a ninety-degree turn and grows straight up, giving the effect of one trunk supporting two trees.

A "barberchair" is when a tree breaks off higher than your undercut and the butt end comes back towards you.

"Albert Lyon was killed that way," says Mac Falkiner matter-of-factly.

"When I first started falling, back in the sixties," says George Walker, "I was working on this big fir and I didn't get all the meat on the back bottom side and the tree barberchaired sideways. It split about thirty feet over my head and started to come down. It pinched my saw, ripped it right out of my hands and shot it out of there just like a bullet. It could have gone right through me. I took off up the hill, over the windfalls and everything like a bear. I was running like hell. And then the tree came down and smashed the stump where I had been standing all to hell. I sat down on another stump up on the hill and I was shaking so hard I couldn't get up. The Cat driver came back and said, 'What the hell's the matter with you?' I must have sat there for a half an hour before I could get up again. That's the only one I had that 'chaired on me.

"Once, my saw hit a wedge that I had drove into the back of the tree. The end of the saw nicked the wedge and the saw flew out and came right across my stomach and ripped all my rain gear. When I lifted my shirt up I had spots of blood across my belly like I had been whipped by a bicycle chain. That's how close I came to getting my stomach ripped open."

"Guff Miskulin once fell this big old cedar that was rotten and hollow in the middle," says Mac Falkiner. "When it came down you could see this bear sleeping in the stump. The bear was more or less in a coma. It didn't wake up, but we knew if we left it uncovered it was going to freeze to death. So we went and got a piece of plywood and built a roof over the stump."

"The biggest tree I ever fell was 14 feet across at the stump," says George Walker. "It took me 6½ tanks of gas and three hours to bring it down. I got a 32-foot log, a 48-foot log and a 40-foot log out of that trunk and she was still 3½ feet across at the top. When it was time to take it off the landing, they couldn't get anything more on the logging truck except that first log.

"In the old days we used to stay in camp. Today they drive back and forth each day. I liked the camps better. The food was good and there was no liquor. You couldn't have booze in camp and you stayed out of the bars. You went fishing at night or swimming in the hot springs."

"It used to be that being a logger was a good way to make a living," says Mac Falkiner. "When I first started in the woods a contract logger was the third-highest-paid person in British Columbia, right behind a doctor and a lawyer. Well, the last time I saw the list the contract logger was in fifty-seventh place. Behind schoolteachers and people working in shops. A butcher makes more than a faller, and with way less risk. It never used to be that way. We used to make forty-five dollars a day in the fifties.

"Today eighty percent of the guys would make their living other ways if they could. It used to be that they would rather log than do anything else."

"Sometimes," says George, "when a tree goes down it's unbelievable. Sometimes it's like the whole forest is exploding."

———————— • ————————

John Koper lives in a log house with a cedar-shake roof. The house sits on five treed acres about a five-minute drive out of town. We are sitting at a sunny table just off the kitchen eating eggs from chickens I can see scratching up the yard. The bacon is from a pig John slaughtered. His wife, Tove, made the thimbleberry jam I am spreading on my toast.

"This house was built by one of the original hippies," says John. "He was part of the big hippie commune that used to be across the road. I got the land and the house for $13,500. That was in 1987.

"The first thing I did when I bought it was turn around and take the logs off half the property. I got $7,500 for the lumber. So it was a pretty good deal. But the house was in rough shape. No one had lived here for a few years. There were no doors and windows and there must have been a couple of years' worth of leaves lying about the floor."

"We lived here the first winter," says Tove, shaking her head, "without windows upstairs. We slept in the dining-room."

"So I had to figure out what to do about the windows," adds John. "The windows that had been here were beautiful. The guy who built the house had helped tear down the old hospital in town and he had taken the windows out of the hospital and built this house around those windows. They were from the 1800s. You could see by the ripples in them that they had been poured and levelled with wood. Anyway, when he moved out he took the windows with him.

Then one day he said he would sell me the windows back for $350.

"I came up with a counter offer. I offered him $200 to rent the windows. I said he could have them back as I replaced them with thermal panes. I only ever put one thermal pane in so far. So these are the original windows that we're looking out of."

We have moved outside now. We are sitting on the steps of the small front porch. Luke, Koper's three-year-old son, is ploughing through a salmonberry patch that stretches along the dirt driveway. Katie, the family dog — a mix with a lot of golden lab in her — is sewn to the boy like a shadow. The forest crowds in on the other three sides of the house.

"Do you worry," I wonder, watching Luke smear another handful of berries onto his face, "do you worry that he'll wander into the bush?"

"Katie looks after him," says John with a nonchalance that is utterly oblivious to my urban apprehensions. "He only went off once, but the dog came and got us and brought us to him. We have grizzlies here and bobcats, but the dog would run them off. They're like brothers, those two."

Two hummingbirds are waging hummingbird war over the red geraniums growing in the tree stump at my knee. They buzz each other like motorized darts. They are, says my bird book, pugnacious birds. But for all their showy belligerence, they inevitably pull up short of physical contact.

A friend of mine living in Maine once wrote about how she would go on early autumn mornings to the Rockefeller Gardens and, if there had been a frost, find hummingbirds lying on the lawn like fallen leaves. They were too cold to fly, she wrote. Almost frozen. And then she told me how she would walk around the grounds with the gardener, picking up the birds and warming them in her hands. You could warm one with your breath she said. A puff of air and you'd feel its heart beating like a propeller on an elastic-band plane, and then it would whirl off like paper and you could pick up another.

A red squirrel is chattering at us from a fir. A sapsucker is working on a nearby birch.

In the freezer on the back porch Koper has brown paper packets sealed with butcher's tape and stamped with black letters: "Venison Steak," "Mountain Goat Burger," "Moose Round Roast" or "Swiss Steak — Elk."

Koper is thirty-seven years old. He was raised in Ontario. His father worked in an American Motors plant. Before he moved to Nakusp in 1983, Koper worked on oil rigs all over, put in a stint as a cowboy in Saskatchewan and apprenticed as a carpet-layer in Toronto.

"I rode rodeo for a while," he says. "I have a picture upstairs of me riding a bronc." There is a pause and a smile. "I wasn't very good."

The saddle from his cowboy days is also upstairs, slung over a chair in his bedroom.

John and Tove came to Nakusp to settle because they had always liked small towns. "When you live in a city you don't know anyone. When you live in a place like this you might not know people well enough to visit, but you wave at them when you see them. I go to town and drive down the street and I wave at people left and right. If I lived in the city I might wave at people once a week. And if someone says, Did you hear about so and so, well, you're going to know who they are talking about. I know a lot more people than I'd ever know if I lived in the city."

"We don't," says Tove, joining us on the porch, "even have locks in the doors."

"I really like it here," says John. "I like living in the bush like we do. I like the remoteness. And I like going to town. If you aren't shy to try your hand at something different, there is opportunity here. People come out here and say they are going to stay and then three weeks later you never see them again. It takes about two years to be accepted. After two years everyone figures that you aren't going to be one of those people that leaves.

"I thought I'd come out here and start up as a floor-layer.

I put an ad in the paper and linked up with an outfit in town that sells carpet. But there was just no way. I had to do something else or we would've had to move. So I figured out which end of a power saw to hold onto and I went into the bush cutting shake blocks."

There are two shake mills in Nakusp. The mills are ramshackled and fearsome factories of thumping hydraulic splitters, whining circular saws and dust. The sort of place where Saturday afternoon movies used to end — with the hero strapped to a log that was stuttering towards a saw blade the size of a kitchen table.

Saddle Mountain Cedar Products, on the side of a mountain on the edge of town, is really just a tin-roofed shed and a collection of vicious-looking mechanical saws. The front of the shed, held up by unpeeled cedar logs, is open to the elements. The place looks as if it might have been here since Van Horne pushed his railroad through the Rogers Pass. In fact it has only been here five years. Like most shake and shingle operations, all the equipment was bought second-hand at auction. You set up, saw and split until all the available old-growth cedar is gone. Owner Ed Wiebe says he has been going for five years now and figures there is maybe eight years of old-growth cedar left in the valley. Until then he has the splitters and saws whacking away at cedar blocks twenty-four hours a day.

John Koper worked as a shake blocker for three years.

"It was fun. I really enjoyed it. I liked working outside in the bush. I liked scouting for new trees."

A shake blocker works the bush almost the same way a prospector works a mountain. He is an independent operator who scouts the hills for trees and, when he finds a stand he wants to cut, lays a claim at the forestry office.

Although logging companies can cut live cedar and sell it to the shake mills, an independent operator like Koper can only go after what are known as "dead and down" trees.

"What you are looking for is an area where a fire went through years and years ago, because cedar is a tree that lasts and lasts and lasts. You can get a piece of forest and you can't even tell there's been a fire because it's so grown up. Maybe it burned back in 1909, but there'll be all sorts of dead cedar lying there or standing there that you can make shakes out of."

Both the "dead and downs" that Koper looks for and the live trees that the larger companies bring down is old-growth cedar. That means all the wood that is sent to the shake mills is likely between two hundred to five hundred years old.

The trees are felled, split and hauled to the shake mill where they are split again — this time into shingles — and then strapped onto pallets and most likely sold to the United States.

"Once I was cutting a tree by the side of the road and I looked down the valley and saw all these dead needle tops — cedars always grow to a sharp point so we call them needle tops. Anyway, I saw this stand so I went for a walk and I found this whole forest of dead cedar. I remember standing there in the middle of them saying, 'Jackpot.' I went running back and got my partner and said, 'Come on. You've got to take a look at this.' I couldn't believe it. It was only about half a mile from the hot springs. Everyone else was looking miles and miles from town. I guess they figured that all the stuff around town was long gone. But there it was. Boy, that was a nice claim. We had some trees in there must have been eight feet across."

A cord of cedar split and delivered to the mill fetches $425.

"I can show you a tree fourteen feet across," says Koper, looking at me carefully. "And I don't show it to many people. I'm afraid they are going to poach it. Poaching is pretty prevalent because cedar is so valuable. You could cut fourteen maybe fifteen cords from a tree that big."

Koper pushes his cowboy hat off his forehead so it's perched on the back of his head. He calls out to his son.

I turn the numbers over in my mind. That one tree, I figure, could bring him over six thousand dollars.

"You going to claim it?" I ask.

"What?"

"The big cedar. Are you going to claim it?"

"No, no. I just like to know it's there. I just like to go see it sometimes."

———— • ————

I think of John Koper a week later on the afternoon I visit the Nakusp Museum. The museum takes up two large rooms in the basement of the town's library. It has its own entrance, however, and on the afternoon I arrive, the door is unexpectedly locked. The sign out front confirms that I have come during business hours so I knock again, but there is still no answer.

"I guess someone didn't show up for their shift," says the woman at the tourist bureau next door. "I can give you the key if you'll lock up when you're finished."

Two minutes later, alone in the dark museum, I fumble my way down the north wall looking for the light switches.

What brings John Koper to mind is the saddle I find in the second room — a deep, scooped-out walnut-leather saddle with a high back, a tall saddle-horn, wooden stirrups and a rope cinch. The saddle is thrown over a saw-horse. The note on the wall says, "RODEO SADDLE ORIGINALLY OWNED BY TOM THREE PERSONS."

The photo of the man on the wall is mounted on a piece of rough wood and framed with an old leather horse collar. It is a picture of a handsome square-jawed cowboy. The cowboy is sitting in a photographer's studio. He is staring directly at the camera. He is wearing beaded long-fringed gloves, a scarf and a cowboy hat. There is a medal of some sort pinned over his heart. The woman standing beside him in the calico dress has her hand on his shoulder.

So this is Tom Three Persons. The first and only Indian to win the Bronc Riding Championship of the World. He won in 1912 — seven years after Alberta became a province and the year an American trick-roper named Guy Weadick convinced four Albertan cattle kings to underwrite a rodeo at the Calgary Exhibition.

Left alone in a museum, it doesn't take much to make a grown man twelve. Wondering vaguely what I will say if someone walks in, I climb into the saddle and lean on the saddle-horn as I read the typed note pinned to the wall. The horse that Tom Three Persons rode to fame was known as Cyclone.

Cyclone was known as the best bucking horse in the world. 129 cowboys tried to ride him and none succeeded. The only person rated as having a chance was Tom Three Persons who at the time of the Stampede was languishing in the Calgary Jail. However the local RCMP relented and Tom was let out of jail to try his luck on Cyclone. After a wild ride the victor was Tom Three Persons. Mastering Cyclone at last. He was a hero of the Stampede audience among whom was the Princess Patricia and the Duke of Connaught. Today more than a half century later his picture hangs in the Blood Reserve Community Hall at Standoff. A permanent tribute to a man who walked out of a jail cell to tame a Cyclone.

I sit in the saddle and look at the other photo on the wall — an out-of-focus shot of the famous ride. The photographer caught Cyclone as he leapt, frozen forever with four feet in the air, back arched, the crowd well in the distance, Tom sitting easy. Long ago someone wrote three words in white ink on the negative.

"Let 'er Ride."

I wander alone around the museum all afternoon, trailing my hand over the wood and glass cases and peering at the dioramas of local heros.

In the far room I come across a section cut from a large cedar. The huge round disc has been sanded, varnished and then stood on its side like a wheel. The concentric growth rings spread from the heartwood as if someone long ago dropped a stone down the centre of the tree and it splashed out waves of wood like ripples in a rock-jarred pond. Someone at the museum has counted and marked the rings by decade. By their calculation the tree lived 277 years — from 1680 to 1957.

I study the stump for nearly an hour. The back of the wood, which hasn't been painted, has the rich, earthy aroma of a cedar chest. Dividing the rings into groups of forty-three — my age — I see that the tree grew the most during the forty-three years between 1790 and 1833 (over seven inches). Its poorest growth over forty-three years was during the last years of its life. During those years, when it must have been at its most magnificent, and over the span of time during which I had been conceived, born and lived long enough to marry and have two children of my own, the cedar did not add three inches to its radius.

I wonder who brought it down. And where. And what they thought about as their saw bit through the wooden years. As they tore through the 1800s did they think about Riel or Sitting Bull, or the railroad that had consumed so much of the western forest? As the sawdust piled up around their feet, were they only thinking of stopping and eating the sandwiches that were wrapped in their rucksacks, or how cold their hands were, or whether they should sharpen their saw? Or did a fleck of wood jump out at their face? Did they hold it and think, my God, that was 1770. Beethoven had just been born, Captain Cook was in Botany Bay. Did they whistle through the life of Mozart, strain through the Seven Years War? Down, then, as the sawdust thickened, through another century, through 1698 — a bad year for trees in the new world, the year paper manufacturing began in North America. And what sound was there when the wood at the centre, the heartwood encased for 277 years, what strangled cry, what thunder, when the first ring saw light, felt air, and the cedar fell? It was 1957. I was nine. The cedar, almost three hundred, had begun its life in 1680. The same year the dodo, the flightless bird, became extinct.

Much of the museum is rooted in logging. And though at first the displays don't seem different from those in any other small town museum I have spent time in, there are some things I have never seen before. A pair of wooden snowshoes fashioned for a horse — four Frisbee-sized wooden discs with leather shoes for the horse's hooves that lace in the front and buckle in the back. A brown canvas duffle bag that was issued to Japanese evacuees during World War II — "Only one bag per person" reads the card in the case.

The more I dawdle over the cases, however, the more the artifacts seem to be washed by a sense of whimsy unfamiliar to most collections. A classic silver trophy in the old style, with curved handles and a distinguished black base, turns out to be the Abriel Trophy, once presented "for the best pyramid of Wagner Apples."

The trophy has been awarded three times — to J.H. Vestrup in 1913, 1914 and 1915.

A whale's tooth and a scorpion in a bottle both seem oddly displaced in a mountain town like Nakusp.

So does the suckling pig. It is preserved in a glass jar and sits on a spinning base so you can count all eight legs and examine both heads from all angles. "Please turn pig slowly" read the handwritten instructions on the counter.

"Freak of Nature" proclaims the caption on the split log near the pig. And, yes, there embedded in the piece of firewood is the leg bone of a fawn, completely encased by the wood. The fawn, the sign speculates, was running from a cougar when it caught its leg in the young cedar and remained wedged there for forty years while the tree gradually swallowed it. It was only discovered by accident when Mr Dieterman split the cedar for his wood stove.

My favourite, however, is a collection of framed works of art by barber, pool hall proprietor and champion checker player Eugene Levesque. Between the wars Levesque set out to create one hundred pictures — each one from a different material. He finished about seventy before he died in 1945. Of the ten or twelve hanging in the museum, my favourite, a piece done in sawdust and on display in the men's room — is called "Evolution." It is a picture of an ape evolving into a man.

Levesque's other works scattered around the museum include a Plasticine evocation of thunderclouds over the mountains, a piece made out of broken Christmas tree decorations depicting two birds, and a picture of a bridge spanning a canyon that Levesque fashioned by pressing different-coloured soaps together. The sun and the years have faded and melted the soaps, giving the piece an impressionistic and almost artful soul.

There is, in one corner, a full-scale model of Levesque's barber shop, complete with brass spittoons, a life-like miner at a checkerboard, a customer laid out in the barber chair and Levesque himself, razor in hand, paying more attention to the game of checkers than the anxious face he is about to shave.

Levesque, it turns out, was a spirited eccentric. And it is his spirit, I learn, that infuses the museum with the whimsy that pleases me so.

Eugene Levesque was born May 15, 1878, in St Boniface, Manitoba. His great-grandmother, Reine Lagimodière, was the the first legitimate white child born in the west. Reine's sister Julie was Louis Riel's mother. When he was young, Eugene Levesque used to play in Louis Riel's house.

"My grandfather always claimed Riel was never hanged," says Milt Parent as we pore over family albums in his basement office. "He believed the church made a deal and Riel escaped to the States."

It is here in Milt Parent's basement, sipping raspberry vinegar and soda and flipping through pamphlets and letters and photos, that I become acquainted with the life and times of Eugene Levesque.

"When Eugene came west his original plan was to go to the Klondike. When that didn't pan out he ended up in Revelstoke, which is where he got into barbering. In about 1905 his appendix ruptured. In those days when that happened you didn't recover. He was very, very sick. But he felt if he stayed awake he could fight the poison. So he had his wife sit with him and rouse him every time he drifted off. He lasted for three days like that. When he couldn't stand it any longer, he told her to let him sleep for one minute and then wake him. And that's the way he built up. First one minute of sleep, then two, then three and so on. My aunt, who was a nurse, said he had a hole in his side until the day he died from where the appendix had drained.

"But he got better. At first he couldn't do much. He got a job that didn't require a big effort — tallying in a sawmill. Then, when his strength had returned, he heard they needed a barber in Nakusp. He came here in 1911.

"He was great with kids. Oh, boy. I spent a lot of time in his house. He started a museum in his attic and kids would bring stuff to the barber store and he would pay them for it. He would pay you for a butterfly or a water beetle if it was one he didn't have. Kids used to go hunting all over town for stuff and bring it to him. There was all sorts of stuff up there. There were life-sized mannequins and crooked wood canes and stuffed animals. Flying squirrels, owls, everything. When I got older and interested in history I began reading old issues of the town paper, and I would come across items about animal attacks, like an owl attacking goats or something. Then I'd realize that he had that owl up in the attic. He collected everything. The pig you saw in the museum was his. It was born on old Sam Henry's farm. Sam thought it was the devil himself when it was born. He was scared out of his wits. I don't think it lived more than a few hours. When Eugene saw it he preserved it in whisky until he could do it properly.

"A lot of the time he used to sleep down at the barber shop, and I remember one night when a bunch of us kids decided to sneak into the museum with flashlights. The attic was a pretty spooky place for a kid to go. I remember going up those stairs with the lights bouncing off the slanted roof. Everyone was on edge. All those eyeballs glaring out at you. I remember one kid kept saying, 'Let's get out of here. Let's get out of here.'

"He had a monkey that lived in the house, too. He came back from Winnipeg once and he brought a monkey with him. My grandmother was furious. It wasn't a small monkey, either.

"Another thing he organized was called 'Old Man's Day.' It was typical of him. He had to be entertaining all the time. You had to be over sixty to go. He'd decorate the house with bunting and pennants. I think the oldest guy of the crowd was proclaimed Granddaddy for the day. Anyway, all the old men would come to the house and there would be speeches and recitations and they would tour the museum and play checkers and horseshoes and the Mrs would serve the goodies.

"The Knights of Pythias picked it up when it finally got too big for him, but they gave up on it after his wife died.

"When he died three-quarters of his museum got taken to the dump. I helped them. They just backed a pick-up truck against his house and kept loading it up. Everything went. I've got bits and pieces here at home. Some went to the museum in town. But most of it went to the dump.

"Eventually the house burned down. It's a vacant lot today."

I go back to the museum one afternoon to see how much of Eugene Levesque's collection I can pick out. What I really want to do is visit with the old barber. If his house was still standing I would knock on the door and ask if I could see the attic. But it isn't and this is the best I can do. I try to make the rest of the museum fade away and see it through his eyes. There is an ostrich egg in a glass case. Lying beside it, an unopened coconut. These were his, I think.

"Yes, those were his," explains Milt Parent when I ask a day later. "In the old days travellers would come through town on the paddle-wheelers. Sometimes they were on around-the-world trips. They'd have these big steamer trunks with leather straps. Hard to believe people like that would come through Nakusp. Maybe they'd get their hair cut in town and Grandfather would show them the museum. Then a package would arrive a few months later. People used to send him stuff."

Growing up in the same town as Eugene Levesque, I think, as I stop for a last look at his moustached mannequin, would have been all right.

———————

It is late. I am, once again, the only paying customer in the museum. On my way out I stop at the front desk and talk with the young woman who has taken my two-dollar entrance fee. Her name is Kathryn Van Immerzeel. She is eighteen years old. Working at the museum is her summer job. For the past year she has been Queen of Nakusp.

"When I was in grade eleven they came around and asked how many of the girls wanted to sign up for the contest. I think there were five of us. Five girls out of thirteen. I was Miss Hospitality. There was also Miss Fireman, Miss Legion, Miss Downtown Merchant and Miss Manor [representing the Manor Restaurant].

"A woman from Vernon came and taught us how to pose. You have to do these little poses. Basically we learned how to act like a queen or a princess. We began classes in April. We had two classes a week for two hours each. We did that for about three months. They taught us speechcraft and how to walk properly. And we practised a group dance routine."

"What did they teach you about walking?"

"They taught us how to make our hips move in and out. And not to swing our arms like soldiers. They taught us to look very ladylike and elegant. The pageant is on the July first weekend. The judges come from out of town."

"How did they judge you?"

"They judged us on different criteria. There are private meetings where they ask you questions about the community and current events. They want to see if you are someone the town could be proud of.

"Then there are the long gowns. You are judged on how they fit your personality. And how well you hold yourself when you walk in them.

"And there is sportswear. You have to pick an outfit or sport you enjoy and a piece of fast music and they see how well you can move in front of people. There's also a casual wear segment. Like tea wear. Nice dresses, you know?

"You're also judged on an impromptu question. This year the question was 'What's the biggest problem facing teenagers today?' The other girls all said drugs. I said getting the incentive and ambition for post-secondary education. I think they liked the uniqueness of that. They liked the ability to think on your feet."

"What does the queen do?" I ask.

"I represented Nakusp at the other pageants around. I went to the pageants at Vernon, Revelstoke and Lumby. There is always a dance for the queens, and if you don't have a boyfriend they provide you with an escort for the night. I think you have to pay ten dollars for the escort. Sometimes the guys were really nice. Others weren't my type of guys.

"I did the raffle draw here in town. And at Christmas there are Santa Claus pictures at the Home Hardware and my princess and I helped put the kids on Santa's knee."

"Did you enjoy it?"

"The neatest thing was being at school and hearing the younger girls say, 'She's the queen.' That was flattering."

"Do you have a boyfriend?"

"Yes. We've been going out for about twenty months now. He gave me a ring in the spring."

"Are you engaged?"

"No, no. At the end of the summer I'm going to school in Alberta. He's going to Vancouver. He wanted to give me something so I'd remember him and be good. We don't intend on breaking up. It's a nice reminder that I'm his girlfriend."

"How did he give it to you?"

"We went for a walk on the beach one school night. Like at seven or eight. We were sitting on some rocks and he said, 'I have something for you.' So I shut my eyes and he put it on my finger. It's so sweet and cute. We're both going our separate ways. That's love in a small town."

"That's how it works?"

"Well. Basically, people here don't date. You don't phone someone up and ask if they'd like to go to a movie or something. You just get together at dances and parties and stuff and then the guy asks if you want to go out with him. There is no ring or anything. You just tell your friends that you're going out with him or her.

"Most of the time you just see the guy at school and at parties. There are no parents involved or anything like that. It's too embarrassing. He doesn't come home for dinners or anything. If you make it past three months you've been going out a long time.

"I guess I've gone out with three or four guys. That was when I was younger. We just held hands. There was nothing else. It wasn't really an emotional relationship. Or a physical one. You just wanted to have a boyfriend.

"When you get older you tend to have more mature relationships. Your families become involved and you lose your girl or guy friends. It's just the two of you becoming a functioning and mature couple. There are thirteen girls in my class. Maybe ten of them have serious boyfriends.''

"Is it difficult in a town this size? Is it hard to find privacy?"

"Yeah. Everyone knows you. Everyone knows what you're doing. It is a restless angry feeling sometimes, like someone is putting a pillow on your face. You walk down one side of the street and there are your friends. You walk down the other side and there are your mother's friends. It'll be nice to get out from the suffocating pillow."

"What do you two do?"

"My boyfriend has a car. A '79 Camaro. White. We used to drive around a lot. Or go for walks and stuff. Basic romantic things like that. Sometimes we go out of town for the day. Like to Vernon or Kelowna. We go shopping. Or just look in stores and dream about things we can't afford and wish that we were older."

———— • ————

I hardly use my car at all while I am in town. I can walk almost anywhere in under ten minutes. At night, if I have nothing to do, I go for a walk along Broadway. After nine the only businesses open on the main street are the milk store, The Hut and the gas stations. In that strange and usually unspoken way that certain jobs are designated to a certain gender, in Nakusp it has been decided that pumping gas is a girl's job. At night, anyway, all the gas stations have young women working the pumps. The girls pump the gas while the boys drive their cars up and down the main street looking for action.

———— • ————

Columbia Machinery and Equipment is in an unpainted wooden building at more or less the end of a dead-end dirt street. You could pick the building up and drop it, as is, into the middle of any cowboy movie and it wouldn't look out of place. It is a small manufacturing business. They make chokers and cables and other things that only a logger would need.

The building is closed the morning I walk by. Peering through the window, I read a sign on the office wall: "ECO FREAKS KISS MY AXE."

———— • ————

One lunch hour I meet a young boy sitting on the back steps of a clapboard house. He is working on a home-made slingshot.

"I got the elastic," he says, "from the hardware store. It cost ninety-one cents a foot. It's slingshot rubber."

His name is Michael. He is twelve years old.

"Do you want to try it?" he asks, holding up his handiwork.

We balance a row of tin cans on a sawhorse by the shed. Michael shows me a handful of pebbles.

"Do you want to see my hockey cards?" he asks as we clear off the row of cans again. He bolts through the back door and comes back carrying a cardboard box and a looseleaf binder. Most of his cards are clumped together with elastic bands in the box. The important ones are in the binder. Each card in its own plastic window.

"That one's worth five bucks," he says, pointing at one page. "That's Clint Malachuk. He's worth $1.25. That's Jaromir Jagr. He's worth $3. Mario Lemieux's worth $8. That's Paul Coffey's rookie card. It's worth $165."

The challenge, with hockey cards, used to be to collect a set. Wealth, like candy, was measured by simple yardsticks. Quantity counted. So did the obscure cards that everyone believed were "hard to get." Kids flipped and swapped and won and lost their cards in a universe that belonged to kids and kids alone.

Today a generation of men have corrupted a part of the world that once belonged to children. They don't give you gum in a pack of cards anymore because the oil from the gum might stain and thus devalue the cards. Some packets cost well over a dollar and contain more cards than a young boy can easily fit in his hand. Instead of living in their own secret universe, anxious children take their cues from their avaricous and retarded fathers and daren't carry their cards in their back pockets anymore.

"Actually, the Coffey isn't worth that much," says Michael, sizing me up. "It's not in mint condition.

"My parents both go to work at 6 A.M.," he explains, when I ask him where his mom and dad are. "I woke up today at nine-thirty and got dressed right away. Then I went to my friend Paul's house. He was up but he hadn't had breakfast so I had French toast with him. We watched monster trucks on TV for a while. Then we came here and looked at my hockey cards. Then we went and got the elastic."

"Where do you get your money?"

"I go up into the mountains and I pick pine cones with my parents. I've done it the last four weekends. It's a four-hour drive to where we go picking. We get up at about 6 A.M. and get home after eight at night. We collect them in twenty-gallon buckets. At the end of the day we clean them here in the backyard. You have to get all the pine needles out. Then you take them and sell them to the tree company. They germinate them and plant them. We get about thirty dollars a bucket."

"What do you do with your money?"

"Spend it."

"On what?"

"Hockey cards."

"All of it?"

"I'm saving for a mountain bike. I have about $205 saved. Are you hungry? Do you want to have lunch with me?"

"Thank you," I say looking at my watch, "but I have to go. Someone is expecting me."

He looks disappointed.

"What are you going to make for lunch, anyway," I ask, not wanting to run right off.

"Do you like Kraft Dinner?" he asks. "Have you heard there's a new recipe for it?"

"No. I didn't hear."

"You add Cheez Whiz. It makes it cheesier."

"I wish I could stay."

"What about soup?" he asks. "I could make some noodle soup. It only takes three minutes."

———————— •———————

I have been eating in my room a lot. I have a small fridge, a hot plate and a toaster. For breakfast I fix cereal and fruit juice and sometimes toast. Lunches I eat downtown, usually at the Broadway Deli. The chef and effervescent owner, Bob Nowak, has introduced a selection of Mexican fare, and I have been working my way through the menu. One day enchiladas. The next day burritos. One day with meat. The next day without. I take some suppers at the Lord Minto, which is the restaurant everyone in town recommends. But it must be coasting on past glory, because I don't favour it, and nothing except the pizza really passes muster. Before long I start returning to my room for supper, too. I buy a few bottles of California Zinfandel and drink the wine out of a tumbler while I juggle pots on my two-burner stove. My first night I resurrect a recipe I use on canoe trips. I boil rice on one burner and sauté a can of shrimps in garlic and butter on the other. I sit on the back stoop balancing my plate on my knees and watch the moon bounce over the mountains as I eat. Another night I cook pasta and toss it with olive oil and broccoli. Sometimes I make do with a bottle of the wine and a can of baked beans. It's a meal I often eat if I come home late and everyone has eaten. On the nights I don't feel like cooking, I go to the Chinese cafe and have a beer or two and a mound of chicken fried rice. I have never had a bad plate of chicken fried rice west of Winnipeg.

———————— • ————————

I find Allison Alder through the classified section of *The Arrow Lake News.*

"JUST DESSERTS"
by Allison
exquisite cakes, pies and pastries made to order

"I'm working on a wedding cake right now," she says when I call. "You can come over, but best wait till I get the kids to bed."

Allison, who is twenty-seven years old, has two children. One is three years old. The other is one.

"There are going to be four cakes, actually. Each one on a stand. I'm kind of nervous about it because I've never made anything this complicated before. I tried it out on the weekend. I built the whole thing and it worked out wonderfully. "This is going to be the last cake I make. Someone reported me and the health inspector called and said if I wanted to make cakes at home I had to have a separate kitchen where the family didn't go. So that's the end of that.

"Which ad did you see, anyway?" she asks.

"The cake ad."

"I also had one in about science tutoring. I had a student for science all year and a few others for biology."

Allison, who has only been in town for a year, has also worked as a substitute teacher at both the high school and the elementary school and at the satellite campus of Selkirk College, teaching English as a second language and grade twelve upgrading. Over the summer she was hired on at the fish hatchery for a few weeks.

"We were clipping the fins of the trout so that they could be identified. We did 100,000 trout in two weeks."

Her husband works in the bush and is gone for weeks at a time.

"As soon as we moved here Mike had to go away to work. I was eight and a half months pregnant. Then when I went to the doctor he said he thought I was going to have the baby early. I was really worried. I didn't even know a babysitter. I thought, what happens if it comes in the middle of the night? I started asking people about babysitters and one morning a neighbour came by with a bouquet of sweet peas and chrysanthemums. She said she had been up all night worrying that I had no one to call. She said I could call her anytime at all.

"It was so nice. I had spoken to a lot of people but I didn't want to say can I call you in the middle of the night? She had the foresight to say that.

"People are friendly like that, but I've been here a year now and I still haven't met anyone my own age and sat down and talked to them. Sometimes I wonder about that. I haven't connected with the young moms. Not yet. In some cases there are four generations of families here and I think people tend to gravitate around that. They're nice to you but they don't make friends with you. It seems to take time to break into the established circles."

It is late now. After midnight. The wind is up and the holly bushes are scratching against the side of the house. We're sitting on mismatched chairs at an old kitchen table with steel legs and a yellow Arborite top. Allison looks around the kitchen and nods.

"People still call it the old Moseley place. We are trying to make it more our own. But it doesn't matter what we do. It is always going to be the old Moseley place to a lot of people in town."

Much around us has been started, but nothing has been finished. There are curtains on some windows but not on others. Wallpaper on half the walls, unpainted wainscotting around and about. I get up to put my cup in the sink.

"Those counters are lower than they should be," says Allison as I put my cup down. "The Moseleys built them like that so their boys could help in the kitchen. I'd love to get them raised up."

———————— •• ————————

"My brother died when he was eighty-four in a skiing accident," says Bert Gardner, leaning over the table. "He got pulled off the lift. There was quite a commotion. Perhaps he shouldn't have been there. But he was a determined bugger."

We are sitting in the window of the Broadway Deli. It is early yet. Gardner, who is eight-one, goes for a two-mile walk every morning along the promenade and then comes to the deli for a chat.

Bert Gardner is old enough to remember the days when the only way you could get to the hot springs on the edge of town was to walk. The tourists used to go by horse train. Bert worked with the pack horses when he was a kid. He learned how to do a diamond hitch without looking because he was too small to see the top of the horse. He remembers prohibition and Bill Pratt who used to run the Leland. If you saw Bill go down to meet the *Minto* wearing a certain hat, then you knew he had a new supply of liquor.

Bert is missing his gall bladder, only has half his stomach and has a pacemaker sewn inside him to keep his heart straight. But you'd never guess it to look at him. He is wearing sneakers and a fishing hat and has the soft comfortable feel of an old windbreaker. He loves to talk.

"I'm just having a hell of a good time. Everybody speaks to me, even the little kids. I met a young fellow the other day. I didn't know who he was but I knew his kid because his kid plays around our house. Anyway, we said our hellos and as they walked away I overheard the father say to the boy, 'That's Mr Gardner.' And then I heard the kid say, 'Dad, that's not Mr Gardner. That's Bert.'

"But I keep thinking I've got to get a clock I can wear on my wrist that will ring every two minutes. Because once I get going, one story leads to another and I just don't know when to shut up."

Bert and I sit in the deli window for the better part of that morning. Him telling stories; me grateful he isn't wearing the watch.

"Smith, that was the brother who died skiing, he went to college the same year the mill burned here in town. My father figured someone had to work, so he and I decided to go to Trail to see if we could find something. We had an old 1928 Chrysler back then. But there weren't a lot of roads. So we drove up to Summit Lake and put the car on the railroad tracks.

"We had it so the two left wheels were between the rails and the right wheels were riding on the outside ties. We soon figured out that if we were going to make it we had to drive at eleven miles per hour. If we went slower we'd drop between the ties and the wheels would spin. Any faster and it bumped the hell out of us.

"Just this end of Slocan Lake there was a big trestle. And we had to cross it. The alternative route was to go to Vernon. But that would have been three times as long. Well, when you're up that high, there are just the tie ends to hold you. No dirt between them and it was a little shaky. But there weren't that many trains in those days so we weren't too worried about that."

One day I want to write a movie that ends with a 1928 Chrysler bucking its way across a trestle bridge somewhere in the Selkirk Mountains. The camera will pull back, back, back . . . and maybe in the distance, maybe on the other side of the mountain we'll see . . . a train coming in the opposite direction. Just a whiff of smoke. Just a hint of anxiety. And then the theme, swell the music hard and high. And freeze the frame and roll the credits.

All morning people drift into the deli with empty coffee mugs. They fill them, pay and joke at the counter, and then back out the front door with a nod or smile for Bert and me.

At ten-thirty Bob Nowak threads a grocery cart through the tables and out the front door. He'll push it down Broadway to the Overwaitea supermarket for his daily shop. He is back in forty minutes with lettuce, melons, onions, tomatoes and other supplies he needs to make today's lunch.

"This used to be my building," says Bert, looking around. "This used to be my electric shop. I think that's why I like sitting here.

"See them trees over there?" Bert is nodding at two spruce trees towering over the front lawn of the old courthouse. "We planted those on July first, 1952."

Today the trees almost obscure the courthouse from the street.

"When I was a kid they used to hold concerts there. There was always singing and dancing in those days. It was all fun and fine until the radio came. When the radio came everything changed. Dad used to sit there every night with the headphones on and he forgot all about us.

"I remember in the early twenties John Henry Stevenson's niece was going to be on the radio singing in a concert from San Francisco. We had several sets of earphones, so Dad invited Mr Stevenson over to listen.

"We had the first radio in town and it was the first time Mr Stevenson had heard one. He sat there listening with tears running down his cheeks. When the concert was over he turned to my father and said, 'And, Mr Gardner, can they hear us just as good?'

"Jesus. Jesus. I have to train myself to shut up. People ask me a question and I know all they want is a yes or a no. But I just can't seem to shut up."

"Tell me about May Bill," I ask.

"So you've heard about May?" he says, smiling softly. "I don't really know too much."

No one in town seems to know "too much" or, if they do, no one seems anxious to share what they know with me.

I know this. That May was brought to Nakusp from Eng-
land as a baby in 1909 by Ernie Bill and his wife, Leticia.
That both Ernie and Leticia were said to have worked at
Buckingham Palace — Ernie as a "gentleman's gentle-
man," Leticia as a lady in waiting. That Ernie's sister,
Charlotte Bill, was nursery maid to the children of the
Duke and Duchess of York (later King George V and
Queen Mary). And that May was said to be a royal child,
born out of wedlock and given to Ernie and Leticia to
raise in Canada.

"Just tell me what you do know," I say.

"Well, she was a nice girl. She was a year older than me.
We used to ride horses a lot together. We'd ride up to the
hot springs in the summer or go for cutter rides in the
snow. We'd skate in the old fair building. They used to
flood it every winter back then, but we can't do that anymore because the climate has changed so.

"Anyway. There was no birth certificate. I think that's
when she became suspicious. They took her back to England when she was twelve or thirteen, and there was no
birth certificate when she went to get her passport."

Some of May's trips were recorded in the local paper:

May Bill, who with her mother is visiting relatives in Eng-
land, has been given the honored privilege of holding in
her arms Princess Mary's son, and the nation's idol. Mrs
Bill, sister of Ernest Bill, is the nurse in charge of the
Royal infant.
Arrow Lake News, March, 1923

While to most of us it has been a thrill to read about the
wedding of the Duke of York and Lady Elizabeth Bowes-
Lyon, to May Bill of Nakusp it was an actual experience to
see the bride and groom on this most auspicious day of
their lives and to shake the hand of some of the noblest in
the land. . . . With here [sic] aunt, who for many years was
the Royal nurse, May was at Buckingham Palace on the
day of the wedding and from Princess Mary's rooms in the

palace viewed the festivities. She had the honor of shaking hands with the Royal bridal pair and described the bride as being a "small dark girl and very pretty." In addition she shook hands with Queen Mary, Queen Alexandra and ex-dowager Empress of all the Russias. . . .
Arrow Lake News, May, 1923

"I had a locket she brought me back from London one time she went," says Bert. "She pinned it on my hat. It stayed there for a long time. But I don't know whatever became of it.

"Eventually May rebelled and had it out with her parents. She left town. I was eighteen and she was nineteen. I took her down and put her on the *Minto* the day she left.

"She went to Vancouver and got a job looking after kids. She was a nanny. I think she also looked after an old couple for a spell. She only came back to town when her parents died.

"She married some guy called Jones in Vancouver. He worked in a machine shop.

"I think she met her real mother one time. The mother was living in California. She was a member of an upperclass British family but she had been thrown out of England because of May. I never learned who the father was.

"She stayed friends with my sister Helen, though, and I think Helen knows the whole story. But she's never told it. Maybe you should speak to Helen. When May died, Helen got all her jewellery."

And so begins my correspondence with Helen Pearson.

Helen lives in Victoria, B.C. She is eighty-three years old. As a young woman she worked as a registered nurse. For years she was in charge of medical welfare at Shawnigan Lake Boys School. We write and then talk on the phone, and she seems to know more than anyone about May. In February, 1992, I fly to Victoria to meet her.

I don't know why I feel compelled to go. I write to the royal archives at Windsor Castle had receive a courteous reply confirming that Charlotte Bill (May's "aunt") was indeed a royal nanny. The woman who writes, however (an assistant registrar in the archives), can't confirm or deny that May's "parents" — Ernest and Leticia Bill — worked in royal service.

> "... our lists of Royal household employees are not complete and so it is possible that either or both of them did work for the Royal Family but I am afraid I cannot confirm it."

I know there are other stories in other towns about illegitimate royals, and I don't know of any that have been proven true. But there is something about May's story that feels authentic. From Helen's letters I learn that, when she was younger, May wondered if "maybe Aunt Lottie [Charlotte Bill, the royal nurse] is my mother and George V is my father." Helen says that May seemed indifferent to this possibility and seemed to shrug off the royal connection.

Later, writes Helen, May "did have some nice trips and when in England found out who she was. Her father was Edward VII — the great womanizer. Her mother who was [also] royal, [was] a very young girl."

In the letter Helen doesn't give me the (alleged) mother's name.

"I didn't give you her mother's name as up to last year May's mother still had a sister living. May's mother was matron of honour at the Queen Mother's wedding and her sister a lady in the bed chamber."

Maybe it is Helen's reluctance to tell me everything she knows. Maybe it is the way she reports May's own disinterest. Certainly nothing I have read about Edward VII dispels the story. In *Uncle of Europe*, his biography of the social and diplomatic life of Edward VII, Gordon Brook-Shepherd doesn't shrink from describing the lusty and amorously adventurous monarch. He calls him the Prince of Pleasure. Edward's wife, Princess Alexandra, says Brook-Shepherd, was "the most courteously but most implacably deceived royal lady of her time." Edward, he writes, worshipped beautiful women, and "that was to produce several tender friendships, as well as a stream of casual affairs and a string of regular mistresses."

So.

So I go to Victoria to meet Helen Pearson. She lives alone not far from downtown in a one-bedroom apartment on the second floor of a three-storey building.

When I arrive, not long after breakfast, she greets me warmly and leads me to the lace-covered dining-room table where we sit for much of the day. Waiting for me on the table is a blue Birks box about the size of a game of Monopoly, tied carefully with red cord.

We open the box and Helen removes the royal memorabilia that May gave her.

There is a small leather-bound prayer book.

"She gave this to me up at Shawnigan," says Helen. It's the order of service for Edward VII's funeral in St George's Chapel, Windsor. There is a flowing, hand-penned inscription on the flyleaf: "To Charlotte Bill in memory of King Edward VII. [Signed] Mary R. Christmas 1910."

There is an aquamarine pearl brooch in a red leather case. "Collin C. Wood and Company, to the Royal Family" reads the gold printing in the satin lining.

"May said her mother gave her that when she went to see her in California," says Helen, turning the brooch over in her hand. "She said it was her mother's favourite piece. When she gave it to me she said it didn't mean a thing to her."

There is a little leather purse.

"That was Prince John's," says Helen. There are four coins inside — a farthing from 1885 and three threepenny pieces — also from the 1800s.

There is a gold snuff box and a lovely leather wallet that opens to display at least two hundred sewing needles of every size arranged like the pipes of a cathedral organ.

"Isn't it beautiful?" says Helen, holding it up in the light.

And there is a large and fine leather-spined illustrated edition of *Grimm's Fairy Tales,* printed in 1909. It, too, has an inscription on the flyleaf. Someone (I can't make out the signature) gave the book to H.R.H. Prince John in July, 1909.

Prince John was the epileptic son of George V who had been Charlotte Bill's special charge. When he died in 1919, Charlotte added a second inscription: "For May in memory of Prince John from your aunt "His nurse" Charlotte Bill."

It is lunch time. Helen fixes us some sandwiches. After we eat I go for a walk in the warm Victoria sunshine. It is only February, but daffodils and tulips are already up. I think over what I have seen. The books and jewellery seem authentic. They seem to confirm the Bills had a royal connection. But I know that already. Just because Charlotte Bill worked at Buckingham Palace didn't prove anything about May's birth, and all of these mementoes could have come to May from Charlotte.

When I come back there is a pot of tea waiting. We sit at the table again and Helen tells me her story.

"For some reason Mrs Bill chose me to be May's friend. May would visit all the time and sleep over on weekends. May called my mother and father 'Dad and Mom Gardner.' She used to say, 'Can I stay for supper?' and Father would say, 'As long as you eat what we put in front of you.' May told me later that she used to hate the salads and only ate them so she could stay.

"May was born in Maidenhead, England, on February 22, 1909."

"Today would have been her birthday," I say.

"Yes," says Helen. "That's right. Her real name was Mary Marguerite. She first became suspicious of who she was when she was a little girl. Someone told her — I think it was a neighbour — that she had been adopted. She told me that one day she asked Mrs Bill if it was true. She asked, 'Who am I? Am I adopted?' She said Mrs Bill shook her and told her never to say that again.

"I think the Bills got a little bit of something for keeping her. In those days everyone was really hard up. And May had things the rest of us didn't have. My underwear was made out of flour sacks. But she had nice underwear and a horse, and I remember the Bills put a bath out back. She had piano lessons and everything.

"She was a little imp. She used to tell her mother that she was going down to my house to study, but she would get on her horse and go downtown.

"I think she was twelve the first time she went back to England. They went on two or three occasions. I think they stayed in Buckingham Palace, but it might have been Sandringham.

"Anyway. When she was a teenager she had a big fight with Mr and Mrs Bill because they wouldn't tell her who she was. And she left Nakusp. She was nineteen when she left. She got a job in Vancouver doing housework and met a man who worked in a garage next door. She eventually married him. He was much older than she was and turned out to be an alcoholic.

"She lived in Vancouver for the rest of her life. I visited as often as I could. One time Princess Mary was in Vancouver and she had a visit with May.

"Everything I know she told me herself. She was called to her mother's deathbed in California. She told me that was the only time that she met her mother. She said it didn't mean anything to her. But that's where she got all this stuff, when she went to see her mother.

"I remember the night she told me who she was. She had come to visit us at the school. My husband slept on the couch that night and May slept in the bedroom with me. It was 1967 or '68. She told me right after we turned out the light. She said,'Helen, I found out who I am.' She said she found out in England. She said she went to the place where you find out who you are. I never told a soul until after she passed away.

"The last time I saw her she was in the hospital. She cried

and cried. I spent eight hours with her and fed her. She was very sick. She had rheumatoid arthritis. She had five operations and had her legs amputated. I guess she knew she wasn't going to live. That's when she gave me all these things. She said, 'I want you to have this.' She was crying and crying. The last thing she said to me was 'I haven't had as nice a life as you had, Helen.' Not long after that she died."

"Do you believe it?" I ask. "Do you think she might have made it up?"

"No, no," she says. "It's all true. She wouldn't have had all this jewellery if it wasn't true. She was actually a granddaughter of Queen Victoria's. I wouldn't have all these things that belonged to royalty if it hadn't happened."

Helen gets up from the table and comes back with an old photo album.

"This was May's," she says.

An enlarged photo falls out of the book and lands face down on the floor. As I pick it up I read the handwritten inscription on the back: "Princess Mary Marguerite."

"I wrote that on all the photos when I found out," says Helen.

We sit and turn the pages of the album without talking. On the very first page there is a snap of the Princess Royal (Mary). "Taken Aug. 3, 1953 at Lalla's, Sandringham," reads the inscription underneath.

There are pictures of the Queen Mother unveiling a memorial (Sandringham, 1953), and of May with her "aunt," Charlotte Bill (also at Sandringham). There is a studio shot of May as a baby wearing a knitted outfit with fur around the collar of her bonnet and ribbons around her neck. And of May as an adult on the *Queen Elizabeth,* May in Dover, May in front of Canterbury Cathedral, May at Stonehenge, May on a "shady lane in Cumberland."

"See how she always keeps her hands hidden?" asks Helen. "That's because they were crippled from the arthritis. She didn't like to shake hands, either. She'd always give you a hug."

I don't know what to think. Helen clearly believes what she has told me. I want to believe it, too. But her belief isn't proof.

I keep thinking of something a friend told me. Before coming west I called my friend, a private detective, and told her May's story and asked her for advice.

"Don't," she said, "try to prove the girl was royal. Just try to find out who her parents were."

I have one more thing to check. Amongst Helen's papers we have come across a copy of May's will. On it is the name and address of the lawyer who represented her. Maybe he knows something. I fly to Vancouver.

There is no listing in the Vancouver directory under the lawyer's name. The next morning I call the Law Society of British Columbia. No, they tell me, he no longer practises.

Maybe he has retired or passed away. Has he sold his practice, I wonder? They check, and I get lucky. It takes half an hour, but they come back with a name and address.

The lawyer has a walk-up office over a second-hand book store in a two-storey part of town. He shares his practice with his son and he remembers the Bill file.

"I think I did some work on it some years ago," he says. "I think we still have it."

He disappears and comes back a few moments later with three manila folders.

"Is this what you wanted?" he asks. Then he leaves me at a corner desk in his office so I can go through the files.

For three hours I shuffle through what remains of May Bill's life. There are letters written from hospital that authorize the sale of her furniture, copies of phone bills that her lawyer paid for her, a document from a cemetery describing the plot where she buried her husband, Hugh Jones. I write down the cemetery address and plot number. Maybe, I think, she is buried beside him.

Finally I turn to the last file. There is a small envelope

stapled to the inside cover. I open it. And there is May's social insurance card. The original copy of her will.

And two copies of her birth certificate.

I unfold the birth certificate slowly and stare at it. I did not expect to find it here.

The date of birth, just as Helen Pearson said, was February 22, 1909. The mother, however, is not the high-society woman that Helen believed her to be. She is listed as Hilda Alice Earl Flynn, dressmaker. The father's name and occupation are blank.

That night I drive across town to the cemetery where Hugh Jones is buried.

"We are closing soon," says the woman on the phone. "I'll leave a map to the grave taped to the door. You might have difficulty finding it. It's really dark down there."

I stop for a beer and a sandwich at a small pub and buy a flashlight at a drug store down the street.

I know that I will not find out any more about May Bill. Her mother's address on the birth certificate is in Plumstead, a poorer section of London. May was an illegitimate child, and though it is still possible, it seems unlikely that her father was the king.

As I drive across Vancouver I think about the photos Helen Pearson showed me. In one picture, May, a young teenager, smiling and wearing a pretty checked dress; her hair in ringlets falling over her shoulders.

I think of May the girl, riding her horse to fool around downtown. May the woman, hiding her crippled hands. May, who had been to Sandringham, always wondering who she was.

It is raining now. The map to the grave is taped to the office door as the woman promised. I wind around the cemetery roads for half an hour. Twice I have to come back to the main gates to start fresh. It is after ten when I find the right section. Instead of tombstones the bronze tablets that mark the graves are set flush with the ground. I park the car and walk across the grass, my flashlight bouncing through the darkness. My shoes soaked through. I wonder what I will feel if I find the grave. What I want to say to May Bill.

I nearly give up.

And then it is there at my feet.

Hugh Jones
In loving memory
1889-1967

But not May. Though she had bought herself a plot beside her husband, she was not buried here.

I don't feel anything.

Three months later, back in Toronto, I track down May's resting spot. She was cremated by the Vancouver Crematorium in 1974. Nobody claimed her ashes. At first it is unclear where they are. They might still be in storage. I get the idea that maybe I can claim them, that I can take them to St George's Chapel and sprinkle them on Edward VII's grave — something I think, she might approve of.

But once again I am too late. May's ashes were stored in the basement of the crematorium for ten years, in a bag inside a box. In 1982 she was buried in a common grave with about five thousand other people.

———————— • ● ————————

My favourite refuge in Nakusp is Olson's Marina. Olson's is more a brotherhood than a business — a home away from home to a neighbourly collection of men with pipes sticking out of their mouths, peaked hats sticking over their foreheads and bellies sticking over their pants. Cindy, the twelve-and-a-half-year-old Chesapeake, sprawls across the doorway. Step over Cindy and you step into an establishment that breaks all the rules of modern merchandising.

Olson's is a big, open and mostly empty room. There are no aisles. The stuff that is for sale — lures, weights, leaders, sinkers and floats — is hung on the walls all around. The rest of the room is given over to the clientele. There's a wood stove. A brass ashtray on a stand. A couple of chairs. A couple of men in the chairs. A coffee pot. And a can of Bullshit Repellent within easy reach of the chairs which, says the label, "helps prevent and cure chronic bullshitting, exaggerated claims, tall stories, political discussions, sales pitches and heart-rending tales." The pop (drinking) and the maggots (fishing) share the fridge in the corner.

Two tourists, a father and his eight-year-old son, wander in to buy the boy a hook and weight. Glen Olson, ex-logger, elbow hooked on the counter, studiously ignores the father.

"What kind of hook do you want?" he asks the boy intently.

The boy doesn't know.

The father tries to interject but Glen pays no heed.

"Would this be about the right size?" he asks the boy, holding up a hook.

The boy nods tentatively.

"Yeah, that would be about right," says Glen. "Would you like a grasshopper to put on it?"

Later, when the father and the boy have left and someone remarks on the moment, Glen smiles and says, "You got to look after your future customers."

In the winter Glen moves the chairs around the stove, and every morning about ten to twelve regulars drift down and hang around the room like smoke.

"Glen," says someone, "how come you keep them candy bars down on the bottom shelf? Ain't no one can see them down by their knees."

"No one but the kids," says Glen laconically. "That's knee level to you, Neil, but that's eye level to a seven-year-old."

"You crooked bastard," says Neil, pouring a coffee he isn't expected to pay for. "I said all along you're a crooked bastard."

Glen is smiling. Or maybe he is squinting. It's hard to tell the difference.

"It's not what you do," chimes in Lloyd Hill from a chair in the middle of the store. "It's what you get caught doing that matters." Lloyd looks as if he is sitting in his own living-room.

They'll sit and talk fishing all winter, until the morning someone comes in with a big one. Then they'll all scramble onto the lake like prospectors.

They fish for the native rainbow trout. A radiant fish with a bright yellow belly, yellow fins and a pink stripe down the side. Some of the trout can grow as heavy as twenty pounds.

"It's kind of hard to explain," says Glen, "but they're so beautiful it's almost a shame to kill them. Sometimes they look like rainbows lying in the bottom of your boat."

And they fish for the pink-fleshed Dolly Varden, which they say tastes like salmon only not so oily.

And also for the kokanee, which is freshwater sockeye salmon. The kokanee still behaves like its saltwater ancestors — spawning in creeks in its third or fourth year and then dying after the spawn. When it is in the lake, the kokanee is a brilliant silver, but when it spawns in a mountain stream, the fish's body turns bright red and the head turns green. The deep red flesh is considered by many around Nakusp to be the finest eating fish there is. Before the dams, of course, salmon that weighed forty to fifty pounds fought their way from the Pacific Ocean all the way to Nakusp.

Outside a car squeals as it pulls to a stop.

"Must be a Dodge," someone says. "Only a Dodge sounds like that."

A man and woman walk into the Marina. The woman is wearing a T-shirt that says "Have six pack will travel." They want to buy some bait. As they pay for their worms, I step over Cindy and out the door. The man and woman emerge a few minutes later, climb into a Dodge Dart and drive away.

"Barns . . . ," wrote the late Canadian architect Eric Arthur, "have joined the ranks of 'endangered species.' No funds from wealthy societies, heritage trusts or governments are spent on the purchase and preservation of our oldest barns, and their demise can be expected."

I have been looking for a barn ever since I read Arthur's lament. I want to find a small and lusty barn, warm in winter and pungent with cattle and hay. I want to stand in the middle of the dust and cobwebs and steaming cow pies and consider the world we have left behind.

The number of farms in Canada has been declining since 1941. Between the wars almost one out of every three Canadians lived on a farm. Today it's one out of twenty-five. Over the same fifty years, the volume of agricultural production has increased by 175 percent — and that's all you need to know about what is happening on Canadian farms.

I stumble on Chris Spicer's farm in my second week in Nakusp.

It is almost in town. His small acreage is hidden behind a thicket of lilac, wild roses and laburnum — a stone's throw, no more, from the marina. Behind the fence, however, beyond the hedgerow and down the lane not twenty-five yards, you feel as if you are miles from nowhere. His barnyard the centre of the world alone.

How do I tell you about Chris Spicer? That he is the skinniest, liveliest, fastest-moving seventy-eight-year-old I have ever met. That he has more energy and moves more gracefully than most men half his age. That his house is a mess and his fields aren't. The rows of onions couldn't be straighter, the carrot tops bushier, the beet tops greener, the muck between the lettuce blacker.

I wander down the lane before lunch and we sit together at the kitchen table and he leans his head back and with hardly a pause tells me the story of his life.

"I came to Canada from Britain after the war. I was at complete loose ends. All I knew was I wanted to start a farm. I started in Newfoundland near the Salmon River, at a place called White's Crossing. There were large flats of land there. It was ideal, really, and I tried my damndest to get a down payment for a place but I just couldn't do it. So I picked up and worked my way across the country.

"In Toronto I met a man who felled dangerous trees. I told him I had never seen the end of a chainsaw in my life, but he needed a donkey at the other end of a mile-long blade, so he hired me. We worked in orchards all over, and I saw enough of Ontario to know that it wasn't for me. Rather too flat, too organized and far too many chemicals for my liking. So I came out here.

"At that time everybody was trying to sell orchards, and I nearly got sucked in. I was this greenhorn Englishman, and I was broke. Then I saw this ad in the paper. A chap needed someone to help him skin mink on a mink farm in Nakusp. Now, I'd never seen a mink in my life. But I needed a job and he took me on."

It was 1948.

"I came to Nakusp on the *Minto*. The weather was appalling. The mink man met me and took me home to this horribly dirty and smelly granary. He had told me he would pay me room and board, but when I got there I found he was sleeping in the granary and if I was going to stay I was going to stay in the granary with him. So I did. He was very poor. He said if I was going to eat with him I'd have to eat mink food. It was a mixture of horse meat and tomatoes and various vitamins. Horse meat isn't that bad. It's actually quite delicious. I grew some Swiss chard and he broke down and bought me some potatoes. Well, all this time the weather had been perfectly terrible and then one morning I woke up and it was bright and sunny and I looked out and I thought, 'What on earth is happening?' The sun was reflecting off the snow and I was surrounded by all these mountains. It was extraordinary. It was like waking from a sleep and stepping into a dream.

"So I stayed on. Next thing I had met my wife. She was a cook at the Bluebird Cafe."

Someone is stirring in the other room.

"That's Jean," says Chris. "She had a stroke a year ago. It was devastating. She was like a shot bird. She is coming out of it now but she may not understand everything you say. It has been a hard time."

Leaning on a four-legged cane, Jean Spicer struggles into the kitchen and falls into a chair on the other side of the table. Chris introduces us.

"I'M-TELLING-STUART-HOW-WE-MET," says Chris a little too loudly, a little too slowly.

"HOW-DID-WE MEET?" she asks with the same tentative cadence.

"YOU-REMEMBER," he says. Then, turning to me. "I was thirty-five. She was thirty-nine at the time. I'd trade her cracked eggs for burnt pies. She'd give me a pie for a dozen eggs. One of them was so burnt I nailed it to the wall."

"IF-YOU-ARE-ONLY-THAT-FAR-ALONG," says Jean, interrupting his story, "I'LL-NEVER-GET-DINNER."

"YOU-CAN'T-HAVE-DINNER," says Chris. "IT'S-NOT-TIME-YET.

"Jean was a wonderful worker. She worked every bit as hard as me. I guess these days you'd say that our children were neglected. We used to put them in a playpen down by the field and they would look after themselves. They'd play or scrap. After she had worked in the fields, Jean would come back to the house and cook. It has come full circle. I'm chief cook and bottle-washer now."

The kitchen looks as if Chris has been doing more cooking than bottle-washing.

"DO-YOU-WANT-TOAST?" he asks "I-MADE-APRICOT-JAM-THIS-MORNING."

Chris pokes around the kitchen looking for the butter.

"HERE-WE-ARE," he says putting the toast in front of his wife. "Here we are," he says to me. "A disintegrating couple in a disintegrating house. We're worn out. The house is worn out. It has been a hell of a strain. Everyone thinks I'm crazy for not putting her in a place, but we're both independent people. And she *is* coming back.

"She couldn't even talk at first. Now she's gained back the twenty-five pounds she lost in the hospital. That's what happens with a bit of loving care. We can feed her the food that she likes here. And I can go out and leave her now. When we first got her home I used to sleep in the chair beside her because she would try to get up in the middle of the night and she'd fall down. I did that for about a month. She still falls down sometimes. But she has a whistle around her neck and when she falls she blows the whistle so I can come and help. Sometimes I'll be down in the field and I can hear her blowing on her whistle like stink.

"Ten days ago I took her up to the Idaho Lookout. I had to pretty near drag her along the path. But we've been outdoors people all our lives. I thought it would be a good thing to do.

"I-AM-TELLING-STUART-HOW-WELL-YOU-ARE-DOING."

Spicer bought the farm from a pair of Channel Island bachelors. They were desperate to sell. They let him pay down the debt by working in the fields. He knew nothing about Canadian farming — the weather, the soil or the seed varieties. And he had never worked with horses. He remembers the two ex-owners peering anxiously through their parlour window as he struggled to plough a straight furrow with the recalcitrant team.

But he had his wife, ten beautiful acres of black muck, a captive market and the will to work. Before long he had a flourishing business selling vegetables to the logging camps and the surrounding communities. In those days the valley was actually exporting fruit, vegetables, milk and eggs. These days, says Spicer with disgust, everything comes from California or Spain. Nothing leaves except the logs.

He kept chickens for eggs, and cows for milk and beef. Jean made her own butter and cheese. The twins, both girls, were born in 1950. They used to dress up the cows. They would paint their hoofs and crimp their hair. The girls taught the cows how to pull them around the yard in a wagon, and how to jump. Sometimes they would hold cow rodeos.

It was 1960 and Diefenbaker was prime minister when the surveyors arrived. They just appeared and began sticking pegs everywhere.

There were public hearings, but the hearings were a smokescreen.

The environmentalists were stuffed. The treaties were signed.

And all up and down the valley, farms were expropriated and then flooded.

"We were horrified. We refused to go. B.C. Hydro seized the title to our land and lawyers came and told us we didn't own our own property anymore. It was the most miserable time of my life."

There is a framed photo of General A.G.L. McNaughton over a door in the kitchen. McNaughton was the highest-ranking Canadian officer in the U.K. during World War II. He fought a long, hard and losing battle to keep the Canadian army from being fragmented. His last great campaign, fought when he was the chairman of the Canadian Section of the International Joint Commission, and another loss, was his bitter opposition to the Columbia River Treaty.

"McNaughton," says Spicer, nodding at the photo, "was a true Canadian of the old style. He'd turn over in his grave if he heard what was going on in the country today. You don't find people like that anymore."

Chris Spicer dug in his heels so deeply that he actually got to keep his house and his barn. But not his low-lying fields. Before they were flooded he hauled hundreds of cartloads of precious black muck to high ground. Today he farms that handmade field and rents other land around Nakusp.

Lee Mitchell is sitting in the doorway of the smallest of Spicer's three barns. Lee, a nurse, works at the hospital in town. Most days, however, she finds a few hours to come out to the farm to lend a hand. She isn't paid. She comes because she likes to. Sometimes she takes vegetables home with her. Today she is swinging her legs in the afternoon sun and clipping roots off stalks of dried garlic.

The garlic is lined up in careful rows that cover the entire barn floor. The bulbs are as big as lemons, each clove almost the size of Lee's thumb. There is enough garlic to keep the whole valley happy.

In the largest of the barns, Janet, one of the twins who returned home when her mother had her stroke, is rinsing bunches of beets the colour of a medieval tapestry. She is standing the wet beets in cardboard boxes. She'll take them to the farmer's market in Revelstoke tomorrow before dawn.

If my boys were fifteen and eighteen instead of five and eight, I would pack them up and send them to work with Chris Spicer for the summer. As it is, all I can do is leave. I take some garlic with me and use it that night in my pasta.

Two days later in a corner grocery store on the edge of town I pick up two shrivelled buds of garlic in one of those little cardboard boxes with the cellophane windows. They have been grown on some chemically pumped-up field in Gilroy, California. It is the only garlic in the store. It costs sixty-two cents. It has probably been shipped to Nakusp by truck.

This is what is called globalization.

On Wednesay I go to the post office to mail some postcards. There is a handwritten sign taped onto the front door.

NOTICE
Funeral Services for
Bertha Millar
Will be held at the
United Church
Friday at 1:00 pm

The woman behind the counter tells me that funerals are the only private notices the post office puts up.

"Everyone sees them that way," she says.

———————•———————

On Sunday I go to the dump. On the gravel road along the side of the mountain there are the usual warnings about hazardous material (forbidden) and garbage-habituated bears (dangerous). "For your own protection," reads the sign about the bears, "do not approach or provoke them at any time."

Bears that hang around garbage dumps, the sign explains, soon lose their natural fear of people.

Well. Yes.

The corollary, of course, is that people who hang around garbage dumps soon lose their natural fear of bears.

The morning I visit the dump, Daniel Sheremeto, the twenty-year-old son of the dump's manager, is sharpening his hockey skills. He is using a pile of rocks instead of pucks and a full-grown black bear as a moving target. After the third direct hit the bear throws a disgusted look over his shoulder, sways slowly away and melts back into the forest.

"He'll be back later," says Daniel, dropping his stick in the dust and climbing inside a large cardboard box. The box once held an electric stove. Sheremeto has cut a door in one side and is using the box as shelter from the sun. He has a chair inside that he can sit on.

A town dump is more than just a place to leave garbage. It is a place where people meet and talk and, often, trade goods. Some people call the dump the trade mart. Sometimes, they say, you drop stuff off. Other times you pick it up.

"Hey, look," says truck driver Ray Lythgoe, already clutching three pairs of shoes and a seat cover he has scavenged. "That's Gordy Matchett. I'll bet that couch is in mint condition. He's fucking rich."

Ron Is Bell is looking for copper, aluminium and brass.

"This here is an old carburettor," he says, pointing to a lump of metal in the back of his pick-up. "It's made of aluminium. It has a few brass screws in it, too. This is an old starter. It's full of copper. You just have to take it apart. The copper is all wound up in there.

"My dad used to do this when I was a kid. He was too sick to work. We lived on welfare. He used to do this to make a few extra bucks.

"Me? I'm not doing this for myself. I'm doing it for my brother. He has a couple of kids and he split up with his wife, but he still has to support them. I'll take this back to him and he'll separate it into different piles and store it in boxes. Then — say he has to go Vancouver — he'll take a load with him and the load will pay for his gas."

"The best thing here are the bottles," says Daniel Sheremeto from inside his cardboard shelter. "If you collected every bottle you saw, you'd get maybe fifteen dollars a day. Lots of people just give them to me." He nods at the pile of bottles beside his feet.

Garbage at the Nakusp dump is separated into three piles. A pile of metal, a pile of wood that is burned two or three times a year, and a pile of household garbage to be squashed with a tractor and then buried in open trenches.

There is also a collection of yellow plastic five-gallon drums alone in the middle of the dump.

"That's motor oil," says Daniel. "We're not supposed to take that here. We're not allowed to bury it."

"What happens to it, then?" I ask.

"I don't know. People are supposed to take it to a regular dump, but I don't know where one is. So they just bring it here. If they don't bring it here, where else are they going to take it? Sometimes people dump it so they can get the cans. Most of the time it just sits until someone from the regional district or Environment Canada does something about it."

I point at a dark stain on the ground and ask if that is where someone has dumped oil.

"Nah," says Daniel. "That was the bear. He got into some vegetable oil."

———— • ————

Every Tuesday evening at seven o'clock the siren on the Nakusp Fire Hall sounds. It echoes off the mountains and lingers in the evening air like wood smoke, reminding the twenty-odd volunteer firemen in town that Tuesday is meeting night. On most Tuesdays no one needs the reminder. On most Tuesdays most of the men are already scuffing around the false-fronted fire hall when the alarm goes off.

For the first hour and half until, say, eight-thirty, the men are supposed to practise drill. The Tuesday I answer the siren, drill means taking the pumper up Highway 6 to test a newly installed hydrant.

"It's sort of a rough ride," says Danny Santano as we build the momentum we'll need to get up the hill and out of town. "The tires get kind of square sitting in the hall all week. It takes a little while for them to round out."

This year Lyle Thompson is the fire chief in Nakusp. During the day Lyle works for BC Tel as a district repairman.

"One of the problems," he says, pocketing the watch he used to time tonight's departure. "One of the *big* problems," he says, correcting himself, "is getting younger people to join. We're finding that younger people would rather play ball than join the fire department. They don't want to get up in the middle of the night. Most of them work in the bush and that means they have to be up at four or five every day. So it's hard. Very few of us can get away during the day if there's a fire. We actually had a guy who got fired last year because he left work to fight a fire. I never thought we'd hear something like that. It was a bit of a shocker. There's a different attitude to things nowadays."

There are certain perks, however. Every fireman gets a free peaked hat and a windbreaker, and twice a year they all take their wives out for supper and the department picks up the bill.

Firemen also get to use the social club — a large wood-panelled and carpeted room above the fire hall. There are four round tables, a TV in one corner and a bar in the other. There is also a desk, a filing cabinet and, on the walls, a dart board, some local maps and a toilet seat painted gold. If you open the lid you expose a pin-up cut from a men's magazine.

In a smaller room on the other side of the stairs there is a shuffleboard table, a pool table, a Ping-Pong table and a game of table hockey. Some of the men bring their kids to the hall when they're looking after them. The kids play in the small room while their dads watch an instructional video or sit around and bullshit.

On Tuesday night after practice there are three bags of potato chips upstairs, twelve firemen, a bottle of rye, more than a few beers, and a lot of bullshit.

Lyle Thompson has been down in Nelson pricing this year's windbreakers. He has some samples with him. He is trying to get the men to agree on the colour and style they are going to order.

There is an hour of noisy debate. The polyester camp squares off against the poly-cotton blends. The no-crest contingent takes on those that want crests on their arms. Arm crests squabble with back crests. Waist-length argues with hip-length, and Danny Santano starts to get silly.

"I want pink," he says.

"Who's going to wear it?" whoops someone at a far table, "you or your wife?"

Lyle is trying to coax the meeting towards consensus.

A cheer goes up from the table farthest from the front. Six men have been flipping coins to decide who pays for the next round of drinks. Someone has just lost.

Lyle says it's time for a vote.

Short jackets win seven to three.

Fifteen minutes later it's eight to two in favour of cotton blend.

"You realize," says Santano, who appears more interested in causing problems than resolving conflict, "that if we choose this one," — he is holding the cotton blend over his head — "we'll have to have it dry-cleaned."

Everyone is nodding.

"Well," continues Danny matter-of-factly, "we don't have a dry-cleaner in town."

One of the coin flippers calls for a re-vote.

"But we've already voted," says someone else at the same table.

And they are at it again.

They are no closer to a decision an hour later when Lyle Thompson stands up to present Richard Friedenberger with a glass-bottomed silver beer tankard.

"Nakusp volunteer fire department, '90–'91," reads the inscription on the front of the mug. Richard, the youngest fireman in the room and one of the newest to join the department, is leaving town to return to school.

On my way out I pause and read the fire department club room rules.

Rule Three: Anyone using the club room at the time of a fire call must not drive any of the department vehicles.

I wonder if there has ever been a fire in Nakusp on a Tuesday night.

The next night I meet one of the firemen downtown. He is out for a walk with his wife and five-year-old son.

"We are going over to The Hut to get an ice cream," he says. "Why don't you join us?"

We take our sundaes to a bench by the lake and watch the sun turn the sky various shades of pink.

Gary is thirty-four. He has a brushcut and wears an earring in one ear. His wife, Dawn, is thirty-two.

"We also have a daughter," explains Dawn. "She just turned eight. She's at the movie theatre tonight with the girls who live next door. She has never gone out like that by herself before.

"She got all dressed up and did her hair with spray and put on new jeans and a pink T-shirt. She was walking around the house for about half an hour before it was time to leave."

Gary and Dawn have just moved to Nakusp from Calgary. They are not used to the idea of their eight-year-old daughter wandering off to the theatre alone.

"We gave her $3.75 to get in," says Gary, leaning on the steel rail with his back to the lake. "She took $4 of her own for popcorn and a drink."

Sometimes the local theatre has $1 nights. One evening Gary took the whole family to the movies for $4. They saw *Teenage Mutant Ninja Turtles*.

Gary used to be a courier in Calgary. He was on the road fighting traffic twelve hours a day.

"It was a living," he says, turning and peering across the water, "but it wasn't a life."

As the light dips from pink to grey, the lake grows still. As the water darkens it also seems to thicken. There is a splash, and we all turn, but only in time to catch the concentric ripples rolling towards us.

"That's a fish that just jumped out there," says Dawn.

"This is right at the end of our street," says Gary. "Sometimes I walk down here in the afternoon and keep going right off the end of the street and into the lake for a swim. Our yard is three times the size it used to be. And we have trees out front. Sometimes we can hear the hummingbirds flying over the house."

"I keep binoculars on the kitchen counter," says Dawn. "When I hear a bird I look at it. You notice things here that you'd never notice in the city."

Dawn is sitting on the back of the park bench. She is resting her elbows on her knees. While she talks she looks straight out at the lake. Her husband and son have moved down by the shore. They are skipping rocks across the water.

"It's so much better for the kids. I don't get as upset with them as I used to. And they can do more here than in the city. In the city my kids were only allowed to go certain places. Like they had to stay on one side of the street and if they were on their bikes I was always watching them.

"Here I just say, 'Go outside and play.'

"For a while I missed the malls. I would find myself with time on my hands and I didn't know what to do. If I was in the city I would've gone to the mall. I used to spend hours window-shopping. I sort of had withdrawal. But that goes away.

"It's just like walking into another dimension. It doesn't happen all at once. I raced around for a couple of months. It takes a while to wind down.

"If it keeps going this well, we'll probably stay here for the rest of our lives. Everyone is happier. Even the cats. In the city they used to lie around the house and sleep. Now one of them even climbs trees. He never climbed a tree in Calgary."

———————— • ————————

That night, in the bar of the Kuskanax Lodge, I meet Murray Creighton. Creighton is a tan and leathery forty-one-year-old New Zealander who, I learn over a few beers, has been living in a house trailer high in the mountains above the Sable Creek. Creighton, it turns out, is a professional shepherd working on an experimental program in reforestation. The project uses sheep rather than chemical herbicides to retard the growth of unwanted underbrush in a reforested area.

Creighton speaks of his dogs and his work with both enthusiasm and passion.

"Back home," he says, "a cowboy is the kid who milks the cows. The rest of us are shepherds."

His trailer is about an hour and a half out of town along a difficult series of logging roads. Directions are impossible. Before the night is over, however, he has introduced me to two biologists who are driving into the mountains the next day and are delighted when I ask if I can tag along.

The network of one-lane dirt roads that clings to the mountains and valleys of interior British Columbia like a spider's web is both complex and terrifying. Complex because there are no signs in here and, once you have navigated the first few crossroads, no way of knowing (if you are new to the area) exactly where you are. Terrifying because eventually you are going to meet a logging truck barrelling through the mountains like a Central American bus. The loggers clear the road in front of them with their CB radios, but if you happen to be bouncing around the back seat of a jeep with no CB, and if you are being driven by a hungover biologist with no apparent fear of what might be drifting around the next blind corner, you can't help but wonder what the hell you are doing.

My notes of the ride are sketchy, hard to read and make no sense. "Bear meat," it says at the top of the page. And then, "Buckyballs," "Assault," "University of Texas," "Explosion," and "Death." Could the ride have been that bad?

Later, I can remember only fragments of conversation about the "buckyball." Somewhere in the United States a scientist has discovered a giant new carbon molecule. The molecule is the same shape as the geodesic dome that sprang from the imagination of that unique American, Buckminster Fuller. In honour of Fuller, the molecule has been named the buckminsterfullerene. Scientists are calling it the "buckyball" for short. It is being hailed as the most important development in chemistry since the discovery of benzene in 1825.

We bounce across a log bridge that clings to the edge of a cliff and down, down, to a river on our left that boils white and wild.

Biologist One, my driver, stops the jeep abruptly in the middle of the bridge, turns, smiles and offers me a beer.

Why not? It has been well over an hour since breakfast.

The mountains, snow-capped now and cloud-wisped, fold, roll and then drop dramatically to the valley floor below us. The mud road we are following twists back and forth, around and over the outcrops. In the distance, our destination — a square of clear-cut forest the size of five football fields — looks deceptively like an alpine meadow, but up close you can see the burnt and ragged stumps that poke through the knee-high vegetation like tombstones.

It is called "The Block," and the climax forest of cedar and hemlock was logged off it in 1984. The clear-cut ends abruptly at the perimeter of the block, and just as abruptly the old forest crowds in like a curtain. It is as if the area has been hacked clear for a housing development.

Many foresters would tell you that clear-cutting a block of forest is not necessarily contrary to the natural world. They say these ugly swaths cut out of the forest aren't dissimilar to the fire damage that lightning storms leave behind. They say clear-cutting is the most effective and economical way to harvest and regenerate a stand of old-growth forest. They say that you can expect far better growth rates in a clear-cut area compared to an area that has been selectively logged, because the block will be more open to the sun and the new growth won't have to compete with the old forest for water and nutrients.

So this block was clear-cut in 1984. Burned in '86 and planted with two-year-old spruce seedlings in '88. The summer of 1989 a crew tramped around the seedlings with hand-held mowers and cut away competing vegetation. Now, two summers later, the five-year-old spruce are hidden by clumps of thimbleberry bushes and a pink ocean of fireweed that waves across the hillside.

If the spruce seedlings are going to thrive, the fireweed has to be controlled. The traditional method is to spray the block with herbicides. But no one is crazy about herbicides these days. That's where Murray Creighton and his sheep come in.

The idea is simple and elegant. Creighton bounds from boulder to boulder whistling commands to the five dogs that work with him. Under his direction the dogs move nine hundred sheep systematically around the block. If Creighton keeps the sheep moving at the right speed, they will eat the fireweed and the thimbleberry but leave the spruce seedlings alone. Without the competing vegetation the spruce will get the head start they need.

By all accounts the project is working. The Alberta ranchers who have provided the sheep should be happy. The sheep will have gained an average of forty pounds each by the end of the summer. That is, admittedly, half the weight gain you would expect if the sheep were pastured on grass, but the ranchers would have to rent grass pasture, and they are being paid to graze their sheep on the mountain. The logging company that is paying the tab should be happy. Even with the sheep rental factored in, the cost per hectare for sheep browsing is $320, compared to $900 a hectare for manual brushing.

Most important, the spruce seem happy. So far they appear to be thriving.

The biologists have come here today because they are worried about the effect the nine hundred sheep might have on the local grizzly population.

"We have a couple of concerns," says bearded biologist Peter Corbett. Corbett is standing near the sheep corral on the side of the mountain.

"First, we're worried about the effect the sheep might have on the natural habitat. So far it doesn't seem like they are having any impact at all. The site doesn't seem to be changing in composition, so in that way they're good for wildlife.

"But we're also worried about the direct impact the herd could have on the bears. There are a lot of grizzlies around here and it is critical for them to load up before they hibernate. On the coast they load up on salmon. Around here they eat huckleberries before den-up. Last year there were lots of berries around. We actually saw bears sharing sites with the sheep and there were no confrontations. This year we have a different situation. There aren't so many berries, and it could be a new ball game. We don't want the bears to turn on the sheep. Not because we are worried about losing a sheep or two; it's the bears we don't want to jeopardize. We don't want to teach them any behaviour that people might resent. We don't want these grizzlies becoming garbage bears. Last year the dogs seemed pretty effective in keeping the bears and the sheep apart. We'll have to see how effective they are this year when berries are a little scarcer.

"We're also concerned about the transmission of disease. No one knows about the abilities of sheep to transmit disease to ungulates. We have seen some foot rot in all three flocks we've brought up here this year, and we need more information before we can give this idea a sweeping endorsement."

Up on the mountain a large white dog is barking loudly. It is one of the maremmas. Unlike the border collies and the huntaways that Creighton uses to *herd* his sheep, the maremmas are used to *protect* the flock. The maremmas live with the sheep twenty-four hours a day and are always on the lookout for something that might be a threat. It is hard to know what goes on in a dog's mind, but it seems as if the maremmas, who look like huskies, think they are part of the herd.

Up on the mountain the dog is barking louder. It is charging the trees in the far corner of the block, but on each charge it stops short, wheels around and bounds back to the herd. Maremmas aren't attack dogs, and that is why they are so valuable here. An attack dog like an akita might launch itself into the woods and get killed by a grizzly that may be doing no more than sniffing around. And that would serve no purpose. The maremma's job is to make the bear take notice. The idea is to keep the predator away from the sheep but allow him to live in the block and share the berries.

"There is no way we are going to allow the wildlife to be compromised," says Corbett, gazing into the trees. "If the bear wants this block enough, she is going to get it. We aren't going to shoot any bears. We'll move the sheep first."

No one is ready to label sheep-browsing operational. Everyone says it is still an experimental technique. Yet everyone connected with the operation seems optimistic. Penny Dewar and Ray Greene of West Coast Browsing are talking of setting up a shepherd school on Vancouver Island. Sitting on the steps of his trailer, Murray Creighton thinks that would be a terrific idea.

"The life of a shepherd is wonderful. How many mornings can you wake up in the mountains with no cars around you and no telephones and sit there and watch a thunderstorm roll down the valley below you, or maybe watch a grizzly eating berries and feeding her cub. If I'm thirsty I just hike down to the creek and lie on my belly and drink all the fresh mountain water I want.

"I'm up every morning at 4 A.M. I lie in bed and watch the sun rise and read for about an hour. I'm reading a book called *Arctic Exodus*. It's about a reindeer drive from Alaska to Canada that happened in the 1930s. After I read, I cook breakfast. Usually I have sausages and eggs, and pancakes or maybe some hamburger. Next I clean camp and go for a run. Then I get my hill stick and my hill pack and get the sheep out of the corral and onto the block."

Murray is smiling at me.

"Jesus was a shepherd, you know."

As I nod earnestly his smile grows wider. I have fallen, I think, for a line he has used before.

"No, He wasn't," he says, laughing. "He was a carpenter. But He had a lot of shepherds around him. It's the most incredible, beautiful life."

On the way home we pull onto a side road an hour out of town and everyone tumbles out. We scramble down a steep path to a clearing in the forest the size of a small chapel. All around us ancient cedars soar into the clouds. I feel as if I have stepped into a painting by Emily Carr. Everything is green and brown. Moss, tree bark, leaves, soil, rock and, before me, a black pool of water the size of a choir stall. This is the St Leon hot spring. There are no markers, no signs pointing the way down the hill. There are no ticket collectors, no towels, no tourists. Just this clearing in the forest, just this stream trickling out of the ground, just this waist-deep pool collecting in the smooth rock face, just these cedars, just us. We peel off our clothes and sink tentatively into the hot water. Feet, hands, buttocks — moving at first like a family of herons fishing, but then as we acclimatize ourselves, slipping below the glassy surface and floating now so that only our heads bob on the top of the pool. Heads floating in the steam.

There is something about hot water. At home I often bath when I am already clean. I turn to hot water the way others turn to liquor. Water, the universal sacrament, unwinds me. It has become a family joke how long I can stand under a shower. I fill my tubs with potions that turn the water aegean blue or oils that make the bathroom smell of pine. I slip below the surface and lie full out under the water and . . . I open. Here in the forest the water bubbles out of the earth itself.

We float in the tree-lined pool for hours. Climbing out to cool down so we can climb in again. Our skin red and wrinkled. Our breathing slow and deep. Our voices softer. Baptised by the heat we drip dry, dress and climb up the path again. Moving more slowly on the way up than on the way down.

———— • ————

One morning, in my car, I happen upon a dirt track. It sails straight off through the conifers like a surveyor's line. There is something familiar about it, something that makes me want to stop, and without knowing why, I pull off the road and park. There is grass growing down the centre of the trail and scrub bush crowding in from the forest, but still plenty of room for my car. Because the path seems so flat and so familiar, I feel an urge to follow it. The trail lingers through the trees like a memory, and I am touched by that odd sensation of entering a room I have never visited and yet knowing somehow where everything is.

Then, abruptly, I know this isn't a path in the woods, and it doesn't lead anywhere familiar. It isn't an old road. It is the old railbed. This gravel path — like the contrails from an unseen plane, like the wake from a boat that has long passed — is what we have left from the age of steam.

And so it is in the small towns across this country. One afternoon in Nova Scotia, driving down the Annapolis Valley, I came across a crew that was actually pulling up the rails. Was it because they wanted the iron for scrap? Could this possibly be an exercise in economic righteousness? Somehow I thought otherwise. Somehow I knew that somewhere in Ottawa someone with his hands on the levers of power understood that if they were going to take the trains, they couldn't leave the train tracks.

This is what we are left with. These gravel waves and, somewhere in our memory, trains floating through the forests like ghost ships. If you follow the dirt trails, they will lead, if you are lucky, to a washed-out bridge, a forgotten lake, a beaver-dammed marsh; or, if luck is not with you, to where some civil engineer has captured the railbed for his road or, worse to an ugly collection of bungalows. I have walked on railbeds in Newfoundland, and now in British Columbia. The rails that stitched us together belong to another time — a time when distances were real and steam, as white as linen, floated over the tracks. And the tracks flashed in the sun like the silverware in the dining-car.

There was a time when all the trains had names. The Flyer. The Local. The Express. There was a time in Nakusp when everyone in town knew the name of all the train crews. Jim Connacher was one of the first engineers in the valley. He died when a bush fire burning from the head of Slocan Lake ignited one of the old trestle bridges. Jim couldn't see the fire ahead of him because there was a sharp bend in the rail just before the bridge. Before the train hit, Jim's fireman jumped to safety, but Jim stayed with the engine and managed to stop the train before the baggage car slid onto the bridge. He saved the passengers, but Jim and the engine went over the edge and Jim was burned to death.

———————◗•◖———————

I find the pole yard not far from where I found the old train tracks. Nakusp, it turns out, produces some of the finest telephone poles in the world. The cedar on the coast may grow faster but it doesn't have the fibre content, and thus the strength, of the poles that grow around the Arrow lakes. Trees that are cut and stripped in Nakusp are shipped across Canada and the United States. The poles are so desirable that they have even left Nakusp for Sweden and Denmark.

The day I visit, fumes from the burner smudge the sky like a dirty eraser. During the day smoke often hangs over the valley, capping the town like a beret, but I never hear anyone complain. Smoke streaks in the sky mean that the pole yard or the shake mill or, better, both, are working, and if that's the price you have to pay to know there'll be cheques on Friday, so be it. Smoke in the sky is as good as money in the bank.

The day I visit the yard, a buyer from the J.H. Baxter Company of California is scrambling over the piles of poles with a moisture meter he carries in a wooden case. The meter looks like something from my high-school physics class. It has a probe with a black wooden handle. The man from California hammers the probe into each pole he wants to test. Every time he knocks the probe into a pole, he twists some dials, grunts and chalks some numbers onto the wood. It is a functional tool, carefully assembled long before liquid crystal displays and digital read-outs.

"I'll only buy poles," he says, squinting into the sun, "with less than twenty-eight percent moisture two inches into the wood at the mid point of the pole."

His name is Fred Lynch. He is wearing blue jeans, a white shirt and thick red suspenders. He seems happy for my company.

"A good pole is nice and straight and has an even taper. And no defects."

"Defects?"

"Like cracks in the wood, or knots or cat faces."

"What's a cat face?" I ask as he swings his meter to the next pole.

"A scar," he says, and he hammers the probe home. Any pole that passes muster he brands with a hammer and initials with a fat piece of chalk.

Later in the day I sit on the ground with my back against a pile of poles and talk with yard foreman Ollie Coates. Ollie started working in the pole business when he was twelve years old. He likes his job.

"It's a very special business," he says, removing his green peaked cap and scratching his head. "You need a different temperament to work with poles than you do to work with lumber. You've got to be different, right from the moment you look at a tree in the forest. In a way, I guess, it's more of a challenge than ordinary logging. You can't treat a pole like a saw log. When you're logging for saw logs you judge yourself by how much wood you take out in a day. You just can't do that when you're cutting poles. Maybe you'll only take down six in a day. You have to have more pride in your work. The poles have to be handled like eggs. They're so easy to damage. If you fall one carelessly and put a crack in the top, then you're going to have to cut maybe ten feet from your pole. And that's a lot of money. The big poles bring the big money, so you can't afford to be careless."

Once they arrive in the yard the poles are peeled and graded. They are ranked first by length and then by quality. Each pole is eventually classified into one of fifty-eight potential categories, depending on the wood fibre, the moisture content, scarring or splits in the wood.

In Nakusp poles are either cedar or jack pine. The standard telephone pole is forty-five feet tall. The rule of thumb is that it takes two years of growth for every foot of height. That means the average telephone pole is ninety to one hundred years old.

The Village Bread and Pastry Shop is opposite the high school.

In the back of the bakery Edith Izairovich is decorating a cake. She drops sugar rosettes in the four corners and squeezes garish loops of icing around the roses and along the borders. As she steps back to take stock of her progress, she runs her forearm across her forehead. Her grey hair is pulled back into a ponytail. She is fifty years old and built like a fire plug.

Now she is writing a message with red gelatin across the middle of the cake. She gets as far as the second D in "BIRTHDAY."

"Accht," she says with disgust when she realizes her spelling mistake. "Too much confidence."

She flicks the offending letter off the top of the cake with a spatula and begins again.

"There," she says, stepping back. And then, not yet satisfied, picking up the green squeezer and adding yet another florid row of icing. "There."

Edith was born in the mountains of Germany. Her husband, Nick, was born in Yugoslavia. Nick is at home asleep. He opens the bakery every morning at 3 A.M. Edith, who says she is the left hand to Nick's right, doesn't begin until five. Soon she'll go home for her rest and Nick will return to wrap up the day. Edith and Nick will have supper together. They have been in the bakery business for over thirty years. They came to Nakusp from Calgary six years ago.

"I wish we had come here thirty years ago when my kids were young. The climate suits me. I garden. I go fishing. I ride my bike to work. It takes me five minutes. In Calgary it took forty-five minutes and I had to ride the bus. Another thing is shopping. It takes me half an hour here. In Calgary it took me half an hour to get to the store. And people care about people here."

As she talks, Edith never stops moving. She pokes at some buns in the oven, begins to roll out some pastry and then stops and looks at the cake. She puts down the roller and picks up the icing again. She adds another swirl.

"There," she says for the third time.

"I was going to tell you about when my husband got sick," she says. "He had cancer. He was very ill. He was in hospital and I was left to keep the shop going. Well, sometimes the pastries weren't what they should be. I had never done pastry before. But people came in and took them and never said anything. They waited until he came back. When he came back he was bald from the treatment. He looked awful. But the only thing people said was, 'You're looking great.' They bought the things he was making. It did a lot for him. It was very important for his recovery. Remember, we were new to town when that happened. Do you understand what I am telling you?

"We left Calgary so we could sell our business to our son. We wanted to give him something so he could make a life. Now he wants to sell that business. He wants to move here, too.

"If I was to tell you the truth, I would tell you that when we moved here I felt like I had come home."

While Edith and I talk in the back of the bakery, Charlotte Poulin has been running things out front. Like all great bakers, Edith and Nick have done very little to the front of their store. There is nothing attractive about their establishment. The lighting is poor, the walls dark, the signage *ad hoc*. There are a few glass-fronted cases filled with pastries, and some wooden shelves with unpackaged bread. The bakery gets by on aroma, and it seems to be getting by very well. While Charlotte slides loaves of warm bread into brown paper bags, I settle cross-legged on the soft drink cooler by the door and pull out my notebook.

Charlotte, too, has a story she wants to tell.

"We left Montreal," she begins, "in August of 1988. We sold everything. Everything except our summer clothes, three forks, three knives, three glasses and three plates. There was the three of us. My husband, my kid and myself. We didn't like the winters anymore and we were going to live in Florida. But when we got there we didn't like Florida, either. We were only there for three hours. Long enough for me to put my feet in the ocean. We had a family meeting there on the beach and decided it was too hot. We were all miserable. Everywhere we looked there were fast-food restaurants. It was just what we were trying to get away from. Everyone was in a hurry. We were doing the speed limit and people were zooming by us honking their horns. So someone said, 'Let's get out of here.' And we did. We got onto the highway and Wayne said, 'I've always wanted to go out west. Let's go to Vancouver.' And that's what we were doing when we stopped here. We were heading for Vancouver.

"It was the Labour Day weekend. Wayne was tired of driving. We needed food and gas. We decided we would camp here for the weekend. We were sitting in the campground right here in town, and the pastor comes and invites everyone to church. Now, we weren't church-goers. We were heavy smokers and drinkers. But we didn't have anything else to do so we said what the heck and we went to church. After the service Wayne was talking to the pastor, and Wayne said if he could get work, he wouldn't mind staying here. And the pastor told him he should meet Ed Wiebe. Ed owns Saddle Mountain Cedar, one of the shake mills. Ed was looking for someone to work for him. He wanted someone who had no experience so he could train them his way.

"That was three years ago. Now Wayne is the foreman at the mill and I'm working part time here at the bakery. We don't drink anymore. Wayne quit smoking three days ago. I used to be angry all the time. The least little thing upset me. I'm not like that anymore. Our lives have changed. I don't know where we'd be if we hadn't stopped in this little town. Somewhere lost in the crowd, I guess."

A woman with two children comes through the front door. Charlotte pauses while everyone chooses a pastry. She picks up her story before she has finished making change.

"Let me tell you something else about this town. My husband had an injury at work. He hurt his back and they wanted to send him down to Vernon for a CAT scan. I didn't get the message that they wanted to go to Vernon until after everything had closed that evening, so I didn't have any money. It must have been eleven o'clock at night when I realized I had a problem. I called the people who run the corner grocery and asked if they could cash a cheque. You know what they said? They said, 'Come on down.' It was like being on 'Let's Make a Deal.' Heck, I cashed a cheque the first day I was in town and no one asked for ID."

The bakery is unusual among Nakusp's small businesses, in that it sells baked goods and nothing else. Many of the other merchants in town have diversified. In the lobby of the movie theatre, for instance, you can rent videos. The town's insurance agent will also book your vacation.

In the big cities, bakeries routinely spring up that specialize in one item — cinnamon rolls, for example — and it's common to find a coffee shop where just about all you can buy is . . . coffee.

Small towns march to a different economic beat. I was once told of a gas station in Trepassey, Newfoundland, where there was a handwritten sign in the window that read: 'We also sell coffins and wreaths." As I travel across the country, I have seen many other examples of economic resourcefulness, but for sheer chutzpah and imagination, none come close to the Nakusp Flower Shop.

The flower shop is on Broadway near the centre of town.

The flowers are squirrelled away at the back of the shop in an old refrigerator with rounded corners — the kind you might see in a summer cottage. The day I visit, there are in the fridge, five vases of flowers, to wit: peppermint and candy-striped carnations, yellow alstroemeria and some white and red-trimmed mini-carns.

The flowers share the fridge with a number of boxes of EQ VALAN — "the most complete parasite control for horses" — for as well as dealing in flowers, the Nakusp Flower Shop is a feed store, a bottle depot, home to one of the town's two lottery outlets, and a pet supply centre (complete with a wall display of products such as Sergeant's Worm Away, Fermalt Hair Ball Remedy for Cats and Kittens, a leather muzzle for a pit bull and fungus cure tablets for fish). The shop is also a garden supply centre with, in the back, a locked room full of pesticides. And a gift store. There is a wall rack of bestsellers by the front door, shelves of magazines by the counter, stationery supplies by the magazines, a line of exotic coffees and a selection of specialty chocolates from West Germany. In the craft section there is a macramé kit, a candy-making kit and a collection of how-to books, including one on string art and another on classic Christmas doilies. On shelves around and about there are china tea cups and coffee mugs with cute sayings, a selection of gourmet teas, wicker baskets, sunglasses, silver spoons, watches for $4.40, kids' games, party favours and small cars. On one shelf there is a box of fluid-filled plastic pouches that, for fifty-nine cents, will remove film from your windshield. There are also plastic pouches of wrapping paper, racks of postcards, shelves of house plants and a bin of remaindered cook-books. The shop, incidently, is no larger than any corner milk store.

If all this should prove too much for me, I am in good hands. The Nakusp Flower Shop is also the town's funeral parlour.

———— • ————

On my last evening in town I go for one last walk. I end up at the marina and, as luck would have it, run into Bob and Judy Nowak. I know that Nowak, who runs the delicatessen, is also involved in the local mushroom trade, and I have been looking for an opportunity to ask him about it. I have learned that mushroom-picking is a lucrative hobby for many people in town, but it is also a secretive one. No one I ask will talk to me about mushrooms. I have a hunch, how-ever, that the loquacious Nowak just might.

The three of us walk down the cement jetty and settle aboard the Nowaks' new boat. There are pillows, blankets and a bag full of beer, and we sit there while the sun slips away and the smoke from the shake mill thins in the cool evening air. If I have to leave in the morning, this is the right place to be tonight, and Bob and Judy Nowak are the right people to be with.

"Mushrooms," says Bob, smiling, as he reaches for a beer. "I guess I found out about them in 1976."

"What happened?" I ask.

"What you have to understand is that the mushrooms that grow around here are highly prized by the Japanese. They are like herring roe, or something. The Japanese will pay upwards of $150 a pound for these mushrooms. The sort of thing they do is buy one of them — one mushroom, not one pound — and take it to their father-in-law as a gift. It is a very special thing. They cut a sliver off a single mushroom and drop it into a bowl of miso soup. The flavour explodes in the soup like ambrosia."

The mushroom Nowak is talking about is the Japanese pine, or matsutake. "The pungently sweet, aromatic odour," says my mushroom guide, "is a distinguishing feature not easily forgotten." The pine mushroom, says the book, grows in the autumn "in the mountains under conifers, or along the Pacific coast under pine and in the thickets of huckleberries and rhododendrons."

"They grow in the most beautiful places in the world," says Nowak, "and this happens to be one of them. They germinate under heavy moss, and when they open up they can be as big as a dinner plate and you can see them two hundred yards away. But they are more valuable if they're just buds, so you want to pick them from under the moss carpets. Sometimes it's like hobbit land in there. You find these little streams trickling down the mountain and the moss, and there is very little underbrush, and then down the hill a little you see all these tiny white mushroom buttons.

"It seems funny now, but not so long ago no one around here knew anything about them. There was this one guy in town who used to go out every fall and come back at the end of the day with burlap bags full of stuff. But he'd never say what he was about. One day somebody picked up on what he was doing. He was picking mushrooms and selling them in Vancouver.

"For a few years he let out to a few people what to look for, and they would go out and pick for him, and he would take their mushrooms and maybe pay them two or three dollars a pound, and he would sell them in Vancouver.

"But it's not like that anymore. It's hard to describe the fever that hits this town in a good mushroom year. In a good year Nakusp will receive over $2 million from mushrooms. At the beginning of the season the Loomis truck arrives in town and all of a sudden three armed guards pop out of the truck. It's the only time of year they have guards like that. Sometimes there is so much action, the bank actually runs out of cash. Everyone goes picking. The kids go picking after school. They'll put a plastic bag on their handlebars and come back with ten or fifteen mushrooms by supper time and walk away with $25. Some people take trips to Europe on what they make in a year. Others have bought four-wheel-drive vehicles. I'd say the average person who does maybe four or five hours will make somewhere between $100 and $350 a day. A good picker can make $8,000 to $10,000 in a season.

"Sometimes the population of Nakusp will double. There will be encampments of maybe 1,500 people. There are normally somewhere between four and six buyers around town. But they'll have satellite buyers working for them, so in all maybe you'll have twenty different places bidding for mushrooms. The pickers go from station to station, and of course people start rumours about how much the different buyers are paying. It can get pretty crazy.

"The whole thing is crazy. There are only a handful of buyers in Vancouver, and they're all friends. And every year they get together and have dinner and all agree that they won't pay more than, say, twenty dollars a pound. And while they are eating they're slipping out of the room and getting on the phone and telling their buyers to go to twenty-one dollars. They're fighting all the time. They all want more product.

"People in town get just as nuts. They'll get hurt, like badly scratched up, or they'll sprain an ankle or something. When they go to the hospital there is a form they have to fill out, and one of the questions is 'Where did the accident happen?' Of course, no one will answer. Everyone protects their favourite spot like it was a secret fishing hole."

Nowak is one of the mushroom buyers in Nakusp. During the two or three weeks of mushroom season he'll have a large refrigerated truck parked behind his restaurant. In a garage out back Nowak and his partner buy, sort and grade mushrooms well into the night. The mushrooms are re-graded in Vancouver and shipped by jet to arrive in Japan less than forty-eight hours after they leave Nakusp.

"You haven't," I say, nearly an hour later, as the rigging on the neighbouring boats clangs in the night, "told me how you got into the business."

"It's hard to believe how it happened," says Nowak, "but it's true. This guy came to town from Vancouver to scout things out. He came to the deli for a coffee and we got talking. At the end of the day he came back and asked if I wanted to work with him. I said 'Sure' and he said 'Good.' Then he handed me $5,000 in cash and said, 'I'm in a hurry. Take this and deposit it in the bank in your name and call me tomorrow with the account number and I'll put another $10,000 in the account. Then I'll phone you and fill you in on what I want you to do.' I took the money but there was no signature. No anything. I had never seen this guy before. Sure enough the next day another $10,000 was dropped in the account. I took a partner and we started buying mushrooms. The first year we made about $500. The next year we made $7,500 each.

"The mushrooms are mostly a quarter to half a pound. We've paid as much as $62 for a Number One. One year we got a freak. A five-pound Number One. We paid $500 for it. We wrapped it and wrapped it and wrapped it, and shipped it to Vancouver air freight.

"Sometimes it's like a fever. If you are paying top price, people will line up at your station for hours. I serve them coffee, and if they are my top pickers, I feed them, too. You have to treat your pickers well or you're going to lose them to another buyer. Some people make a fortune. There's one guy in town who picks for me who has worked in the bush all his life. He knows the forest like the back of his hand. He's maybe the best picker around. He once made $40,000 in a three-week season."

I say goodbye to Bob and Judy and take the long way home. I walk the length of the promenade along the shore of the lake. Then I wander up to the ballpark.

During the spring just about everyone in town plays in the local slow-pitch league. But summer is here and the last tournament of the season is over.

I climb over the stubby wooden fence and walk around the bases and out to the pitcher's mound. All around me the trees bleed into the blackness of the mountains.

Three weeks ago, in the bottom of the ninth inning with two men out and two men on base, twenty-four-year-old Stuart Klassen made the catch of his life on this field to end the slow-pitch season and clinch the championship for his team, the Rusty Nails. The opposition hadn't lost a game for two years and were so sure of winning that they hadn't bothered to bring the trophy. When the game was over, someone had to be sent home to fetch it.

Klassen was playing centre field when the last man up cracked the ball and Steve was yelling, "Catchable, catchable, it's catchable!" He must have yelled it three or four times, and while he was yelling and pointing, Stuart was running back as hard as he could, pumping towards the fence, and then he was jumping, jumping up into the mountains and into the trees. He was moving so perfectly that when the ball hit his glove he had his eyes sort of closed, and when he brought his hand back over the fence he was squeezing just as hard as he could, because he didn't know for sure whether the ball was in there or not. Then he opened his glove and the ball was lying in the leather like he had plucked the moon out of the sky, and everyone was jumping up and down and hitting him on the back, and some of the girls were crying.

I am running around the bases in the night, now. Coming fast towards home. Thinking to myself as I run that every catch should be so splendid. Every memory so grand. Stuart Klassen drove up to Halfway Creek where his wife was waiting, and by the light of a campfire he told her about his catch. The moment seared in his mind forever.

Like the picture over the fireplace of the *Minto* burning on the lake.

Ferryland
NEWFOUNDLAND

*People in this town don't carry any money. You don't need
any money in this town. All you need here is your name
and your face.*

CYRIL O'KEEFE

I came to Newfoundland in June, 1991, before the big cut in the cod quota, but during the coldest spring anyone could remember.

"Colder," said someone earnestly, "than 1928."

I poked around St John's for a day and then another I hadn't counted on — wandering around the harbour, up and down the steep hills and in and out of the pubs. Jan Morris is right. It *is* Canada's most entertaining city. On my third morning I stopped a tourist — a man from Port William, Nova Scotia — and asked him to take my picture in front of the sign that marks the beginning of the Trans-Canada Highway.

"Get the billboard in the back," I told him.

"MILE ZERO — CANADA BEGINS RIGHT HERE."

The 7,821-kilometre highway that unfolds west from where I was standing — St John's to Vancouver Island — is the longest national highway in the world. Astonishingly, when it was officially opened in the summer of 1962 (six years behind schedule), nearly half of the Trans-Canada Highway, about 3,000 kilometres of it, was unpaved.

As I drove out of St John's I thought back to the two friends I visited the afternoon I left Toronto — a man and a woman who had both spent years working in Newfound-land. We drank beer on the woman's balcony and when I got up to leave, the man offered me some travelling advice.

"Remember," he said. "You're going..." and he paused to make sure I was listening "you're going to another country."

Newfoundlanders will tell you there are only two types of people who live in their province. "Townies" live in St John's. Virtually everyone else lives by the ocean and is, therefore, a "bayman."

It is an hour's drive from St John's, south along Highway 10, to the bay I have come to visit. Ferryland dangles off the south-east corner of the province like a worm on a hook. The highway loops along the ocean as if it was following the French Riviera. But here the coastline is jagged, scoured by glaciers, sculpted by the wind. Out the passenger window on the right side of my car are the scrubby logged-off barrens. Through the driver's window on my left are the bays, the heads and the offshore islands. And still some lighthouses. For every indent there's a harbour, for every harbour there's an outport slipping into the sea. And rocks. Rocks everywhere. Rocks in the fields, rocks along the road and rocks spilling into the ocean. Rocks mashed as much now by memory as by waves. For here is where recorded history began in Canada.

Looking at my map, I am driving *down* the page from St John's towards Ferryland. But locals would say I am moving *up* the coast. Up the "shore," actually. The "southern shore," as opposed to the "south coast," which is somewhere else.

Sometimes the road wanders away from the ocean and I twist in my seat, wondering how something that large can vanish so completely. Then I crest a hill and there is the water again — big, brilliant, blue.

It is at the top of such a hill that I come on my bay. Up the hill and through the trees and then, *pow!* The ocean and the town. And icebergs, as far as I can see.

I park on the gravel shoulder. So this is Ferryland. A handful of houses strung along the highway like coloured beads. From the hill I am standing on at the north end of town to the hill at the south it is just under five kilometres. And then it's trees again on your right and the ocean on your left. There are no sidewalks here; few, if any, parallel lines. There is only the highway and, from time to time, a side road drifting casually up into the hills on the right or down towards the water on the left. The side roads are wide enough for one car — two in a pinch — and they connect only a dozen or so houses before they rejoin the highway like sweeping U-shaped driveways. There aren't many of them and they never wander too far out of sight. They have names like "Horse Nap Lane" or "Quarry River Road" or

"Sunny Hill," but there are no numbers on the houses, and in the phone book everyone's address is simply listed as "Ferryland." You go to the post office for your mail; as for visiting, everyone knows where everyone lives. People like me are given directions.

"Go to Paul's Store. You know Paul's Store? And then turn left and we are the third house on your right." Or, "We are beside the doctor's."

The harbour is both perfect and perfectly placed — midway between the hill on the north and the hill on the south side of town. It is called The Pool and is protected on one side by a sloping peninsula that tilts out two kilometres towards Ireland, and all around by a cluster of islands that are characteristic of sunken coastlines. The peninsula that protects the harbour is called The Downs. Among the islands are Nancy's Portion, Ship Island, Goose Island, Kelly's Island, Costello's Island and Isle of Boise (pronounced "boys").

Behind the town there is a third hill that overlooks the harbour and is called The Gaze because there was once a time when someone would be posted there to keep a weather eye for the ships (privateers or Royal Navy) that would heave into Newfoundland's outports and press able-bodied men into service. Whenever a mast was sighted on the horizon, a flag was raised or a fire lit and fishermen out in The Pool scrambled for shore and made for the woods. The lake behind The Gaze, where the kids swim and "trout," is Merrymaking Pond. Is there anywhere else in Canada, I wonder, where the name of a fish can so easily become a verb? The pond is only one of many landmarks whose names echo local history — There is also the Cornfields, The Groves, The Battery, Forge Hill, and Fox Hill, where the pirate Peter Easton is said to have buried part of his loot.

There are two gas stations in town, two fish plants, one old stone church, one general store, a handful of convenience stores, a school, three graveyards and 795 people

— double, maybe, the number who lived in Ferryland two hundred years ago.

I have been warned there will be nowhere to stay, so am surprised when I drive into town and find The Downs Inn. I bang hopefully on the door and then, heart sinking, cup my hands against a window in the three-storey clapboard building beside the church. It is badly in need of paint. Maybe, I think, no longer in business.

There are two phone numbers on the sign by the road-side. I drive to the local grocery store and try them both.

"We don't open till next week," says the man who answers the second number. "And the Mrs is out till supper."

"Supper would be fine. If I came at supper could I stay?"

"Oh, yes. You can stay. And would you be wanting a meal?"

Mrs Costello is waiting at the inn when I arrive. It used to be the convent, she explains. Her son, Gerard, bought it and opened the inn a few summers ago. He lives "to town," which is St John's, seventy-five kilometres north and an hour "down" Highway 10. Mrs Costello and a girl from here look after things.

The girl won't be starting for a week. Mrs Costello lives in the house next door with her husband. I'll be alone in the inn. She gives me a front door key and says I can come and go as I please. She will cook dinner for me at night. It will be ready at six. We agree I will make my own breakfast. I don't want to feel I am dragging her out of bed or, for that matter, myself.

She takes me upstairs and shows me my room. It looks over the highway and down at the harbour. Some nights the wind comes up in great gusts, crashing into the inn and rocking it so it seems as if I am sleeping in one of the boats across the road.

The next morning I stand at my bedroom window and look out across the water and think, "Out there is

Europe. You can't get much closer without getting in the water."

Downstairs I find a box of Kellogg's Corn Flakes beside a bowl on the kitchen counter. There is orange juice in the fridge. I fix toast and tea as well. We settled on a price last night — thirty-five dollars a day including anything I want to eat at breakfast. Dinner is twelve dollars extra.

After I rinse my breakfast dishes I get into my car and drive aimlessly from one end of town to the other. Back and forth and back again. I don't know how or where to start. There is no main street in Ferryland to walk down, no newspaper office to drop in on, no shopping district to poke through.

The houses are as scattered and often as colourful as the dories that bob in the harbour. Half are the flat-roofed square two-storey clapboard homes you see on New-foundland postcards. The others are newer bungalows. Later I learn that virtually no one in town has a mortgage. When you turn twenty you buy a lot from a relative for a dollar. Then you spend the next four years building a bungalow in your spare time. Your friends and neighbours help. For a town where the resale value of a home is inevitably below the construction costs, there are an unreasonable number of new homes. In Ferryland it seems that getting married without a bungalow is a greater sin than having a child out of wedlock. I will meet more than one young woman who is living at home with her parents and young child, waiting until she and her fiancé get their bungalow finished so they can marry and move out.

A few people commute to jobs in St John's. Some of them stay "to town" for the week. Reg Clowe, who lives with his wife, Margaret, in the last house in Ferryland, has a trailer he baches in Monday to Friday. He keeps it parked behind an Irving gas station. His neighbour across the road, Ken O'Keefe, works in construction and commutes to St John's every day. But most people in Ferryland are tied to the local fishery. They might set cod traps within a stone's throw of the shore or go out onto the Banks a week or two at a time. They might work at the fish plant here or in Fermeuse or Cape Broyle. Whatever they do, it is both blessed and cursed by the sea.

The town is Irish Catholic. The one church, beside the inn, might have washed ashore from County Kerry. It is one of the last old stone churches in Newfoundland. I will hear two stories about the stones. One is that they were carried here, one by one, by boat from Stone Island at the tip of Cape Broyle Head. The other story is that the rocks were part of a fort that once stood on one of the islands in the harbour. The bronze statue in the church-yard and the crucifix inside were salvaged from a ship that went aground near the doctor's house in 1926. For years the SS *Torhamvan* lay beached yet proudly intact, almost in the harbour, and the generations since the twenties have watched while she slowly rusted, twisted and washed away. All that is left of her today are two huge boilers still sitting on the gravel isthmus. The two boilers, that is, and the crucifix and the statue in the stone church.

Ferryland has always had a complicated relationship with shipwrecks. Men have risked their lives to pluck people off foundering ships. Yet the same men would be lying if they told you there hadn't been nights, when times were lean, that they had asked the Lord God to send them a boat. The night the *Torhamvan* went down a goodly supply of paint, soap, lard and macaroni made its way into a number of homes before the wreck commissioner arrived to impound the cargo.

Ferryland is a community where social gatherings are often left more to destiny than design. Five cars parked in front of a house on a Saturday night are as good as an invi-tation in the mail. Wherever a group gathers there is likely a song to be sung, a story to be told and a bottle of Lamb's Light Rum in a paper bag to drink.

"I even keep her bagged in the cupboard at home," says one schoolteacher early on a Friday evening. "That way I don't have to see how much I've drunk."

Most everyone will have "mug-up" before they go to bed. It might just be a cup of tea, but sometimes it's a feed of fish. People still go mumming here during the twelve days of Christmas. When mummers call on their neighbours, they always go in disguise, often as a member of the opposite sex. Mummers are welcomed in and given a drink. The game is to guess who has come calling and, if you guess right, to remove their disguise. Sometimes the visitors are boisterous and uninhibited. Other times garish mummers will sit stoically at the kitchen table without speaking — a nod or maybe a grunt all they offer to the questions thrown their way.

Nearly every house has a wood stove and therefore a woodpile in the yard. In Ferryland people build their woodpiles before they cut and split their wood. The thin tree trunks are leaned on end, one against the other, so the woodpiles resemble tepees. The piles are balanced this way so the wind can dry the wood. God knows the sun won't. Most men cut their own wood in the winter, and many of the men still use horses. Today the horses are supposed to be tethered in the grass by the roadside or pastured in a yard close to home, but you can still see a "scatter" horse wandering free around Ferryland. Not so long ago it was the habit to fence in gardens rather than livestock. It was not unusual to look out your kitchen window in the morning and see ten or twenty horses leaning over your fence trying to get at your lawn.

Things have changed since the highway came. Like all outports, Ferryland used to be a community of paths. The wheelbarrow was the main form of transportation then. You pushed it down to the docks to meet the schooner and back again. They only paved the road to town in the 1960s and things have changed, but not so much that Susie Kavanagh can't still keep a cow in the middle of town. The cow starts bawling and kicking her stall every morning about ten o'clock if Susie hasn't appeared to milk her.

"We always kept a cow in the old days," says Susie, who is maybe the last woman in Ferryland still milking. "We'd kill a calf every year. We had to, or we would've starved. I wouldn't eat our own meat, but the kids did."

Every morning Susie, who is in her sixties, lugs her milk pails into the kitchen and scalds the milk for an hour in a big pan on the wood stove. After the milk has set for a day she skims the cream off the top, and every few days, when she has enough cream, Susie makes butter.

"I churns it for about an hour and a half and then washes it out," she says. "That's what me kids were raised on — molasses bread, bakeapple jam and cream that thick on top." Susie is holding her thumb and index finger about as far apart as she can get them.

She keeps her milk in Pepsi bottles or jam jars or whatever she can get hold of, and lots of people come around to the house to see if she has any milk to spare.

———————— • ————————

Bert O'Keefe is working his way across the church lawn on his knees.

"I forgot my knee pads," he says, shaking his head.

O'Keefe is seventy-six years old. As he crawls forward, he shoves an aluminium crutch out in front of him. He is holding a pocket knife in his right hand and a white plastic bag in the other. He sticks the knife into the ground and pops out a weed, shakes the root clean and shoves it into his bag. Bert O'Keefe is harvesting dandelions.

"They used to graze sheep here and you couldn't get dandelions or nothing. If I get another bag like that one," he says, pointing behind him, "I'll have a fine lot to take home. I stores them in water. They'll keep like that for a week. And they don't smell. You put a bag of greens in water and they stink."

O'Keefe is wearing an old peaked hat, a windbreaker and big rubber boots. His face is as weathered as the stone walls of the old church; his accent is about as thick.

"There's about three feeds back there," he says nodding. "When they boils down they gets smaller."

He thrusts the knife, pulls, shakes and stuffs another weed into his bag. Dumble-dor, it's called by some in this province.

"I read in the *Reader's Digest* where this is the best green you can get," he says, "It's got all the vitamins you need."

As I follow him around the yard my tongue feels like it is made of wood. Words drop out of my mouth thick and woolly. His words seem to be dancing a jig.

There is a mickey of Lamb's Light Rum sticking out of his windbreaker pocket.

"Pure spring water," he says, taking a swig "Right out of the rock, boy."

"I thought it was rum," I say.

"No. It's water. But we used to make wine out of these roots." He swings the bag of dandelions up to my face. "It makes the best wine. You just got to boil down the water and strain the dandelion off."

The wind is blowing hard now off The Downs, and Bert slips the hood of his jacket over his peaked cap. I huddle closer to the wall of the church and watch silently as he uses the handle of his crutch like a rake to gather a pile of leaves that are just out of reach. It is cold. My wife told me on the phone that back home in Toronto the kids are playing in the backyard with the hose. Here there is only this. The sound of his knife tearing at the dry ground, his breath coming hard. The wind.

———— • ————

Mrs Costello tells me another guest will be checking in. He'll be arriving after midnight, she says. Would I leave the light on in the hall? His name is Robert. He comes from Twillingate.

I meet Robert the next evening at dinner. He is twenty-five years old and has come up the shore to a job at the fish plant in Fermeuse. He is a refrigerator engineer. His job is seasonal. He has left his wife and child at home.

At first I resent his intrusion. I have been enjoying my dinners alone, but as there are only two tables in the dining-room, and as we are the only two people eating, it seems ridiculous for us not to sit together. As we get to know each other I come to look forward to his company.

Robert Linfield is, I learn, the son of a sea captain. His father once owned a long liner and went to the seal hunt. In 1986 Robert followed his father to sea. He spent eight months as a deck-hand on a 250-foot scow that had a shipping contract for CN and ploughed the outports from Labrador to the south coast, delivering everything from chickens to refrigerators. Some people, he says, can cope with the sea; some can't. Robert went back to school and got his engineer's papers.

At dinner he wears a crew-neck sweater with no shirt showing under it. The sweater and his dark hair, which is cut short, give him the appearance of a Norwegian sailor. As we sit opposite each other, passing Mrs Costello's sweet pickles back and forth across the table, Robert tells me about growing up by the sea.

"I used to go sealing with me dad. It's a bloody business, sealing is. Same as any other kind of slaughter. Sometimes we'd go swatching when the wind was in on the land. I was out there once and suddenly there is an ice-breaker coming up through the channel between me and the shore. I had to make haste to get up in front of it so I could make it back to land. But before I could do that the wind switched and caused the ice to slacken so instead of being compacted against the shore it started to spread out and there were spaces between it. Well, boy, I was coping some fast, then. Coping is when you jump from one pan of ice to the next. Sometimes the pans don't hold your weight and you might have to run across three or four small ones to get to one big enough. I was in a bit of a panic. I was carrying a rifle and a big gaffer that you use to kill the seals and to keep your balance on the ice. A couple of times I had to jump when I knew I couldn't make it and I ended up in the water and had to pull myself up on the ice. I knew I wasn't going to drown. I had a lifejacket on. I was just heading for land, boy. But make no mistakes — that water was cold.

"A lot of people get snow-blind or ice-blind out there, but that never happened to me. It's a hard racket. It's bred into you, I guess."

The town doctor tells me that the seal hunt was a rite of passage for young men who lived in Newfoundland. Until you've been on the ice, you are a "landlubber," and that's almost synonymous with coward. After you've been out, you're a "swiller."

Robert may have left the water, but he has something to say about the ocean every night.

"I was always by the water, I guess. When I was a kid I spent all my time on the beach. We used to play in the tidal pools. We'd get crab and kelp and lobsters and sticklebacks and baby lumpfish."

As he rhymes off his childhood conquests, Robert's foot taps up and down in rhythm.

"We'd fish from the rocks and catch anything that would take our hooks. I remember these little things that looked like mermaids. They were tiny things with little heads and two little wings that came down to a tail. They were like little angels."

Another night he tells me about his time on the mainland.

"I went up to Ontario during the summer of 1987. I worked for Kruger Paper. Oh, I missed the ocean, boy. Sometimes the roar of traffic can sound like the sea, but it's not the same. Oh, I loves it, boy. I loves it. The smell. The salt. Even when I was young I loved it. I used to get sick constantly. I'd go out with me dad and be sick all day long. Yet when I got home I'd want to go out again. I did that for years before I got used to it.

"Oh, I was some homesick that summer I was away. I'll never go back to the mainland again. Not even for a holiday.

"I love it here. I get up in the morning and look out the door, look over the water and that's happiness for me. That's happiness. I just loves the water, boy. I just loves the water."

———————— • ————————

There are icebergs in the harbour and this morning I drive up onto one of the hills to get a better look. I sit in the car and try to count how many icebergs I can see. Each one is tremendously large. Yesterday, under the grey sky and before the chill wind, the ice offered no comfort. Today it is sunny. The water where the sun reflects off the ice is a brilliant aquamarine. It looks like a poster of a Caribbean island. I count eleven icebergs. One looks like a mountain range; another is low, flat and swooping like an aircraft carrier.

Across the road I can see people in the graveyard leaning on shovels, talking, hammering. I wander over and meet Jim Hall. Like me he has been watching the ice.

"They look like a row of starched white shirts drying on a line," he says. "I'd love to get out there and crawl on one."

The blue of the water, the white of the ice, the snap of the wind. Each iceberg looks like a frozen cloud dropped from the sky, bobbing, almost billowy, on the ocean. Except they aren't bobbing. They are, all of them, grounded. They are stuck around the harbour, and while they are stuck here, the fishermen are stuck on land. The nets are all repaired. The boats are ready. Everyone is just . . . waiting. A wave-worn iceberg will roll, and if you are too close when it rises out of the water it can take your boat and flip it like a coin. You can't set the cod traps, anyway, because when the ice shifts it will cut them. And even if you did set the nets, the water is cold with the ice, and slobby. The capelin won't come till the water warms.

Capelin, members of the smelt family, are the small fish that herald the arrival of the cod. Every spring the capelin swim into the bays by the millions to spawn on the beaches. The cod, who eat the capelin, follow them in. The female capelin, valued in Japan for their roe, are a lucrative fishery in themselves. For the week or two (or less) that the capelin are spawning, everyone joins the fishery. Whether they are out in boats working nets, picking fish that roll onto the beaches by the thousands, or working in the plants or on the docks separating the "he's" from the "she's," there is work enough for everyone over seven years old. Last year the fishery lasted only four days, and this year the word is that the Japanese technicians, who arrive in each outport to oversee the plants, will be buying even less.

So everyone is . . . waiting.

Waiting for the first boat to pull in with a load of fresh fish. Half the town will be down to the dock to greet it. It's a spring ritual in Ferryland.

"I always look forward to that day," says artist Stewart Montgomerie, who lives right on The Pool. "You think of that first feed of fresh fish all winter. You never have to pay for it. You go down to the wharf and someone will say, 'Hi, Stewart. You want a fish?' And they'll clean it up so fast you'd swear there was a zipper in it."

Waiting on ice. Ice torn from ice. The correct word is "calved." Calved, then, from some glacier in some Greenland fjord. When an iceberg breaks up, the smaller pieces are called growlers or bergy bits. When one scrapes the bottom, as they all are here, an iceberg can gouge a trough fifty feet deep in the ocean floor.

One morning I walk out to the old lighthouse on the Ferryland Head and get close enough to an iceberg to almost get lost in its geometry. They are bigger than you'd think — this one unexpectedly dwarfing a thirty-five-foot boat as it forces its way through the choppy swell. And more colourful. Blue, sometimes, along the edge where ice has freshly broken off; brown and full of sediment if one should roll after scouring the sea ground; green, even black where the ice is highly dense and bubble free. My glacier is, this sunny morning, all angles and dramatically aquamarine like the Aegean Sea. I know now that Lawren Harris understood what he was painting.

Someone tells me that there was an American around who was planning to make millions of dollars by breaking icebergs into pieces the size of tennis balls. He was going to ship the ice balls south, melt them and sell them as bottled water.

Someone else said that the icebergs are so dense that the Americans used to bounce artillery shells off them.

Always, it seems, when we are talking about ice there is an American with an idea lurking somewhere on the edge of things.

And all the time the ice just sits there. Icebergs ringing the harbour like marshmallows. As dangerous as sharks. As frustrating as a locked door. No one is going fishing until the icebergs go. And no one knows when they are going.

———— • ————

There is a handwritten notice in the post office:

If you wish to have a
family plot or single grave
cleaned up, decorated
or a headstone put in position
please call 555-2264
thank you

"I don't get as much work as I used to," says William Shannahan as he drives me to the cemetery in his blue 1988 Chevy pick-up.

"These days people seem to do their own graves."

As he pulls onto the shoulder, Shannahan points at a man kneeling among the gravestones. The man is working with a hammer.

"See? There. He's doing up a grave for Father's Day."

Shannahan is sixty-one years old. Like many men in Ferryland he worked a spell at the American military bases. He was forty-six when he was laid off, and he would have gone to the fishery had he not had the good fortune of running into Mr Campbell.

"I'd never seen him before. He came from the mainland somewhere. I don't know if it was Alberta or Toronto. Somewhere up there on the prairies."

The only photograph that Shannahan has left of his mentor shows Campbell in his mid fifties — a hefty man with longish grey sideburns, cigarettes in the pocket of his short-sleeved white shirt, and his hand travelling towards a beer. Campbell himself travelled from town to town with his portfolio of graveyard photos, asking the Mrs if she would like him to decorate a grave perhaps.

"He asked me right out if I'd like a job and I said, 'Sure I'll work for you,' and I started then and there that afternoon."

It was a profitable partnership. Campbell went door to door lining up jobs and collecting money. Shannahan worked in the graveyards — propping up the headstones, levelling off the graves, covering them first with concrete, and then topping the concrete with a scattering of coloured stone chips before finally enclosing each grave with a knee-high picket or wrought-iron fence. For the two summers Campbell came to Newfoundland, Shannahan fixed graves all the way from Calvert to Trepassey.

"He made some money, my son. I don't know how often he sat at my kitchen table and counted out five or six thousand dollars at the end of a week. I'm telling you the truth. Five or six thousand dollars. I should have taken a picture of him counting the money. I used to do all the work and he would collect all the money. But he taught me everything and paid me honest right up and if my kids were around he would slip each of them twenty dollars, too. He'd count it into piles and then sit back and say, 'There's more money in the dead than in the living.' "

The graveyard we are poking through is quite unlike any graveyard I have ever seen. Each family of stones is fenced off from the rest, giving the sloping field the appearance of a petting zoo. There are wrought-iron fences and white picket fences and split-rail fences with miniature hearts cut into the rails. There are plastic flowers and there are wreaths. The tombstones are straight and proud and ordered and, like the houses where these people once lived, not in rows but scattered helter-skelter around the hill.

Wayne Barnable is repairing the fence around his Uncle Ronald's tomb.

"I am doing it for my aunt," he says, smiling, the hammer we saw from the road dangling by his thigh. "She knew the fence was down and I knew she'd want it right for Father's Day."

"Here," says Shannahan a few moments later. "Here's one I done about ten years ago." Shannahan has dropped to his knees and is running his hand over the concrete slab that covers the grave. He flicks at the little pieces of coloured stone embedded in the cement.

"She's held up pretty good, my son. Pretty good for ten years."

"How much do you charge for that?" I ask.

"We used to charge $250 a grave. Now I charge $300. For $300 I'll level the ground right down, pour an eight-inch foundation, then cap her with two inches of good white finishing cement, add the coloured chips and a fence, boy. That's just how Mr Campbell taught me. That's stuck down right good. We worked all up the shore together, and I guess if you went up to the prairie provinces you could see Mr Campbell's work all over."

Shannahan is stretched out on the grass now, as at home in the graveyard as if he were on a picnic. Windbreaker, jeans and sneakers. The wind pulling at the tufts of hair sticking out from under his peaked cap.

I go to the cemetery often after that. Whenever I have no one to talk to I drive up the hill at the south end of town and park on the wide gravel shoulder. There is always another car there, always someone fixing something. Always someone happy to stop and talk.

This is where I meet Jim Hall. Hall lives in Yarmouth, Nova Scotia. He is married to a woman from Ferryland and is in the graveyard working on his father-in-law's grave.

"He died in the middle of last winter. And when you dig a grave around here you don't use a back hoe. It's just not the way it's done. Some of the men in the family came down with a couple of shovels and a bottle of rum and dug it. We waked the body for three days at home. He was never alone for those three days. After the funeral his six sons carried the casket from the gate to the grave. There are still a lot of Irish traditions that are strong around here.

"I'm just smoothing the ground off a bit today. I guess we'll eventually get a fence like the others. I was inquiring yesterday and it cost $760 for the aluminium fence around Smokey Curran's grave."

It is Jim Hall who explains to me why the fences are here. I have heard several theories, but it is Jim's explanation that rings true.

"They started with them to keep the sheep out. When the sheep were running loose they didn't want them coming to the graves and eating the flowers and such, so they built the fences."

"So why are you going to build one today? Seven hundred

dollars is a lot of money." I don't need to mention that sheep no longer run free in Ferryland.

"We're putting one up," Hall says smiling, "because everyone has one."

Another day I find a tombstone that told me more about the beginnings of this country than anything I have ever read in any book.

"In Fond Remembrance," it reads, "of the Children of Phillip and Ellen Keough."

Phillip and Ellen, God rest their souls, lived in the late 1800s. They had six children. And I don't know anything else about them except that the first to die were the twins, Mary Catherine and John, three years old, on May 3, 1878. Five months later ten-year-old Mary Ann died, then a week after that five-year-old Nicky. Three years passed before ten-year-old Eddie went and another six months before Stan, eight months, died, too.

Maybe when death is all around you, maybe when everyone's children are dying, maybe when the winter blows cold and the nights are dark and your ten-year-old daughter gives a little cough and your heart seizes and you look at your husband with frightened eyes and then the priest comes and then she dies, maybe you find a way to make sense of things. But how, after five have gone, could you have a sixth? And how, when your last boy dies, could you plant a crop, go to church, milk a cow, eat a meal, smile, laugh, carry on?

———————————•———————————

I eat all my meals at the inn, which is, save for the take-out place down the road, the only place to take dinner in town. My meals come with both food and instructions.

"This is our salt cod. I don't know whether you know it or not. This is the sauce. You can put it on the cod. Or not. Whatever pleases you." Jackie, the student hired to work for the summer, and Mrs Costello, who does the cooking, hover in the kitchen while I eat in the dining-room. There is a china bell that I am to ring if I need anything.

"If someone needs anything they should just ring it," announced Mrs Costello when she set the bell at my right elbow during my first dinner. I was alone in the dining-room at the time. Then, as an afterthought, she returned and gave it a self-conscious shake. "It should ring."

Occasionally one head or the other appears at the serving window that joins the two rooms.

"Is everything all right, sir?"

"Would you like some more, sir?"

"Will you be taking coffee or tea tonight, sir?"

"No, thank you, Jackie."

"Will you be taking coffee or tea tonight, sir?"

"No, thank you, Mrs Costello."

Dinners are plain, plenty and pleasing. I eat fresh fish from the fish plant and last summer's cod that Mr Costello salted himself. I eat Marshberry Upside Down Cake that Jackie has baked. She uses berries that Mr Costello's brother picked last fall before he passed away. When I ask, Gerard Costello brings me lobster he buys from the Clowe family and joins me at the table the night he cooks them. There are home-made rolls at every meal.

———————————•◀———————————

Rhonda O'Keefe is an upfront and outgoing twenty-four-year-old woman who spent a year and a half living in St John's. She worked in a clothing store part of the time, and she didn't like it there at all.

"It just wasn't for me. To start with the money wasn't good. By the time I had paid my rent there was nothing left. And I missed everything here. I used to be a town councillor and a Kinette. I used to be at meetings all the time and I missed everything. The feelings. The peacefulness. The sea.

"Here if you have something on your mind you just go for a walk by the sea. I even missed the air. My skin used to get really dry when I lived to town. It's more than nice here. I'd love to be successful and independent, yet there is a big part of me that would just like to get married and settle down and have a couple of kids. I think that's in every woman though she's not about to admit it.

"People are so distant in the city. They're not nearly as trusting as here. We're probably too trusting. Lots of people don't even lock their doors.

"And family ties are really important. Three days ago I was up to the graveyard and visited my great-great-grandfather's grave."

"Great-*great*-grandfather?" I ask, trying to keep up.

Rhonda looks at her hand and, like a schoolgirl doing a math problem quietly chants the generations off on her fingers.

"Jimmy, Augustus, Thomas, Valentine. Great-great," she says, looking back at me. "He was a shipbuilder. We still have some of the wooden tools that he brought with him — wooden levels and things like that. He died in 1872. He has one of the oldest headstones there. It's kind of knocked down and I was thinking of doing it over. There is a Celtic cross and shamrocks up on top and they're starting to fade and I was thinking they should be cleaned. Maybe some time this summer. After that I went and visited with my grandparents on both sides."

"What do you do when you visit?" I ask.

"I just talks to them."

"What do you say?"

"What did I say to my grandfather?"

"Yes."

"I said I was going to the club that night and I said, 'I'll have a drink for you.' "

"What else?"

"Well, then I went to see my uncle. I sat on the bench that they have there. And I was just talking, and I said a few prayers, and I said I'd have a scuff for him, too, because he loved to dance so.

"And then I went to see my brother. I had a younger brother. He was born with a hole in his heart and he died when he was just a baby. So I visited with him, too.

"I sat down on the grass. There's a little lamb on the tombstone and I was touching the lamb and thinking about how old he would have been. He would have been twenty-two if he hadn't died. And I was wondering what he would have been like. And what it would have been like to have a younger brother. I prayed and I asked him to pray for me. I was thinking of him as a little angel in heaven. And then at every grave before I go I say, 'May your soul, and all the souls of the faithful departed, through the mercy of God, rest in peace. Amen.' "

"Do you pray at night?" I ask.

"Yes."

"How do you pray?"

"I say my prayers."

"Like what?"

"I usually start by saying, 'Thank you for everything I had this day. Thank you for my friends. Thank you for my family.' Then I say all the standard stuff. Our Father, Hail Marys, the Glory Be's, Acts of Contrition, all of them. If there's something special happening then I'll say a special prayer. Like during the Gulf War I said a prayer for peace every night. Or if someone is sick I'll say a prayer for them."

Rhonda looks at me and smiles. We are sitting at the kitchen table in her parents' home. The lace tablecloth is covered with a large piece of clear plastic. There is a wood stove, some plastic flowers and, on the wall beside the spoon collection, a picture of John Paul II. The inscription on the photo says "May God Bless This House."

"We're covering some ground now," says Rhonda. "Do you want a mug-up?"

There are no banks in Ferryland. The closest bank is in St John's, an hour away. So everyone who lives here does some or all of their banking at one of the town's six stores. Paul's Store at the north end of town is the biggest and therefore the busiest.

Paul's sells gas; hardware, plumbing, electric and fishing supplies; floor coverings; dry goods and groceries; and has the only liquor and beer outlet between Bay Bulls and Trepassey — all under one roof.

Fraser Paul is one of the two brothers operating the family store.

"At least half our business is done on credit," he explains. "We have to work like that. I would prefer cash but we are in the country and credit is part of country living. A lot of people here don't have bank accounts. So what we do is set up a credit limit on a two-week or monthly basis. We sit down and talk with our customers and base the limit on what a person needs and what they can afford. At the end of the two weeks, or whatever it is, we expect to be paid in full, and then they can start charging again. People bring their pay cheques here and we cash them, deduct what they owe us and give them the balance. We're taking a bit of a chance. There are seven fish plants within fourteen miles and we have to have a fair hunk of change on hand to settle the cheques. But that is the fashion of living in the outports. It is something that has just went from one generation down the line. That's just the way it is.

"The whole system is based on trust. No one takes a receipt when they leave. We have a little book for each customer and we write down what they bought in the book. I've never had to take anyone to small claims court to settle or anything like that. If there's a problem I get on the phone. I find that is much better than sending invoices in the mail. If they get a note in the mail they might be ashamed to come in and you could end up losing their business. This way if there's a problem we talk about it and work something out, and then everything is out in the open. That way you don't have to be enemies.

"A lot of business goes out the road. A lot of people go into St John's to do their shopping. I thinks if this community wasn't as well off I would do better. If we weren't doing so well people wouldn't have good cars and then they'd have to do more country shopping. Then I could work on getting a bank here, and I could bring in more clothing."

More clothing maybe. But probably not more fresh food. Fruit and vegetables have never been plentiful in Newfoundland. Paul's, the biggest store for miles, has more bags of ice cubes (eighty) and fisherman's salt (an entire annex of seventy-five-pound bags at $5.50 a bag) than bags of apples (four bags at five pounds) or potatoes (seven bags at ten pounds).

Newfoundland's only agricultural export is the blueberry. Much of everything else has to be imported. At Paul's the day I visit there are three cabbages, twelve turnips, five bags of carrots, a box of onions, two oranges, three lemons, five grapefruit, sixteen tomatoes, two cauliflower, one broccoli, three green peppers, the four bags of apples, the seven bags of potatoes, a solitary head of lettuce that looks as if it is left over from last summer and fourteen of the ubiquitous kiwi fruit. For four months every year Fraser says he is able to get cabbage, turnips and greens (the tops of turnips) grown locally. Like Albert O'Keefe, everyone digs their own dandelions. If you want any better you have to drive to St John's.

There is more diversity among the dry goods. If I wanted a pair of rubber boots I could choose from among the $10,000 worth of stock that Paul keeps on hand. And I could choose between knee rubbers, hip rubbers, what I call Billy boots and a variety of others.

In fishing supplies there is everything from a faded box of squid jiggers at fifty-nine cents each ("Those will be there a lifetime," mutters Fraser. "They're not worth nothing.")

to swivels, pulleys, lines, trawl hooks and gaff hooks.

Paul also sells school supplies, the plastic wreaths I have seen at the cemetery, candy, cigarettes, ice cream, and he rents videos. The big sellers at the liquor counter are Lamb's Light Rum and Golden Wedding Whiskey.

Paul's closes every night for an hour at supper time between 5 and 6 P.M.

"People say we should stay open," says Fraser, "but, boy, when you're doing fourteen-hour days it's important to sit down for an hour. People get used to it."

There was once a branch of the Bank of Nova Scotia in Ferryland, but it only lasted three years.

"People never used it," says teacher and businessman Loyola Sullivan. "They might have used it to cash their cheques, but they never got into the habit of depositing money. They figured everyone would know how much money they had if they left it in the bank. So everyone kept their money at home. No one ever had to go to the bank for a loan because no one needed a mortgage. You build your home as you can afford it. And what you can afford depends on the fishery. If it's a good year, you do a lot. If it's an off year, you slow down.

"You have to understand that the credit system is very significant around here. In the old days you got credit from the fish merchant who bought your fish. He usually owned the local store as well. The accounts used to be settled annually. He would pay you for your fish every fall and you'd pay off your account at his store. There was traditionally little money left over.

"Today everyone is paid every two weeks. So you take your cheque to the store where you go for groceries. It is not uncommon for people to run their bill up to one thousand dollars. They pay it down when they get their income tax back, or their child tax credit, or maybe if they have a big week in the fishery. Accounts tend to linger a bit in the winter, but not in the summer."

"What about paying bills," I ask. "What about the light bill, or the phone bill?"

"Most of us go to the post office. You don't need a cheque book. You just take the cash to the post office and buy a money order."

———— • ————

Everyone has their time away. For the men over fifty, "away" meant the American bases. For years Gander, Stephenville, Argentia, Greenland and Goose Bay were the places men turned to when the fishery turned bad. They built the bases, painted the barracks, unloaded supplies and picked up the garbage for American servicemen. When the Americans left Newfoundland, Newfoundlanders peeled off the rock for the factories of Upper Canada and the oil fields in the west. Now young people dreaming of money and adventure go to Yellowknife.

Yellowknife. Someone said they counted fourteen people who had left Ferryland for Yellowknife last year alone.

Lisa Clowe will be leaving at the end of the summer. Lisa is twenty-four years old. She is going to be married on July 26. Until the wedding she is living at home with her three sisters, her mother, her father and her seventeen-month-old daughter. Lisa's fiancé (and the father of her child) is teaching school in Ontario. He'll be home for the wedding as soon as the school year is finished. Lisa followed Keith to Ontario last year but had to live an hour away with his sister in Owen Sound. Keith is teaching in a Catholic school and it was understood that Lisa couldn't move in with him unless they were married. Lisa and Keith wanted to get married in Ferryland.

Nearly half the town will be at the wedding. There will be a mass at the church in the afternoon and then supper at the parish hall in Fermeuse.

"There'll be about four hundred for supper," says Lisa, sitting at her kitchen table. "It's too bad you aren't going to be around. You could see a real Newfie wedding."

Lisa's mother comes into the kitchen and peeks into a pot simmering on the stove. A whiff of steam and the strong smell of game fills the kitchen. Turr soup for supper. Lisa's brothers shot the birds yesterday near Burns Head Rock.

"There'll be a cold plate supper after the service," says Lisa. "Mom and Dad will buy the food in bulk and then distribute it to the ladies around. Some ladies will get potatoes for salad. Others will get cabbage and do up cole slaw. The hams and turkeys and roast beef will be cooked around and then taken to a store to be sliced. Cookies and all the sweets will be made by family mostly. My mom made the wedding cake a couple of weeks ago. A lady in Cape Broyle will do the decorating.

"The morning of the wedding they'll all get together at the hall at ten or eleven and everyone will start cutting out the suppers. They'll cut out maybe 375 plates and put another 25 or 30 away and serve them at midnight for anyone who gets there late or wants some more."

Then Lisa and Keith will pack up everything they own and, like thousands of Newfoundlanders before them, make the long drive from the rock to Upper Canada.

"I have mixed feelings about leaving. It's like any change in life, I guess. I'm looking forward to making a fresh start. Just the three of us as a family. Keith has a permanent job in Ontario which is something he wouldn't get for a while around here. But I am going to miss all this, my family, my friends. You get used to a way of life and I have lived here for twenty-four years. It'll be lonely, I suppose, but I'll get used to it. Here you know everybody and everybody knows you. I don't know what the people are going to be like where I am going. Keith says everyone minds their own business and don't associate with each other too much. He says there is only one function every year at the school where he's working — a closing dance. Here there are all sorts of things — a Christmas party, Easter parties, barbecues in the summer. All sorts of things."

Christine Walsh was nineteen when she left Ferryland, moved to St John's and enrolled in hairdressing school. She got a job in a beauty salon and worked in town for two years before she gave up and came home to live with her parents.

"I got tired of living in St John's. I thought I'd come home for a few months and then do something else. But before long people started phoning for me to do their hair and I've been working here for five years now. People phone me and I goes to their place."

Christine has come to the inn to cut my hair. She has brought her equipment with her in a shoulder bag. We have moved a chair into the centre of my room and she has covered me with a plastic cape. I feel self-conscious and embarrassed. I have never had a woman come to my room to cut my hair before.

"Do you want to wash it or what?"

There is a sink in the corner of my room. The shower is across the hall. I am unsure whether Christine is offering to wash my hair, or suggesting I leave the room and wash it myself.

"Whatever you want," I mumble. "I washed it last night."

"We can just wet it down, then," she says.

"Do you do mostly men or women?" I ask.

"Mostly women. But I have some men customers. I do perms, colors, cuts and everything that goes with it." Hair begins to drift around my feet. "I don't do dead people, though."

"Dead people?"

"I was asked once. The man from Fermeuse called looking for me. I was out doing someone's hair. He found someone else before I got home. I don't think I'd have done it, though. I'd be afraid of having nightmares."

I am struck by the notion that you would have to sit a dead person up to trim their hair. As I ponder how they do that, I wonder what is going to happen to my hair, which is now all over the floor of my room.

"Is it fun doing this?" I ask. "Do you like it here?"

"Yes. It's more personal than St John's. I know more about my customers here. I'll cut someone's hair and then I'll stay and have tea or supper. Sometimes I feel like I am part of the family."

"Is it a good business?"

"It has its ups and downs. February and October are really slow. It's busier in the summer when there are weddings and proms. On a busy day I can do ten or twelve cuts. On a slow day the phone doesn't ring at all. You know what? I make more money here than when I was in town working full time. Most of the places in St John's only pay minimum wage."

Downstairs the front door slaps open. Gerard, who owns the inn and is living on the top floor for a few days, comes bounding up the stairs. He slows noticeably when he passes my room and hears a woman's voice. I should say something, I think, but Christine is still talking.

"For a while I wondered if I should get a place. Like a store or something. But there are not a lot of places for rent around here. Anyway, I enjoy this. I am not stuck in one place. I get to stop at the store between calls. I like to move around a lot."

Gerard is coming downstairs again. I have to say something.

"Do you have a boyfriend?" I blurt a little too loudly.

"Yes," says Christine, looking at me strangely.

"Are you going to get married?" I almost shout.

Downstairs the door slaps shuts behind Gerard.

"We'll probably get married next year. We are building our home now. We're planning to get married as soon as the house is finished, and it's just about finished.

"His dad's a carpenter and he's been helping. Plus he gave us the land. All our money is in the house. It's cost us about forty thousand dollars. We go there in the evenings and on the weekends. We've been at it two and a half years, going at it bit by bit. It's just a three-bedroom bungalow.

"Well, that's about it," she says, standing back. "Go see if it's OK."

I get up from the chair and go over to the mirror by the sink. Hair spills out of my lap and onto the floor.

"It's fine," I say, running my hand over my head. "How much do I owe you?"

"Ten dollars." She folds the cape and slips it into her bag. "And who," she says, looking at my hair on the floor, "gets to clean this up?"

I thought maybe she brought a little vacuum. I thought maybe she took the hair with her.

"I'll do it," I say, dropping quickly to my knees and pushing my hair into a tidy pile in the corner.

I stand up and give her twelve dollars.

"It looks," she says, standing by the door and surveying the little pile of hair by the bureau, "like a rat died in the corner."

Downstairs, just as she is leaving, she turns.

"I was talking to my brother last night on the phone. He lives in Ottawa. He said he dreamed that the capelin were rolling on the beach and he was walking along taking pictures of them."

I stand on the porch and wave as she drives away. Across the road the ice hasn't moved in the harbour.

The next time I see Gerard, I make a point of mentioning the haircut.

For all their trips down the road, travel at home can be difficult. Except for the freight line in Labrador that they use to haul iron ore to the St Lawrence River, Newfoundland, like Prince Edward Island, no longer has a railroad. The trans-island passenger train was the Newfie Bullet. (You can read about her in the Bible, sir, that's what they used to say. They'd pause and fix you with their eyes and say. That's right, my son, in the Bible, right where it says, "The Lord made all things that creep and crawl.") Well, the Bullet left on its last twenty-mile-an-hour (average speed) trip across the province on July 2, 1969. The 547-mile run from St John's to Port-aux-Basques used to take twenty-seven hours and forty-five minutes. Once the highway was in, who wanted to do that? The end of a seventy-one-year tradition. You could still ride the Bullet today if the passion seized you, but you would have to go to Bolivia, Chile or Nicaragua where the engines, rolling stock and even some of rails are now being used. The trucking industry killed the freight trains. Oh, some of the mixed freight-passenger trains on some of the branch lines hung on into the eighties, but they are gone now, too. And gone with them the days when you'd hear stories about a blast of wind in the Wreckhouse area that blew fifteen cars off the rails. Wind! Or the winter day so cold that the God-damn track froze and cracked under the train. Cracked, sir! Today buses cross the island along the east–west axis, but if you want to travel north–south you have to go by taxi.

Albert Lawlor drives the taxi that passes through Ferryland every day on its way to and from St John's. The vehicle he drives is a bit of a hybrid. The front half is a cab from a standard pick-up truck. The back half, where his passengers sit in rows, is the same as the compartment, without the glass bubble and customized stool, that Pope John Paul II used when he toured North America in September, 1984. Essentially Albert Lawlor drives the Popemobile up and down Highway 10 every day.

Albert leaves Cappahayden every morning at 7:45 A.M. and picks up passengers in the outports all the way along the coast. People phone the night before to book their rides.

"The phone starts ringing at about six o'clock at night and will keep going until midnight or later," says Albert, sitting in his tidy kitchen. "Sometimes it'll start again as early as 5 A.M. I keep a pad of paper and a pencil by the bed. I can write the names down without waking up. All I needs is the name. I know where everyone lives from here to Tors Cove. I go right to their houses to get them and then I drop them wherever they want in town."

Albert's taxi-van looks like a small school bus. There are five rows of seats and an aisle down the middle. Room for twenty passengers plus Albert, although sometimes he carries as many as twenty-five.

"It's busiest around Christmas, though Mother's Day or Father's Day can be just as bad. And Mondays and Fridays during school because you have the university kids going back and forth. It's always a laugh. Everyone yacks about what Bill Rowe's been up to on the 'Open Line Show.' Everyone listens to Bill Rowe. I keep it on in the taxi. And there's lots of news, you know, back and forth, like who's won bingo. Things like that. Sometimes it can be very comical. Sometimes I am in stitches all the way to town."

It costs nine dollars for the one-hour drive from Ferryland to St John's. But Albert doesn't only drive passengers. He runs messages, too.

"Lots of individuals call and get me to do messages for them. The minimum charge for a message is five dollars. Like if I was to take an envelope for you and drop it off at the Jiffy Cab stand in St John's, that would be five dollars. Sometimes people do that if they want to get some money to their kid in university. I use the stand as a kind of base. I leave the envelope there and the kid can come and pick it up. I do other things, too. Like they will ask me to pick up a bike at Canadian Tire or take a pair of skates in to get repaired. I'd charge maybe twelve dollars for the bike and seven dollars for the skates.

"I pick up a lot of floor covering, too. Carpets and canvas. I lay it down under the seats. I charge ten or fifteen dollars depending on the size."

Albert also does messages for businesses along the southern shore.

"I do work for all the fish plants around. I'll pick up hydraulic hoses or hairnets or rubber gloves — all sorts of things. Also for the phone company. I pick up at least ten boxes a week for the phone company. You know, phones, wire, gauges, that sort of thing. I also do all the school supplies. Toilet paper, stuff for the art room, what have you. And I do deposits for a few of the grocery stores along the way. I put money in the bank for them. And church supplies, too. Candles, bingo cards and a drop of wine for the priests."

"Where do you get the wine?"

"It's special wine. Altar Wine, the label says."

"But where do you get it?"

"In town. At the British Confectionery Company."

When he has finished running his messages it is usually time for Albert to start picking up people for the ride home.

"Going home is always fun. Sometimes the boys have had time for a beer or two. On the way back they'll get to singing. It's never dull."

Like everything along the shore, how you pay Albert is up to you. Some people pay when they get to St John's; others at the end of the day. Others don't even mention money.

"They don't have to pay right away. And if they don't, I won't say anything. Ninety-five percent of the people are honest. If they don't pay right away they go out of their way to pay as soon as they can."

———————— • ————————

There is a load of cod at the fish plant that's come from an offshore boat. Twenty-five people are called in for two days' work. Splitting the fish is the top-paying job in the plant. A splitter makes ten dollars an hour. The rest of the men here — the header (who cuts off the heads), the sculper (who cuts out the cheeks and tongues) and the salters — make eight dollars an hour.

After they are split and gutted and headed and washed, the cod fillets are stacked like fur pelts five feet high on wooden pallets. The pallets are buried with shovels of coarse salt so only the tails show. From the far side of the plant the rows of cod look like stacks of firewood under an early snow.

The fish are left to cure for twenty-one days. As the salt draws the moisture out of the cod the piles will shrink by almost two feet.

As it was when the cod fishery began, and as it has always been, most of this salted cod will be shipped to Europe. To Portugal, Spain, Norway, Greece and Italy. It will be packed and shipped after the twenty-one days of curing — shipped "wet salted," it's called. The curing process will be completed in Europe, where the fish will be sun-dried and then sold.

Cod fillets are also sold fresh and frozen into the American and British markets — mostly out of Boston. But these days you are actually paid a premium for a large fish if it is salted.

———————— •• ————————

I am the only man invited to Lisa Clowe's shower. The shower is held in the community hall opposite the inn. There are sixty of us there. The youngest person is four years old. The oldest is sixty-five.

We are invited to the hall for eight o'clock. As we arrive we are each given a picture of a bride that Lisa has cut out of a bridal magazine. We are supposed to pin the picture to our blouses. It's a game. Any time I see someone crossing their legs, I can remove their picture and add it to my chest. The person with the most pictures pinned to their chest at the end of the night wins a Pyrex dish.

I lose my picture in the first five minutes.

We play card games and bingo, and the little girls have as much fun as the adults. There are prizes for everything — a carrot peeler, a dish cloth, a spatula.

"Just what I needed," laughs one woman as she ticks off her bingo.

At about ten, the bridesmaids — the only ones in skirts (the rest of us are wearing slacks) — gather at the front of the hall and open the presents that have been piled on a long banquet table. Lisa sits at the head of the table and watches.

"Thank you, Mary. Thank you Laura," she says as each gift is held up. There are oven mitts and towels and a set of dishes from the bridesmaids, and envelopes with money.

"We got $470," announces the maid of honour.

Everyone nods. There is a rustle, a murmur of approval.

"That's good. That's good."

There is coffee and pop. Sandwiches and cake. There are paper tablecloths over the long banquet tables. We use Styrofoam cups as ashtrays.

———— • ————

Another night driving south of town I pass a building with a lot of cars parked in front. I can't see a sign, but it looks more like a club than a house, so I take a chance and stop to see what is happening.

"Three dollars to get in," says the lady at the table by the door.

The woman's name is Shirley Maher, and behind her people are drinking and dancing and smoking. It looks like any small town legion hall, except the music is louder.

"Three dollars," she says again. "The money is for June Oates."

June Oates is her brother-in-law — a fisherman who worked offshore on a gillnet boat. A month ago they found a brain tumour and took him to St John's for an operation. He hasn't been out on the boat since. June has two boys — one four, one five. Three dollars to get in, but most people are giving five or ten or twenty.

The next night I visit Shirley Maher at her home. We sit at the kitchen table and drink coffee.

"I've been getting donations all day. People've been at giving me cards with twenty or fifty dollars in them. We're up to about sixteen hundred, and there'll be more. A lot of the fishermen say when the fish start coming they'll give a hundred pounds on each trip. That'll be about fifty dollars every time they go out.

"No one'll see his family hungry. That's how it works here. We help each other. We'd do the same thing if someone's house burned and they had no insurance or if someone had to fly a child to Halifax for an operation."

Shirley lives in a new house, not far from Paul's Store on the Quarry River Road. There are two other houses on the road.

"We were three and a half years building this house," she says. "We put every cent we had into it. Sean did most of the work himself. He paid a carpenter to help with the framing and an electrician and a plumber. But that was all. I had Julie when I was eighteen and I lived at home for four years after she was born and Sean lived with his parents.

"Most people build the way we did. My uncle gave us the land for one dollar. We put up the basement and covered her in and then whenever we got a thousand dollars we did some more work. When he wasn't fishing, Sean was working on the house. We finished in October of '88 and then we got married and moved in. Julie was four years old."

In the fall Sean hunts moose and sets snares for rabbit.

"If he gets a moose we'll keep a quarter and give the rest away. You can only eat about a quarter of a moose a year."

Like most women in Ferryland, Shirley makes a moose stew if her husband brings her a moose. She bottles the stew in Mason jars.

"You never heard of bottled moose? I'll have to give you a jar."

She disappears into a cupboard and comes out holding a glass jar half full of greyish meat.

"You don't have to freeze it or anything. Just leave it on the shelf and heat it up when you want it."

I make a label that says "Moose in a Bottle" and leave it on my bureau at the inn. I smile each time I see it.

"We snare rabbits, too. I guts them and puts them in the freezer with the fur on. That way they don't get freezer burn."

They salt and freeze their own fish. And put up some cod tongues every year. In the spring Sean cuts the wood they heat with. A permit to cut eight cords costs five dollars. In the fall Shirley hires a babysitter and goes berry-picking with a carload of her friends.

"We goes to the side of the road somewhere between Cappahayden and Trepassey. We get partridge berries and blueberries and bakeapples. Everyone picks bakeapples. I got ten gallons last year. I make bakeapple jam."

In the winter there are card clubs. They play "45's" or "Jack for Your Partner."

"We went to Montreal once to see a hockey game. I wouldn't want to live there for the world. It was too fast for me. I wouldn't feel safe. We went walking on St Catherine Street one night and I was nearly up on Sean's back. We went in a taxi back to the hotel and I thought, 'If I'm not killed in the plane I'm going to die in this taxi.'

"I feel safe here. We leave the doors open all the time. I leave things out on the lawn. Sean has only taken the keys out of the truck maybe six times in the eight years he's owned it. I never look outside when Julie goes out to play. She goes trouting in the river or up the shore to the ponds. I don't worry. Everyone is friendly."

On my second Friday in Ferryland I wake up and there is fog everywhere. We can see the highway from the inn, but the sea and everything beyond is gone. Saturday the wind is up from the north-east, but the fog is still with us. At noon a sound like distant thunder rolls over the town. Some time during the night one of the icebergs in the harbour must have foundered. It is a good bet that she has started to break up in the choppy swell, but no one knows for sure what is happening on account of the fog.

Sunday morning the evidence is in. The beach is covered with hundreds of pieces of ice, most the size of refrigerators. They look like frozen waves that have beached up and down the coast. This is what the fishermen have been waiting for.

After breakfast I walk over to the shore and bump into Gerard Costello. He is standing beside his pick-up truck with a pick-axe. The back of the truck is half full of broken bits of glacier.

"That's five-thousand-year-old ice," he says, smiling. "I just about have enough to last all summer."

It pleases me that someone else is as interested in the ice as I am.

"I'll serve it to tourists in their drinks," he says, wading back into the water to tackle another piece. "Have you ever had it? It pops and crackles in the glass. It's something to talk about, anyway."

———————•———————

Later that night, watching television I receive an illuminating lesson in social hierarchy.

"Watch the news tonight, and every weeknight, at six o'clock," says the local announcer, pausing only a beat to add, "six-thirty in Labrador."

———————•———————

On Monday, gannets, large black-and-white sea-birds, have begun plunge-diving all over the bay. They tuck their wings against their stout bodies and drop into the ocean from as high as fifty feet. They look like soccer-ball bombs. It is another good sign. It means the capelin are here. The cod can't be far behind.

There are twelve fishermen who set cod traps in the heads and bays around Ferryland. In the old days their fathers would rush out like prospectors every March and throw out anchors and markers to lay claim to their favourite trap berths. It was first come, first served, and it was far from a satisfactory system. The March ice would inevitably sever the anchor lines, and the markers would float away, leaving the berths open to the next "first" person to claim them. The trap men used to spend most of the spring trying to save their berths from the ice and each other. Some time in the thirties someone decided there must be a better way.

So every April, in a tradition unique to cod-trap fishing, the fishermen in Ferryland get together and hold a draw for the berths. Each berth represents a particular square of ocean floor over which the designated fisherman can set up his bungalow-sized cod trap for the season. The berths, which were laid out years ago, all have names. Among the ones drawn for this year in Ferryland are: Bread and Cheese Cove, The Wash Ball, Vin's Gulch, The One Gun Battery, Kelpy Rock, Sinking Rocks, Goose Island and The Butcher's Hole. The men get together at the community hall and put their names in one paper bag and the names of the berths in another, and one by one the berths and names are drawn and thus assigned for the year.

It is a system that seems to work, though not without discussion, and sometimes some rancor.

There are enough cod berths around Ferryland that every fisherman is guaranteed to get two and sometimes three spots to set his nets. Some berths, however, are better than others. So the first order of business every year is to decide which are the best twelve berths and to hold a draw for them, that way ensuring that everyone gets at least one good spot. After the number-one berths are drawn, separate draws are held for the number-two and number-three spots.

The inshore fishery is an intensely personal business. The men here in Ferryland are friends and neighbours. Yet they are also in competition. And every year there are plenty of issues to confront.

This year there are five:

* If Kenneth and Gerald Hynes are both going to fish out of the same boat, should they each be allowed to draw for a number-one berth? (Yes. After years of complaining about the inherent unfairness of the two working together and getting two number-one berths for the one boat, it is decided that Kenneth and Gerald can do what they want.)

* Should a fisherman who only owns two cod traps be allowed to draw for a third berth? (Yes.)

* Can Terrence Kavanagh hand over his right to a cod berth to his brother Leo? (Yes. Leo has worked with Terrence for years. So Terrence can pass the berth on.)

* Can Wayne Hynes' berth rights pass to his father? (Yes. Wayne, a hemophiliac, died over the winter. He and his father fished together for years. The fact that the berth is in Wayne's name is a technicality.)

* If Gerald Costello wants to retire from the fishery, can he draw a number-one berth and then sell it and all his equipment to Phonse Kavanagh's son Loyola? (No. He can sell his equipment but not his berth or the right to draw for it. The right to a berth can only be passed from fathers to sons. Or from a boat owner to someone who has worked on his crew for years.)

All the drama and intrigue of the international fishery is played out at the local level. Just as Canada squabbles with France over fishing boundaries, so, too, does Ferryland debate boundaries with the town down the coast, Calvert. The disputed area is around Goose Island.

Years ago the berth known as Goose Island belonged to the outport of Calvert, but Mike Devereaux, a Ferryland fisherman, took to going out every spring and claiming the spot for himself. For a long time no one in Calvert protested, and when they finally did Ferryland fishermen

felt Devereaux had acquired some sort of squatter's pre-
rogative for their community. The debate simmered for
years before both towns finally agreed to turn to the government to settle the matter. Goose Island was awarded to
Ferryland. In return, however, Ferryland had to hand over
to Calvert the berth called The Bite of Goose Island. The
boundary between the two communities thus became
blurred, and each season the possibility of renewed squab-
bling hovers offshore like a summer fog.

Disputes can just as easily break out between two fishermen in the same community. The issue is usually the same.
Someone feels a neighbour's trap is encroaching on his
berth.

The fisheries officer in each community has the power
to rule on such matters, but it is not often they choose to
wield their power arbitrarily. The correct placement of a
cod trap is more steeped in tradition than anything, so
when there is disagreement, fishermen are more likely to
turn to someone long in experience than to call in the
long arm of the law. Someone whose knowledge of the disputed berth is beyond doubt is asked to reset the traps,
and his view of things will prevail for the remainder of
the season.

Phonse Kavanagh has set cod traps around Ferryland since
he was a boy.

"Fishing," he says, "is my life, I loves it out there."

Phonse is slouched in a chair in the downstairs sitting-
room at the front of the inn.

"It's a good way to live. Not a great way to make a living,
but a good way to live. I'd settle for half of what I could
make on the land in order to stay on the water. I go at it
twelve months a year. When the season is over I get to work
on my gear in the twine store. You're your own boss. You're
out in the fresh air. Everything about it is a pleasure. It's a
pleasure to set the traps and it's a pleasure to haul them
out and see fish in them.

"I think the best time for me is in the fall of the year when we go out and trawl. You should be out there with us on a sunny day. We have a forecastle on the boat now, and if it's cold you can pop in there and have a mug-up. Nothing beats it.

"I can only speak for myself, but I can't say that it's hard times being a fisherman. For me it would be harder to get up at seven and drive to town and work until five. For me I'd rather get up before dawn and go out on the water. I like getting out of bed early in the morning and singing out at a buddy on another boat. Though I am ashamed to tell you that I never get up before four-thirty these years. I used to get up at three, but I don't do that anymore. We have it better now financially than we did thirty years ago. Now you can get fairly good UIC. When I started you couldn't get a God-damn cent.

"As far as I'm concerned we are living the life of Riley. I have three sons and they all fish with me. I like working with my sons. Though I must admit I get cranky sometimes. I am happy my sons are in the fishery, and as long as they have the same attitude I have, I hope they stay in it."

"How has it changed?" I ask. "Is it different now?"

"The fish are smaller than they used to be. When I started you used to draw up your trap and pull out the big ones and let the smaller ones go. You did that because you had to split the fish in them times. The stuff we're bringing in now we would have throwed away twenty-five years ago because it was too small to split.

"In the old days when you pulled out your net — say you had two thousand pounds of fish in it — maybe you'd have two hundred pounds of small ones caught in the mesh. Today if you pull two thousand pounds, you're going to have about five hundred pounds meshed."

Phonse Kavanagh and I talk about fish and family for about an hour before he brings up the church.

"This used to be the convent," he says, nodding at the room.

"I know."

"It's been a long time since I've been here. It hasn't changed much."

The convent was built in 1914. It was used by the Presentation Sisters until Gerard Costello turned it into The Downs Inn. There are still plaster religious statues in the halls.

"I was a good Catholic," says Phonse, looking around. "I spent a lot of time helping the church. At bingos and all that. But I don't do that no more."

On January 12, 1988, people in Ferryland learned that their parish priest, Father James Hickey, had been arraigned on charges of gross indecency. Father Hickey turned out to be one of the first of what soon seemed like an endless parade of Catholic Fathers in Newfoundland charged with sexual impropriety involving young boys. Because, perhaps, he was one of the first, the news of the charges blasted Ferryland like a hot, sour wind, leaving everyone gasping for breath. The news blew into town at dinner time. Dishes were broken and hands burned as it sucked through the kitchens and caught more than one homemaker half-way between the stove and the table.

"I was sitting having supper," says Phonse, "and my daughter went to the phone and she came back and said, 'Father Hickey is up on a sexual charge,' and I said, 'That's enough of that. Don't say that no more,' and I got up from the table and walked away. And there it was on the TV.

"I've never went to the church since. I regret it, too. But I'm not going in again. It was a big let-down and it hurt. A lot.

"I used to love to go and see the nuns. I used to love to go to church and hear the choir. I wouldn't think of doing anything on a Sunday without going to mass. I used to live for that stuff. Now I don't even know the church is there. I do in my mind, but I don't go."

Phonse Kavanagh is leaning forward in his seat. He is

wringing his hands as if he is trying to squeeze something out of them. He is looking at me as if he wants help.

"Phonse?" I say.

Not half an hour ago he told me how one after another of his three brothers died. Ambrose, killed by a car as he was walking along the highway to Calvert. Clarence, killed by a forklift on the American base in Greenland. France, in an automobile accident on his way home from fishing in the middle of winter. Phonse had shook his head, even chuckled ruefully as he told me about their deaths.

And now he is looking at me and wringing his hands.

"Phonse?"

"We're all going to die. And I'm not saying it was great that my brothers died. But as far as I'm concerned it was worse to hear about Father Hickey than it was to hear about any of my brothers. I had a belief. I had . . ."

Phonse pauses, looks away and then, shaking his head, starts again.

"It was just really upsetting. If someone dies, sure, it's upsetting, but you get over it. With time you get over it. But this keeps living. It lives in your mind for a long time.

"And you can't do the things that you used to do when you were in pain. Confession, receive, say prayers. But you think you should. Then you look at the priest and you say to yourself, why should I tell him anything? He's worse than I am."

"I am not surprised to hear that," says Father John McGettigan two days later, when I tell him about Phonse Kavanagh's confession.

"Death . . . is a part of life. It's something that you expect. But what happened here, you never associated with the priesthood. You have to remember that the degree of trust between the priest and the community in these outports was awesome."

Father McGettigan and I are talking in the gracious front room of the parish presbytery. Along with the doctor's house, the old court house (which in the sum-mer now serves as a roadside museum) and The Downs Inn, the presbytery is one of the homes you would notice if you drove quickly through Ferryland. Father McGetti-gan is fifty-eight years old. He became the priest here in the Holy Trinity Parish less than a year ago. Because of the shortage of priests, he is also the priest for the Parish of Immaculate Conception and the Parish of the Holy Apostles, covering twelve outports in all. He conducts four masses every weekend.

"The parish priest," he continues, "used to be the fac-totum. Years ago they used to come to the priest for every-thing. They'd come about the fishery. They'd come when they wanted a letter written. They even came when they were having trouble with their teeth. The priest ran the schools. It was the priest who developed new methods of farming and passed them around the village. It was the priest who organized all the youth and sports activities. Remember, it's only since Confederation that we've had any sports organizations in the outports.

"The trust that used to be there has been destroyed. It used to be when I came to a new parish my credibility was accepted. Now I have to establish it.

"It's not necessarily a bad thing to be called to task like that. And in some other ways good has come from it. A sense of dependence has been removed. People have become more responsible for their own lives. And this is good. People used to hand too much responsibility to the clergy."

There is a knock on the door and Father McGettigan apologizes as he gets up to answer it. There is a brief and muffled conversation. I overhear the priest excuse himself.

"I have someone with me right now. Perhaps another time. Perhaps you could come back later."

The front door closes and there are footsteps on the porch. Father McGettigan rejoins me in the living-room.

"He wanted to take the pledge," he explains, sinking into the couch across from me.

"The pledge?"

"You don't know the pledge? There's a card."

He lifts himself out of the couch again, disappears around the corner and comes back holding a wallet-sized card. It looks like something the YMCA might award for passing a swimming test.

```
            PLEDGE
THIS IS TO CERTIFY THAT

- - - - - - - - - - - - - - - - - - - - - - - - - - - - - - - - -
    HAS  TAKEN  A  PLEDGE  OF  TOTAL  ABSTINENCE

FOR - - - - - - - - - - - - - - - - - - - - - - - - - - - - - - -

(SIGNED) REV. - - - - - - - - - - - - - - - - - - - - - - - - -

DATE - - - - - - - - - - - - - - - - - - - - - - - -
```

The date printed on the reverse side is July 19, 1959.

"If I wasn't here now," I ask, "what would you have done?"

"I would have brought him in and he would have taken the pledge."

"How?"

"We would have formulated a prayer together."

"Like what?"

"Oh," Father McGettigan throws his head back and closes his eyes, "something like 'I, so-and-so, pledge to abstain from all alcoholic drink for a period of so many months and with the help of God's grace I will remain faithful to this pledge.' It is like an oath. I'd go and get the Bible and he would have knelt down and put his hand on the Bible and taken it in the form of an oath."

"How long do they usually pledge?"

"It depends. It depends on a lot of things. Sometimes

they come because they've promised their wives that they're going to stay off the booze for a while. That's why they want the card. They want to take it home and show their wife that they meant it.

"I had a fellow once and when I asked how long he wanted he said, 'For life.' I guess I looked surprised because then he said, 'Oh, Father, whenever I takes the pledge, I always takes it for life.'

"Most of them keep their word. Some, you know, would never be able to stay away from liquor except as an act of faith.

"I had one man once . . ." Almost imperceptibly Father McGettigan has slipped off his priest's collar and become what all outporters are at heart — a storyteller. "I had one man once who came and wanted his pledge lifted. 'Me brother's son is getting married,' he said, 'and I don't think I would have taken the pledge, Father, if I had knew a wedding was coming up.' "

"What did you say?"

"I asked him what his intention was when he took the pledge. I asked him if when he took it he had intended to have it lifted.

"My uncle John used to tell a story. He was a priest, too — Monsignor John McGettigan. I was named after him. He was the priest right here in Ferryland in the early 1920s and one night in the middle of a fierce winter storm a man knocked on the door. He said, 'Father, I am sorry to bother you but I think you have to do a sick call at home.' Well, my uncle thought someone must be very sick to bring this man all the way from Aquaforte in the middle of this storm, so he set off with him and it was so bad that the man had to lead the horse all the way to Aquaforte. Anyway, they punched their way through the snow and when they got there the man said, 'Father, will you wait outside for a minute.' Well, he thought he was going in to tidy up or warn them the priest was there. So he waited a bit and when no one came out to get him he thought he had better go inside. Well, the man was living alone in there. And he had changed into his pyjamas and was lying in bed waiting on my uncle. I guess he had the flu or something, but he must have thought he was sick enough that he needed the priest.

"Another time — now this was a long time ago when I was younger and people had a good deal more faith — a fisherman came to me at the beginning of the year and said, 'Father, I was wondering if you would come out in the boat with me and bless me traps. We've been having a goodly trouble with the ice this year, Father, and could use a little help.' Now this was over in LaManche. So I went out in the boat the next morning and sure enough there was a large iceberg nearby, and I said a few prayers and got a salmon for my trouble and we went back in. Well, the next day I was over in Cape Broyle which is just up the shore a spot and another fisherman came up to me and I could see he was quite upset. And he said, 'Father, is it true what I heard that you were blessing the ice in LaManche yesterday?' And I said, Yes, I had been up there. And he said, 'Well, Father, it would best you stay away from now on because the ice broke up last night and floated down here and tore up all our traps something wicked.'"

On Friday and Saturday nights the teenagers hang out at Bernard Kavanagh's Snack Bar. The Snack Bar is no more than a take-out window with a deep-fryer and a parking lot grafted onto one of Ferryland's convenience stores. The kids start arriving after dinner. The older ones drive their parents' cars. The younger ones either walk or are dropped off. The kids gather in a small adjacent room with chipboard walls. The room is big enough for a pool table, five video games, a pin-ball machine, a public phone, a big old juke-box in the corner and, the night I stop in, twenty-five teenagers. Fifty cents buys you a game of pool or five songs on the juke-box.

When I arrive there is a couple leaning against the video game farthest from the door. The girl, whose back is pitched against the machine, has her arms wrapped around the boy. Her hands are on his bum and she is pulling him against her. Two other girls are playing pinball. The rest of the kids are flicking in and out of the hall like guppies.

All of these kids will have a job of some sort in the summer. The lucky ones will be employed on a local "project" — the museum, the ball field or the swimming pool. The rest — all of them, in fact, at one time or another — will work "to the fishery."

"I was cutting out cod tongues when I was six," says fifteen-year-old Colin Croft. "I used to go out with me brother. I made four or five hundred dollars my first summer."

"I made fifteen hundred dollars last year," says Jody Ryan. "Picking capelin and cutting tongues."

"I made four thousand," says Brent Sullivan. "I worked on me father's boat."

I want to talk quietly to one of these kids, but this is hardly the place to do it. When I ask the most talkative boy, fourteen-year-old Jody Ryan, if we might get together for a chat, he looks horrified.

"Don't go calling me, boy. Don't you go calling me."

"Why?" I ask. "What's the matter?"

"Just don't you go calling me," he says and abruptly turns and slips outside with his friends.

A few days later I do call. I speak to his mother. I explain who I am and what I am about.

"Jody mentioned you," she says. "I told him it was all right. I told him he could talk to people. That he didn't have to be so, I don't know, suspicious. It's hard here after everything that's happened."

We arrange for Jody to come over to the inn. When he

comes, we sit in the front room. The same room where Phonse Kavanagh and I sat. He is comfortable again. Happy to talk.

He is in grade eight. He plays Peewee hockey. He is a good student. His best subject is science.

"I got an eighty-five percent average in me science last year. I didn't have to write me final exam."

His father is away — a drilling supervisor working in the Middle East. He is away for two months at a time, then home for a month. It's been like that for fourteen years. He phoned today from Qatar for Father's Day.

I tell Jody that I was surprised to learn how much money some of the kids were making in the summer.

"You can make some good money when the capelin roll in," he says. "When the capelin are running you watch the wharf all the time. When you see a boat come in and she is nearly level to the sea you go down and ask the fishermen if you can pick. They let maybe twenty-five people work on each boat. There'll be a scatter adults, but eighty percent of the people picking are kids. It takes maybe a half an hour to do each boat. That's maybe 15,000 or 20,000 pounds of capelin. What you do is put the she's in a pan and flick the he's onto the wharf. The he's are taken out to sea and dumped. Last year they paid $7.50 a pan. It takes ten or fifteen minutes to pick a pan. You can usually do three pans on each boat."

"What about cutting tongues?" I ask.

"That's different," says Jody. "Down to the plant there is a chute that comes out the wall and goes into the offal boat. After they've filleted the fish, what's left comes out the chute and falls into the boat. Kids stand by the chute and grab the fish heads as they go by and puts them aside until there is a break and then cuts out the tongues. There's maybe five kids down there every day. When a big fish comes out everyone fights to get him.

"The two best places to be is on either side of the chute, right where it comes out of the plant. That way you get first choice of the fish. But you've got to get there at three o'clock in the morning to get that spot. I done that once. I sat there and waited and waited for the plant to start up. I cut eighty pounds of tongues that day and I made over $160. I started cutting at eight and finished at six. You can sell the tongues for $1.50 a pound, minimum. If you can't find no one to pay that the plant will buy them from you for $1.25. I sell mine to the Surf 'n' Turf in St John's for $2.00 a pound and sometimes to Angus O'Connell. He pays $1.75 and sells them to St John's for $2.00.

"If there is tourists around then I rips them right off. Sometimes I sells tongues to the tourists for $2.50 a pound.

"Terry Kavanagh is the best kid at the tongues. His Dad puts his bucket beside the plant and that saves his place every morning. We're younger. If we put our buckets down like that they wouldn't be there when we came back.

"Like I told you, last year I made about fifteen hundred dollars. I spent it on sneakers, plus I got a four-wheeler, and I put what I had left towards it. You are supposed to be sixteen to drive a four-wheeler but as long as you wear a helmet the cops don't bother you."

"What do you do for fun?" I ask.

"Sometimes we go swimming at Merrymaking Pond. It's all fresh water up there. We changes in the bush. I collect hockey cards. I got the whole set this year."

"What about if you were unhappy? Where would you go?"

"If I was sad I'd go out by the lighthouse. I just sits down and looks at the whales and thinks about things. When I lose a game at hockey I sometimes go out there and just sits and thinks about the game."

———◼•◼———

One afternoon Robert Linfield comes back to the inn after visiting his wife and child in Gander. "I see where the capelin are rolling in at Witless Bay," he says.

"What?" I ask, surprised.

"I just drove by. Something was happening. There were people all over the beach."

There was a time when so many capelin came in the spring that you might sink to your knees in the roe if you tried to walk along the beach. Though it is not like that anymore, there are often seventy-five or more people working a beach when the capelin come in to spawn, each person with buckets full of live fish. This is something I want to see.

It is only half an hour down Highway 10 to Witless Bay. But when I get there, there is no sign of capelin anywhere. I soon abandon my search, park on the dock and console myself by watching three men loading crab shells onto a garbage scow that they are going to dump into the bay. After half an hour I ask the man operating the fork lift where a fellow might buy some crab.

"Right at the plant, my son," he says, nodding at the large warehouse at the end of the wharf.

He takes me into the plant and I buy a pound of freshly cooked crab legs right off the assembly line. They hand them to me in a clear plastic bag. I drive from the wharf to the general store and buy half a dozen hotdog rolls and a six-pack of beer. I balance the bag of crab on the beer case and eat half the meat and drink a beer as I drive back to Ferryland. I find a St John's radio station that plays old rock and roll, and I couldn't be happier even if Robert had been right about the capelin.

———— • ————

Cyril Barbour said to come over to his house any night and he'd get out his guitar and play me some music.

"Years ago Sunday morning was the time for music. Before or after mass. You'd be after having a scatter drinks and singing a few songs. A lot of it was chin music. No instruments."

Cyril lives down by the water with his wife, Mona, and their four children. Sammy is thirteen. Colin is eleven. Matthew is four. Katie is fifteen months.

We're sitting around the kitchen table talking about Colin's ears.

"The doctor was talking to us about whether we should be after having them pinned back," says Mona.

"He said Colin would have to wear bandages for weeks after the operation and then bind them for three months at night after that," says Cyril.

They are looking at me expectantly.

I am looking at Colin's ears. They are big. But they are the kind of ears a boy could grow into if he were given time.

"They look OK to me," I say.

"We decided not to have them done," says Cyril.

"But we have to be careful because they get burned in the sun," says Mona. "It can cause skin cancer."

Cyril is an auto-body mechanic. He commutes to St John's every day.

"It's hard. My eight-hour day is eleven and a half hours. In the winter it can take three hours to get home. Sometimes you don't know if you are going to make it. Sometimes I stay to my mom's."

Mona works part time with the dentist and, when the capelin are running, part time at the fish plant.

"Tell him about the whale, Daddy," says Colin.

"We'll be singing some songs first, Colin," says Cyril, reaching for his guitar. "This is the first song I ever wrote about me. I call it 'Good Times and Memories,' but most people who hear it call it 'Barbour's Song' because it is about me."

When he has finished singing, Cyril smiles at his wife. The kids smile at both of them. For a moment the kitchen is silent.

Colin is the one who breaks the spell.

"Tell him about the whale."

Cyril rests his guitar on the floor.

"I was sixteen when I got my first boat," he says. "It was a twenty-seven-foot skiff. One day I was out in the bay with my brother Dave. You couldn't get the jigger down, there were so many herring and mackerel that day. You'd get it down two fathoms and there'd be three fish on it.

"Anyway, we were fishing away and Dave said something and I looked over and his eyes were bulging so far out of his head that they were almost lying on his cheek. The skiff was rising up in the air. I thought it was just the swell, but she kept rising and rising and I looked over the side and all I saw was this big black whale.

"The whale was rising up to get air and we were rising with him and I thought, 'We're gone now.' And then he . . . sank down. Sank down as nice as can be. He didn't flip down, which is the regular thing they do. He sank. The skiff was nearly swamped but she stayed afloat. Though it did take us two hours to get back, we had had such a fright."

Colin is watching me closely, more interested in my reaction to the story than the story itself.

"Once when we was out on the rocks a whale came so close to me and Bradley that the splash hit our face," says Sammy.

"Must have been quite a whale," says Cyril.

He disappears and comes back a moment later with two black suitcases. He opens the larger of the two and takes out a sparkling red accordion.

And that is when the music begins in earnest. Cyril picks up his guitar, Colin picks up the squeeze box, Matthew picks up a pair of spoons, and Mona picks up Katie and dances around the kitchen as the men work their way through "Turkey in the Straw," "I'se the B'y," and "Forget Me Not." The second time through "Turkey in the Straw," Matthew puts down his spoons and runs out of the room. He reappears a moment later waving a pair of black leather loafers.

"Those are his dancing shoes," says Cyril, nodding at his son. And we all clap in time and stamp our feet while Matthew spins, twirls, taps and slips his way through a medley of reels.

At the end of the music we burst into applause and Matthew bows, so proud of his performance that he almost applauds himself. Katie, who is also down on the floor is still dancing, or doing the fifteen-month-old equivalent — twirling around with her arms out-stretched, bouncing off the refrigerator.

"This song is about my daddy," says Cyril. "It's called 'Daddy's Hard Working Hands.' " He twists shyly in his chair so he is facing the stove instead of directly across the table at me.

When the telephone rings a moment later, Sammy answers it quietly and lays the receiver on the chair. Who-ever has called has to wait for the end of the song before they can speak to Cyril.

Later, after the instruments have been put away and the kids have gone outside to play, the talk turns, as the talk often seems to turn in Ferryland, to the Catholic Church.

"It tore the heart right out of us when we heard about what'd been going on," says Cyril. "Knowing that the priest that married us, Corrigan, and the priest that bap-tized our children, Hickey, were doing those things. It tore the hearts out of everybody."

We fall silent for a moment and then Cyril leans for-ward and fixes my eyes with his.

"I went to church regularly for ten years here," he says. "We used to go to church every Saturday and every Sunday. And I was refused communion by three different priests. They wouldn't give me communion until I changed my faith, and I wouldn't change my faith because I don't believe the Pope is the Vicar of Christ. The last priest didn't think I was good enough to be a Christian. He said it would be sacrilegious to give me communion. What a pile of crap.

"It is an awful feeling, you know, to be in a church for ten or fifteen years and not be allowed to take communion. I always felt like I was only half a Christian.

"Once I asked one of the priests what would happen when I died. I asked him if he would bury me. And you know what? He didn't answer me.

"And all the time they were doing these things to me they were victimizing our children. And lying about it."

Everyone in town is upset. Someone tells me that the money collected at mass and at the bingo has fallen off by about fifty percent. What hurts the most, someone else says, is that we all have them priests' pictures in our family albums — standing there with our children as if they were some kind of special.

"I don't trust any priests anymore," says Cyril. "There were nights and nights Mona and I stayed up talking until dawn. We would go to bed mad. And we'd get up mad. Knowing our children were down there. My son used to be an altar boy. We're left tossing and turning. Wondering and wondering. We were mad for two years.

"My wife is Catholic. My kids are Catholic. I was raised by my parents to read the Bible. I read the Bible at nighttime. But I don't go to church anymore. I kneel down at home and I say my prayers. I can live a Christian life by myself. And I don't mind about my kids anymore. It's their choice to do what they want."

———— • ————

Bill Morry is telling stories on Farley Mowat. Again.

"I knew," he says, slouched in the leather chair in his wood-panelled living-room, "that God-damn boat wouldn't float. I advised him not to buy it. The boat was condemned. I know the guy he bought it from. He could have had a better boat for a lot less money. He was lucky he wasn't drowned. Farley had these illusions of doing things the old way. He didn't want shelter on it. He wanted a tiller instead of a wheel. I tried to explain that he was going to have trouble seeing where he was going. But he just sat there on the couch drinking rum and didn't listen. And then when he went aground he couldn't get up front fast enough to get the anchor out. I could've told him that."

The Morry family bought the property where we are sitting tonight over two hundred years ago. Morrys have lived and worked in Ferryland as merchants — buyers and sellers of fish — ever since.

"Farley used to come and stay here. Here at the house." Pat Morry, Bill's wife, has been uncharacteristically quiet up until now. "In those days there was nowhere to stay in town and we ran a bit of a hospitality home. It wasn't an official thing. People would come along looking for somewhere to stay and I was embarrassed that there was no place to send them. So we'd take them in.

"Farley stayed here on and off maybe six months in all," says Bill, stepping on his wife's sentence with the casual neglect that comes with forty-nine years of marriage. "He is an unusual character. I got a great kick out of him."

While Bill is fixing drinks, I ask Pat about the ring I have heard about.

"He wants to know about the ring, Bill," she calls to her husband.

"The ring," he says, reappearing. "I found it when I was maybe eight or nine. I was playing by the water. Near where the river comes down from the priest's house. It was laying there in the sand. My father took it to St John's and had it appraised. It had a big ruby and settings for two diamonds, but one was missing. It was a Queen Anne setting. Mother wore it for years. Where is the ring now Pat?"

"Peter has it. We gave it to Peter."

"We've found all sorts of other things you know," says Bill. "Grape-shot and cannon-balls. You find that sort of stuff all the time when you're gardening. Once I found a chain-shot, which is two cannon-balls chained together. They are designed that way so they tumble when they're shot. They are supposed to tear down masts when they hit a ship."

It is late and I am tired. But the Morrys don't seem in any hurry to go to bed. Bill fixes another drink and we sit in the dark room, and as the wind makes the house creak like a ship, he tells me about Captain Kidd and Blackbeard and the great pirate Peter Easton. The ring that Morry found when he was a boy is the only tangible evidence of the treasure that Easton is said to have buried somewhere, or so the story goes, up a stream that runs into the Ferryland beach. There are three streams that fit the description. The other clue to the treasure's location is that the pirates are said to have stepped into the stream to wash yellow clay from their boots after they finished burying the loot. There's never been a boy in Ferryland who hasn't spent some of his summers poking into strange-looking rock piles and digging into the stream banks where the clay is streaked with yellow.

There is only one lamp left on in the room. Pat has moved onto the couch now. I am almost dozing in my chair. And Bill is still talking.

"Little changed here, you know, until the radio and TV came. Until the radio and TV it was the same for me as it was for my grandfather."

Bill's grandfather was Thomas Graham Morry, son of John Morry who was born in Ferryland around 1848. Thomas Graham was the fourth generation of Morrys born in Newfoundland.

Bill's father was Howard Morry. In 1965, when Howard was eighty years old, he sat down and wrote a document called "The Memories of Howard Morry." It begins with an apology:

Things I remember which I know will be of interest to folks in years to come. I only wish I had to jot down all the stories I heard when we were young and in the long winter evenings. Poor folks would sit in the twilight and dusk up to 9 P.M., perhaps later, in some cases to stretch out the little drops of kerosene they had, in others, like our own home, to sit and talk and sing songs and sometimes hymns.

My dad was a Church of England man and could play the concertina. I can see him now by the glow of the fire, sitting and playing and singing out the old hymns: Nearer My God to Thee, Rock of Ages, A Few More Years Shall Roll, etc., and his brows would go up and down with the tune.

Pat stirs, "Before TV people used to come visiting. The Lunenburg sea captains used to follow the squid schools up here and they would come visit when they were in harbour.

"Oh, it was a fun time. Bill would get out his guitar and they'd sit here and sing and drink booze. There would be dances in people's houses. And eating and drinking and singing. And then we'd wheel them back to the boats the next morning.

"It all started to change when the radio came. And it kept going with the TV."

I loved to go to some of the old sailors' houses and there were lots of them then. They'd talk about shipwrecks, foreign ports, brave deeds, etc., and sing "Come all ye's" and ballads for hours. Some of the owners of the houses were very poor but that did not make you less welcome. If you could get a couple of pipes full of tobacco or a few coppers and give them to him, or lay it on the window bench, it would be thankfully accepted. Fellows that did not have anything else, and there were quite a few of them, would bring a few sticks of firewood.

"I guess we had the first TV set around here," says Bill. "We got our set three or four months before the broadcasts began. It was a big change. The more people got TV's, the less you saw of them.

"At first they all came here to watch the wrestling. The same bunch came week after week and they all took the same spot. One week Paddy Crane didn't show up so I sat in his chair and soon after I settled down sure enough he came in. Well, he just sat down right behind me and he got so wound up he took off his tie and then his jacket and finally his shirt. He was sweating like a bull and pounding away on the back of the chair like it would come apart. I had to move away but Paddy didn't notice a thing. We wouldn't normally watch the wrestling but everyone came over so we'd put it on.

"But I guess the TV ruined everything."

In the long winter evenings we used to slide over the hills and skate, young and old. And at nights there were always folks on the road. At each crossroad, the first fellow to come along would wait for his chums to come there from the other lanes. Then sometimes we had dances on the bridges, especially in the fall and lovely moonlit nights.

We'd go some nights to Aquaforte and Calvert, go some nights as far as Rocky Pond Bridge which was wooden. The girls and boys would come over from Cape Broyle and we'd dance there and any fellow who had a gal would see her home. Other nights we'd go to the quarry bridge to dance. The Aquaforte crowd would be down there. The music was mostly accordion or mouth organ, but sometimes we'd have to lilt it for a dance, for hours. We danced polka, the bridges were too rough for waltzing, that was left for dances and fairs, etc., in the hall.

"Before the TV everyone depended on everyone else," Bill says. "You visited. You helped each other. It was like the Mormon system. I've walked from here to St John's. And the biggest hazard was putting on twenty pounds. In those days people would know you were walking and they would invite you in for a cup of tea. Only it wouldn't just be a cup of tea, it would be a whole meal.

"The night my mother had her stroke people got out on the road with shovels and they shovelled the road all the way from here to St John's so they could get her to the hospital."

I'll just break off here to tell of my grandfather Sullivan.

His brother had a haberdashery over in Dublin and he was out here some years when he had a letter telling of his brother's death and that there were two large crates of goods left to him. They were being sent to him by the first boat coming to Newfoundland and calling at Waterford on the way over. Eventually he got word they arrived in St John's. Then a long wait. None of the boats calling here could get the bales down their hatches, so one brought it on deck. On the day of arrival all the harbour that could walk went down on Carter's wharf to see what Sullivan got from Ireland.

Well there was another problem, there wasn't any horse or cart big enough to get the crates on to bring it to his home so he decided to open them on the wharf. First one, the biggest one, was filled with — of all things, ten dozen tall silk hats, so he knew he wouldn't sell them. He gave them around to the neighbours as they came along and his son told me, for years afterwards you'd see fellows fishing with Beaver hats (he called them) and when it came to the squidding ground, to look around and see maybe twenty or thirty men squidding away and now and then get their hats knocked off by someone with a squid. For the squidding ground was always a place for jokes.

"My mother was quite a woman," says Bill Morry. It is so dark in the room now I can barely see. I sip my Scotch and close my eyes. Bill keeps talking.

"She came from Scotland. I guess she missed the old country. Anyway, my father got some money together and said she should go home and have a visit because he wasn't sure when he would get any money together again. I think he had saved a thousand dollars, which was a hell of a pile of money in those days. He said, 'Frederis, go and have a good time. Stay six months. We'll get along all right.' Well, there were eight children but we had a maid and off Mum went. She was going to stay to St John's for a few days with relatives and then off to Edinburgh. I remember my father sitting by the fire saying, 'Mother will be well on her way to Scotland by now.' And then after a week or so a schooner came into the wharf and somebody came running up to the house and said, 'Mr Morry, there is a big box on the boat addressed to you.'

"It was only about a hundred yards down to the wharf so we all rushed down and sure enough there was a terrific big freight box sitting on the deck, and then all of a sudden my mother climbed out of the forecastle. My father said, 'Frederis, what are you doing here?' And she said, 'Well, Howard, I thought of you and the children and I just couldn't go.'

"She had met a German music professor in St John's who had come to Canada before the First World War and wanted to go back home. He had this big grand piano he wanted to sell before he left. Mother bought it for nine hundred dollars and I guess she used the last of her money to have it shipped home. It was huge, only a foot short of a concert grand, and it took half the men in town and a jury-rigged sling to get it off the boat. They set it down on a sled and wrestled it up the hill to the house with brute strength. I remember my father standing there saying, 'How in the name of God are we going to get it inside?' It was the fall. There was snow on the ground. They finally had to take out some of the windows and part of one of the walls. Once it was inside, the piano took up nearly half the room. I remember my mother playing and everyone standing around the piano. We all had to sing our own songs. It was a beauty. Black ebony."

It seems to me that Pat Morry has drifted to sleep on the

couch. I am, myself, floating in some half world half-way between sleep and wakefulness. The light, the Scotch and Bill Morry's voice wrap around me like fog.

"Mother was supposed to go to Edinburgh again in 1929. Maybe it was 1930. Anyway, she went off to St John's and once more I can remember Father saying that he supposed she was on the high seas by now, and he hoped she had a good trip.

"Now, in those days it was the habit of fishermen to cure their fish on flakes [wooden-framed racks on which fish are dried in the sun], and it was also the habit for everyone to help each other out. On the weekend the kids would often do the work and I remember we had all been sent down to work on the Currans' flakes when we saw this cavalcade of cars coming up the road. There were maybe three or four cars in a row, which was a lot of cars in those days, and they were all blowing their horns. The one in front was an old square-back Dodge. Well, we all turn up the road and here it is but Mother is driving the old Dodge. And once more father said, 'Frederis, what are you doing here?' and Mother said 'Howard, I just couldn't go.'

"She had been staying with the relatives again and they happened to own the Dodge dealership in St John's and she had bought this big old square car. It sort of looked like a pick-up truck. 'Well, this is all fine, Frederis,' said my father, 'but how are you going to keep it in gas?' She had it all figured out. She was going to go taxiing. And for years that's what she did. She drove people back and forth to St John's and picked up supplies and things.

"Mother taxied until the car packed it in. But Father never learned how to drive. They would take the car into a big meadow by the house and the handyman would sit in the front and try to teach him. He'd say, 'Now, Mr Morry, there is a fence over there.' But Father could never turn in time. He was always running into the fence. And it was a large meadow. That was the only car they ever owned. When it was finished they never got another.

"I think he gave her money for a third trip, but by then he knew she wasn't going to go. She went down to St John's again and bought things for the house. And I think she used some of the money to help my brother at university. She was only gone about three days that trip."

———————— ▪•◂ ————————

One morning I decide to leave my car at the inn and set off on foot. I only have to walk a few minutes before I relearn an old lesson. If you really want to understand a place, you can't do it from an automobile.

I am standing on the gravel shoulder beside a vacant field, a hill sloping towards The Gaze. I must have driven by this field over one hundred times. Except now I can see that the field isn't vacant at all. It is an overgrown and forgotten graveyard, right in the centre of town. I can't believe I have driven past it so often and never noticed the tombstones slanting out of the ground.

I climb the wire cow fence and wander through the uncut grass, absent-mindedly brushing the stones with my fingers as I pass each one. Most of the inscriptions are too faded to read anymore. Many barely poke above the grass. It is as if the ground itself was rising up in slow mounds to swallow them. The stones, I think, looking at the harbour, mark the field like icebergs, floating through time, ninetenths of their memory below the surface. Memory and memorials slipping away together.

These are graves from the early 1800s. Maybe earlier. For there are mounds here with no stones at all.

I sit there among them, under the sun with the wind and the sea in my face, and as I sit I remember a passage I read near the end of Howard Morry's diary.

. . . Don't go home without going to Aquaforte. There is an American privateer sunk there and 'twould be an interesting place to go, it's easy to see her and any of the

Windsors will show it. And get the view out the harbour from the highway up above Mort Windsor's. Then to Fermeuse. Go to Bill Trainor Senior's, tell him I sent you, it's a very historical place. They live in Admirals Cove. He'll show you around. Then to Renews — Go to Steve Chidleigh or old Jim Devine — but I expect that Jim is too old by now. There is a gun there, the oldest, I would say, in Newfoundland. It's Queen Elizabeth's time and is of brass. I warned Steve not to let anyone take it away. Please warn him too, for Renews is quite a historical place, Steve will be able to tell you, and there is a Miss Jackson who was a school teacher in Fermeuse for a while, that knows a lot of history. That's all for today. I'm going to have a few drinks and for a while think I'm forty instead of eighty. Bye now. I'll write a few little stories some day when I'm in the mood.

I sit there for a long time, fingering the wiry grass and following the clouds as they drift across the sky, and the ice still here in the harbour, the sea grass on the downs, the oats.

NOTES

Maple Creek

1 The Great Sand Hills that I skirted on my way to Maple Creek are a unique, sparsely populated and little-known part of Saskatchewan. "No trails, no wood, no water" was the warning about the region printed on one map in the 1880s. Today there are some good-sized ranches in the hills — both sheep and cattle — but there are also parts of the rolling landscape where grass gives way to sand and you'd swear you were walking on a beach or standing in the desert. The sand hills are crawling east with the prevailing winds, covering trees and shrubs as they go. They are home to mule deer and antelope, buck-brush and sage, hawthorn and stunted polar and the kangaroo rat — a rodent so adapted to its dry home that it is able to suck all the moisture it needs from nibbling on dry seeds.

2 The word Nikaneet shows up spelled "Nekaneet", both around Maple Creek today and in historical documents. I opted for the spelling used on Government pay sheets recorded right after the survey in 1913. On treaty payment records in the 1880s the chief, Kah-Nikaneet, is most often referred to as "Foremost-man" or "Front-man" which is an English translation of his name. The prefix "Kah" is a term that some Maple Creek locals might not be familiar with. Kah-Nikaneet is what "Foremost-man" would have been called by his friends and family.

3 A good account of the Cypress Hills Massacre (and one
   that I drew on) can be found in Wallace Stegner's
   evocative ode to the south-west corner of Saskatchewan
   — *Wolf Willow* (Viking Press, 1962), re-released as a Penguin paperback in 1990.

   Paul F. Sharp's *Whoop-up Country* (University of Okla-
   homa Press, 1973) and J.G. Nelson's *The Last Refuge*
   (Harvest House, 1973) provide more scholarly
   approaches to the event.

   Much about the Cypress Hills (including details of
   the massacre) can also be found in Grant MacEwan's
   book, *Sitting Bull: The Years in Canada* (Hurtig, 1973).

   Parks Canada published a pamphlet on the massacre
   ("Cypress Hills Massacre National Historic Site"),
   which includes suggestions for further reading.

   As to the aftermath, the pamphlet reports that "in
   1875, five of the wolfers faced an extradition commission in Helena, Montana, and a year later three more
   (who were arrested on the Canadian side of the 49th
   parallel) stood trial in Winnipeg. They were all
   released on contradictory or insufficient evidence. The
   case was finally dropped in 1882 as no new evidence
   came to light."

   MacEwan recounts how the release of the accused in
   the Montana extradition hearing was "greeted by some
   of the wildest scenes of celebration the western frontier
   had experienced. Bonfires lit the streets of Helena all
   night and citizens drank and sang."

   MacEwan pinpoints the killings, on the spring day in
   1873, as one of the most important focal points in Canadian history.

4 Curator Donny White, of the Medicine Hat Museum
   and Art Gallery, isn't as convinced as Ben Broderick
   that the metal button Broderick showed me came from
   the Battle of the Little Big Horn.

   "There are other possibilities," says White.

The famous march west was hard on the uniforms issued to the North-West Mounted Police. New supplies weren't quick to come from the east. Many photos from the period actually show men wearing buckskin when they were on patrol.

White has heard stories of Mounties being outfitted in surplus American cavalry uniforms — presumably purchased from Fort Benton. John Peter Turner makes reference to this in volume 1 of his book *The North-West Mounted Police.*

Recounting the forces early days in the Cypress Hills — the days before Fort Walsh was built — Turner describes the appearance of a large band of Sioux at Superintendent Walsh's camp. The Indians explained they had been driven across the international boundary by American soldiers. "The visitors," writes Turner, "were disposed to be friendly until they noticed two constables wearing parts of United States uniforms purchased from traders to replace their own worn-out apparel." When they saw the American uniforms, says Turner, the Sioux became excited.

"Walsh was busy at a small table. The Union Jack floated above him on a temporary staff. A Sioux spokesman approached and asked through an interpreter who the strangers might be, and upon receiving a reply, exclaimed that the white chief was lying; that he and his men were Americans in disguise."

The tension (which was considerable) was broken without incident when a second and larger band of Indians — a group of Cree, enemies of the Sioux — appeared over the hillside. The Sioux fled.

White says that he has never seen a photo from the period that shows mounties wearing American uniforms. But even if the practice was rare, the incident Turner describes, and stories of American Army deserters fleeing into Canada, provide other explanations for how the button I held came to be at the Moorhead Creek.

Dresden

1 There are a number of editions of Josiah Henson's autobiography available for reference. The various editions differ — sometimes in language and sometimes in the period of his life they cover. At least two editions (which I relied on) are still in print. The first, dated 1849 (*The Life of Josiah Henson: Formerly a Slave*), is only seventy pages long. This is the version of Henson's life that Harriet Beecher Stowe is said to have read. Afterwards she is said to have met with Henson in Andover, Massachusetts, and it is this meeting that people say she drew on when writing her novel (see below). This edition has been reprinted since 1965 and is available from Uncle Tom's Cabin Museum in Dresden, Ontario.

   A longer volume (*Truth Stranger than Fiction: Father Henson's Story of His Own Life*) was originally printed in 1858. This 212-page edition includes an introduction by Harriet Beecher Stowe. It was reprinted in 1973 and is available from Corner House Publishers in Williamstown, Massachusetts.

2 To what degree Harriet Beecher Stowe based her novel, *Uncle Tom's Cabin,* on the life of Josiah Henson is a debatable question.

   The Ontario Heritage Foundation knows where it stands on the subject. The text of the historical plaque on the lawn in front of Uncle Tom's Cabin Museum in Dresden reads as follows:

   In this house lived the Rev. Josiah Henson (1789-1883) whose early life in slavery provided much of the material for Harriet Beecher Stowe's novel "Uncle Tom's Cabin". Born in Maryland, Henson escaped in 1830 to Upper Canada. In 1841, he and a group of abolitionists purchased 200 acres in this vicinity and established a vocational school known as the British American Institute for fugitive slaves. A sawmill and a grist mill were built, and a considerable number of former slaves settled here. After emancipation was proclaimed in 1863, many returned to the United States, but Henson continued to occupy this house until his death, and is buried nearby.

Some scholars are less certain of the Henson/Stowe link. Stowe herself was ambiguous on the subject. In the face of accusations that her novel was inaccurate in its depiction of the life of slaves, she published, in 1853, a work called *A Key to Uncle Tom's Cabin: Presenting the Original Facts and Documents upon which the Story is Founded* . . . One source Stowe cites in her *Key* is Henson's autobiography. However, the title of the *Key*, says Robin W. Winks in his definitive and immensely readable *The Blacks in Canada*, was "less than honest; for the documentation she brought together in the *Key*, while amply supporting much that she had put in her novel, had not been in her possession at the time Uncle Tom was created; quite simply the *Key* was a post hoc attempt to buttress a thesis already expressed."

Harriet Beecher Stowe could clearly have read Henson's book and might even have met Henson before she wrote *Uncle Tom's Cabin*, as some people contend. In *Romantic Kent* (Kent County Council, 1973) local historian Victor Lauriston recounts a story that you can hear around Dresden today.

> One day in the middle 40's there came to the Dawn Settlement from Andover, Mass. a little, alert woman named Harriet Beecher Stowe. At the Elgin Settlement, at Shrewsbury, at Chatham, she had talked with escaped slaves, gleaning facts for a story she was writing entitled "Life Among the Lowly." Now she talked with Josiah Henson. His gentle piety, his amazing trust in God, his utter unselfishness, impressed her deeply. Then and there she found the leading character for the book the world was to know as "Uncle Tom's Cabin."

There are also accounts (one of them by Stowe's son and grandson) that have Henson visiting Stowe in Boston or Andover before *Uncle Tom's Cabin* was written.

Winks, however, argues that if Stowe and Henson did meet, it's more likely they did so after her book was published. He also argues that "nothing said publicly by the author of *Uncle Tom* gave real substance to any contention that Josiah Henson and Uncle Tom were one and the same."

Henson, says Winks, though often introduced as Uncle Tom on the speaking circuit, was "careful not to make the claim explicit himself." The two, he says, "did reinforce each other," but he questions a direct creative link.

There are two letters worth mentioning here. They were both written by Stowe and they perhaps best give a sense of the debate and the "evidence" cited by both sides.

You can find one (a personal letter that eventually appeared in the *Windsor Daily Record*) reprinted in Daniel G. Hill's book *The Freedom-Seekers* (Book Society of Canada, 1981):

> It is also true that a sketch of his life, published many years ago by the Massachusetts Anti-Slavery Society, furnished me many of the finest conceptions and incidents of Uncle Tom's character . . . in particular the scene where he refuses to free himself by the murder of a brutal master. The real history of Josiah Henson in some points goes even beyond that of Uncle Tom in traits of heroic manhood. He once visited me in Andover, and personal intercourse confirmed the high esteem I had for him . . .

The second letter, as quoted by Winks (and written six years later), was to the editor of the *Indianapolis News* and said that Uncle Tom was "not the biography of any one man."

Winks says that the real significance of the Canadian claim to Uncle Tom is "precisely this":

. . . as Canadians came increasingly to assign Tom's role to Henson, as the myths of the North Star, the Underground Railroad, and the fugitives' haven "under the lion's paw" grew in the post-Civil War years, when these myths no longer could be tested, Canadians came increasingly to congratulate themselves upon their lack of prejudice and to contrast themselves favorably with the immoral and once slave-ridden United States.

The True contrast was favorable enough, indeed; but that the greatest, the best-known, the most pious black fugitive of all time should have sought out Canadian soil for his resurrection bred a growing Canadian self-satisfaction with racial conditions above the forty-ninth parallel. If Uncle Tom came to Canada, could conditions need improving? No year has passed since the late 1860s without a stream of self-congratulatory Canadian newspaper accounts, editorials, and memoirs appearing in April or September of each year — on the anniversaries of the outbreak of the Civil War or of the passage of the Fugitive Slave Act — in which Henson has not been cited as sufficient and sole evidence to prove that Canadians shared none of the American racial virus, that in this one area, at least, the pressures of continentalism has been successfully resisted. That Henson himself allegedly wrote that "in Canada, black children are despised"; that many Canadian Negroes had considered Henson self-serving and sly; that to Negroes "Uncle Tom" was becoming a pejorative term — all were ignored in the recurring annual flush of pride in the presence of "the real Uncle Tom's grave" on Canadian soil.

3 The history of slavery in Canada may have been well documented, but it was never taught to me in school.
Records of slavery go back to the beginnings of the

European settlement of Canada. Oliver Le Jeune was brought at age six from Madagascar and lived for twenty-six-years — most of them as a slave — in Champlain's Quebec. At the time of the conquest, there were over 3,500 slaves listed in local records. One-third of them were black, the rest were *panis* (Indians).

Many people have argued that slavery in New France never compared with slavery as it was practised in the southern United States. While conceding that practices may have differed, Robin Winks writes that it was slavery nevertheless:

If slavery in New France was among the most benevolent expressions of the institution in North America, nonetheless it was slavery, with accompanying potentialities toward the dominance of one man, and of one race, over another. That these potentialities were limited in comparison to the English colonies by the lack of trade, the *Code Noir*, customs that grew independently in New France, and to some extent by the church, is clear. . . .

The chief reason slavery gained little hold in Canada arose from the fact that the French remained in possession of the northern tier of the New World while the British were acquiring the West Indies, which could exploit immediately, obviously, and profitably a system of slave labor. To say that slavery could not be adjusted to the economy of New France, even to the fur trade, is to go too far; although to say that it would have been difficult to establish it — that the active intervention of the state would have been required — is correct. Slavery, if not dependent upon, certainly thrived upon one-crop, mass-production, gang-labor economies; and against such, a few beaver hats did not signify. From the outset the Canadians were, to use Edward Gibbon Wakefield's phrase, "earth-scratchers."

The number of slaves in Canada increased dramatically following the war of American independence. Many Loyalists fleeing the emerging American Republic brought their black slaves with them to British North America.

Before the lieutenant governor of Upper Canada John Simcoe (himself a Loyalist) legislated against slavery (Upper Canada was the only Canadian province ever to do so) slavery had already been abolished in the American Northwest Territories. And so, as Daniel Hill recounts in *The Freedom-Seekers*, there was a time when black slaves were actually swimming across the Detroit River from the Canadian shore to seek their freedom south of the forty-ninth parallel.

"By 1807," writes Winks, "slave owners in the Western District of Upper Canada had suffered such losses to Detroit . . . that ten of the owners petitioned the Lieutenant-Governor, Francis Gore, to stop 'the Evil, . . . the Facility of Escape to the American States.' "

While it is worth noting that Canadian slave owners did not employ overseers, and that a slave was more apt to be dealt with by the courts than by the sting of a whip, it is also important to acknowledge that the practice of slavery did exist in Canada for almost two hundred years. It existed with the sometimes benign and the sometimes active collusion of the state and various levels of society.

Perhaps what Canadians can be most proud of is the role the courts of this country played, both in refusing the extradition of fugitive slaves and, more than the politicians, causing the practical end of slavery in this country. The most thorough treatment of the story of slavery I found was by Winks in *The Blacks in Canada: A History* (McGill-Queen's University Press/Yale University Press, 1971). I recommend this book to anyone wanting to pursue the topic further.

St-Jean-de-Matha

Donat Gadoury's achievements appear on the back of a small autographed poster he hands out.

SES TOURS DE FORCE

LÈVE DU DOIGT (*) 425 lbs*

LÈVE DE TERRE (*) 700 lbs*

LÈVE DE TERRE (*) 1,000 lbs*

LÈVE DE TERRE (*) 1,500 lbs*

LÈVE DU DOS (*) 3,500 lbs*

Foxwarren

1   Pat Falloon was the first draft choice of the San Jose Sharks in the 1991 NHL draft. Falloon was the second player chosen overall in the draft. The first player to go was Eric Lindros in the now famous Quebec Nordiques fiasco. Falloon proved to be a wise pick for the Sharks. In his rookie season (1991-92) he led the team in goals scored (25).

Though the Sharks didn't fare so well on the ice in their first NHL season, they were a sensation in one area — merchandising. Items with the Sharks logo were so hot in 1991-92 that reporter Al Strachan projected (*Globe and Mail,* February 29, 1992) that only one other sports team in North America would sell more licensed goods — the Chicago Bulls of the National Basketball Association. Strachan reported that in Los Angeles, Pat Falloon's jersey (number 17) was actually outselling Wayne Gretzky's. Up in Edmonton, when a local Oilers outlet ordered seven hundred team jackets, five hundred were black and white — the Sharks' colours.

2 If Garth Jacobs had taken the same truck load of wheat to the grain elevator in the summer of 1992 (a little over a year later), he would have received $1,138 for his load. That is an additional seventeen percent *drop* in value.

Ferryland

1 I chose to visit Ferryland for many reasons. Because when I visited they were still fishing for cod there much the same way they fished for cod when Lord Baltimore chose the bay to be the capital of his Plantation of Avalon. Because the great pirate Peter Easton is said to have lorded the Atlantic from Fox's Hill for two years before Baltimore arrived. Because I liked the sound of the name (Fairyland?). And because I was enchanted with the lore that wisps up like candle smoke every time someone mentions that magic name, Avalon.

Avalon is the legendary British island said to be the home of the Holy Grail, the resting place of King Arthur, the burial spot of St. Patrick.

It was Sir George Calvert (later Lord Baltimore) who named this stretch of the New Founde Land, Avalon. (An examination of Calvert's motives for choosing the name can be found in a fascinating paper called "The Role of Religion in Lord Baltimore's Colonial Enterprise," by R.J. Lahey, Maryland Historical Magazine, vol. 72, no. 4, 1977).

Calvert was a principal secretary (one of two) to James I. He bought his plantation and named it in 1620. The first group of a dozen colonists were dispatched in August 1621 under the command of a Welsh soldier, Captain Edward Wynne. When he came himself to Ferryland in the summer of 1626, Calvert (now Lord Baltimore) was so struck by his plantation that he returned the following season with his wife and children. But the next winter was unusually harsh. Baltimore wrote a pleading letter to Charles I that he had

> . . . met with difficulties and encumberances here which in this place are no longer to be resisted, but enforce me presently to quit my residence and shift to some other warmer climate of this New World, where the winters be shorter and less rigorous. For here . . . I found . . . which other men for their private interests always concealed from me, that from the middle of October to the middle of May there is a sad face of winter upon all this land; both the sea and land so frozen for the great part of the time as they are not penetrable, no plant or vegetable appearing out of the earth until the beginning of May, nor fish in the sea, beside the air so intolerable cold as it is hardly to be endure. . . . My house hath been a hospital all this winter, of a hundred persons fifty sick at a time, myself being one, and nine or ten of them died. . . . I am determined to leave this place to fishermen that are better able to encounter storms and hard weather, and to remove myself with some forty persons to your Majesty's dominion Virginia."

Having established, perhaps for the first time, the one truth Americans share concerning their northern neighbour — that you can't believe a Canadian when he talks about snow — Baltimore scurried south to

Maryland to sow the seeds of the town that still bears his name. The official crest of the city of Baltimore still includes a cod fish. It was originally placed there in honor of the Newfoundland colony which remained in the Calvert family yet a while.

The plantation of Avalon was only the fifth attempt to colonize the island of Newfoundland by the British, and is today, one of the earliest settlements that still exists in North America.

Historians can't agree on exactly what it was that Baltimore had to say about his Canadian winter. In some publications Baltimore is reported to have written about the sad "fare" rather than sad "face" of winter. Not having seen the original letter and assuming the difficulty here is Baltimore's handwriting (it is easy to imagine how an "r" and a "c" could be squabbled over), I have opted for "face" over "fare." The poetry pleases me. The "sad face of winter" is a turn of phrase Hugh MacLennan might have coined and as great moments of art are often unintentional, we might as well give the phrase to Lord Baltimore.

2   What Jan Morris really says about St John's in her book *City to City* (Macfarlane Walter and Ross, 1990) is this: "Of all the cities I have written about, anywhere in the world, none has given me more enjoyment than St John's, Newfoundland, the most entertaining town in North America."

3   The relatively unknown Peter Easton, says Rev. E. Hunt in the *Dictionary of Canadian Biography*, "was the leading corsiar of his day and one of the most famous in the whole annals of piracy. He possessed all the requisite skills for his infamous trade but he was neither a blood thirsty monster nor a swashbuckling cut-throat. On the contrary, he proved himself an outstanding navigator, an able, brave, and bold seaman, an expert tactician,

and highly competitive in gun-laying. He controlled
such seapower that no sovereign or state could afford
to ignore him and he was never overtaken or captured
by any fleet commissioned to hunt him down.''

In the 1600s European governments often strengthened their navies by licensing private vessels to engage
in warfare through what were known as Letters of Mar-
que. The so-called privateers were licensed to attack
and capture the merchant fleets of hostile nations. It
didn't take much imagination for a number of privateers who had lost their licenses to move from licensed
piracy to freestyle manoeuvres. Easton, a young Englishman, was one of the most successful of these free-
booters. Some have ranked him along with Captain
Morgan and Captain Kidd as one of the greatest pirates
in the western Atlantic.

Before he fled to Newfoundland (to avoid what
would have been a treasonous confrontation with Sir
Henry Mainwaring) Easton reputedly commanded a
powerful private navy that operated off the coast of
Cornwall.

In Newfoundland he built a fort at Harbour Grace
and then moved south and established headquarters
for two years in Ferryland (1612-14). From Newfoundland Easton is said to have attacked the Spanish colony
founded by Ponce de Leon on the Caribbean island of
Puerto Rico and intercepted and defeated the Spanish
plate fleet on its way from South America to Spain.

He retired from piracy not long after leaving Ferryland to live in splendour on the Mediterranean coast.

4   The Pool at Ferryland harbour may soon become one
of the most important archeological finds in Canada.
Archeologists working underwater in the Pool have
recently identified the remains of a Basque whaling
boat. The ship is made of European oak and is about
fifty feet long. Work on the find is just beginning, but

the picture that is starting to emerge is that the boat was an early seventeenth century (possibly late sixteenth century) European vessel that was probably unloading supplies or taking on dry cod. Meanwhile, archeologists working on the shore think they have pinpointed the location of Lord Baltimore's house.

One chilly afternoon when I was walking on The Downs, I was surprised to see a scuba diver bubble up in the middle of the Pool. It was Roy Skanes, one of the archeologists working on the Ferryland site. I watched him peel off his drysuit and load an old wooden anchor (a killick) into the trunk of his car. Then I joined him for a rum and a chat.

"The fascinating thing about the Pool is the continuity of fishing from the seventeenth century to today. Europeans have lived around here since the middle of the sixteenth century — even earlier seasonally. And if you look at the men fishing here today, they are working essentially the same way that men were working in the seventeenth century. They are fixing up stages and slipways and wharfs and when they get fish they're taking off the head and cutting out the backbone and splitting the fish for salting or whatever. When I was here last year I took a batch of photos and I went back to the university and took out some old pictures and you can see exactly the same thing going on.

"What we have underwater in the harbour is a fish-bone layer at least two metres thick. At the bottom of the fish-bone deposition we're finding artifacts that are French and Cornish that seem to be from the late sixteenth century. Slightly above that there is a thick deposition of seventeenth century north Devonware. There's lots and lots of that. And all the way up you gradually get artifacts that are more and more modern.

"Intermixed with the bones is all sorts of organic material — wood, leather, rope, clothing, shoes — all of it well preserved because it's waterlogged. What we're able to do is date otherwise undatable material from the level in which we find it.

"We're getting some really good bone selections, which is giving us a good idea what people were eating in those days. We are finding pig, sheep and lots of seal and dog.

"Last year we found a 'chill' — a lamp for burning fish oil. It was the only one like it that has ever been found in Canada. No one knew what it was. We had to send it all over to identify it. We found out that it was most probably exported from Plymouth.

"Ferryland," Skanes said, putting his drink down carefully, "could turn out to be as important to archeology as the site at Red Bay in Labrador."

5 The cod fishery that I witnessed while I was in Ferryland is over for the time being. Whether or not the Canadian government's two year moratorium on cod fishing will save the stock is, as I write, being debated both by scientists and fishermen.

Cod have been fished off the shores of Newfoundland for centuries, certainly from the early 1500s and possibly earlier. That the fishery should collapse so completely after four hundred years is a sobering thought with ecological implications that range far wider than the industry itself.

For Newfoundlanders, however, nothing could be worse. The very history of the island (and thus the early history of Canada) is in many ways the history of the codfish. For years the fishery was controlled by merchants from the south west of England. These West Country Merchants (or Merchant Adventurers) opposed any colonization of the island. They recognized that permanent inhabitants would eventually take over the fishery they so profitably controlled from Britain. They prevailed upon both king and parliament to enact legislation that would discourage and even outlaw overwintering on the island, arguing that a migratory fishery provided the training ground for the British Navy. Their arguments were so successful that they inhibited the settlement of Newfoundland for nearly 150 years.

The First Western Charter (1634) decreed that the captain of the first British boat to arrive in each harbour every spring would automatically become the admiral and governor of the harbour until the fall. These factotums of the West Country Merchants pursued their "responsibilities" with vigour. Fisherman and shore workers bold enough to overwinter might see their houses razed. Whippings and even hangings were also recorded.

Although the impetus for colonization was never snuffed out, a significant permanent population wasn't established in Newfoundland until the turn of the nineteenth century.

As for the cod themselves, when the fishery was healthy most of the round-bodied fish taken in the inshore weighed 3 to 25 pounds (*Encyclopedia of Newfoundland and Labrador* says an average cod weighs about 5 pounds). Cod, however, have grown as long as six feet and the heaviest cod on record weighed 211 pounds. (It was caught, on a line trawl, off the coast of Massachusetts in May, 1895.)

Cod are voracious eaters that feed mostly on other fish, but articles taken from cod stomachs include a bunch of keys, a hare, a partridge, a white turnip, a book bound in calfskin and a large piece of candle.

REPRISE

I am thinking again of the evening I spent at Bob Edgett's boxing club in Sackville, New Brunswick. I can almost smell the hot sweat inside, almost hear the pop of the punching bags, the hiss of breath before each punch. I remember Barry Wood's father showing me the pencil lines on the wall where he and Bob had charted his late son's growth. That's when he was twelve, he said. That's a year later. And I remember the youngest boy there that night, watching me scribble in my notebook, and then shyly asking if I was almost finished. Not quite, Patrick, I said. Not quite. When it's finished, he asked me, will you mark The End? Sure, I said, I'll do that.

THE END